PADMAPRIYA SRIVATSA
ADVOCATE
Flat No. 001, Suramya Apartments
Opp: Sharada Kalyana Mantap
Kunjibettu, UDUPI - 576 102.

NATION AND FAMILY

NATION AND FAMILY

Personal Law, Cultural Pluralism, and Gendered Citizenship in India

Narendra Subramanian

Stanford University Press
Stanford, California

Stanford University Press
Stanford, California

©2014 by the Board of Trustees of the Leland Stanford Junior University.
All rights reserved.

No part of this book may be reproduced or transmitted in any form or by any means, electronic or mechanical, including photocopying and recording, or in any information storage or retrieval system without the prior written permission of Stanford University Press.

Printed in the United States of America on acid-free, archival-quality paper

Library of Congress Cataloging-in-Publication Data has been requested.
ISBN 978-0-8047-8878-6
ISBN 978-0-8047-9090-1 (electronic)

Typeset by Westchester Book Services in Adobe Garamond Pro Regular

For my parents,
K. S. Subramanian and V. Vasanthi Devi,
who initially drew my attention to family law

CONTENTS

Tables and Figures   ix
Abbreviations   xi
Acknowledgments   xiii

1. Indian Personal Law: Toward a Comparative Theoretical Perspective   1
2. Nationalism, Recognition, and Family Formation   18
3. Official Nationalism, Multiculturalism, and Majoritarian Citizen Making: The Formation of the Postcolonial Policy Frame   91
4. Recasting the Normative National Family: Changes in Hindu Law and Commonly Applicable Matrimonial Laws Since the 1960s   137
5. Minority Accommodation, Cultural Mobilization, and Legal Practice: The Experiences of Muslim Law and Christian Law   199
6. Nationalism, Multiculturalism, and Personal Law   266

Notes	289
References	321
Index	361

TABLES AND FIGURES

TABLES

1.1	Nature of Change in Personal Law Soon After Independence/Regime Change	6
1.2	Effects of Changes in Personal Law Since the 1970s on Women's Rights and Individual Autonomy	7
2.1	Influences on Multiculturalism and Personal Law	47
2.2	Features of Community Discourses and State-Society Relations That Influence One Another	47
2.3	Regime Type and Change in Personal Law	57
2.4	Policy Regarding Minority Personal Law	66
2.5	Nationalist Discourses and Personal Law	71

FIGURES

2.1	Discourses of Community, State-Society Relations, and Personal Law	46

ABBREVIATIONS

AICU	All India Catholic Union
AIADMK	All India Anna Dravida Munnetra Kazhagam
AIDWA	All India Democratic Women's Association
AIMPLB	All India Muslim Personal Law Board
AIWC	All India Women's Conference
BJP	Bharatiya Janata Party
BSP	Bahujan Samaj Party
CBCI	Catholic Bishops Conference of India
CNI	Church of North India
CPI-M	Communist Party of India-Marxist
Cr. P. C.	Criminal Procedure Code
CSWI	Committee on the Status of Women in India
DMK	Dravida Munnetra Kazhagam
DMMA	Dissolution of Muslim Marriages Act
DUD	Darul Uloom Deoband
DUMI	Darul Uloom Manzar-e-Islam
EFI	Evangelical Fellowship of India
FLN	Front de Libération Nationale

HAMA	Hindu Adoptions and Maintenance Act
HCB	Hindu Code Bill
HMA	Hindu Marriage Act
HMWRSRMA	Hindu Married Women's Right to Separate Residence and Maintenance Act
HSA	Hindu Succession Act
ICMA	Indian Christian Marriage Act
IDA	Indian Divorce Act
ISA	Indian Succession Act
JWP	Joint Women's Program
MWPRDA	Muslim Women (Protection of Rights on Divorce) Act
MWVA	Mussulman Wakf Validating Act
NCCI	National Council of Churches of India
NCW	National Commission for Women
NCWI	National Council of Women in India
NFIW	National Federation of Indian Women
PMK	Paattaali Makkal Katchi
PWDVA	Protection of Women from Domestic Violence Act
RJD	Rashtriya Janata Dal
Shariat Act	Muslim Personal Law (Shariat) Application Act
SMA	Special Marriage Act
SP	Samajwadi Party
UCC	Uniform Civil Code
UPA	United Progressive Alliance
WIA	Women's Indian Association
YWCA	Young Women's Christian Association

ACKNOWLEDGMENTS

My earlier research examined certain ways in which public actors sought to express cultural specificity and reduce socioeconomic inequality in India. While continuing to address these questions, this book explores some themes in much greater detail—especially the interactions of states, nationalisms, and legal institutions with gendered inequalities, and the interplay of religious discourses and secularist policy frames. This project took over a decade of research, reflection, and writing, in the course of which I accumulated many debts, intellectual, professional, and personal, not all of which I am in a position to mention here.

My work on this book was made possible by grants from the Social Sciences and Humanities Research Council of Canada, the *Fonds pour la Formation de Chercheurs et l'Aide à la Recherche*, the Shastri Indo-Canadian Institute, and the McGill Faculty of Graduate Studies, in addition to a Canada in the World Research Grant jointly offered by the Social Sciences and Humanities Research Council of Canada and the International Development Research Centre.

I made several research trips to India between 2000 and 2007, during which I gathered valuable documents at the Indian Law Institute Library, the Nehru Memorial Library, the Supreme Court Judges Library, the Centre for

Women's Development Studies Library, the Census of India Library, the offices of the Census Commissioner, the Joint Women's Programme, the All India Democratic Women's Association, the All India Muslim Personal Law Board, the Young Women's Christian Association, the Church of North India, the Lawyers Collective, and the Human Rights Law Network in Delhi; the Darul Uloom Nadwatul Ulama and the Firangi Mahal in Lucknow; the Imarat-e-Shariah in Phulwari Sharif, Bihar; and the family court, the high court, the Tamil Nadu Legislative Assembly Library, and the All India Democratic Women's Association's office in Chennai. Moreover, I was able to access materials from the offices and personal collections of Rajeev Dhavan, Kirti Singh, Bina Agarwal, and Gargi Chakravartty in Delhi, and Justice K. Chandru, Sudha Ramalingam, V. Suresh, Geetha Ramaseshan, K. Shantakumari, Sheila Jayaprakash, P. V. S. Giridhar, and D. Sharifa in Chennai. This was supplemented by materials that I gathered at and through the McGill University libraries, the library of the School of Oriental and African Studies in London, and Indlaw.com.

Many individuals made me more comfortable during my research trips to India, helped me access people and materials crucial for my research, and shared with me their thoughts and experiences. My parents, K. S. Subramanian and V. Vasanthi Devi, offered me the hospitality of their homes in Chennai. My father also made arrangements for two of my stays in Delhi. My mother connected me to various people who aided my work. My late grandmother, Gomathi Ammal, also made my visits to Chennai more pleasant, as did Rani and Ravi. Dr. G. R. Sundar of the Bharatiya Vidya Bhavan, L. Krishnan, Saurabh Khanna and his family, and Chanda made me at home in Delhi, as did Saleem Qidwai in Lucknow, the late Mr. Pradhan Jwala Prasad and his family in Patna, and Chandan and Vanita Nayak Mukherjee in both Thiruvananthapuram and Delhi. The following people put me in touch with various interviewees and helped me access crucial research materials: the late Vina Mazumdar, Geetha Ramaseshan, Rajeev Dhavan, Bader Sayeed, K. Shantakumari, P. V. S. Giridhar, Sheila Jayaprakash, S. S. Rajasekhar, Mythily Sivaraman, Mr. N. Gopalaswami (former secretary, Union Home Ministry), Dr. Tahir Mahmood, Kirti Singh, Dr. Qasim Rasool Ilyas, Jyotsna Chatterji, Maja Daruwala, Yoginder Sikand, Saleem Qidwai, Maulana Khalid Rashid, Maulana Anisurrahman Qasmi, Justice Shivaraj C. Patil,

Mr. P. S. Krishnan (former secretary, Union Welfare Ministry), Justice S. Muralidhar, Usha Ramanathan, and Bina Agarwal. In addition, the late Vina Mazumdar, Rajeev Dhavan, Dr. Tahir Mahmood, Jyotsna Chatterji, Justice S. Muralidhar, Bina Agarwal, Justice R.C. Lahoti, Justice S. Rajendra Babu, and Yusuf Hatim Muchhala were particularly forthcoming with valuable information. Bina Agarwal was kind enough to involve me marginally in her ongoing efforts to promote the extension of inheritance rights in agricultural land to Muslim women throughout India by bringing agricultural land under the purview of the Shariat Act.

Three senior scholars encouraged me to embark on this project at an early stage—Stanley Tambiah, the late Myron Weiner and Marc Galanter. I am grateful for the comments of various scholars on parts of the manuscript or on papers or presentations that discussed aspects of this project. They included two reviewers for Stanford University Press. as well as the reviewers of articles based on the project published in *Law and Social Inquiry, The Journal of Asian Studies*, and two edited volumes. Of the reviewers of the book manuscript, Yüksel Sezgin read the penultimate draft and later let me know that he had been a manuscript referee. The other reviewer read an earlier draft of all chapters except the Conclusion. Alfred Stepan commented on the drafts of various chapters as well as on my presentation at a workshop to which he invited me at Columbia University, and encouraged me to elaborate on certain ideas. Werner Menski and Sylvia Vatuk offered me valuable suggestions in response to a number of papers, as well as conference and seminar presentations.

I also benefited from the comments of Donald Horowitz, Marc Galanter, Ann Waltner, Wael Hallaq, Marie-Ève Reny, Yoginder Sikand, Mitra Sharafi, Gopika Solanki, John Bowen, Rupa Viswanath, Donald Davis Jr., Rina Verma Williams, David Gilmartin, Christopher Tomlins, Roger Karapin, Barbara Metcalf, Jeffrey Wasserstrom, Gérard Bouchard, and Minakshi Menon on papers that paved the way to the book, and of Sanjay Subrahmanyam, Srimati Basu, Mitra Sharafi, Marc Galanter, John Bowen, Muhammad Khalid Masud, Lawrence Cohen, K. Sivaramakrishnan, Josh Cohen, Clark Lombardi, Martin Lau, Rajeev Bhargava, Christophe Jaffrelot, Mrinal Satish, Gérard Bouchard, Hanna Lerner, Jean Cohen, Sally Merry, Lauren Benton, and Jan Michiel Otto on presentations based on this project at public lectures, conferences and workshops. Donald Horowitz, Mitra Sharafi, Marc Galanter, Jeff

Spinner-Halev, Ahmet Kuru, and Tamir Moustafa alerted me to references in the comparative literature. While I benefited considerably from the generous comments and suggestions I received from these scholars, I bear sole responsibility for the book's claims and arguments, which do not coincide with their ideas in various respects.

Many colleagues provided me the opportunity to present my work on this project at academic and public venues, through which I gained much valuable feedback. Gerald Larson invited me to a workshop at the University of Indiana at Bloomington, Rajeev Bhargava organized a talk at Jawaharlal Nehru University, and Ashok Kotwal at the University of British Columbia. K. Sivaramakrishnan invited me to present aspects of this project twice, initially at Stanford University at a conference he organized with Akhil Gupta, and then at Yale University at a workshop that he put together with Gilles Tarabout and Daniela Berti. Along with conferring on me the honor of delivering one of the annual Neelan Tiruchelvam Memorial Lectures at Colombo, Tambirajah Ponnuthurai, Sithie Tiruchelvam and Radhika Coomaraswamy had me present my work at the International Centre for Ethnic Studies there. Besides, Tuli Banerjee arranged a talk at MIT, Martha Bailey at Queen's University, Gary Jacobsohn and Gretchen Ritter at the University of Texas-Austin, Karine Bates at the Université de Montréal, Gérard Bouchard at Harvard University, John Bowen at the Institute for the Study of Muslim Civilizations–Aga Khan University, Mitra Sharafi at the University of Wisconsin-Madison, Alfred Stepan and Jean Cohen at Columbia University, and Priya Darshini Swamy at Leiden University College The Hague. In addition, I benefited from presenting aspects of my work on the project at three of the annual conferences on South Asia at Madison, Wisconsin, and at annual meetings of the Association for Asian Studies, the Law and Society Association, the American Sociological Association, and the Association for the Study of Nationalities.

A number of research assistants enabled me to access and organize materials, gather citations, and complete the bibliography—Maren Zerrifi, Gopika Solanki, Aparajita Narain, Jaya Gupta, V. Sriranjani, Shiva Poudel, Julie Thekkudan, Sohini Guha, Zeynep Kadirbeyoglu, Pahi Saikia, Marie-Ève Reny, Arshad Amanullah, Shelly Ghai, Megan Gerecke, Alexandra Rallis, Alessandra Radicati, Parminder Chopra, and Clara Boulianne Lagacé. Juanita Jara del Sumar and April Colosimo guided me as I finalized the bibliography and citations. I am grateful to Michelle Lipinski, Stacy Wagner, and Frances Malcolm for piloting the manuscript through two rounds of review and helping me edit and finalize the manuscript, James Cappio for copyediting it carefully to best convey the intended meaning, and Michael Haggett, Melody Negron, and Emily Smith for overseeing the production of the book.

The support provided by various people helped see me through the past decade and my work on the book—especially Dr. Douglass Dalton, T. K. V. Desikachar, Dr. V. R. Seshadri, Rose Toussaint, Dr. Patricia Csank, Nathalie Crevier Chabot, Sam Noumoff, Anthony Paré, Dr. Benjamin Zifkin, Pierre-Marie Toussaint, and Jean-Sebastien Langlois. This was above all true of Mini, who continued to give me her love and her companionship.

NATION AND FAMILY

CHAPTER I

INDIAN PERSONAL LAW
Toward a Comparative Theoretical Perspective

IN 1985, CONSERVATIVE MUSLIMS IN INDIA resisted a decree by the Supreme Court to grant alimony to a Muslim woman. They considered it contrary to Islamic law, and thus to depart from an important way in which the Indian state recognized religious identity. Women's organizations and social reformers defended the judgment for upholding women's rights, constitutional law, and universalistic moral principles, and Hindu nationalists supported it for prioritizing Indian national integration over a Muslim insistence on difference. The involvement of various organizations in nationwide demonstrations and debates over this case, *Mohammad Ahmed Khan v. Shah Bano Begum*, commonly called the *Shah Bano* case, brought the distinct personal laws that govern India's major religious groups the greatest public attention they had received since the 1950s.[1] The dramatization of a sense of damage to the Muslim community pressed the woman to renounce her alimony and parliament to pass in 1986 the Muslim Women (Protection of Rights on Divorce) Act (MWPRDA), meant to overturn the judgment. Hindu nationalists and some modernists claimed that the Act accommodated a misogynistic tradition and undermined the prospects of social reform. However, this was not so.

The woman's lawyers demanded alimony based solely on particular interpretations of Islamic legal traditions, which were among the grounds of the court's judgment too. Muslims had not reacted much to earlier alimony decrees in favor of Muslim women, but many of them opposed this judgment because it cited claims that Islam was incompatible with women's dignity (albeit without supporting these claims), independently interpreted Islamic texts, declared that commonly applicable criminal laws could override Muslim law, and called for uniform family laws. The Muslim opponents of the judgment included some who favored or were at least open to the requirement of alimony, as well as the inclusion of other provisions favorable to women in Muslim law. Some reformers, including the leader of the woman's legal team, had reservations about the judgment, but supported it nevertheless because they favored the requirement of alimony, they did not wish their reservations to be used to hinder Muslim law reform, the case pitted a prosperous lawyer against a housewife in her late sixties to whom he had been married for four decades, and the alimony decreed accounted for a small share of the man's income. Although the MWPRDA was meant to relieve Muslim men of alimony obligations, the courts subsequently interpreted it according to reformist understandings of Islamic traditions and constitutional principles, to maintain Muslim women's alimony rights. This reflected the grounds on which the personal laws of the religious minorities were changed from the 1970s—the concerned group's statutes, traditions, practices, and initiatives, rather than commonly applicable laws alone. Some of these changes increased women's rights and led to convergence in certain features of India's major personal laws, even while these laws bore the influence of distinctive religious-legal traditions. This partly resolved the tension between the recognition of religious traditions in personal law and the reform of personal law, and weakened conservative resistance to social reform.

Why did many believe nevertheless that Muslim difference had undermined women's rights? Ruling elites had focused their efforts to promote the modern Indian family on the laws of the Hindu majority since independence. They misunderstood Muslim demands to be governed by distinct personal laws as resistance to changes in these laws, and attempted no changes in the minority laws until the 1970s, although certain minority traditions and initiatives supported reform. These choices accompanied the growth of a public rhetoric that equated the Hindu, the Indian, and the secular-modern, and contrasted this triad with the Muslim, minority difference, and resistance to modernity. This discourse acquired force although the notions of Indian modernity that shaped Hindu law reform had mixed implications for gender relations, and although Muslim law gave women greater rights in certain respects than Hindu law even after Hindu law was reformed in the 1950s. It influenced how many people understood *Shah Bano*, but did not determine subsequent legal change and cultural mobilization. Rights organizations valued recognition more from the 1980s, and shifted their attention from uniform family laws to culturally grounded personal law reform, thus contributing to and reinforcing the pattern of legal change.

Nation and Family explores personal law as an important arena in which official nationalism, multiculturalism, secularism, and citizenship were formed and expressed in India since independence. It poses the following questions: Why were distinct personal laws retained after independence? Why were changes made only in Hindu law until the 1970s? Why did minority law reform begin from the 1970s? Why was personal-law reform in India modest, yet significant, when viewed in a comparative perspective? What explains the specific nature of the major legal changes? What effects did these reforms have on gender relations and individual liberties, and thus on the quality of democracy?

I. A COMPARATIVE PERSPECTIVE ON THE FORMATION OF PERSONAL LAW

The forces that shaped Indian personal law become clearer when they are placed in a comparative context. States recognize difference in many societies by applying distinct personal laws to specific cultural groups. While recognition is particularly important to represent culturally inflected interests in diverse societies, multicultural institutions and policies often provide unequal rights to citizens, and impede individual liberty, policy change, and cultural exchange. If multiculturalism has such consequences, it could erode some of the foundations of democracy, or prevent democracy from realizing one of its major promises—the attainment of levels of equality in rights and life chances sufficient for citizens to be autonomous political actors. Many consider both the recognition of cultural specificity and the reduction of social inequality crucial to the stability and quality of democracy in most contexts. A major task of democratic governance in culturally diverse societies is the reconciliation of the goals of cultural accommodation and the promotion of social equality.[2]

The tensions between recognition, equality, and liberty are especially pronounced in the domain of personal law or family law. Personal-law systems govern practices like marriage, divorce, marital separation, alimony, property division on separation and divorce, adoption, guardianship, and inheritance. They support unequal rights for the genders in various ways because they are shaped according to understandings of group norms, and the norms of most groups that these systems govern give the genders unequal rights in family life, or at least did so when these legal systems took shape. Besides, policy makers particularly incorporated gender-unequal norms into group law during crucial phases of state formation when they did not prioritize gender equality, and conservative forces often successfully resisted efforts to change these laws thereafter, by presenting such changes as threats to group identity. Moreover, personal laws constrain individual autonomy, as they usually give individuals little choice about the laws that govern them, and accept dominant understandings of group norms.[3]

Many colonial states in Asia, Africa, the Middle East, the Americas, and the Pacific Islands recognized distinct family laws for various cultural groups, and most postcolonial rulers retained many features of colonial personal law. The formation of postcolonial family law in these societies aroused many related tensions: between national consolidation and cultural accommodation; between the pursuit of modernity and cultural authenticity, variously conceived; between recognition and individual liberty; and between the aims of promoting gender equality, recognized in many constitutions and transnational human rights discourse, and the gender-unequal rights recognized by the existing personal laws. Moreover, personal laws that applied to specific religious groups and drew upon religious norms required reconciliation with the aims of the secularist states that recognized these laws to limit and change the public roles of religion. Liberal-democratic secularist states (and states that presented themselves as such) also had to reconcile the recognition of religion in personal law with their goals, actual or proclaimed, to promote religious freedom and to treat different religious groups similarly. Some of these tensions became associated with policy debates in Europe and Canada too, with the growth of demands that different personal laws govern some recent Muslim immigrant groups, and the emergence of community courts that resolved some disputes within these groups.[4]

Many of the cultural traditions that personal laws recognize are diverse and dynamic, and their implications for contemporary life are contested. This provides states considerable space to introduce culturally grounded personal-law reforms that reduce inequalities, promote liberties, and treat various religious groups similarly. Projects to build nations, maintain or change cultures, and form citizens influenced the forms in which contemporary states recognized traditions and the extent to which they appropriated the authority to regulate family and intimacy from lineages and religious elites. States retained much of colonial personal law, which upheld lineage authority in various ways in Lebanon, Syria, Algeria, and until recently, Morocco, where the social groups that valued the sources of these laws or had an interest in the types of family relations that these laws supported had considerable policy influence. In Turkey and Tunisia, ruling elites prioritized the promotion of their visions of modernity and the control of the state over religious, ethnic, and kin institutions, and changed personal law extensively soon after they came to power, although this reduced their support and generated much social conflict. They empowered the nuclear family and increased women's rights through the secularization of family law in Turkey and the reform of Islamic law in Tunisia. In Senegal, Libya, Egypt, Jordan, Iraq, Iran under the Pahlavis, Pakistan (until the 1970s), India, Sri Lanka, Bangladesh, Malaysia, Indonesia, and the Philippines, ruling elites were allied with modernist urban elites, as well as with traditionalist religious, ethnic, and kin leaders, and wished to maintain and broaden their support. Their vision of indigenously rooted forms of modernity and their inclination to accommodate traditionalist leaders led them to make modest changes in personal law based on group norms, changes that increased the autonomy of the nuclear family and women

TABLE 1.1 Nature of Change in Personal Law Soon After Independence/
Regime Change

	Extensive Modernist Reform	Moderate Modernist Reform	Limited Change
Countries	Turkey, Albania, Tunisia	Senegal, Libya, Egypt, Jordan, Iraq, Iran,[1] Pakistan,[2] India, Sri Lanka, Bangladesh, Malaysia, Indonesia, Thailand, Philippines	Morocco, Algeria, Lebanon, Syria, Malawi

[1] Iran under the Pahlavis, not since the Islamic revolution
[2] Pakistan until the 1970s

in certain respects and maintained the authority of patrilineages and men in other respects. (Table 1.1 indicates these patterns of development in personal law in various representative countries soon after decolonization or soon after a regime that distinguished itself from its predecessors by claiming to be modern assumed power). Moreover, further reforms were introduced in the Philippines, most of Indonesia, west peninsular Malaysia, Bangladesh, India, Egypt, and Morocco a generation or two after independence because ruling elites became more oriented to social reform, and reformist mobilization grew stronger. Starting in the 1970s the increased influence of conservative leaders over either national or state governments induced changes in personal law that reduced women's rights and constrained individual autonomy in Iran, Pakistan, Sudan, northern Nigeria, Afghanistan, east peninsular Malaysia, and Aceh, Indonesia.[5] (Table 1.2 captures the trends in several countries since the 1970s).

The different approaches taken to nation formation, the recognition of religion and cultural diversity, and the regulation of family life are part of the larger trend of the emergence of distinctive forms of modernity and reconstructed traditions across the world since the eighteenth century, in the course of state centralization, colonial and other transregional exchanges, and capitalist development. Scholars have noted the influence of differences in social structure and culture, and variations in cultural and political mobilization and state-society relations, on polity type,[6] the nature and level of industrialization,[7] patterns of secularization and change in religious practice and values,[8] the nature of nationalism and politicized ethnicity,[9] and the character of recently re-formed traditions.[10] This book extends these considerations of

TABLE 1.2 Effects of Changes in Personal Law Since the 1970s on Women's Rights and Individual Autonomy

	Significant Increase	Moderate Increase	Limited Change	Significant Decrease
Countries/Regions	Morocco	Philippines, Indonesia,[1] Malaysia,[2] Bangladesh, India, Sri Lanka, Jordan, Egypt, Senegal	Algeria, Lebanon, Syria, Malawi	Aceh (Indonesia), Malaysia,[3] Pakistan, Afghanistan,[4] Iran,[5] Sudan, Nigeria

[1] Most of Indonesia, but not Aceh over the past decade
[2] West peninsular Malaysia and nonpeninsular Malaysia (provinces of Sabah and Sarawak)
[3] East peninsular Malaysia (provinces of Kelantan and Terengganu)
[4] Especially under the rule of the Taliban, 1996–2001
[5] Especially soon after the Islamic revolution

alternative modernities to the analysis of patterns of recognition of religion, forms of secularism, and approaches to social reform and the regulation of family life.

India, with its complex and cross-cutting variations along the lines of religion, language, and caste, is the preeminent instance of the use of multicultural policies to maintain democracy and represent culturally inflected interests. It therefore offers a fine locus to consider the engagement of policy makers and political and cultural mobilizers with concerns of nation formation and recognition. The major forms of cultural accommodation are federalism, the formation of states largely along the lines of language use, the use of a range of official languages by the national government and the state governments, the introduction and later expansion of preferential policies in education and government employment largely based on membership in particular castes or tribes, the provision of political representation and special civil rights protections to the lower castes (called "scheduled castes" since 1936) and tribal groups (called "scheduled tribes"), the restriction of land rights to the members of certain tribal groups in the regions of their prolonged habitation, and the recognition of different personal laws governing the larger religious groups and many tribal groups. The book's examination of the formation of postcolonial Indian personal law engages the literatures on nationhood and recognition, postcolonial cultural politics, secularism and contemporary religion, and legal institutions, social identities, and gendered citizenship. The book explores the influence of discourses about the nation and its religious and other cultural groups and traditions, along with certain aspects of state-society relations on personal law, multiculturalism, and secularism in postcolonial India, in new ways.

The formation of personal law and certain features of nationalist and cultural mobilization under colonial rule set the stage for the construction of official nationalism, secularism, multiculturalism, and personal law in postcolonial India. The rest of the chapter outlines major features of these colonial experiences, as a background to the discussion of postcolonial personal law in the later chapters.

II. OVERVIEW OF EXPERIENCE IN COLONIAL INDIA

The colonial state recognized religious norms as the main basis of personal law in India. Certain religious norms were incorporated into the common-law framework in which the rest of the legal system operated, after being vetted according to the variously applied standard of compatibility with "justice, equity and good conscience." Of the laws governing the major religious groups, Hindu law and Muslim law were based on common law-influenced interpretations of prior religious and religious-jurisprudential traditions and some aspects of British law, both English and Scottish, while the main statutes of Christian law, passed in the 1860s and 1870s, drew largely from British legislation of the nineteenth century. Hindu and Muslim personal law were sometimes called Anglo-Hindu and Anglo-Muhammadan law, to capture the ways in which they amalgamated British and Hindu or Islamic legal traditions. Distinct personal laws were also applied to Parsis and Jews, both of which were small communities in British India. The census estimates Hindus, Muslims, Christians, and Sikhs to account for 80.5 percent, 13.4 percent, 2.3 percent, and 1.9 percent respectively of India's population currently, and Parsis and Jews for less than 0.1 percent of the population each. The population shares of the Hindus and the Muslims were 69.5 percent and 24.3 percent respectively in colonial India.[11] The book focuses on the three major personal-law systems of India, the Hindu, the Muslim, and the Christian. Bodies of customary law were applied to various tribal groups, and to the majority of residents of certain regions, particularly in the Punjab and the North-West Frontier Province in northwestern colonial India. Personal laws were presented as based largely on authoritative religious texts and the understandings of various religious scholars, Indologists, and Orientalists, while customary laws were said to be based primarily on the customs of various groups, gleaned primarily by anthropologists. Moreover, the state courts recognized certain customs specific to sect, language group, region, caste, and tribe as bases on which litigants might depart from the rules of their religious group's personal law if they could demonstrate that these customs were undisputed and long lasting.

State courts considered personal-law cases, but administrators also provided space for various community courts to consider such disputes without necessarily accepting their verdicts or implementing them. Various social groups pressed their concerns in the state courts as well as in community courts, and certain new religious institutions and caste associations developed new community courts.

A. Religious Mobilization and Colonial Personal Law

New forms of religious mobilization emerged in response to certain features of the colonial context: the exposure, particularly of Western-educated elites, to post-Enlightenment ideas; the formation of European understandings of Indian religious traditions, primarily with reference to certain major texts; the presentation of British cultures and practices as civilized and superior; the dissemination of liberal European and Christian missionary criticisms of various features of local religions and cultures; a decline in the influence of non-Christian religious norms and religious elites over governance; the classification of the population into enumerated religious groups in censuses; and the state's tendency to allocate resources and make policy partly based on religious identity. These changes encouraged the mobilization of religious communities across wide territories, efforts to reform religious practices to meet certain standards of colonial modernity, initiatives to purify religious practice to conform more closely to particular interpretations of religious norms and texts, and attempts to gain official recognition for certain reformed / revived religious norms.[12]

Different South Asian words were translated as "reform" and "revival," and served as flags for initiatives that had varying implications for social inequality and the relationships between religious groups. Some mobilizers interpreted religious traditions or sought to change them to support the reduction of certain social inequalities—for instance, by urging greater education among women, the remarriage of widows, less authoritarian relations between spouses, and interaction on more equal terms between differently ranked castes. Others upheld the privileges of the upper castes and other groups of higher status, and restrictions on the rights of female kin and children. Efforts to reduce inequalities were more often presented as innovative among Hindus, and as a return to the egalitarian features of the religion's founding texts and practices among Muslims. Religious mobilization enabled cultural exchange across religious boundaries in some respects, but policed these boundaries with greater vigilance in others.

Religious mobilization sometimes addressed personal law and the criminal laws pertaining to family life. It did so much more among Muslims than among Hindus, as traditions of religious law were better formed before British rule, and the authority of religious elites depended far more on their expertise in religious law, among Muslims. The *ulama* (Islamic religious scholars / religious elites) initially opposed the restriction of the scope of Islamic law to personal life, but shifted from the late nineteenth century to a defense of Muslim personal law as it operated in the state courts. They accommodated themselves thus to the rule of colonial law, and linked Muslim personal law to the recognition of Muslim religious identity. The adoption of such a posture by the guardians of the faith encouraged others to equate Muslim personal law with *shari'a*, the moral norms indicated in the Qur'an and the practices of the early Islamic community, which are the primary sources of Islamic jurisprudence. However, *qazis* (Islamic religious judges) continued to mediate family disputes.[13] Moreover, the major religious institutions that emerged from the mid-nineteenth century, especially the Darul Uloom Deoband (DUD), built new institutionalized religious court systems and urged their followers to seek these courts rather than the state courts, particularly when they were disappointed with certain interpretations of Muslim law in the state courts. Muslim reformers educated mainly in secular institutions also contested certain ways in which the colonial courts interpreted Muslim law.

The common-law convention of following precedent became an important part of personal-law adjudication in the state courts, especially after the courts ended the regular consultation of Hindu and Muslim religious scholars in the 1860s. This reduced flexibility in adjudication and marginalized certain processes through which religious norms and approaches to adjudication had changed before colonial rule. It particularly limited the role in official Muslim law of *fiqh* (a form of jurisprudence as well as substantive rules developed on the basis of ongoing dialogue among Islamic jurists to construe the implications of authoritative texts for new social predicaments and new kinds of disputes) and *ijtihad* (innovative methods of legal interpretation that were used more often than orthodox Sunni religious scholars claimed). However, many Muslims revived such deliberative processes through which intellectuals tried to arrive at consensus. Some Muslims educated in secular institutions revived *ijtihad* as a way to wrest the authority to interpret the meaning of Islam for contemporary life from the *ulama*, and to arrive at norms conducive to greater economic success in the colonial and postcolonial contexts. Many *ulama* also continued their engagement in *fiqh* to orient Muslims in a context of growing secularization, state consolidation, and interreligious competition; to deduce ways to resolve disputes in religious courts; and to suggest approaches to Muslim personal law in the state courts. This gave classical forms of Islamic legal reasoning a continued and somewhat autonomous existence despite their incorporation into colonial law.

Both secularized Muslim intellectuals and the *ulama* piloted some changes in Muslim personal law. The former were primarily involved in the passage of the Mussulman Wakf Validating Act (MWVA) of 1913, which approved bequests to family members (parents sometimes used bequests to give property to their daughters rather than to extended kin). Both groups participated in passing the Muslim Personal Law (Shariat) Application Act (the Shariat Act) in 1937, which made Islamic law rather than local custom the basis of the regulation of Muslim personal life, and the Dissolution of Muslim Marriages Act (DMMA) of 1939, which increased women's divorce rights. These agents passed the Shariat Act to limit the legal relevance of regional custom, which they tended to consider un-Islamic—perhaps Hindu—as well as to consolidate Muslims as a political and cultural community by applying the same laws to them in many respects. But landholding elites ensured the continued application of custom to the inheritance of agricultural land because they wanted patrilineages to retain control over such land rather than cede control to individual kin, especially women. The concern that the limited divorce rights of the majority of Indian Muslim women, who followed the Hanafi school of Islamic law, would lead some of them to resort to apostasy as a means to access divorce led some major *ulama* to draw from the Maliki school of Islamic law, followed in parts of north Africa, to enable Muslim women to divorce their husbands if they were found to have abrogated their spousal obligations, for instance through adultery, desertion, or cruelty.[14]

Mobilization regarding Hindu law was based less on prior traditions of jurisprudence and more on new forms of dialogue between religious normativities, customs specific to region and caste, and post-Enlightenment ideas. Colonial bureaucrats considered the *shastras* (classical Hindu texts of the first millennium BCE and the first millennium CE) the bases of classical Hindu law, much as the Qur'an and the *hadith* (reputable narratives of the early Islamic community) were sources of classical Islamic law. However, the *shastras* had mainly provided moral guidelines and suggestions for dispute resolution by community institutions rather than rules to govern regulation by states and religious institutions, differing in this respect from Islamic law and Christian canon. Colonial Hindu personal law was based largely on certain important commentaries on these *shastras* from the end of the first millennium and the beginning of the second millennium CE, as well as precedents in the colonial courts, as reflected in the texts of Hindu law compiled by British Orientalists, colonial administrators, and lawyers and judges.[15]

Hindu traditions were open to diverse forms of *achara* (normative practice).[16] This made it easier to credibly present customs specific to region and caste clusters as part of a pan-Indian Hindu tradition. Certain customary practices that predated colonial rule or emerged in the colonial period were the bases of demands regarding the content of Hindu law. Colonial Hindu law recognized some precolonial customs, while transforming them by giving them the fixity of precedent.[17] The central place of Hindus in predominant colonial and nationalist constructions of India also suggested links between particular group customs and Indian national culture. These factors made it easier for cultural mobilizers to attempt the consolidation of the Hindu community around the customs of certain groups, as the Hindu nationalists did around the customs of their core support groups, the upper and upper-middle castes of northern and western India. Community courts run by village and caste associations resolved disputes with reference to changing local norms. They presented their approaches as either based in Hindu traditions or meant to enable the progress of their communities in changing social contexts. However, Hindu religious elites and religious institutions did not attend to the maintenance of classical forms of religious education and reasoning as much their Muslim counterparts did.

Religious figures, caste and other community mobilizers, and modernist intellectuals conceived projects of Hindu reform and spirituality based on amalgamating precolonial Indian mentalities and post-Enlightenment Western outlooks in various ways. Such forms of reasoning were used to urge, variously, the homogenization of Hindu law as well as the maintenance of customary exceptions to these laws, and to both maintain hereditary inequalities in rights and status and to reduce some of these inequalities. They influenced changes in Hindu law, such as the extension to widows of lifetime shares ("limited estate") in their deceased husbands' property through the Hindu Widows Right to Property Act of 1937. These changes were more limited in scope than those introduced in Muslim law in the 1930s. Two Hindu Law Committees considered more extensive changes in Hindu law in the 1940s.[18]

Muslim elites voiced demands to retain a distinct personal-law system most strongly, but this was also the preference of most mobilized members of the other religious groups. This included many Sikhs who wanted the customary law of Punjab, where the group was concentrated, to govern their family lives after independence as it had in the colonial period, as well as various Hindus who preferred different versions of colonial Hindu law. Some Muslim religious elites also wanted religious law to once again regulate commerce and crime, but did not press this claim, as they realized it was not feasible.

Ideas of administrative efficiency, legal rationality, public order, health and morality, individual liberty, the revitalization / reform of religious and other cultural traditions, and the protection or occasionally the empowerment of weaker groups also motivated bureaucrats and legal elites to consider changes in family law. The initiatives of cultural mobilizers, legal elites, and bureaucrats led to other family-law reforms in the colonial period; the most important of these set and then increased the minimum marriage age and the age of consent, and enabled the remarriage of Hindu widows. Moreover, they set the stage for postcolonial debates regarding family law.[19]

B. Indian Nationalism and Legal Reform

The Indian nationalists who became politically dominant after the First World War varied in their understanding of the nation, their inclination to recognize cultural difference, and the relative emphasis they placed on the revaluation of indigenous traditions and the transformation of these traditions to meet colonial standards of modernity; they engaged to different extents with particular social and religious currents. Despite these differences, the majority of them agreed about certain features of social reform. They aimed for culturally grounded reforms in social practice and personal law that would promote post-Enlightenment ideals such as social equality and individual liberty in certain ways, but did not propose to systematically vet personal law with reference to these ends. Virtually none of them wished to follow the Turkish example of rapid secularization of certain areas of public life, attacks on religious institutions and symbols, and the importation of Western institutions and legal systems in their entirety, although they shared a commitment to build a secular state with Turkish republican leaders.

Jawaharlal Nehru, who became the most influential modernist nationalist by the 1940s, favored the formation of a centralized state that would foster economic development along the lines followed by industrialized societies during the interwar period, the establishment of parliamentary democracy, the adoption of official multiculturalism and secularism, and the judicious promotion of social equality through measures such as land reform, the provision of preferential policies for the lower castes, the promotion of women's education and employment, and the enhancement of lower-caste access to public spaces such as places of worship. He considered these the appropriate ways to revive the earlier national glory associated with kingdoms led by Hindus, Muslims, Buddhists, and Jains, and to promote interreligious cooperation. While valuing syncretic cultures, Nehru wished to recognize certain distinctive features of group culture. Modernists like him wished to change the personal laws, and initially Hindu law, to promote equality and liberty, but largely based on the relevant group's legal and normative traditions as they saw them.[20]

The more conservative traditionalist Indian nationalists, such as Bal Gangadhar Tilak and Madan Mohan Malaviya, viewed the nation as an aggregate of distinct cultural groups with largely static cultural traditions. They resisted efforts to promote caste mobility and reform the personal laws to give women greater rights and extend individuals greater liberties, and were wary of syncretic practices. Such conservatives opposed an increase in the age of consent from ten to twelve in the 1890s, an increase in the minimum age of marriage for women from twelve to fifteen in the 1920s, and efforts to increase Hindu daughters' inheritance rights and give both Hindu men and women divorce rights in the 1950s. Both their celebration of certain Hindu festivals as Indian nationalist rituals and their efforts to maintain social boundaries enabled them to build alliances with Hindu nationalists, who connected Indian national revival to Hindu political and cultural supremacy, valued the cultures of the upper and upper-middle Hindu castes of northern and western India, and wished to assimilate other groups into many of these groups' practices.[21] This alliance led the opposition to Hindu law reform in the 1940s and 1950s. While the Hindu nationalists voiced a preference for a Uniform Civil Code (UCC) even then, they focused on preventing most proposed reforms in Hindu law or preventing the application of these reforms to their support groups.

Mohandas ("Mahatma") Gandhi was the most influential among the less conservative traditionalists. He considered precolonial India a collection of static and autarkic villages, wished to revive such a nonindustrial nation, and imagined a national tradition in which castes were interdependent occupational groups of equal status and landlords used land to benefit the entire village. To promote this vision, he organized improvements in the social conditions of the lower castes, tried to reduce untouchability practices in some villages, and supported initiatives to end child marriage and to give the lower castes access to temples.[22] Along with pluralist modernists like Nehru, he valued syncretism while wishing to recognize difference, and took the reform of Hindu society to be the main basis for making the Indian citizen. Moreover, most Indian nationalists, whether traditionalist or modernist, did not engage closely with mobilization among the religious minorities and were unfamiliar with the religious discourses in which these efforts were largely conceived, and so took the norms valued by the more influential minority leaders to represent the cultures of these groups.

The less conservative traditionalists and modernists were predominant in the leadership of the Indian National Congress (Congress Party) of the 1940s, and included the party's two most popular leaders, Gandhi and Nehru. These informal factions thus had greater influence over early postcolonial policy, especially the initial proposals about personal law. However, conservative traditionalists and Hindu nationalists also accounted for a significant section of the political elite and the first two postcolonial parliaments, and so had a voice in policy making. As the movement to form Pakistan as a separate country for the Muslims of British India grew, certain major Congress Party leaders came to an agreement to continue the recognition of a distinct Muslim law with some Muslim religious elites that preferred to remain a part of India. Their focus on reforming Hindu society and their distance from non-Hindu cultural mobilization made them inclined to reform Hindu law, and to take minority accommodation to require the retention of the minority personal laws in their existing form. This was the case although various Muslim leaders had initiated more changes in Muslim law than had been made in Hindu law in the last colonial decades, and were open to further changes if the majority of Muslim political representatives favored them.

III. ORGANIZATION OF THE STUDY

Chapter 2 develops the major arguments of the study by comparing Indian experiences with trends in various other developing societies in which personal laws specific to religious groups, sects, or ethnic groups that were based partly on religious and other cultural norms were recognized in the early twentieth century. It argues that the discourses of community that influence policy makers and popular mobilization interact with certain aspects of the relations between state and society and that these two factors influence approaches to cultural accommodation and personal law. This argument is developed through a critical exploration of the literature on family law and legal change, state formation, nationalism and cultural politics, secularism and public religion, and multiculturalism, with reference to the aforementioned experiences. Chapter 3 examines the formation of the Indian state's approach to personal law in the first postcolonial decade, the reasons for the focus on changing Hindu law, and the specific changes introduced in Hindu law in the 1950s. It highlights the introduction of rights to divorce—largely based on spousal fault and granted after a period of judicial separation, to indicate the forms of family life that state elites valued—and the compromise over inheritance rights, which indicated the intention to empower women while partly accommodating conservatives who wished to maintain patrilineal authority over property. Chapter 4 explores the changes that judges and legislators made in Hindu law since the 1960s, especially the increase in divorce rights—based on mutual consent or spousal fault without an intervening phase of judicial separation—and the extension of greater rights to daughters over family property. Chapter 5 discusses the experiences pertaining to the laws governing India's two largest religious minorities, the Muslims and the Christians. It highlights the reasons why policy makers did not change these laws soon after independence although support for personal-law reform was comparable among Muslims and Hindus. Moreover, it investigates the changes in cultural and legal mobilization, litigation patterns, and policy makers' knowledge and values that contributed to reforms in the minority laws since the 1970s—notably the extension of alimony rights and restriction of unilateral male repudiation among Muslims, and an increase in divorce rights and the equalization of divorce rights for men and women among Christians. This chapter also identifies certain ways in which policy elites' majoritarian nationalist visions and limited knowledge of minority traditions and initiatives restricted the accommodation of culturally grounded demands for minority law reform. The Conclusion summarizes the major findings and indicates the likely directions of change in India's personal laws over the next decade or two. It highlights certain lessons that may be drawn from the study about how multiculturalism and secularism may be revised in India and some other developing countries, and the forms of cultural discourse and political mobilization that would enable such policy changes.

CHAPTER 2

NATIONALISM, RECOGNITION, AND FAMILY FORMATION

I. STATES, KIN GROUPS, AND FAMILIES

Analogies between patriarchal authority within families and lineages and the authority of the sovereign over subjects were motifs of early modern Western political theory, deployed to reinforce the authority of both sovereign and patriarch.[1] They reflected the presence of patriarchal authority and patrimonial states, as Weber characterized them, in various societies.[2] Lockean social-contract theory severed the link between patriarchal and state authority, locating the latter alone in the consent of the governed. It presaged the efforts of centralizing states to consolidate their power through the appropriation of the authority to regulate family and intimacy from lineages and religious elites, but not the specific ways in which crucial agents framed these projects and the extent to which they redistributed such authority. The modes of regulation of the family were recast over the past two centuries in various societies in ways that provided individuals different choices about how they practiced intimacy and family life, and changed the relationship between patriarchal and state authority in different ways. European states had patrimonial features well after they began to centralize their authority, and many of the states in developing societies retained neopatrimonial characteristics until now. Some of these states limited the authority and autonomy of prior social institutions, and thereby consolidated their authority and became more deeply embedded in society (for example, France and Turkey). Others accepted the continued authority of these institutions in various social arenas at a cost to their own power (for example, Lebanon and Morocco). And many others consolidated their authority partly by building alliances with such institutions with which they shared various regulatory functions (such as, Egypt, India, and Indonesia).[3]

Nancy Cott highlighted the connections between Lockean contractualism and the formation of modern American family law.[4] She showed that analogies between membership in the American republic and partnership in a marriage, based on consent and perhaps official validation in both cases, reinforced the state's promotion of monogamous marriages as well as connections between the potential to head a household and political rights. The rhetorical link between political rights and the possibility of heading a household, she demonstrated, supported the extension of the franchise to black men as well as the recognition and encouragement of marriage among African Americans after emancipation, and this in turn provided a normative and rhetorical basis for women to demand the franchise as well as greater authority in marital relations. Cott's account alerts one to a variety of dimensions along which proposals to make family register, influencing mobilization and policy. However, the conception of the United States as a republic of equals did not determine the specific changes introduced in family law from the late nineteenth century on, such as the more systematic enforcement of heterosexual monogamy and the requirement of marriage registration; similar changes were introduced around the same time in some other predominantly Christian countries such as Britain and France, and somewhat later in certain predominantly Muslim countries such as Turkey and Tunisia, although the nation was imagined rather differently in these societies: in association with images of the Crown, the Anglican Church, and the "freeborn Englishman" in Britain; as republics born in opposition to the alliance of monarch and religious institutions in France and Turkey; and in connection with Arab and Muslim identity, and with Islamic normative and legal traditions, in Tunisia.[5]

States did gain greater authority over the regulation of the family since the nineteenth century, as scholars such as Mary Ann Glendon and Lawrence Friedman show regarding the United States and Western Europe.[6] However, they did not always wield this authority in ways that enabled the realization of individual liberty and social equality, as Friedman claims. Some of the changes they introduced in family law enabled these ends. This was the case regarding the decrease in the authority of family patriarchs over spousal choice, the increase in room to effect marital separation and divorce, the enhancement of the inheritance rights of women and younger siblings and of women's custody and adoption rights, and the more extensive specification of the economic consequences of spousal separation and divorce, such as in the form of alimony obligations. But the growth in the scope and intensity of state regulation until the mid-twentieth century restricted the types of conjugal relationships citizens could enter, typically to monogamous heterosexual unions formally registered as marriages, and punished alternative forms of family and intimacy.

Michel Foucault and certain scholars who adopted his analytical approach showed that the changes in legal systems and socialization patterns that occurred in the West from the seventeenth century to the early twentieth century, and in various colonial and postcolonial societies since the nineteenth century, shaped conjugality along these lines. Foucault showed that modern European discourses about the body, health, pleasure, and sexuality emerged from Christian practices like confession and penance, and shaped predominant norms as well as some alternatives to these norms. Some of his followers explored the formation of new forms of morality, classification, regulation and punishment in Asia, the Middle East, and Africa through the engagement of modern Western discourses with various indigenous religious and cultural traditions and forms of reasoning.[7] In the latter societies, which experienced colonial rule or Western hegemony, the gaps between legal frameworks and public moral sensibilities were especially large. The engagement of Western and indigenous discourses with one another served both to orient citizens to colonial institutions or institutions influenced by Western precedents and to construct alternatives more suitable to these societies. These culturally rooted social visions accorded value to different conjugal and kinship practices; they varied in the importance they accorded the nuclear family rather than lineages, and the extent to which they promoted monogamy and patrilineal kinship instead of preexisting alternative practices. To the extent that states promoted monogamy and gave patrilineal bonds priority, they restricted the inheritance and maintenance rights of women and children who were involved in polygamous relationships or followed matrilineal customs, they motivated groups to modify these customs, and they marginalized these practices.

The transfer of authority over family life from lineages to states was far from complete in many postcolonial and postimperial societies, as we saw in the Introduction. States assumed such authority, empowered the nuclear family, and increased women's rights through major changes in family law in Turkey and Tunisia, as well as in Morocco over the past decade. They barely disturbed lineage authority or changed personal law in Lebanon, Syria, Algeria, and, until recently, Morocco. And they increased the autonomy of the nuclear family and women in certain respects and maintained the authority of patrilineages and men in other respects in Indonesia, Malaysia, Bangladesh, India, Sri Lanka, Iraq, Jordan, Egypt, Libya, and Senegal. Moreover, further culturally grounded modernist reforms were introduced since the 1970s in Indonesia, west peninsular and nonpeninsular Malaysia, Bangladesh, India, Egypt, and Morocco, in contrast with the diminution of women's rights in certain respects and the increase in the influence of religious elites through the same period in Iran, Pakistan, Sudan, Nigeria, east peninsular Malaysia, Afghanistan, and Aceh (in Indonesia) (see Tables 1.1 and 1.2).

Mounira Charrad explored the reasons for the complete transfer of authority over the regulation of family disputes and the promotion of the monogamous nuclear family in Tunisia—in contrast with the continued recognition of lineage authority in various respects in Algeria and Morocco, which shared with Tunisia the predominant influence of the Maliki *madhhab* (school of Islamic law) and the experience of French colonization.[8] She traced the way family law was formed to the relations between states and lineages, the latter being the most important form of social organization in much of the Middle East and in various other regions too. Charrad claimed that Islamic law in its precolonial and colonial forms upheld the authority of the patrilineage. She argued that the Moroccan Crown chose not to reform colonial Islamic law because it was closely allied with lineages; that the Algerian regime, which included groups with different relations with lineages and varying views about the main desirable family unit, was indecisive regarding family law until it chose to maintain much of colonial law in an unsuccessful effort to stem the growth of Islamist opposition a generation later; and that the Tunisian regime, from which urban reformists ousted rural conservatives soon after independence, consolidated the state's prior autonomy by assuming the authority to resolve family disputes, authorizing the nuclear family, and increasing certain rights of women.

Charrad identified some reasons why states assumed the authority to regulate the family to varying degrees and used this authority in different ways. But her analysis did not clarify why the state used such authority to secularize family law in early republican Turkey and increased women's rights to inheritance and autonomy from their husbands more than the reform of Islamic law did in Tunisia, although state-lineage relations were similar in the two countries. Moreover, it did not shed light on the ways in which nation and family were made in countries such as India and Indonesia, in which religious practices were more diverse than in North Africa, religious and language boundaries cut across one another, patterns of social organization and kinship varied across region and ethnic group, distinct religious law systems as well as norms and customary laws specific to region and ethnic group influenced family regulation, and important nationalist understandings engaged in different ways with various religious and cultural traditions. This is crucially because Charrad, like Cott, did not attend to cultural constructions of nations and understandings of the forms of modernity and types of traditions appropriate to build or maintain in particular societies.[9] Explanations with greater comparative scope need to attend to the links between modes of imagining the nation and approaches to regulating family life.

As states became more centralized and presented themselves increasingly as representatives of nations from the eighteenth century onward, the relationship of states to religious groups, sects, ethnic groups, lineages, and families was often conceived with reference to the proclaimed character and destiny of nations. Gendered familial norms were important aspects of nationalist narratives, which varied in how far they urged the retention rather than the reconstruction of predominant social practices, the practices they sought to retain, and the ways in which they aimed to change others. Discourses about nations, their constituent cultures, and the forms of modernity and variously reconstructed traditions appropriate for particular nations and cultural groups influenced projects to make citizens, recognize religious and other cultural groups, and shape the family. This book explores, in a comparative perspective, the formation of official nationalism, multiculturalism, secularism, and personal law in India, in mutual interaction.

II. NATIONS AND MODERNITIES

Postcolonial theorists explored the connections between the way nations are imagined and approaches to family life. They highlighted how the hegemony of colonial discourse pressed anticolonial nationalists to make claims to both modernity and cultural authenticity, as colonial discourse typically took rigid cultural traditions to drive much of local social dynamics, presented colonized societies as backward, valued certain forms of cultural distinctiveness, and upheld the preeminent value of modernity. Partha Chatterjee understood many features of anticolonial and postcolonial cultural politics in terms of these goals.[10] He believed that to assert their sovereignty over the cultural realm, anticolonial nationalists felt compelled to reject the paternalistic social reform initiatives of colonial states. Moreover, he argued that they resisted the "rule of colonial difference," which refers to organized distinctions between colonizers, settlers, and the colonized and those between different colonized groups, which were central to colonial state-society relations. Anticolonial nationalists, he claimed, initiated reforms meant to produce authentically national (rather than Western) educational institutions, literary forms, and families while resisting the agency of colonial states in social change; once these nationalists controlled postcolonial states, they gave the state's backing to such reforms. While building nations that were at once modern and culturally authentic, postcolonial states were said to refuse recognition to popular discourses of communities other than the nation they claimed to represent because they felt driven by the universalizing narrative of capital and prioritized the nation they took themselves to embody.[11] Chatterjee and Mahmood

Mamdani claimed that, in the process, postcolonial regimes rarely made a definitive break from colonial despotism and Western forms of polity and economy.[12] Chatterjee uneasily juxtaposed his skepticism about the feasibility of multiculturalism and the transcendence of colonial hegemony in postcolonial societies to suggestions that opinion among the concerned groups, ascertained through systematic community consultation, should guide postcolonial cultural policy.[13]

The above claims were not based on a systematic examination of colonial law, the social reform agendas of anticolonial and postcolonial nationalists, and postcolonial multicultural policies. Careful empirical accounts of colonial law demonstrate that colonized groups, including some of subordinate status, found some space to negotiate jurisdictional boundaries, group boundaries, and rights under colonial law. Colonial administrators were sometimes willing to cede them such space either for administrative convenience or to gain support and limit discontent. Colonized groups used mixed strategies of pressing their interests through state courts, resorting to community courts that certain states recognized, and contesting some features of colonial law. Some of them came to value certain features of colonial legality, and linked aspects of colonial personal and customary law with their identities, even if these legal systems were products of cultural exchanges between the colonizers and the colonized. This meant that the retention of features of colonial personal law and the adoption of imperial precedents did not necessarily undermine postcolonial assertions of rights and authenticity.[14]

While certain conservative anticolonial nationalists resisted the social reform efforts of colonial states, many other nationalists gave such initiatives their carefully circumscribed support. For instance, in India, only the more conservative nationalists, such as Bal Gangadhar Tilak and Madan Mohan Malaviya, opposed the efforts of colonial officials and liberal Indian professionals to increase the age of consent for girls in the 1890s, and to ban child marriage in the 1920s. Many other important Indian nationalists, including modernists such as Gopal Krishna Gokhale, Jawaharlal Nehru, and Mohammad Ali Jinnah, as well as less conservative traditionalists such as Gandhi, supported these reforms, and Nehru and Gandhi also supported many of the Law Commission's proposals of the 1940s to change Hindu law. The latter

Indian nationalist leaders were not at the forefront of these reform efforts, but some of their supporters were, especially those in the major women's organizations of the last colonial decades, the All India Women's Conference (AIWC), the National Council of Women in India (NCWI), and the Women's Indian Association (WIA). These actors did not feel that their participation in certain social reform initiatives of colonial officials compromised their efforts to build a culturally indigenous nation or their opposition to colonial rule, because they either found or sought to construct domestic cultural bases on which to reshape the family along these lines. This was dramatized by the AIWC's choice to support the efforts of the government-appointed Hindu Law Committee in the 1940s, even while the Congress Party was engaged in civil disobedience to end colonial rule.[15]

Visions of national and group culture influenced the social reform proposals of anticolonial nationalists and postcolonial cultural policies. There was considerable contention over postcolonial social reform amidst the hegemony of nationalist discourse. Conservative nationalists, some of whom were represented in postcolonial regimes, resisted many reform proposals in countries such as Tunisia, Egypt, Pakistan, India, and Indonesia. Such conservatives dominated other postcolonial regimes, such as those of Syria, Lebanon, and Malawi, and these regimes did not attempt major social reforms. The disagreements among nationalists over social reform extended across the colonial and postcolonial periods in many societies, and thus did not derive mainly from attitudes toward colonial state agency. Rather, they were based on alternative understandings of the cultures and desirable courses of the nation and its constituent groups, and on the links of specific nationalist organizations and tendencies with particular social groups.

Drawing from Chatterjee the understanding that postcolonial cultural politics and policy were often framed in terms of modernity and authenticity, I address the following questions that he did not: Under what conditions did postcolonial states introduce social reforms? What determined the approaches states took to recognize difference and promote culturally inflected forms of modernity? Various public actors developed understandings of the forms of modernity appropriate for particular colonial and postcolonial societies based on precolonial indigenous traditions, colonial knowledge about local society, forms of ongoing cultural mobilization, and earlier social changes in the modern West. They used such understandings to frame social reforms as based on aspects of local culture, and thus to counter conservative efforts to discredit reform for causing cultural deracination. This study identifies certain understandings of indigenous forms of modernity influential in India and other former colonies, and sketches their influence over personal law.

Understandings of the forms of modernity appropriate for a nation, region, or cultural group emerged in various colonial and postcolonial societies, "internal colonies" such as Scotland, Catalonia, and Quebec, and other societies considered less developed when their links to other world regions increased (such as Italy, Ottoman Turkey, Russia, Japan, China, the southeastern United States, and Brazil in the later half of the nineteenth century). These models encompassed aspects of the political economy (particularly the forms of state engagement in the economy, types of property rights, and patterns of property and income distribution), state formation (such as the nature of the bureaucracy and the military, the extent of state centralization, the forms of political representation, the character of state-society links, and the patterns of state engagement with religion), and public culture (such as the public roles of religion and features of the languages of mass communication, public ritual, and everyday life). Their authors thus did not only mark the distinction of their societies (especially from more developed societies), make claims to sovereignty, and build culturally rooted social projects within the "spiritual realm," as Chatterjee characterized it. Intellectuals, cultural and political mobilizers, and policy makers articulated such visions because they felt that viable strategies of economic development, state building, and cultural formation needed to take account of crucial features of the local society, and wished to frame their projects as culturally authentic. These understandings influenced the patterns of formation of polities and political economies, forms of secularization and religious practice, and types of nationalism, politicized ethnicity, and recently constructed traditions.[16]

These models varied in the social spheres to which they paid greatest attention. Some emphasized the need for the state to intervene in the economy more and in a different manner in later-developing societies than it had in previously industrialized societies, to enable economic growth, stabilization, redistribution, and poverty alleviation. They prescribed varied forms of state intervention such as the establishment of tariff barriers for infant industries, the easier provision of investor credit, the development of infrastructure, the direction of investment into desired sectors, the maintenance of peasant and artisanal production, the promotion of small industrial firms, state ownership of the commanding heights of the economy, and state ownership of much of agriculture and industry. Alexander Gerschenkron emphasized the distinctive features of these visions and their consequences for policy and economic change in Europe, and his lead was followed by scholars of state-led industrialization in East Asia such as Chalmers Johnson, Peter Evans, and Alice Amsden. Christopher Hill highlighted how important actors linked such economic strategies to narratives of national history.[17] Political leaders like Lee Kuan Yew popularized aspects of these accounts, and connected them to features of religious culture.

Various intellectuals and political elites in colonial societies drew on the ideas developed earlier in Central and Eastern Europe and East Asia, added the claims that colonial rule had hindered industrialization and incorporated colonized societies into the world economy on a subordinate basis, and argued on these bases for building postcolonial developmental states. Moreover, they felt that postcolonial states needed to give special attention to promoting national cohesion and cultural decolonization, managing ethnic, religious, and racial conflict, and maintaining or changing the social structure. Such arguments were deployed in favor of the retention of collective land ownership tied to lineage power and customary law in parts of sub-Saharan Africa, the Middle East, and South Asia; the redistribution of land from European settlers to indigenous groups in various settler societies; and the maintenance of existing forms of the division of labor (especially in agriculture) or a return to imagined precolonial political economies in various colonies. Many important actors believed that the predominantly non-Christian religious cultures of much of the Middle East and Asia were important reasons to craft distinctive social projects, emphasizing either specific religions (particularly Islam, Hinduism, Confucianism, and Buddhism) or the common features that they saw in the different popular religious cultures of their societies. Political leaders and nationalist intellectuals made Islam central to their understanding of national distinctiveness in much of the Arab world and Central Asia, but more of them valued the common features of the religious cultures of Indonesia and to some extent India. Both kinds of constructions of national religious culture influenced proposals to revitalize the nation, accommodate diversity, and shape personal law.

Arguments to build distinctive forms of modernity were voiced early and in especially influential ways in India. Claims that colonial rule was associated with the drain of economic resources from the colonies, the destruction of precolonial life-worlds, and the promotion of religious and ethnic conflict emerged particularly early in India, in the nineteenth century, and were crucial aspects of the anticolonial nationalist visions of the early twentieth century. Gandhi offered a particularly totalizing and popular critique of these features of the colonial encounter. While his preferences to build an agro-artisanal economy and devolve most governance functions to the local level were far removed from the determination of modernist nationalists like Nehru to promote industrialization, Gandhian traditionalists and the majority of modernists agreed that India needed to be independent of the global economy and imperial powers. This enabled the modernists to appropriate aspects of Gandhi's critique of colonialism in favor of their plans to build a developmental state and consolidate parliamentary democracy, as well as to pursue certain goals that Gandhi shared—building national solidarity while recognizing difference, and constructing a secular state that accommodates many features of public religion. Along with various traditionalist allies, the modernists built broad social coalitions that supported versions of this agenda and the dominant Congress Party. The agenda of the modernists included the culturally grounded reform of colonial personal law to promote individual autonomy and reduce gender inequality in certain respects, while maintaining the continuity of the nuclear family, various gendered social roles, and perhaps aspects of lineage authority.

III. STATE-SOCIETY RELATIONS, DISCOURSES OF COMMUNITY, AND PERSONAL LAW

Individuals, social groups, associations, social movements, and political parties imagine projects to make society and family, mobilize in their favor, and sometimes reframe them in light of contention with alternative projects on offer in society. They thus influence the projects that states adopt, as well as the social responses to these projects, which reorient state projects to varying degrees. Most analyses take the interaction of interests, institutional orientations, ideas, and meanings to influence such projects. They vary in how they understand (a) the formation of interests and institutions, (b) the interactions between the formation of interests and institutions, the emergence and circulation of ideas, and the generation of meaning, and (c) how states (or different groups of elites that have significant influence over the state or particular state institutions) formulate projects and propose policies meant to realize those projects.

An older scholarship understood the array of organized interests and institutions in society to shape the goals and actions of states.[18] It was unable to account for the varied policies that states adopted in similar social contexts, and for the special influence that states exert when they gain a near monopoly over the legitimate use of force. Scholars that emphasized state autonomy highlighted the definite preferences that public officials have in their specialized policy arenas (in contrast with the indifference of many social actors about various policies), and the resources and influence they often have to shape societal opinion to favor or to at least not obstruct their preferences, and to override powerful interests that remain opposed to their preferred course. While some of these scholars focused on the autonomous formation of the preferences of crucial policy elites,[19] others emphasized the ways in which the history of state formation and the resulting structure of the state channeled collective action, and shaped policy makers' incentives and goals.[20] The former versions gave inadequate attention to the factors shaping the preferences of state officials, and both they and the latter disregarded the frequency with which powerful groups influenced these preferences or diverted policy makers from their priorities.[21]

Other accounts of state centralization and state-led social change overemphasized how far state actions are driven by objectives to maximize control over resources and practices and to maintain stable regimes.[22] A variety of policies may be considered compatible with such goals in many contexts, and the groups, ideas, and values with which state elites feel greatest affinity influence their perception of the policies most suitable to these ends and the polices they adopt. Moreover, these explanations do not adequately consider the conditions under which states may be unable to overcome certain forms of resistance or prefer to accommodate them by devolving aspects of social regulation to authoritative social institutions. Friedman adopted such an analysis of the formation of family law, which shared these problems. He claimed that the state's greater control over family regulation in Western societies enabled greater social complexity, individual liberty and social equality, and he inadequately recognized the frequent tensions between these ends.[23] This approach did not capture why states retain prior personal-law systems or change them in particular ways.

Other scholars took state-society relations to determine the social projects that states undertake and the capacity of states to pursue these projects, without assigning causal primacy to the actions of states or social groups. Their "state-in-society" approach stressed the porousness of state-society boundaries in many contexts, the frequency with which fragments of states ally themselves with different social groups locked in contention with one another, and the ways in which state-society boundaries get constituted through such interactions and alliances. This approach's emphasis on the influence of conflicts between particular state institutions, groups of state elites, and alliances of different state-society fragments over policy formation was valuable.[24]

Because personal laws lend the state's recognition to particular social norms, the formation of these legal systems involves ongoing passage across the boundaries between state and society, and this study draws on various valuable insights of the state-in-society school to understand these processes. It nevertheless differs from some assumptions that much of the work of this school shares: social structure determines interests and the groups that have the capacity to mobilize significant alliances; old elites defend enduring practices that reproduce their dominance and ideas that uphold their authority, often in the name of tradition; emergent elites and groups generate and embrace new ideas that promote alternative practices and forms of solidarity; and the structure of states and the relationships of states or fragments of states with particular social groups determine the projects that states pursue.[25] This book's consideration of the different directions taken by nationalism, multiculturalism, and personal law in postcolonial societies indicates that interests are constructed in different ways in societies with similar patterns of resource organization and distribution; that a variety of practices can often be credibly presented as having the force of tradition in a given society or social group; and that the discourses of community salient in particular societies or among specific social groups influence how individuals construct their interests, the projects of social change launched in society, the alliances formed in favor of these projects, the projects which particular state institutions or segments thereof promote, and how states or state-society fragments modify these projects in view of their interactions with social forces. Analyses focused on state-lineage relations, such as those of Philip Khoury, Joseph Kostiner, and Mounira Charrad, and some of the essays in Julia Adams and Charrad's *Patrimonial Power in the Modern World*, adopt versions of the state-in-society approach whose explanations of state initiatives to reform society and family have the shortcomings indicated above.[26]

Most accounts focused on state autonomy, state centralization, and state-society relations attend inadequately to the ways in which beliefs, ideas, and values influence how social groups construct their interests and mobilize to promote them, and how state elites perceive the interests in society, set their goals, and respond when their initiatives face resistance. They recognize the nearly universal tendency of states for over a century to claim to represent particular nations, but the influence that discourses of the nation and its crucial cultural cleavages exercise over the projects that various social groups support and that states adopt is not central to their analyses. Rather, they implicitly understand official nationalism and forms of social classification as concomitants of state-building processes, and the studies that adopt these approaches to the examination of nation-states and nationalism make this understanding explicit.[27] This is particularly a problem for studies of postcolonial societies, in which understandings of the nation, its proclaimed cultural distinctiveness, and its constituent cultural groups are crucial motifs of public debate, and for analyses of policies to recognize and perhaps change national and group cultures.

Poststructuralists gave central importance to how discursive practices simultaneously shape subjects, disciplinary institutions, and state projects. Foucault explored the disciplinary practices employed by social institutions such as clinics, schools, and churches as well as by state institutions, and the forms of knowledge that accompanied such articulations of power. He considered such practices pervasive in effect because they not only constrained action, but also formed individual dispositions, popular mobilization, and responses to policies.[28] Certain other scholars who adopted these methods were more attentive to the tensions within disciplinary practices, which provided scope for varied responses from subject populations, including some that resisted the hegemony of disciplinary institutions.[29] They examined the elaboration of colonial knowledge about colonized societies, which influenced the classification of subject populations in censuses, land surveys, and revenue settlements, meant to render the peculiar customs of these populations legible, in James Scott's usage, and open to bureaucratic management.[30] Some of them highlighted ways in which colonized groups creatively fused knowledge originating in Europe and in the colonies in the course of colonial encounters with precolonial norms both to orient themselves to colonial institutions and to devise alternatives to them.[31]

Colonial knowledge and classification schemes exercised significant influence over colonial personal law and customary law systems. They influenced the choice of the cultural groups to be governed by distinct personal law systems, the traditions incorporated into these legal systems as well as those that were not enforced on grounds such as morality and public order, and the considerations guiding changes in these systems. Postcolonial theorists emphasized the enduring influence of colonial knowledge and institutions over postcolonial projects. In the process, they underestimated the autonomy of postcolonial responses to colonial strategies. Although they were influenced by ideas that emerged during colonial encounters, personal laws were presented as recognizing precolonial norms and practices, and sometimes as ways of delegating the governance of the family and perhaps land control to precolonial institutions and elites. Partly for this reason, colonized groups drew not only on colonial knowledge, but also on precolonial traditions as they interpreted them in light of current predicaments, practices that emerged in interaction with colonial governance while remaining somewhat independent of it, and postcolonial ambitions (often expressed in nationalist discourses) to frame litigation strategies and devise projects to maintain or change personal law and social practices.[32] This study attends to the influence of postcolonial visions of the nation and its major constituent cultures on projects to make state, society and family.

IV. RELIGIOUS NORMS, SOCIAL STRUCTURE, REGIONAL CUSTOM, AND FAMILY LAW

Friedman reconstructed the changes in Western family law since the late eighteenth century as aspects of the formation of a legal culture of modernity, involving the interrelated processes of legal secularization, the replacement of group-specific norms with universalistic rules, and the realization of individual liberty and social equality.[33] Various other teleological accounts of legal development shared such an understanding.[34] These narratives suggested a close connection between the recognition of religious and other group-specific norms and restrictions on forms of family, intimacy, and kinship. They indicated that the accommodation of such norms in various colonial personal law systems limited the export of modern Western legal systems and their culture of liberty and equality, and considered the legalization of difference a major barrier to constitutionalism, the rule of law, and the extension of rights in postcolonial societies.

Archana Parashar adopted such a perspective on Indian personal law, and attributed the modest character of postcolonial reform to the "religious nature" of the major personal-law systems. As she took religious law to necessarily restrict women's rights, she misunderstood the Muslim law reforms of the 1930s to have subjected women to the "rigorous control of the high culture Islamic law" because they applied Islamic law rather than regional custom to Muslim family life.[35] However, these reforms provided women greater inheritance rights and divorce rights.[36] The assumption that religious laws limited reform also prevented Parashar, Rajeswari Sunder Rajan, and Susan Okin from recognizing the judicial reforms in Indian Muslim law from the 1970s.[37]

Contrary to such understandings, family laws that were framed in religious and other culturally specific discourses followed very different trajectories. The religious laws recognized by colonial states underwent little change after independence in Lebanon, Syria, and Algeria, but changed to provide women greater rights (and individuals greater liberties) around the same time in Tunisia, and to a lesser extent in Indonesia, Thailand, west peninsular Malaysia, Sri Lanka, India, Pakistan, Iran, Iraq, Jordan, Egypt, Libya, and

Senegal. Moreover, such legal systems changed in a conservative direction since the 1970s in Iran, Pakistan, Sudan, Nigeria, Afghanistan, and east peninsular Malaysia, in contrast with the modernist reforms introduced through this period—especially in Morocco and to a lesser extent in Indonesia, Malaysia, the Philippines, Bangladesh, India, and Senegal.

The more extensive modernist reforms changed family law along many of the same lines that certain largely secularized family law systems followed. Nuclear families and individuals gained greater authority in family life in Tunisia in the 1950s, as had happened only a few decades earlier in most industrialized countries and around the same time or a little later in some predominantly Catholic industrialized societies such as Italy, Spain, and Portugal. Morocco adopted the Tunisian reforms over the past decade and went further in certain respects, especially regarding matrimonial property and spousal authority in family life. Moreover, some official religious laws provided women certain rights recognized only in a minority of largely secularized family law systems. For instance, many courts granted women shares in matrimonial property equal to those of their husbands under the rubric of Islamic law in Indonesia, and Moroccan legislation gave women these rights as well a decade back. These shares were greater than divorcees get in about half the states in the United States and in many other industrialized regions.[38] This was possible because religious discourses were reconstructed in these societies, and could be elsewhere too under appropriate conditions, to support most family practices that gained recognition in conjunction with legal secularization in industrialized societies from the mid-nineteenth century until about the 1970s. Moreover, the view of the marital bond as fragile in classical Islamic law and certain customary laws has affinities with how marriage was reconstructed and no-fault divorce rights granted in most industrialized societies since the 1960s.

Religious discourses did limit legal reform in various societies in certain ways, however. For instance, even the most extensive Islamic law reforms, seen in Tunisia and Morocco, did not alter the unequal shares of parental property (in a 2:1 ratio) that the Qur'an prescribes for sons and daughters and other male and female kin with a similar relationship to the decedent.[39] Moreover, Islamic law reform marginalized certain kinship practices and sexualities that had enjoyed some social acceptance but were considered contrary to

Islamic norms, such as matrilineality in parts of Indonesia, Malaysia, and India, and alternative sexualities and transgendered behavior in Malaysia and the Philippines.[40] Changes in family law had such mixed effects on rights not only in countries with religious laws, but also in those with largely secular family laws.

To understand the directions taken by official religious laws over the last century, we need to plot the different relationships between the mobilization of religious and other cultural communities, the enactment of kinship, and the formation of states and nations. Four assumptions underlying Charrad's approach to these questions merit critical examination: (a) classical Islamic law supports the authority of the patrilineage, a claim that is of broad relevance as many more states recognize some form of Islamic law than any other kind of religious law today; (b) urban groups counter lineage power because they are less dependent on agriculture, the main source of lineage resources and authority, live in more nuclearized households, and are more influenced by the modern Western valuation of companionate marriage and autonomous nuclear families; (c) under conditions of prior state autonomy and significant urbanization, centralizing state elites and urban groups reform cultural and religious traditions to promote nuclear family autonomy; and (d) family nuclearization aids women's rights.[41]

While Islamic legal traditions uphold male authority over many family practices and recognize inheritance rights mainly based on relationships with men, their prescriptions reduce the authority of the patrilineage in certain ways. For instance, the fixed inheritance shares that they prescribe for individuals, including women, are not conducive to patrilineal property control.[42] This led to conflicts between *ulama* and landed elites at different points over inheritance practices in various societies with strong lineages.[43] Urban groups vary in the extent of their dissociation from agricultural property, and nuclearized households may find extended families both constraints and sources of support. This renders uncertain the relationship urban groups have with lineages and cultural traditions that uphold lineage authority, and thus the extent of their support for initiatives to limit lineage power and increase nuclear family authority. The implications of family nuclearization for women's rights depend crucially on the nature of authority relations in the nuclear family. Discourses of nation and community influence the kind of family units and the types of familial gender relations that both urban and rural groups value most.

Echoing Charrad (though without referring to her work), Mytheli Sreenivas linked the emergence of ideas of the conjugal family in India to the growth of new mercantile and professional elites and their competition from the nineteenth century with landholding elites, which defended the authority of the patrilineal joint-family.[44] She took better account of ongoing changes in family forms than Charrad did, but presented only fragmentary evidence that class status was closely connected to the positions taken in debates over family life. In attempting to align positions in these debates with the occupational specialization of agents, she misrepresented some of these positions.[45] Ritu Birla's more empirically detailed and conceptually nuanced analysis showed that the joint-family remained crucial in the organization of mercantile activity in colonial India, and that many aspects of the legal construction of the Hindu joint-family as an entity that controls property were results of efforts to promote commerce.[46] This was a reason why fewer mercantile and professional elites favored granting individuals control over ancestral property than over property accumulated through professional activities. Thus, individuals from these groups piloted the passage of the Hindu Gains of Learning Act, which assured professionals full rights in the property they acquired by virtue of their education as early as 1930, even if joint-family resources had funded their education. But many of them resisted efforts to make ancestral property readily divisible into individual shares in the 1950s, and accepted this change only in 2005.

While social structure did not determine preferences regarding personal law and family life in the ways that Charrad and Sreenivas indicated, there are some affinities between particular social groups and certain projects of family formation. Urban professionals with limited connections to agricultural land favor the autonomy of the nuclear family and sometimes that of individuals in certain respects. However, they vary in the activities over which they favor giving nuclear families control, the extent to which they prioritize such authority for the nuclear family, and in whether they seek to promote these ends by secularizing law or reforming religious law, adopting Western precedents or reforming indigenous traditions. Rural elites and urban professional groups with significant landed property tend to favor the shared control of extended kin over ancestral property (especially land) and various forms of clan authority. Those embedded in patrilineal kinship practices particularly support the rights of agnatic kin. The majority of colonial personal laws upheld such forms of property control as well as other forms of authority for extended kin, and certain precolonial normative and juristic systems supported them as well. Legal elites, which play crucial roles in initiatives for legal change, tend to draw their visions of authentic legal tradition largely from colonial personal law and customary law, rather than from the older cultural and jurisprudential traditions that these legal systems are said to reflect. By way of contrast, religious elites and certain ethnic elites more often base their personal law agendas partly on precolonial traditions.

Charrad paid inadequate attention to the diverse ways in which the kinship practices upheld in classical religious texts were enacted in particular social contexts, the various sources from which colonial personal laws were drawn, the different relationships that systems of religious personal law had with local customs, and the particular ways in which different groups felt that their social identities were tied to classical religious law on the one hand and local customs on the other hand. Due to her focus on a region where the Maliki *madhhab* developed in interaction with patrilineal forms of kinship, she did not consider the rather different forms of "practical kinship" enacted as normatively Islamic and enforced as Islamic law in different societies.[47] John Bowen, Michael Feener, Mark Cammack, and Michael Peletz showed that kin relations developed among Muslims in Indonesia and Malaysia through the interaction of pre-Islamic matrilineal and bilateral practices with the largely patrilineal norms of the Shafi'i *madhhab* that is said to govern these groups.[48] *Qadis* (religious judges) often mandated inheritance according to *adat* (ethnic or regional customs, many of which predate the influence of Islam in the region and differ from the prescriptions of Islamic jurisprudence). Even the authoritative texts of the main school of Shia law (the *Ithna Ashari*) prescribed bilateral rather than patrilineal inheritance outside the nuclear family, influenced by the predominantly bilateral kinship practices of Iran and Iraq, where the majority of the world's Shias live.[49] The variety of inheritance practices followed by Muslims, some of which were encoded in texts of religious law, are among the many indicators that world religions assumed different forms in interaction with specific social contexts.

Even if they were framed as religious laws, colonial personal laws incorporated many customs specific to region or ethnic group, as well as common law or civil-law conventions. These customs had uncertain relations with the texts on which colonial policy makers mainly based their understanding of religious law. Some of them governed members of many religious groups. Colonial courts recognized many such customs in Indonesia, where various colonial intellectuals and officials considered such customs rather than Islamic law the main basis of family practices especially regarding inheritance, although Islamic law was said to govern the country's Muslim majority. They also recognized the inheritance customs followed by the majority of Indian Muslims, which did not give women the shares in family property that classical Islamic law prescribed. Thus, colonial personal law was in most cases some steps removed from the classics of religious law. It often influenced what colonized groups considered of cultural value, and to the extent that it did so, postcolonial rulers faced popular expectations that they would recognize many family practices that the texts of classical religious law did not support. This was less the case among Indian Hindus. Colonial officials constructed official Hindu law based importantly on particular Hindu religious texts (especially the *Mitakshara* and the *Dayabhaga*) that upheld many of the customs of the dominant castes and lineages of particular regions. They systematized different schools of Hindu law based on these earlier texts, and applied them to the residents of specific regions. This aligned the Hindu law in force with certain prevalent customs.[50]

The perceived relationship between religious law and custom influenced how groups connected their identities with religious law on the one hand and regional custom on the other hand. Indian Hindus saw ethnic and regional customs more often as the prescriptions of religious law, while Indian Muslims (particularly religious elites) felt that the customs of their religious group departed from their religious law in crucial respects. As a result, Muslim religious elites demanded that the rules of classical Islamic law rather than the customs of landed elites be applied to Muslim inheritance, and faced the resistance of Muslim landed elites, who ensured the continued application of regional custom to land inheritance. Among Hindus, the majority of religious elites and landed elites made common cause in opposing personal-law reform on the grounds of religious tradition as well as indigenous custom from the late nineteenth century until the 1950s.

Besides, groups vary in the stake they feel in religious law. Indian Muslim religious elites had a greater stake than their Hindu counterparts because expertise in religious law was more important to their authority. As a result, they mobilized Muslim personal law as an important domain of religious identity from the late nineteenth century, and remained closely engaged with Muslim law adjudication and legislation thereafter. By way of contrast, Hindu religious elites largely withdrew from debates about personal law after parliament introduced moderate reforms in the 1950s. Resistance to Hindu law reform came primarily from the social elites of patrilineal groups thereafter.

The norms of specific ethnic groups and regions supplemented religious jurisprudence more in societies in which predominant nationalist discourses highlighted cultural similarities and cultural exchanges across religious boundaries. This was especially the case in Indonesia. Sensitivity to regional culture also depended on the level of government that was responsible for family law, being greater in federal polities in which the state governments assumed much of this responsibility—such as Malaysia, the United States and Canada—than in unitary polities such as Britain or in federal polities such as India's in which the federal government assumed primary responsibility.

Bina Agarwal explored the implications of kinship practices for orientations to family law in South Asia. She argued that regional differences in customs regarding inheritance, marital alliances, and postmarital residence influenced women's rights to inherit land, as well as their effective access to land. Agarwal demonstrated that the customs of patriliny, village and kin exogamy, and patrilocality, predominant in northern and western India, Pakistan, and Nepal, limited women's ability to access resources, especially land, to which they were legally entitled. The greater prevalence of bilateral and matrilineal inheritance, and village and kin endogamy, and more varied patterns of postmarital residence in southern and eastern India, Bangladesh, and Sri Lanka were more favorable to women's access to land. Moreover, Agarwal showed that these customs influenced state-specific land legislation, which overrode national-level Hindu laws regarding the inheritance of agricultural land until recently, seriously limiting women's land rights in northern and western India.[51] These regionally specific practices influenced the Hindu law debates of the 1950s and the 2000s, in which legislators from the north and the west especially opposed changes that would have enabled women to access ancestral property. They were also crucial to the introduction of such changes initially in the southern states. Furthermore, they influenced people's positions on marriage and divorce law, which Agarwal did not discuss. Representatives from northern and western India particularly resisted allowing kin endogamy and increases in the rights to marital separation and divorce. This was especially the case among those from the upper and upper-middle castes, which followed norms of kin exogamy and marriage indissolubility the most.

V. SECULARISM, THE RECOGNITION OF RELIGION, AND MULTICULTURALISM

Certain states that claim to be secular recognize personal laws that draw from religious norms and govern specific religious groups or sects. Tensions arise between their secularist claims and their application of religious laws. Secular states aim to restrict or change the social roles of religion to promote various ends. Liberal-democratic secular states and states that present themselves as such claim that their interventions in religion are meant to ensure individual liberties, treat different religious groups similarly, limit religious discrimination in society, contain religious and sectarian conflict, and promote social equality to levels necessary to produce an autonomous citizenry. An important body of literature indicates that secularist institutions and policies depend on, and perhaps ought to reflect, the nature of religious practices and religious institutions, the prior engagement of states with such practices and institutions, and the visions of religious toleration, equality, and freedom salient in particular societies.[52] These studies trace the higher resistance to the recognition of religious norms and the greater restriction of religious symbols in public life in France than in the United States to such factors as the role of anticlericalism in restricting the monopolistic power of the Catholic Church in France and the greater prevalence of religious practice in recent decades in the United States. Similarly, they attribute the greater accommodation of religious norms and greater attention to the state's equidistance from religions and religious groups in India than in France and the United States to the higher public relevance of religion and greater intensity of interreligious conflict when a sovereign state was established there.[53] These considerations are taken to have motivated the recognition of religion as a basis for social and cultural rights (for example, to distinct educational institutions and personal laws), but not for political rights (for example, separate electorates) in India. In highlighting the extensive accommodation of public religion in India and the correspondence of these arrangements with certain popular expectations, this literature refutes the claims of T. N. Madan and Ashis Nandy that India's secular institutions did not engage with crucial public cultures infused by religious norms and therefore drew support only among a narrow elite. We will see, however, that such criticisms were applicable to Turkish secularism.[54]

Gary Jacobsohn offered such a contextually specific understanding of three models of secularism: American assimilative secularism that seeks to preserve religious liberty in the private sphere while urging political assimilation in the American republic; Israel's visionary secularism that involves the coexistence of the vision of Israel as a state of the Jewish people with commitments to preserve religious liberties and cultural autonomy; and India's ameliorative secularism, committed to transform enduring social inequalities related to religious belief and practice while ensuring cultural autonomy. He considered these models responses to religion's role in social life and national identity, and understood features of family law as expressions of these models. While the American state's determination to subsume the claims of religious groups to the supremacy of civil law led to the penalization of alternative family practices related to minority religious norms (specifically, Mormon polygyny), the inclination of the Israeli and Indian states to accommodate religious minorities led them to accept polygyny among Muslims while banning the practice among their religious majorities. Jacobsohn claimed that the Indian state was more likely than the Israeli state to reform Muslim law and introduce uniform secular family laws if opinion among the concerned groups supported these steps because the Indian state alone had ameliorative ambitions.[55]

These authors contributed significantly to understanding varieties of secularism, but slipped too readily from an empathic understanding of official secularisms to the conclusion that religion was accommodated appropriately in various societies. They paid inadequate attention, for instance, to phenomena that meant that Western states engaged very unequally with specific religious groups and sects, a problem which became more glaring as these societies became more diverse in religious practice, such as the association of the British state with the Anglican Church; the incorporation of Judeo-Christian visions in the Constitution and aspects of the legal system in the United States; and the reluctance of states in Norway, Sweden, Denmark, and the Netherlands to extend non-Christian religions the recognition they had given Christian sects that had lived for long in their societies. Nor did they consider whether the religious laws of Israel and India best reflect religious practices, reform initiatives, and the requirements of tolerance. The ban on polygyny among the majority and not among Muslims was related to public opinion in Israel but not in India, where bigamy was practiced and accepted about as much among Hindus as among Muslims when the practice was banned among Hindus soon after independence. Even in Israel, polygyny was practiced among some Mizrahi groups (Jews from the Arab world, Caucusus, Central Asia, and Ethiopia) when they migrated to Israel. As the Israeli political and judicial elite prioritized changing practices among the Jews, but not among the Muslims, they applied the civil law banning polygyny (and other civil marriage laws) much of the time in the rabbinical courts, but accepted the continued validation of polygynous marriages in the Muslim courts.[56]

Major understandings of Indian secularism identify the main reasons for the maintenance of distinct personal laws, but do not effectively account for the postponement of change in the minority laws or the specific changes made in Hindu law. Jacobsohn and Rajeev Bhargava argued that the focus on Hindu law reform reflected the greater support for personal-law reform among Hindus and a commitment to minority accommodation. In a similar vein, Paul Brass, James Chiriyankandath, Subrata Mitra, and Alexander Fischer attributed the choice not to change the minority laws after independence to the agreement that Congress Party leaders had reached with certain Muslim elites to maintain distinct Muslim laws.[57] These authors ignored the compatibility of minority accommodation with changes in minority laws based on the relevant group's norms, practices, and initiatives, and misunderstood the relative strength of reformist mobilization. Significant initiatives to change social life and personal law had emerged among Muslims from the 1920s. They led to some reforms in Muslim law in the late 1930s, and made many Muslim elites open to further changes if they were based on Islamic norms and significant Muslim mobilization.

The most important change made in Muslim law was the passage of the Shariat Act in 1937, initiated by various Muslim political and religious elites, which required the application of Islamic law rather than customs specific to region, caste, or lineage to Muslim family life. This increased the rights of most Muslim women in colonial India, to whom the courts had applied patrilineal customs, particularly to inheritance. Muslim women were thereafter entitled to half the share of similarly positioned male kin in family property. The resistance of Muslim landed elites to the shares that Islamic law gave women in family property led to a compromise that exempted agricultural land from the purview of Islamic law, as we saw. As a result, patrilineal customs that gave women no shares or very limited shares in family property continued to govern most Indian Muslims with regard to agricultural land.[58] The majority of the Muslim landed elites that had pressed for this compromise wound up in Pakistan after 1947. The resulting decline in the power of Muslim landed elites in India significantly reduced opposition to extending the Shariat Act's purview to agricultural land, and the majority of *ulama* would have supported this change because they considered the inheritance shares prescribed in the Qur'an to be immutable features of Islamic law. Moreover, the Indian Constitution, adopted in 1950, moved succession to agricultural land from the sole jurisdiction of provincial governments to the concurrent jurisdiction of the national and the state governments, removing procedural obstacles to the passage of national legislation to this effect.[59] Despite this, the Shariat Act was applied to the inheritance of agricultural land soon after independence in West Pakistan (today's Pakistan), but not in India, where only two state governments made this move.[60]

Certain Muslim legal and political elites proposed other Muslim law reforms by the 1940s, such as requiring families with means to provide their daughters' dower, giving women control over their dower and the right their husbands already had to repudiate their spouses, and restricting unilateral male repudiation.[61] Policy makers did not consider such changes or an increase in divorce rights for Christians, which various Christian organizations demanded from the 1950s. Besides, Hindu law reform initiatives faced considerable resistance. Thus, support for personal-law reform was no stronger among Hindus than it was among Muslims and Christians, and influential Muslims and Christians had highlighted culturally specific grounds to change their personal laws.[62] Nevertheless, policy makers changed Hindu law and Hindu law alone soon after independence, because most political elites primarily engaged initiatives among Hindus, imagined the nation primarily with reference to various Hindu cultural sources, and conceived projects to reshape the nation and reduce deep inequalities mainly with reference to such sources and initiatives.

Gyanendra Pandey, Partha Chatterjee, and Aamir Mufti noted that the majority of Indian nationalists, both cultural pluralists and those who sought Hindu hegemony, shared such orientations in the late colonial period, but the literature has not explored the consequences for postcolonial recognition.[63] Many aspects of Indian multiculturalism had a Hindu-majoritarian orientation, not only regarding personal law but also preferential policies and state responses to autonomist and secessionist movements. Preferences in education, government employment, and political representation, along with special civil rights protections, were extended to the Hindu lower castes (scheduled castes) and tribal groups and later to lower-caste individuals practicing other religions of South Asian origin such as Sikhism (in 1956) and Buddhism (in 1990), but not to lower-caste Muslims and Christians even though the latter groups faced much the same constraints and indignities as the former. This discouraged lower-caste conversion from Hinduism to Christianity and Islam, contrary to the state's claim to promote religious freedom.[64] The formation of Pakistan as a country for India's Muslims led many policy makers to consider the religious minorities most likely to favor secession. They therefore more readily accommodated autonomist and secessionist movements that emerged among predominantly Hindu cultural groups (such as the Dravidian and the Assamese movements), while repressing such movements more often if they grew among predominantly non-Hindu groups (such as the Naga, Kashmiri, and Sikh movements).[65] Various scholars did not address the influence of religious identity over preferential policies and policies toward ethnic movements.[66] The manner in which these policies took religious identity into account was contrary to the Indian state's claim to equidistance from the various religious groups. Bhargava and Charles Taylor nevertheless misleadingly deemed the state's maintenance of such a "principled distance" from religious groups a major distinctive feature of Indian secularism. The asymmetries in the Indian state's engagement with religious groups weakened efforts to build interreligious understanding, to reduce durable inequalities, and to represent the country's different religious cultures in the emergent nation.

Jacobsohn understood early postcolonial Hindu law reform as meant to realize the constitutional principle, based in liberal public reason, of ameliorating deep inequalities; Bhargava took it to be aimed to make personal law more just with respect to gender. However, the main sources of these changes—notions of social reform based on Hindu normative traditions and the model of the heterosexual and monogamous nuclear family that Western law provided at the time—were not based on a liberal imaginary and did not urge the systematic reduction of gender inequalities. The former encouraged the maintenance of lineage control over property and limits on mate choice and divorce rights; the latter influenced reductions in the rights of women in matrilineal groups or in polygynous relationships. Moreover, a preference to maintain broad support led policy makers to accommodate conservatives by placing serious limits on women's access to ancestral property and strengthening men's right to the conjugal company of their spouses.

VI. CENTRAL ARGUMENTS IN BRIEF

The book explains the course of personal law with reference to two sets of mutually interacting factors: features of state-society relations and the discourses of community that are salient among ruling elites or groups with significant influence over policy. The relevant features of state-society relations are social structure, the nature of state-society engagements under the predecessor regime, the coalitions that the regime or segments of the regime have and aim to build, and the projects of state elites to change state-society relations. The discourses of community that exercise greatest influence are those about the nation, its cultural groups, and its traditions.

The ways in which two category couplets—nation-community and modernity-authenticity—are deployed in discourses of community matter. The particular forms in which the nation-community and modernity-authenticity dyads are articulated influence the imagination of crucial group boundaries, the dynamics of the society, the nature of state institutions, and the boundaries and engagements between state and society in the present and in the projected future. Such forms of imagination of community in turn influence the construction of states and state-society relations, and how certain actors experience these phenomena.

The two crucial explanatory variables, state-society relations and discourses of community, develop through such interactions with one another, and their interactions shape various policies, particularly those pertaining to the recognition, transmission, and transformation of cultures. Figure 2.1 and Tables 2.1 and 2.2 capture these relationships.

We first consider the links each of these variables has to patterns of nation formation, recognition, and family law. Then we explore the interaction of these variables and the effects of these interactions on multiculturalism and family law.

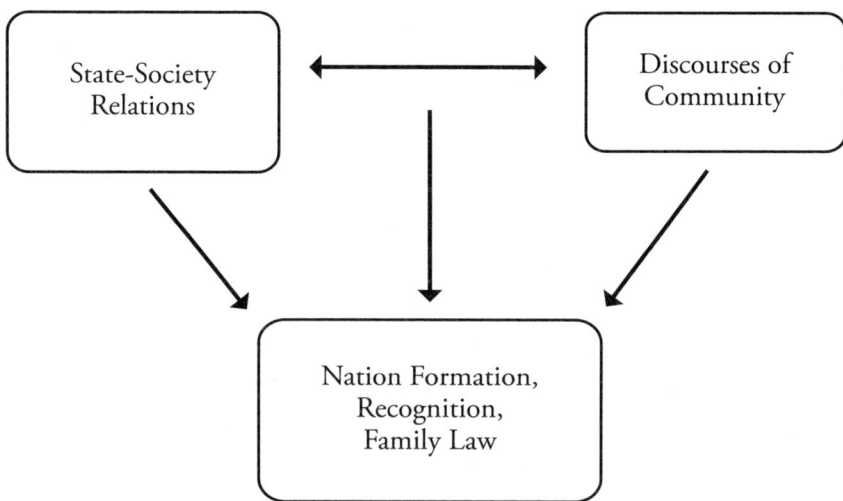

FIGURE 2.1. Discourses of Community, State-Society Relations, and Personal Law

TABLE 2.1 Influences on Multiculturalism and Personal Law

State-Society Relations	Discourses About
Social Structure	Nation
Prior State-Society Relations	Cultural Groups
Regime Coalitions	Traditions
Projects of State Elites	

TABLE 2.2 Features of Community Discourses and State-Society Relations That Influence One Another

Couplets Used in Discourses of Community	Features of State-Society Relations
Nation-Community	Group Boundaries
Modernity-Authenticity	Social Dynamics
	Nature of State Institutions
	State-Society Boundaries & Engagements

VII. CENTRAL ARGUMENTS ELABORATED

A. Regimes and Coalitions

The kinds of social coalitions that regimes have and aim to build influence the course of family law. Societies in which traditional elites such as agrarian lineage leaders enjoyed considerable authority and professional, commercial, and industrial elites were weak tended to produce regimes dominated by or heavily dependent on traditional elites. These traditional elites tended to retain prior personal laws that upheld the authority of lineages and kin groups. These conditions obtained in postcolonial Lebanon, Syria, and Morocco and to some extent in Algeria, and they ensured the retention of most colonial personal laws. Catchall regimes that aimed to build links with a wide range of social groups and social visions introduced only limited social reforms, especially if mobilized groups were sharply divided over reform. This was the case in postcolonial Egypt, Jordan, Sri Lanka, India, Malaysia, and Indonesia. Vanguardist regimes, which valued the social projects they wished to pilot more than building broad coalitions, promoted extensive social reform even if this led to considerable conflict and narrowed their support. They closely associated these projects with the groups among which they retained support while they transformed society. These groups could be either modernists, such as socialists and communists drawn largely from the urban middle and working classes, or religious elites and other groups that preferred either the extensive public recognition of religion (as sections of the lower middle classes did in various societies) or the reinforcement of kin group authority (as powerful agrarian groups tended to). The vanguardist projects were modernist in early republican Turkey and early postcolonial Tunisia, and conservative in Pakistan, Iran, Sudan, northern Nigeria, Afghanistan, and east peninsular Malaysia at different points from the late 1970s.

To take some examples of regimes dominated by traditional social elites, the maintenance of community courts was an aspect of the agreement that forged the Grand Alliance that gave the clan leaders among Lebanon's various sects political representation. The elites that led these courts retained the existing personal laws. The close alliance of certain factions of Algeria's ruling Front de Libération Nationale (FLN) with conservative lineages, like the restriction of the Syrian regime's support mainly to the minority Alawi sect since the late 1960s, restrained the reformist inclinations of certain regime members. The Moroccan monarchy's reliance more on rural lineages than on the urban groups aligned with the nationalist Istiqlal party also predisposed it not to alter colonial Islamic law until the growth of civil society mobilization changed its calculus over the past two decades.

The experience of Egypt is representative of the approaches of catchall regimes. The Free Officers regime that came to power in 1952 and whose successors retained control over the national government until 2011, upheld a secular understanding of the nation and claimed to represent a socialist understanding of public religion. This suggested that the regime might either secularize family law or substantially reform Islamic law. Either approach could have drawn on intellectual and political currents that had been vigorous in the country since the late nineteenth century. Secular nationalism was influential in the anticolonial movement, particularly among the legal elite; Islamic modernists such as Muhammad Abduh and Muhammad Rashid Rida pioneered innovative religious reasoning that influenced policy debates around the Islamic world; and the women's movement had begun to take root. These forces urged the government to change Egypt's personal laws extensively, building on the minor changes introduced through the first half of the twentieth century.[67]

While the regime felt some inclination to follow this path to consolidate its modern image, it also considered the assistance of *ulama* in major religious institutions such as al-Azhar University important to broaden its support and contain militant Islamist organizations such as the Muslim Brotherhood. Many influential *ulama* opposed substantial increases in women's rights and individual autonomy in family life. As a result, policy elites abandoned plans to draft a modernist code of family law that would draw from Islamic legal traditions but apply to all citizens; they restricted themselves to transferring jurisdiction over personal law in 1955 from religious courts to state courts that drew their judges from both Islamic educational institutions and secular universities. They periodically made modest changes in Islamic law thereafter, but were reluctant to make far-reaching changes that major *ulama* and Islamist organizations did not consider to be grounded in Islamic traditions, especially once Islamist organizations resumed their growth in the 1970s. When there was considerable opposition to a law that enabled earlier wives to divorce their polygamous husbands, passed in 1979 through presidential decree after little public consultation, the Supreme Court struck down this law and parliament altered legislation accordingly. Subsequent reform initiatives were more cautious. They increased women's rights to maintenance and divorce, obliged women to obey their husbands in fewer activities, and decreased the ability of men to secure their wives' conjugal company; these measures promoted companionate marriage and women's education and workforce participation. But they left much space for men to act against their wives' interests, such as by requiring them to give up their jobs, repudiating them unilaterally, or concurrently marrying several women without the consent of their earlier wives.[68]

Similar concerns limited personal-law reform in Malaysia, Sri Lanka, and Jordan. The much greater vigor of electoral competition made broadening support a more compelling concern for the major parties of Malaysia (the United Malay National Organization) and Sri Lanka (the United National Party and the Sri Lanka Freedom Party). These parties gained support primarily by presenting themselves as effective representatives of their country's ethnic majority, among whom preferences regarding family law varied. To maintain support among the ethnic majority that overlapped considerably with the religious majority in these countries (Malays being largely Muslim and Sinhalese predominantly Buddhist), they had to contain challenges from Islamic and Buddhist religious institutions and movements. They did so by upholding moderate modernist understandings of religious norms and personal law, thereby allying themselves at times with religious parties and movements and limiting the appeal of these organizations at other times.[69] Concerns to contain Islamist mobilization and to limit discontent among the substantial Palestinian population similarly limited the Jordanian monarchy's reforms.[70]

The scope of personal-law reform was modest yet significant in Indonesia, much as in the countries just discussed. However, reform there was more extensive than in these countries in some respects, and more ambitious proposals were seriously considered at some points since the late 1980s. Different ideological tendencies and social visions were represented in the nationalist movement and the early postcolonial political elite—religious pluralists and proponents of an Islamic state, cultural indigenists who valued *adat* and supporters of the types of Islamic jurisprudence formed mainly in Arab contexts, and proponents of social equality as well as those who wished to maintain gender, age, and class hierarchies. In order to reconcile these diverse perspectives and contain the secessionist demands that emerged from certain "outer islands" other than Java, from particular Christian and animist groups, and from some Islamic modernist organizations, the early postcolonial political elite agreed on the doctrine of *Pancasila* (five principles), which included the recognition of a Supreme Deity rather than a specific religion. Moreover, religious pluralists such as Sukarno had greater influence, and deleted from an earlier draft of the constitution a phrase that obliged Muslims to live according to Islamic visions of justice and be governed by Islamic law. Nevertheless, Muslim marriage and divorce cases remained under the jurisdiction of the Islamic courts, which were centralized and professionalized along the lines of the civil courts, and were offered greater state resources. Besides, such courts were established in some of the outer islands for the first time after independence and gained jurisdiction over inheritance in these regions (while they governed only marriage and divorce elsewhere in the country between 1937 and 1983), whereas only minor changes were made in Islamic law throughout the country until the 1970s. These choices were made to contain the resentment of Islamic organizations about Islam not being given official primacy and the omission of a constitutional commitment to maintain Islamic law, and to preclude the reemergence of an Islamist insurgency such as had engulfed parts of Java in the first postcolonial decade.

The authoritarian New Order regime that ruled Indonesia from 1966 to 1998 retained its predecessor's secularist inclinations and resisted demands to give Islam greater constitutional significance. It initiated various important personal-law reforms, such as requiring Islamic court approval for male repudiation, authorizing the Supreme Court to supervise the Islamic courts and consider appeals of their verdicts, extending jurisdiction over the consequences of divorce to the Islamic courts, and offering litigants throughout the country the choice to have these courts consider their inheritance cases. Moreover, an official compilation of legal rulings that was meant to guide Islamic court decisions departed in many ways from the rules favored by the majority of *ulama* of the Shafi'i *madhhab* that governs most Indonesian Muslims.

Even through this period of greater personal-law reform, concerns to maintain broad support, limit Islamic resistance, and gain the support of certain Islamic scholars and institutions for their development projects deterred authorities from implementing more ambitious proposals, such as to transfer jurisdiction over marriage to the civil courts, to change Islamic inheritance rules according to the bilateral practices predominant in the country, and to equalize on this basis the inheritance shares of men and women with a similar relationship to the deceased. At the same time, the concerns of secular nationalists deterred policy makers from giving the Islamic courts sole jurisdiction over inheritance cases. While legislators did not devote much attention to changing the laws of the religious minorities, the civil courts that considered family disputes among these groups generally did so with reference to the relevant *adat*; they accepted bilateral and matrilineal practices as well as other customs favorable to women (such as the joint ownership of marital property of which both spouses are entitled to shares when they get divorced or when their spouse dies), and sometimes applied such customs to groups among which they were not prevalent based on novel constructions of a "national *adat*," which was said to be based on the "living law of society" and used to promote more egalitarian customs. After the transition to democracy in 1998, Islamist movements increased the scope of Islamic law and ensured that Islamic law was interpreted more conservatively in some of their regions of strength, particularly in Aceh where *shari'a* was made an important basis of the entire legal system.[71]

Despite the recent conservative developments in certain regions, the changes in personal law in much of Indonesia since the 1970s promoted women's rights, individual autonomy, and variety in kinship practices more than in most countries that had catchall regimes. They favored such ends more than the legal changes in Senegal, Libya, Egypt, Jordan, and Malaysia, where Islamic law also governs the majority of citizens.[72] The changes in the personal laws of Indonesia's Muslim majority were roughly comparable in character with the changes introduced in Hindu law in India since the 1970s. But the laws of the religious minorities were changed more extensively and earlier in Indonesia. Reforms were less extensive in Indonesia in various respects than in Tunisia and Turkey, whose experiences are discussed later. However, a proposal of the Ministry of Religious Affairs to equalize the inheritance shares of men and women with a similar relationship to the decedent, based on the understanding that this custom was prevalent among some ethnic groups and should be promoted among other groups, would have changed Islamic law more dramatically in Indonesia than was done in Tunisia. The Islamic laws recognized by all states give men twice the inheritance shares of women similarly related to the deceased based on the Qur'an, and only in Indonesia did policy makers consider the equalization of these shares.[73] Thus, among the countries that saw modest reform, the most extensive changes were introduced or seriously debated in Indonesia.

Regimes were particularly associated with vanguard groups and willing to launch social reforms at the cost of alienating other groups in early republican Turkey and early postcolonial Tunisia. Turkey's republican regime relied largely on the support of urban reformists and transplanted many Western social, constitutional, and legal precedents even though this caused considerable conflict. It banned various religious institutions (specifically, Sufi orders and the tombs of Muslim saints), closed religious courts and religious schools, and ended the recognition of Islam as a state religion, but simultaneously increased state control over mosques, their officials, and their practices. In 1926, it made the Swiss Civil Code rather than Islamic law relevant to family disputes. Women gained various rights in family life as a result—for example, to inherit shares in family property equal to those of their brothers, and to get divorces on grounds identical to those available to men. Moreover, polygyny and male repudiation were banned, the age of consent to marriage was increased to fifteen for women and seventeen for men, Muslim women were allowed to marry non-Muslim men, fathers were no longer preferred to mothers as child custodians, and marriage registration was required, making it easier for women to gain the economic benefits of marriage. Even after overt resistance to the regime declined, many litigants avoided state courts in rural areas, seeking unofficial courts that resolved family disputes with reference to Islamic and customary norms. Moreover, certain features of prior Islamic law were retained, albeit without official acknowledgement. For instance, the man was deemed the head of the family, was made responsible for his wife in various respects including the management of her property, and was allowed to bar his wife's workforce participation. (Various Western family law systems gave men similar authority over their wives until the early twentieth century.) Women could remarry only three hundred days after their earlier marriages ended while men faced no such restriction. Besides, judges were allowed to base matrimonial verdicts on custom and tradition on matters not covered by statute.[74]

The modernists led by Habib Bourguiba who assumed control over the Tunisian state right after independence were based mainly among the urban middle classes and unionized working classes. Much like Turkey's early republican rulers, they narrowed their coalition by expelling their main opponents, the pan-Islamist faction of the ruling Neo-Destour Party led by Salah ben Youssef. They centralized power, limited the authority of lineages and religious elites, and introduced extensive family law reforms based on innovative interpretations of Islamic law. Tunisia saw the most extensive Islamic law reforms until the Moroccan monarchy adopted most of the Tunisian precedents and went further in certain respects in 2004.[75] The Tunisian rulers prioritized the reforms sufficiently to adopt them soon after independence even though mobilization in their favor was weak, especially on the part of women's organizations, and they aroused significant opposition. By way of contrast, the major reforms happened in Morocco nearly fifty years after independence, only once they were backed by effective civil society mobilization; reforms were passed in Indonesia at different points after more ambitious proposals were abandoned because they faced resistance.

The different sources of the Turkish and Tunisian reforms especially influenced the inheritance provisions. While the changes in Tunisia retained the 2:1 Qur'anic ratio in the inheritance shares of men and women who had a similar relationship to the deceased, the secularized Turkish family law was not bound by this constraint and equalized these shares. However, women's likely shares in family property were increased in other ways in Tunisia: by limiting testamentary rights to a third of one's property, prohibiting the donation of one's property to *waqf* (public trusts, many of which are run by religious institutions)—thereby also limiting the resources of religious institutions—increasing a wife's share in the absence of male agnates, and giving the claims of daughters and sons' daughters priority over those of male agnates. Many of the other Tunisian reforms were similar to those in Turkey. For instance, religious courts were discontinued, polygamy was criminalized, the divorce and custody rights of men and women were equalized, the registration of marriages and divorces was required, and adoption was allowed in both countries. The husband's authority over his wife was limited less in Tunisia than in Turkey until spousal authority was equalized in both countries over the past decade. But women gained more rights in certain respects in Tunisia than in Turkey—for example, mutual-consent divorce was made available in Tunisia alone, and the minimum age of marriage was made the same for men and women in Tunisia; it remained higher for men in Turkey until 2002. The similarities in the reforms in the two countries show that Tunisian policy makers interpreted Islamic legal traditions in tune with much the same modernist goals that their Turkish counterparts derived from secularist reasoning. The Tunisian regime contained conservative resistance and the operation of unofficial courts much sooner than the Turkish republic did, giving official law fuller and quicker influence over the resolution of family disputes.[76]

Critiques of the monarchy's elitist modernization efforts and secularist nationalism, along with calls to reinstate Islamic authenticity, influenced the Iranian Revolution. They shaped the conservative project the postrevolutionary regime pursued once the faction led by Ayatollah Khomeini and likeminded religious elites marginalized its former allies (including secularist democrats, egalitarian Islamists, and certain traditionalist Islamists), vested preeminent authority in an unelected religious jurist who was the state's Supreme Leader and guardian of Islamic values, and gained a decisive voice in the elected parliament.[77] The regime reversed many of the Pahlavi monarchy's reforms, including in family law. For instance, it returned family law to the religious courts' jurisdiction, removed women judges from these courts, made the judicial approval of male repudiation unnecessary, gave fathers and their kin priority over mothers as child custodians, deemed divorces based on old-regime legislation invalid, deprived women of the divorce rights they had enjoyed if their husbands contracted other marriages without their consent, reduced the minimum marriage age to nine, reinstated temporary marriages, and enabled the stoning of adulterers.

These features of the postrevolutionary Iranian regime and the extent to which it changed family law bore affinities with the experiences in Turkey and Tunisia. However, women had participated extensively in the Iranian revolution, and Khomeini and his allies wished to retain their support to compensate for expelling their faction's ideological competitors from the regime. They claimed that Islamic norms as they understood them could offer women greater rights and dignity than the monarchy's Westernization had, and they deployed dynamic forms of Islamic jurisprudence to justify the institutions they established. This lent some legitimacy to the innovative religious reasoning used by certain public intellectuals not closely linked to the regime to support extensive public roles for women. Moreover, the demand for women's labor increased because of the decline of the male population during the war with Iraq through the 1980s.

For the above reasons, policy makers reinstated many rights that women had enjoyed earlier. For instance, through the 1980s and 1990s, extrajudicial divorces came to be accepted only if there was mutual consent; the judicial approval of unilateral repudiation was required once again; and judicial approval of divorce was made contingent on efforts having been made to reconcile the spouses, the woman's deferred dower having been paid, and arrangements having been made for the father to support his children if he was not given custody of them. Moreover, standard officially approved marriage contracts gave women the delegated right to divorce husbands who took concurrent wives, and to receive payment for housework they had done during the course of their marriage, as well as half of the matrimonial property if their matrimonial faults were not the bases of the divorce. Women were reinstated as judges in family courts, which were required, moreover, to have at least one woman judge. The courts relied on Pahlavi-era statutes in areas of family life not covered by postrevolutionary legislation, often gave women child custody while holding their husbands or husbands' kin responsible for the children's economic support, and did not decree stoning. Such changes accompanied increased public roles for women and helped secure the regime wider support (especially when cautious reformers occupied the Iranian presidency) than the Turkish republic enjoyed through its first generation, without containing demands for further women's empowerment articulated in innovative Islamic discourses.[78]

As part of its efforts to reinforce Pakistani identity after the secession of Bangladesh by giving religious norms and symbols added public relevance, the Pakistani dictatorship of the 1970s and the 1980s incorporated conservative Hanafi interpretations into Islamic law, applied Islamic law to the assessment of evidence and certain types of crimes, and reversed some minor reforms introduced by earlier governments, This gained it the support of the small Islamic parties as well as of less organized conservatives. The vision of public religion that motivated the president, Zia-ul-Haq, led him to persist in this course although it provoked the concerted opposition of the Shia minority and various women's organizations and reformist organizations.[79]

Thus, the kind of coalitions that regimes aimed to build and the ways in which they sought to engage with society influenced the extent and nature of the changes introduced in personal law. Table 2.3 summarizes these patterns.

However, the following features of state elites also crucially influenced the debates and conflicts that determined regime composition, the states' approaches to engaging with society, and the course of personal law: the nationalist discourses framing their orientation, the forms of modernity they embraced, the ways in which they formally and informally classified cultural groups, their understandings of group cultures, their valuation of cultural authenticity, and the weight they gave personal law as a realm in which to assert modernity and cultural authenticity. We now consider the relationships between modes of imagination of the nation and approaches to personal law.

TABLE 2.3 Regime Type and Change in Personal Law

Extent of Change in Personal Law	Type of Regime		
	Vanguardist	Catch-All	Led by Traditional Elites[1]
Extensive	Turkey, Tunisia (Modernist)		
	Nigeria, Iran, Pakistan, Sudan, Afghanistan, east Malaysia, Aceh[2] (Conservative)		
Moderate		Senegal, Libya, Egypt, Jordan, Iraq, Iran, Pakistan, India, Sri Lanka, Bangladesh, Malaysia, Indonesia, Thailand, Philippines[3]	
Limited			Algeria, Morocco,[4] Lebanon, Syria, Malawi

[1] Regimes over which groups such as landed elites, patrilineage leaders, and religious elites, that valued the earlier personal laws and whose interests and authority these laws upheld, had considerable influence
[2] Nigeria since the 1980s, primarily regarding the laws of the Muslim majority; Iran since the Islamic revolution and especially in the 1980s; Pakistan since the late 1970s; Sudan since the late 1980s; Afghanistan especially under the rule of the Taliban; east peninsular Malaysia since the 1970s; and Aceh since the last decade
[3] Iran under the Pahlavi monarchy; Pakistan until the 1970s; West peninsular and nonpeninsular Malaysia
[4] Morocco until the last decade

B. Modes of Imagination of the Nation

Most contemporary states present themselves as representatives of nations—a claim they deploy to build affective links with citizens, the majority of whom they typically consider part of the nation they aim to represent. This is a means through which the widespread impression in contemporary societies that the state is autonomous and regulates social action intensively is partly reconciled with the sense (also frequently encountered) that popular sovereignty ensures a close connection between the vitality of states and the welfare and cultural identities of citizens.[80] Many states also articulate discourses about particular religious groups and ethnic groups with which they claim a special connection, and thereby cement links with these groups.

The discourses of nation and community that states and political elites employ do not only serve the purpose of building support and legitimacy and increasing the chances that their commands carry authority. They also frame the social visions of many state officials and various other social actors in many ways. For instance, they influence how these individuals view the major constituent groups in their societies; the norms, capacities and dispositions of these groups; the social roles these groups should have; the institutions that would best recognize the qualities and roles of these groups; the relationships between these groups and the nations of which they are a part; the relationships of these groups with groups and traditions based in other states; and more generally the courses they wish their societies to follow. These discourses also frequently influence popular expectations regarding state action and the language in which certain groups raise demands, whether in support of or opposition to state initiatives. Thus, they significantly affect the state-society interactions accompanying the formation and implementation of various policies.

Discourses of nation and those of community develop through mutual engagement. The nature of political community is central to nationalist narratives, which vary, however, in how they see the nation's constituent cultures and how they seek to forge community. These narratives vary in whether they consider the nation culturally homogeneous or diverse; and if they see the nation as diverse, whether they consider the cultures of the constituent groups to be entirely distinct or to overlap. Even discourses that present the nation as diverse vary in whether they construct national culture primarily with reference to the cultures of the most numerous or powerful groups, or also the cultures of minorities and subordinate groups; whether they seek to recognize the specificity of minorities or urge their assimilation; and whether they conceive the nation in terms of the ways of the dominant religious group or sect, a nondenominational religiosity, or a secular culture connected to predominant social practices and political institutions. Moreover, nationalist discourses vary in whether they see national cultures as static or dynamic and in whether they wish to maintain or revive social and cultural forms, channel indigenous sociocultural dynamics in new directions, or borrow institutions and mores from other societies. These features of the way the nation, its cultural groups, and its traditions are imagined, influence various policies, particularly those pertaining to the recognition, transmission and transformation of cultures, such as policies regarding education, language, religious communication and conversion, the promotion or restriction of intergroup interaction, the reduction, maintenance or widening of group inequalities, and systems of family law.

The connections are particularly close between discourses of nation and community and patterns of regulation of family life, because many actors consider certain forms of family and intimacy central to particular group or national cultures. They are explicit in personal-law systems that are framed to reflect group cultures, thus urging individuals to construct their interests in family life importantly in terms of how they see group norms. For instance, they lead many who wish to give individuals greater conjugal autonomy and property control, as well as many others who wish kin groups to control such matters, to understand and present their preferences as part of particular constructions of group normative and legal traditions. In such contexts, proposals that are given a credible basis in popular constructions of group culture have greater chances of acceptance. To the extent that salient discourses give certain cultural groups a privileged position in the nation, projects to change the personal laws of these groups tend to be framed as ways to make both group and nation.

i. Homogeneity / Diversity. While official French, Turkish, Chinese, and Argentinian nationalist narratives emphasize cultural homogeneity, the diversity of national cultures is central to official narratives about Indonesia, India, Lebanon, Kenya, Nigeria, Belgium, and Switzerland. Discourses that emphasized cultural homogeneity while being formally inclusive led state elites to resist the recognition of the nation's religious and linguistic minorities in France and Turkey, and to transfer religious minority group members to neighboring countries in exchange for members of the religious majority in Turkey.[81] In certain other countries such as Israel and Pakistan, where national culture was defined almost exclusively in terms of the ways of the dominant religious majority, policy makers acknowledged certain cultural differences and maintained some forms of minority recognition that predated the formation of these nation-states, such as distinct personal laws. However, they did not try to inculcate in the minorities the values they promoted among the majority. For instance, they changed the majority laws to promote the family norms they valued, but did not change the minority laws much. Policy makers changed Muslim law in Pakistan at different points, initially in a somewhat modernist and later in a decidedly conservative direction, but not the laws of the Hindu and Christian minorities to which they devoted little attention.[82] The Israeli legislature introduced significant changes in civil marriage law and the Supreme Court ensured the somewhat systematic application of these laws in the rabbinical courts governing the Jews, but not in the religious courts governing the country's Muslims, Druze, and Christians. In applying the standards of civil marriage law to family disputes among Jews alone, the Supreme Court reflected the Israeli elite's view that minority practices were unimportant to nation formation, and their unrealized hope that limited intervention in certain minority religious practices would restrict the mobilization of the minorities against their political and social marginalization.[83] The Pakistani and Israeli states also enabled population transfers similar to those in Turkey.[84]

The Egyptian state periodically reformed the laws of its Muslim majority, but did not change Coptic Christian law after the 1930s, and disbanded the lay Supreme Communal Council that had earlier changed the latter set of laws. Along with the incorporation of *shari'a* in the constitution, this reflected the implicit view of Muslims as central to the nation that coexisted with official emphasis on an Arab identity that embraced Christians too.[85] For similar reasons, the legislature and judiciary changed the laws of Bangladesh's Muslim majority, but not those of its Hindu, Christian, and Buddhist minorities even though official nationalism focused on Bengali speakers (including Hindus and Christians).[86] However, in some cases in which the nation was defined significantly with reference to its religious and ethnic majorities, minority representation in regimes ensured changes in minority recognition. Although the Malaysian legislature focused on changing Islamic law from the 1970s, it also began to apply civil laws rather than personal laws to non-Muslims at the same time and changed these civil laws periodically thereafter, with the support of the ethnic minority parties that were crucial partners in ruling coalitions.[87]

Among nationalist discourses that emphasize diversity, those that consider group cultures entirely distinct urge the accommodation of these cultures in ways that limit cultural exchange, while those that highlight cultural overlap are more open to enabling cultural exchange. For instance, the former type of understanding led the Lebanese and Syrian states to maintain the jurisdiction of community courts over their various personal laws; by contrast the Egyptian and Indian states, whose emphases on the Arab and Indian identities respectively shared by all their citizens led them to give state courts jurisdiction over personal law and to consider the introduction of uniform family laws. The judges who staff community courts bring distinct social visions to bear on how they interpret their communities' personal laws, and maintain differences between these personal laws.[88] Personal law systems tend to converge in certain respects when interpreted by the similarly trained and professionalized judges of state courts, even if they are said to rest on distinct statutes, jurisprudential systems, and cultural formations, as happened in India. Moreover, in India and Indonesia, where nationalist narratives highlight cultural similarities across religious and ethnic lines, courts construed personal-law provisions in light of distinctive group traditions, customs shared by various religious groups, and statutes applicable to all citizens or the residents of particular states. This led them to apply similar alimony provisions throughout India, similar rules regarding acceptable marital alliances in particular regions of India, and the same customs concerning matrimonial property in Indonesia to different religious groups although the relevant features of statutory and uncodified religious law were rather different.

While nationalist discourses emphasized that various religious groups shared certain cultural practices in India and Indonesia, the predominant discourses among political elites and religious scholars varied in other respects. In Indonesia, ruling elites defined belief in a nondenominational Supreme Deity as a central aspect of membership in the nation (although Confucianism, Hinduism, and certain of the country's folk religions are not monotheistic), and understood the customs of the archipelago, shaped by Buddhist, Hindu, Islamic, and Christian influences as well as by folk spiritual practices, to constitute national culture. In India, official discourse presented the partially overlapping cultures of the major religious groups as central to the nation, without expecting religious belief of its citizens. While the Indian narrative was similar to Indonesian nationalism in its cosmopolitan pluralism, it coexisted with the wide prevalence of the view that Hindu practices were based in indigenous cultural traditions while the ways of Indians practicing religions of foreign origin were not. This led many public actors to see Hindu norms as central to Indian national culture, in contrast with the mores of Indian Muslims, Christians, Parsis, and Jews, which they took these groups to share with their respective transnational religious groups. They especially saw Indian Muslims as having greater affinities with Muslims in other countries than with India's non-Muslims, despite the considerable cultural similarities between the inhabitants of particular regions of India.[89] This contrasted with the predominant view in Indonesia that the country's Muslims were embedded in the cultures of the nation, which other religious groups shared, These contrasting views existed of the relationship of the country's Muslims to national culture although the influence of Islam began earlier in India.

These discourses about the relationship of Muslims to indigenous culture encouraged Indonesian policy elites to promote similar changes in the practices of Muslims and other religious groups, and made both policy makers and certain religious elites comfortable about incorporating the bilateral customs of many of the country's ethnic groups in Islamic law. The rather different views of most policy makers and Muslim religious elites in India made them disinclined to change Muslim practices in ways for which they could not find support in distinctively Islamic norms, and reluctant to incorporate the bilateral and matrilineal practices of certain Indian Muslim groups into Indian Muslim law. Along with the limited understanding that most policy makers had of Islamic norms, the visions many of these elites had of Indian national culture and Muslim mores seriously limited changes in India's Muslim laws and kept the rules of this personal law system particularly distinctive.

ii. Nations and Minorities.   The ways in which nationalist discourses framed cultural differences were related to how minorities were constituted in the course of state formation and nation making, especially in the formative phases of these processes. Centralizing states and the initial mobilizers of territorial communities generated new public categories such as citizen, town dweller, and worker, which were linked to emergent practices more than to ancestry, faith, and custom. They frequently regarded minorities as resistant to full incorporation in such categories, and thus as troubling constraints to the formation of modern public spheres. Various state builders and mass mobilizers typecast groups such as the Jews and minority Christian sects of modern Europe, the "natives" and enslaved populations of settler colonies, various cultural and religious minorities of postcolonial states, and many recent immigrant groups in Europe and the Americas along these lines.[90] Some of them barely incorporated minority cultural traditions, practices, and initiatives into their ways of imagining national culture and destiny. (The reconstruction of settler colonies as racially exclusive nations in southern Africa and parts of the Americas were stark instances of this trend). They typically engaged too little with minorities to be aware of many aspects of the dynamism and internal diversity of these groups. Nationalists who paid limited attention to diversities within the nation, such as those of France, China, and Turkey, and those that associated national culture largely with the dominant majority, such as the state elites of Israel, Pakistan, Bangladesh, Thailand, and the Philippines, viewed various minorities along these lines. The former typically tried to assimilate minorities, while the latter were willing to accommodate minorities on the margins of national life. To the extent that their engagement with minorities was limited, certain pluralistic nationalists, such as many in India, also marginalized these groups in certain respects.

Aamir Mufti highlighted such patterns in the construction of European Jews and Indian Muslims, but did not address differences in predominant stereotypes of minorities that influenced whether and how they were accommodated.[91] While certain minorities were typecast as backward and resistant to post-Enlightenment modernization projects, others were considered particularly educated, open to new currents, or enterprising, perhaps in devious ways that required the ethnically unmarked citizen (typically a member of the majority) to distrust them.[92] Ruling elites' stereotypes of Muslims fit the former pattern not only in some countries in which they were minorities (such as India, Thailand, the Philippines, and various European countries), but also in some in which they were the majority (as in much of the Arab world during colonial rule). Various mercantile groups (or groups typecast as such) were seen as wily and enterprising (for example, Jews in Europe, Chinese in Southeast Asia); certain minorities that had close links with colonial powers were considered modernizing agents with uncertain affinities with the nation (such as Christians in Syria, Lebanon, Egypt, India, and Indonesia); and some groups were considered enterprising yet difficult to incorporate in public life (such as European Jews).

Only a few official nationalist discourses incorporated minorities and their traditions significantly. They include the Canadian myth of dual founding nations, the multinational vision of the former Yugoslavia and the binational conception of the former Czechoslovakia, the multiethnic understanding of countries such as Belgium, Nigeria, and Lebanon, and the postimperial and postmonarchic reconstructions of British and Spanish identity respectively. These pluralistic nationalisms included only certain minorities, and some of them resisted the accommodation of other minority groups. For instance, Spanish, Yugoslav, and Czechoslovak nationalisms did not include the Romany, and Canadian nationalism was belatedly and only partially modified to embrace indigenous groups. Nevertheless, pluralistic nationalisms construct minorities differently from how homogenous and majoritarian nationalist discourses do.

Initiatives emerged in various societies to gain recognition for certain minorities, and international agreements and international organizations addressed these concerns, particularly after the United Nations adopted the Declaration on the Rights of Persons Belonging to National or Ethnic, Religious and Linguistic Minorities in 1992. Recognition enabled the closer integration of certain minorities into public spheres, mass politics, and state institutions. However, discourses that placed minorities at the margins of political communities often encouraged state elites to accommodate only dominant understandings of minority cultures, empower traditional elites as group representatives, consider reformists unrepresentative of group opinion, and make forms of recognition insensitive to emergent currents. They also induced policy makers to give less priority to promoting the practices they encouraged among most citizens to minorities. Many modernist state elites considered conservative minority elites less of a constraint to their authority than conservative majority elites, and this further reduced their inclination to promote minority reform. The resulting patterns of accommodation reinforced minority marginalization from various spheres and induced various minority-group members to orient themselves primarily toward their own communities, even while these institutions lent certain group members added authority and resources, and made others too feel that they could maintain some practices they valued. Groups that nationalist discourses typecast as backward tended to be accommodated in these ways—for example, the Muslims of India, the Philippines, Thailand, and Israel, and the Hindus of Pakistan and Bangladesh.

State elites tended to approach minorities considered attuned to education, enterprise, and modernity differently. They were more likely to register support for social reform among these groups and to consider it appropriate to promote similar practices in them and the majority. Policy makers also better understood opinion and initiatives among minorities that played important roles in regimes, as certain Christian groups did in Egypt and Indonesia and the Chinese and Indians did in Malaysia. Such stereotypes and circumstances prompted Egyptian policy makers to authorize the secularized reformers of the lay Coptic Orthodox Supreme Communal Council to introduce a reformed Coptic personal status code in 1938 and consider the introduction of uniform family laws in the 1950s; led Indonesian judges to apply customs that granted women greater rights to the religious minorities; led to the application of new civil marriage laws to Malaysia's religious minorities in the 1970s and the ongoing reform of these civil marriage laws thereafter; and induced Indian legislators and judges to effect convergence in certain features of Christian and Hindu law. However, certain minorities that were typecast as having modern inclinations were marginalized in regimes and official nationalist discourses, and the forms in which they were recognized did not remain sensitive to emergent currents. For instance, many nationalists took Christians to have affinities with the West and their transnational religious institutions even though many Christians had opposed colonial rule in Egypt and India. This led the Egyptian regime to sideline Christians and halt Coptic Christian law reform to accommodate the Coptic Church from the 1940s onward rather than continue to empower lay liberals, and dissuaded Indian policy makers from granting concerted Christian demands for adoption rights, since they feared this would increase the group's share of the population. Table 2.4 indicates these patterns.

iii. Cultural Change / Cultural Stability. Ruling elites that prioritized cultural modernization changed personal law most extensively, as in Tunisia and Turkey. Those that valued cultural maintenance or revival, as in Syria, Lebanon, and early postcolonial Morocco, were disinclined to change personal law. Those that wanted cultural continuity in some respects and cultural

TABLE 2.4 Policy Regarding Minority Personal Law

Stereotype of Minority Group	Predominant Vision of Nation		
	Homogeneous	Majoritarian	Pluralistic
Backward	Assimilate in Civil Law—e.g., Muslims in China, France	Little Change—e.g., Muslims in Philippines, Thailand, Israel;[1] Hindus in Bangladesh, Pakistan	Little Change—e.g., Muslims in Lebanon, India[2]
Modern	Assimilate in Civil Law—e.g., Christians in Turkey	Moderate Modernist Reform—e.g., Chinese in Malaysia,[3] Copts in Egypt[4]	Moderate to Extensive Modernist Reform—e.g., Various Ethnic Groups in Indonesia, Christians in India[5]

[1] Civil marriage law was not applied much in Israel's Islamic courts.
[2] Muslims were a minority in Lebanon when postcolonial personal-law policy was formed, but became the majority later. Muslim law was changed in India since the 1970s, but not extensively.
[3] Civil laws were applied from the 1970s to Malaysia's non-Muslims, among whom Chinese are the largest ethnic group.
[4] Reform was early but not sustained in Egypt.
[5] Reform was late in India.

change in other respects introduced moderate personal-law reforms, and such elites were predominant in most postcolonial states, including Libya, Egypt, Jordan, Iraq, Pakistan, India, Malaysia, Indonesia, Thailand, and the Philippines.

If ruling elites wished to abandon many aspects of indigenous culture and adopt the ways of more privileged societies, they transplanted various institutions from these societies, as happened in early republican Turkey. Political elites that preferred to channel indigenous cultures in the directions they favored drew their social reform proposals significantly from interpretations of indigenous religious traditions and customs, and this was the predominant pattern in India and Indonesia.

iv. Modernity / Authenticity. Discourses of nation and community engage in different ways with concerns of modernity and authenticity. Certain nationalist and cultural mobilizers frame their projects as primarily driven by considerations of authenticity; others say they are primarily seeking to promote modernity. However, even narratives that place rhetorical emphasis on authenticity engage considerations of modernity in some ways. For instance, the overwhelming attention in official postrevolutionary Iranian discourse to building an authentically Islamic and Iranian public life coexisted with an engagement with Western institutional precedents, some of which were adopted during the Pahlavi monarchy. A specific fusion of considerations of authenticity and modernity shaped the dual character of the postrevolutionary Iranian state—as an Islamic state led by an unelected supreme religious jurist and a republic governed partly by representative institutions. Similarly, nationalist discourses that emphasize considerations of modernity are also often supplemented by concerns to maintain connections to authentic national, regional, or ethnic cultures. For example, this was the case with official discourses in early republican Turkey and Iran under the monarchy. They urged the adoption of various Western mores and institutions, but also attended to the uniqueness of national identity, which they located partly in the non-Islamic features of the cultural heritage of their societies and considered crucial sources of social cohesion.

The majority of nationalist and communitarian projects give considerable attention to both modernity and authenticity, particularly in late-developing societies. They reconcile or fuse these considerations by presenting the changes they promote as emanations of group culture that would yield contextually appropriate forms of modernity. Official Indonesian and Indian nationalism are representative of this pattern. They presented these nations as based in the overlapping cultures of their various religious and ethnic groups, drawing inspiration from these portraits for their efforts to form secularist states that engaged with various religious norms and practices and to build developmental states that engaged with existing forms of social organization while gradually reducing socioeconomic inequality.[93] These states adopted policies that were opposed by important religious institutions and leaders; for example, the Indonesian ruling elites' refusal to declare the establishment of an Islamic state and to make a constitutional commitment to maintain Islamic law, and the Indian state's ban on caste segregation in temples and its introduction of divorce rights and enhancement of women's inheritance rights in Hindu law. But these choices were grounded in interpretations of these societies' religious and other cultural traditions that enjoyed significant support. As a result, they occasioned far less conflict than various religious policies did in Turkey and Tunisia.

The regimes from which they assume power influence, but do not solely determine, the models of modernity and authenticity that the mobilizers of nations and communities adopt, and how they base particular changes in state and society on such models. The leaders of the early Turkish republic wished to end the state's close association with major religious institutions and religious traditions. This was an important reason why they relied heavily on certain European experiences in which the state had seriously curtailed the power of religious institutions, particularly those of France and Prussia, to end the recognition of a state religion, secularize the legal system, and limit religious symbols in public life. (They also drew from these precedents because the Ottoman reforms of the nineteenth century had been based primarily on French ideas and experiences, and many of the military officers who led the early Turkish republic had been trained in Prussia). The influence of French and Prussian experiences and ideas also led them to prioritize the centralization of authority. This motivated them to establish control over the major Sunni religious institutions (as well as various ethnic and kin institutions), which ironically reproduced aspects of the Ottoman state's engagement with them and gained some acceptance for this reason. But state control over Sunni institutions, the repression of various other religious institutions, the restriction of religious symbols, and the wholesale import of Western institutions also aroused considerable opposition in a society in which many were mobilized to maintain important public roles for religion and indigenous norms.

As their political visions developed mainly in the course of opposition to an indigenous monarchy (although they also briefly resisted European imperial powers), Turkey's republican leaders were less concerned to revalue indigenous cultures and were comfortable about adopting many Western precedents, including in family law. Nationalists who opposed colonial states were ambivalent about prior experiences in imperial societies and the institutions established in their societies under colonial rule, and sought authentic indigenous cultural bases for more of their projects. This was a crucial reason why most anticolonial Muslim nationalists around the world wished Islamic law to remain a major basis to regulate family life, even while they differed on the form they wished to give Islamic law. The majority wished to retain much of colonial Islamic law in Morocco, Lebanon, and Syria; the more influential anticolonial Muslim nationalists in Tunisia wanted to adopt alternative interpretations of Islamic law that promoted women's rights and nuclear family autonomy; and some anticolonial Islamists preferred to apply conservative understandings of Islamic law to more areas of social life in various societies. Some of the ideological successors of these Islamists shaped policy a generation after independence in Nigeria and Sudan.

Many anticolonial nationalists did retain certain colonial institutions and borrowed other institutions from imperial societies, presenting these choices as necessary to promote modernity. However, a concern to structure state and society along indigenous lines often led them to alter these institutions or supplement them with others, in view of their societies' specific features. For instance, Indian nationalists were critical of the serious limits within which colonial representative institutions had enfranchised Indians, and aimed to increase the authority and representative character of these institutions. This led them to borrow parliamentary democratic institutions from Britain, but they departed from British models to adopt federalism as a means to enable the governance of a much larger and more diverse society. Moreover, they allowed the formation of states along the lines of language use to accommodate more of the country's vernaculars and language groups, avoided associating the state with a particular religion in view of the country's religious diversity and its experience of considerable religious conflict, and tried to introduce strong local government institutions based on precolonial traditions of village governance.[94] Moreover, they abandoned colonial institutions that they believed had weakened national cohesion, such as electorates based on religious identity, even while recognizing various social and educational rights based on religious identity to accommodate religion's important public roles.

Certain nationalists and community mobilizers who replaced domestic regimes were also ambivalent about the institutions they inherited. This was the case with Iran's postrevolutionary leaders, importantly because the monarchy they replaced was closely allied with Western powers and adopted various unpopular Western institutions. They believed the representative institutions that existed under the monarchy had failed to capture popular will, and Ayatollah Khomeini specifically felt that the enfranchisement of women was contrary to Islamic norms. However, Khomeini took genuine popular will to have crystallized during the revolution, so that postrevolutionary representative institutions elected based on universal franchise could represent the citizenry. These institutions were based largely on the model of the French republic, which had also influenced representation under the monarchy, but they were framed now as contemporary incarnations of Islamic traditions of *shura* (popular consultation). To ensure that they would pursue the authentic Islamic projects of their architects' imagination, their decisions were subject to the approval of two unelected entities, the supreme religious jurist and the Council of Guardians composed largely of religious scholars.

In the sphere of family life, modern Western states promoted the authority of the nuclear family, monogamy, patriliny, and, since the mid-twentieth century, more equal rights for the genders. Various Asian and African cultural traditions and personal laws (and earlier European traditions and legal systems as well) recognized the authority of larger kin groups and greater rights for men and agnates, and some of them recognized bilateral and matrilineal kinship practices. The culturally grounded modernists of Asia and Africa promoted the autonomy of the nuclear family and the reduction of gender inequality in certain respects. They framed these aims in discourses of nation and community, modernity and authenticity, which shaped the specific changes they sought in family life and how they related these changes to the other ways in which they wished to make state and society. Conservatives framed the social practices and institutions that they defended in alternative discourses of nation, community, authenticity, and sometimes modernity as well. Various features of state-society relations influenced the pace at which modernists and conservatives promoted the forms of family life they valued and the extent of their success.

Table 2.5 summarizes the relationships between certain features of nationalist discourses and personal law policy.

C. Explaining Policy Trajectories

We have seen that certain features of state-society relations and the discourses of nation and community prevalent among ruling elites influenced the approaches of states to the personal law systems that they inherited. We will now consider how these factors interacted, and how their interactions influenced personal law.

TABLE 2.5 Nationalist Discourses and Personal Law

Personal Law	Emphasis of Nationalist Narratives		
	Modernity/Cultural Change	Authenticity/Change Amid Continuity	Authenticity/ Cultural Stability
Extensive Reform	Turkey, Tunisia		
Moderate Reform		Senegal, Libya, Egypt, Jordan, Iraq, Iran,[1] Pakistan,[2] India, Sri Lanka, Bangladesh, Malaysia,[3] Indonesia, Thailand, Philippines	
Little Change			Morocco,[4] Lebanon, Syria, Malawi

[1] Iran during the Pahlavi monarchy
[2] Pakistan until the 1970s
[3] Most of Malaysia saw moderate modernist reform. East peninsular Malaysia alone saw conservative changes from the 1970s
[4] Morocco until the 1990s

Certain features of personal-law policy correspond with particular forms of state-society relations—specifically with the nature of social structure, state-society relations under the predecessor regime, the social coalitions that crucial state elites had or aimed to build, and the way these elites wished to restructure state-society relations. For instance, personal-law reform was most extensive and promoted nuclear family autonomy most in countries such as Turkey and Tunisia, where the state was already somewhat autonomous of crucial social institutions, ruling elites viewed certain sections of the urban middle classes and working classes as the national vanguard, and these elites prioritized increased state control over religious, ethnic, and kin institutions even though this seemed likely to provoke significant opposition. Personal-law reform was more limited in societies such as Senegal, Libya, Egypt, Jordan, Iraq, India, Sri Lanka, Malaysia, and Indonesia, where regimes were allied with modernist urban elites, as well as with traditionalist religious, ethnic, and kin leaders, and wished to consolidate their support among both sets of groups. Reforms were barely attempted in Lebanon, Syria, Algeria, and—until recently—Morocco, where lineage leaders had more influence, ruling elites were either lineage leaders themselves or depended heavily on the support of kin groups, and professional, commercial, and industrial elites were weaker. Changes in personal law reduced women's rights and individual autonomy where conservative religious elites were important leaders, members, or supporters of regimes, as was the case in Iran, Sudan, and northern Nigeria since the 1980s, and in Afghanistan while the Taliban ruled the country from 1996 to 2001.

However, social structure and prior state-society relations did not determine the social coalitions that state elites sought to retain or build, the projects of these elites to restructure state-society relations, or the discourses of nation and community in which these elites conceived these projects. In many of these countries, significant sections of the political elite wished to launch different projects and articulated distinct discourses of nation and community in response to the same conditions. In some, the regime at least initially included factions oriented toward very different projects and committed to different nationalist visions. Conflicts over alternative conceptions of the nation were important aspects of the competition over regime composition; they shaped regime support, and how regimes changed state-society relations. They specifically influenced how these regimes changed personal law, and in the process made the nation and recognized its cultural groups.

i. Cases of Extensive Early Reform. In the countries that saw the most extensive early personal law reform, Turkey and Tunisia, political forces that articulated distinct discourses associated with different policy agendas emerged in response to Ottoman and French rule, and were initially represented in the new regimes. The early Turkish republic included not only the faction led by Mustafa Kemal Paşa (Atatürk) that favored extensive Westernization and secularization, but also Turkic cultural nationalists inclined to revive certain pre-Islamic Turkish cultural norms as they imagined them, and to build links with other "Turanist" groups in Central Asia, and modernist Islamists who wished to change society as suggested by their reconstructions of Islamic traditions. In including secularists who wished to limit the public role of religion as well as reformers that valued various religious norms, Turkey was similar to some regimes that changed personal law less, such as those of postcolonial India, Indonesia, and Egypt (although the latter regimes included more conservatives). The Neo-Destour Party that led the Tunisian nationalist movement through the last two decades of colonial rule and assumed power from the French included not only the Islamic modernists led by Bourguiba and based among urban groups, but also pan-Islamists closely connected to religious elites and rural lineages. It included fewer secularists and at least as many conservatives as the contemporaneous Egyptian, Pakistani, Indian, and Indonesian regimes, which reformed personal law less.

These factions could have coexisted longer, but this would have required compromise regarding social policy and personal law. In Turkey, a viable compromise could have involved the import of fewer Western institutions, the greater accommodation of indigenous cultures and perhaps also religious norms and symbols, and aspects of Ottoman personal law. The main ideologue of Turkic cultural nationalism, Ziya Gökalp, imagined a pre-Islamic Turkic family life organized around monogamy, bilateral kinship, and somewhat egalitarian norms, which could have inspired the incorporation of the country's more egalitarian customs (real and imagined) into religious law, as happened in Indonesia. Certain Islamic ideas developed through then-current innovative religious hermeneutics could have inspired extensive Islamic law reforms along the Tunisian lines. In Tunisia, the very different preferences of the Neo-Destour Party's modernists and pan-Islamists regarding personal law meant that their cohabitation would have required that both sides accept the kind of moderate reforms seen in countries such as Egypt, India, and Indonesia.

However, the Turkish and Tunisian regimes changed family law far more. The Kemalist and Bourguiba factions of the respective regimes based their strategies on particular modernist nationalist visions, and to give them full effect, they severed their links with former allies who were more attached to religious institutions, predominant interpretations of religious traditions, or aspects of lineage power. They used the prior autonomy of the states they inherited to increase state control over social institutions considerably and to repress their opponents.

Other features of the social vision of ruling elites also influenced the change of personal law in Turkey and Tunisia, making it more extensive than in India. The Turkish regime had fewer members who valued conservative religious norms, the Ottoman regime had given public religion and the religion of the majority much greater roles than India's colonial state had, and the Turkish republican leaders were determined to limit various Ottoman legacies (in contrast with Indian policy makers' ambivalence about British colonial legacies). Moreover, the dominant leader of the Turkish republic

(Atatürk) used the popularity he won by having led the Turkish War of Independence to gain greater leeway to shape policy than his Indian counterpart (Nehru) enjoyed. His social vision was also far more elitist, devaluing both dominant religious institutions and various forms of popular religion, and his inclination to establish an authoritarian regime made it less crucial to maintain broad support.

That Nehru was far more inclined than Ataturk to consolidate democracy, maintain broad support, accommodate various religious practices and aspects of popular culture, decentralize power, and promote social change gradually was partly the result of these leaders' institutional contexts and earlier political experiences. Nehru became the leader of an institutionalized party that had existed for over six decades and that had support across ethnic, religious, class, and urban/rural boundaries, considerable ideological diversity, a culture of compromise, experience of participation in representative institutions, and excellent prospects of consolidating its dominance in a competitive multiparty democracy. Atatürk's role as a military officer shaped his political vision. When the republic was founded, Atatürk led one of the intensely competitive factions of the newly formed Republican People's Party, which had support primarily in cities and among the Turkish majority, weak institutions, and an uncertain trajectory. These circumstances reinforced Nehru's inclination to consolidate democracy and Atatürk's to build a centralized dictatorship. These inclinations led Nehru and most other Congress Party modernists to compromise with conservatives over personal law, while leading the Kemalists to rapidly secularize family law even though this eroded the regime's support and impaired political stability.

The leaders of postcolonial Tunisia, much like those of the early Turkish republic, did not prioritize either the formation of democracy or gaining broad support. This made them willing to expel conservatives from the Neo-Destour Party and establish a one-party dictatorship, in a process that was eased by the sharp factional boundaries in the party. The greater fluidity of factional alignments in the Congress Party reinforced the preferences of the modernists to craft careful compromises with conservatives.

Both the Turkish and the Tunisian regimes introduced extensive social reforms, but framed them differently in crucial respects—as part of a project of secularization in Turkey, but as a way to revitalize public Islam in Tunisia.

This was because ruling elites adopted Western precedents far more in Turkey. Even modernist Arab nationalists such as Bourguiba gave religious identity and Islamic law considerable importance in their constructions of nationhood, to overcome colonial hegemony and the associated devaluation of Islamic public cultures.[95] The Turkish republic emerged, by way of contrast, mainly in opposition to the indigenous Ottoman rulers who were closely associated with the *ulama* and their institutions. As a result, its leaders did not feel as pressed to uphold indigenous culture, and were more inclined to embrace Western experiences, including the separation of religion and state in many respects (uneasily combined with state control over various religious institutions), to distinguish themselves from the Caliphate. Reform initiatives based on religious and other indigenous traditions were also strong in early twentieth-century Turkey, but lost out to the Kemalists.[96]

The different ways in which reform was framed in Tunisia and Turkey influenced the content of family law and induced a divergence in state-society relations. Statutory law gave women greater inheritance rights and autonomy from their husbands in Turkey than in Tunisia, as we saw earlier. But because public religion was important in both societies, the religious framing of reform in Tunisia contained resistance more quickly, gained the state courts greater acceptance, and enabled greater regime stability than rapid state-led secularization did in Turkey. This was the case although many *ulama* and conservative Islamists sharply contested the interpretations of Islamic law incorporated in the Tunisian reforms. The Neo-Destour Party was able to maintain its dominance over Tunisia without using much repression from the mid-1950s (when its conservative wing was suppressed) until popular protest ended the rule of its successor party, the Rally for Constitutional Democracy, in 2011. The rapid reduction in the accommodation of religious norms and religious symbols, the suppression of certain religious institutions, and the imposition of state tutelage over others made the Turkish republic much less popular. As a result, through the first decades of the republic many citizens approached community courts, particularly in rural areas, and supported movements that favored the greater acceptance of public religion even later. Moreover, these conditions limited the popularity of the Republican People's Party, which led the country through the first republican generation, and the party lost power whenever free elections were held, to parties that aimed to accommodate religion more in public life. This in turn led the military to overthrow these elected governments several times and rule directly, to curb religious movements and public expressions of religiosity, and maintain the form of secularism adopted in the 1920s.

ii. Cases of Moderate Reform.   The modernist leaders who led the early postcolonial regimes of Senegal, Libya, Egypt, Jordan, Iraq, Iran, Pakistan, India, Sri Lanka, Malaysia, Indonesia, and Thailand conceived the nation significantly along culturally indigenous lines. This made them unwilling to adopt as many Western institutions as in Turkey, and impelled those that adopted some form of secularism (in Senegal, Egypt, India, and Indonesia) to also accommodate various public roles for religion. Moreover, the way that Tunku Abdul Rahman, the United Malays National Organization, and the National Alliance in Malaysia; Leopold Senghor and the Socialist Party in Senegal; the Hashemite dynasty in Jordan; the Gaddafi regime in Libya; the Ba'ath regime in Iraq; and the major Sinhalese parties in Sri Lanka balanced considerations of authenticity and modernity meant that they aimed for only moderate cultural changes.[97]

Sukarno and many of Indonesia's Nationalists, Gamal Abdel Nasser and Egypt's Free Officers Regime, and Nehru and certain other modernists in India's Congress Party wished to introduce more extensive social and personal-law reforms, for which they could count on the support of various mobilized groups. However, they also embraced encompassing visions of their respective nations, which reinforced their inclination to maintain broad coalitions. Many Indonesian nationalists considered folk, Hindu, Buddhist, Islamic, and Christian traditions to have shaped national culture. In a similar vein, India's pluralist nationalists upheld a national culture that was a composite of the country's various religious and ethnic cultures, and the Free Officers regime espoused a vision of an Arab nation including the country's various religious groups. Such inclusive visions dissuaded the Egyptian and Indonesian regimes from forming Islamic states. Further, to maintain broad coalitions, the modernist leaders of India, Egypt, and Indonesia tempered their transformative ambitions given that some of their allies preferred to retain various forms of social dominance, including gendered and patrilineal patterns of family authority. This discouraged the introduction of uniform family laws in Egypt and India, motivated the reversal of certain reforms in Egypt, and limited the promotion of egalitarian customs in Indonesia until the 1970s.

iii. Cases of Limited Reform. Among the countries that saw limited personal-law reform at least until recently, Lebanon is an illuminating case. The maintenance of distinct personal laws under the jurisdiction of community courts was an important aspect of the Grand Alliance that gave Lebanon's sects political representation. It cemented alliances between clan leaders and religious elites, and was an area of consensus among the political elite of various sects between whom sharp conflicts emerged over the terms of sectarian representation, resource distribution, and the definition of the nation. The Lebanese National Movement proposed to change the personal laws as part of its efforts to build a cohesive nation and a strong state, but its defeat during the civil war doomed this initiative. The situation differed in Morocco; the focus of Moroccan nationalism on the monarchy gave the kings considerable leeway, which they used to maintain colonial personal law soon after independence as they depended heavily on lineages, but to change it extensively in 2004 in response to the growth of civil society mobilization.[98]

The socialist ideology of certain members of the FLN that formed Algeria's one-party state inclined them toward personal-law reform, and similar features of the Ba'ath Party suggested this possibility when it seized power in Syria in the 1960s. Reform did not happen in Algeria because the FLN initially wanted to retain its links with conservative lineages and was later reluctant to provoke opposition to reforms, which might strengthen the Islamist opposition. Neither did it happen in Syria because the faction of Hafez al-Assad, drawn largely from the military and the Alawi sect, expelled many socialists from the regime, lost support among the Sunni majority and Christians, and was reluctant to narrow its coalition further through risky reforms. The Syrian experience contrasted with that in Iraq, where the Ba'athists under Saddam Hussein interpreted their socialist heritage to require significant changes in religious practice and family life, and did not allow the restriction of their support mainly to a minority sect (Arabic-speaking Sunnis) to deter them from personal-law reform.[99]

Thus, discourses of the nation and its traditions were important foci of competition over regime composition and state-led social change in various societies, and specifically influenced multiculturalism and personal law. The debates over regime trajectories gave considerable attention to personal law in Turkey, Tunisia, Lebanon, and Indonesia, and some attention to it in countries such as Morocco, Algeria, Libya, Egypt, Jordan, Iraq, Iran, Pakistan, India, and Malaysia. In Syria, Sri Lanka, Thailand and the Philippines, political elites attended less to personal law, but their debates over nation formation influenced personal law.

iv. Minority Law Reform: The Indian and Indonesian Experiences. Nationalist discourses and religious discourses affected not only the laws governing religious and ethnic majorities, on which the earlier discussion focused, but also those that applied to minorities. A comparison of the Indian and Indonesian experiences highlights their effects on minority laws. Both postcolonial regimes had support among the different religious groups in their societies, and among groups whose preferences varied about the public role of religion and the specific religious norms to be recognized.[100] Wishing to retain such support and limit secessionist inclinations among their religious minorities (and in Indonesia, among certain Islamists too), they retained various multicultural colonial legacies, introduced new forms of cultural accommodation, and adopted versions of secularism that accepted extensive public roles for religion. Official discourse advocated respect for different religions and depicted the nation as based in various cultural traditions; the governments retained diverse personal laws with moderate changes. Amidst these similarities, the changes in India were mainly in Hindu law, while changes were made in many of Indonesia's personal laws through the first postcolonial generation. Moreover, Islamic law was changed more extensively in Indonesia.

When Dutch Orientalists began to systematize their understandings of local practices in the late nineteenth century, just as colonial officials sought to regulate Indonesian society more closely, they saw *adat* rather than classical Islamic law as the main basis of family practices, particularly inheritance patterns. Some of them claimed that Islamic law had not influenced Indonesian practices much, while others more accurately took Islamic law to have interacted with prior customs to shape the lived Islam of Indonesia. On these bases, they encouraged the recognition of *adat* in the religious courts, urged that Islamic law be applied only to those practices that it had shaped, and transferred inheritance from the jurisdiction of the Islamic courts to that of the civil courts in 1937. While accommodating *adat* in these ways, Dutch officials also formalized a system of Islamic courts in 1882 and helped implement their verdicts.[101]

Colonial intellectuals tended to understand Hindu religious practices as based in Indian spiritual traditions, in contrast with the religious practices of India's Muslims, Christians, Parsis, and Jews, which they took to have originated outside South Asia. This led the colonial courts to apply a partly homogenized Hindu law to all residents of India who practiced religions of South Asian origin, including the Sikhs, Buddhists, and Jains, although these groups did not claim a Hindu identity. These courts recognized various customs specific to region and caste among all religious groups. When doing so among Hindus, they understood many of these customs as aspects of territorially rooted schools of Hindu law—the *Dayabhaga* school applied mainly in Bengal, and different versions of the *Mitakshara* school applied in northern, western, and southern India. But they saw the regionally rooted customs of groups practicing religions of foreign origin as departures from their religious traditions and religious laws, rather than as specific South Asian Muslim, Christian, Parsi, and Jewish religious practices. These understandings created a tendency to equate the Hindu and the culturally indigenous, and sometimes to place all groups practicing religions that emerged in South Asia in the Hindu category.[102]

The main responses of nationalist and religious mobilizers to these features of colonial knowledge and colonial institutions had a bearing on personal law. Although certain colonial officials hoped to promote ethnic solidarities as alternatives to Islamic identity by recognizing *adat* rather than Islamic jurisprudence, Islamic norms remained significant to how most Indonesian Muslim intellectuals and political mobilizers constructed their cultural repertoires. Nevertheless, colonial understandings that *adat* represented practices on the ground reinforced the tendency of Indonesian Islamic scholars and *qadis* to construct Islamic law in light of *adat*. Moreover, these ideas led many of these actors not only to return to the Qur'an and the *hadith* (reputable accounts of the early Islamic community) to construct purified Islamic traditions as many Islamic scholars did elsewhere, but also to demonstrate the relevance for contemporary Indonesian contexts of the principles they derived from these sources. This led certain influential scholars, especially Hasbi Ash Shiddieqy and Hazairin, to point toward the development of an Indonesian *madhhab* that would replace the patrilineal Arabian customs incorporated into classical Islamic jurisprudence, especially its inheritance provisions, with bilateral Indonesian customs. Many other religious scholars gave considerations of *maslaha* (public interest) greater importance in their reformulations of Islamic law. These approaches were meant to help create an official Islamic law sufficiently connected to current social practices and predicaments that it could more effectively promote social change and thus be the country's living law. The efforts to develop a distinct Indonesian *madhhab* were unsuccessful, but led Islamic scholars to connect their jurisprudence systematically to the findings of cultural anthropology. They also encouraged scholars trained in *pesantren* (Islamic schools) to engage significantly with those trained in secular institutions, and Islamists to engage with secularists in developing their policy perspectives.

Orientalist representations of *adat* (but not classical Islamic traditions) as crucial to indigenous culture also influenced nationalist discourses. They led many Indonesian nationalists to give indigenous customs shared by members of different religious groups, some of which had their origins in folk, Hindu, and Buddhist traditions, a central place in Indonesian national culture, construing such constructions of the nation as compatible with the Islamic identity of the majority of its citizens. Modernist nationalists such as Sukarno especially valued the more egalitarian customs, and this influenced how they presented *Pancasila* (five principles, including the recognition of a Supreme Deity) as a basis for the postcolonial nation-state. These features of religious and nationalist discourse influenced how certain religious as well as secular jurists envisioned an authentic national *adat* drawn from various customs of the archipelago that nonetheless had affinities with constitutional values such as equality and liberty; these jurists proposed the revision of both Islamic law and the rules applied to non-Muslim family life in light of this notion. These features crucially enabled the extensive judicial recognition of bilateral customs, the Supreme Court's grant of equal inheritance shares to sons, daughters, and widows in some cases, and the serious consideration given at times to the systematic legislative equalization of the inheritance shares of men and women with a similar relationship to the deceased (contrary to the 2:1 Qur'anic ratio to which most Islamic courts adhere).[103]

In contrast with Indonesian experiences, colonial knowledge about Indian society prompted many Hindu mobilizers to claim that Hindu traditions alone were based in indigenous culture, and to attempt to assimilate Sikhs, Buddhists, and Jains into the Hindu fold. It also influenced the tendency of many nationalists to justify giving Hindus primacy in the Indian nation not only because they account for the demographic majority, but also because they considered Hindu norms the most reliable elements from which to construct an authentic indigenous national culture. As a result, various individuals and organizations envisioned the Indian nation based mainly or exclusively on Hindu sources, and focused their projects on the Hindu community.[104]

Certain cosmopolitan Indian nationalists, of whom Nehru was most influential, rejected association of the Hindu with the culturally indigenous, and aimed to build a territorial nation not based on religious identity. However, they remained allied in the Congress Party with those who framed their pluralism in primarily Hindu idioms such as Gandhi, and with others who connected Hindu and Indian identity more intimately. The growth of conflict between religious groups through the last colonial decades reduced the engagement of Hindu political elites with minority initiatives, while the formation of Pakistan increased the weight of Hindus in the political elite, giving Hindu-centered understandings of the Indian nation greater influence.[105] As a result, the postcolonial state framed its multicultural policies based on limited engagement with minority initiatives and traditions, centered its projects to build an indigenous and modern nation and reduce enduring social inequalities on the Hindu community, and focused its efforts to promote the modern Indian family on Hindu law reform.

Rather than contest the colonial view of Islamic traditions as foreign to local society by demonstrating that these traditions had taken root locally (as their Indonesian counterparts did), the majority of Indian Islamic scholars viewed South Asian customs for which they could not find justification in classical Islamic discourse as "Hindu," and encouraged Muslims to abandon them. Moreover, they highlighted the connections of their jurisprudence and religious reasoning to Arabic and Central Asian approaches more than to South Asian experiences.[106] This distanced Indian Islamic discourse from cultural currents among non-Muslims; rendered it less comprehensible to non-Muslims; limited the realization among many Muslim and non-Muslim reformers that they shared common goals such as the reduction of the practice of dowry, the extension of marriage networks, and an increase in the age of marriage; and specifically led many non-Muslims to underestimate Muslim reformist initiative. These circumstances, combined with the tendency of Muslim reformers to associate some of their goals (such as the reduction of dowry and the influence of caste over marital alliances) with the abridgement of Hindu influence, limited alliances between Muslims and others over social reform even though certain practices that cut across religious boundaries could have served as bridges between the reform projects launched among different religious groups.

These features of Indian Islamic discourse reinforced the tendency of most Hindu mobilizers not to register ongoing Muslim reform initiatives and to consider changes in Muslim practices of marginal relevance to building the Indian nation. As a result, early postcolonial policy makers barely changed Muslim law until the 1970s. Certain civil society organizations that mobilized members of various religious groups engaged more with Islamic discourses from the 1980s; they helped increase awareness of these discourses among policy makers (particularly judges), and thus enabled some changes in Muslim law. However, these developments did not lend Islamic norms influence over the laws that regulated family life among most Indians—the matrimonial laws applicable to all citizens (such as those concerning alimony) or Hindu laws.[107] Moreover, the view among most Islamic mobilizers that certain indigenous customs favorable to women, such as the matrilineal and bilateral practices prevalent among some Indian Muslim groups, were incompatible with Islamic traditions hindered the incorporation of those traditions into Indian Muslim law, in contrast with their adoption in Indonesia. The Indian experience contrasted sharply with the decisive influence that individuals trained in Islamic religious institutions exercised in Indonesia's Ministry of Religious Affairs, which supervised the Islamic courts until 2004. Some of these individuals proposed reforms in Indonesian Islamic law framed through innovative religious reasoning, and they ensured the implementation of some of their proposals.

The ruling elites of India and Indonesia shared the goals of building modern and culturally indigenous nations while maintaining broad support. Religious and nationalist discourses led them to view somewhat different personal-law policies as conducive to these goals, and to follow policy paths that differed in certain respects. Indonesian policy makers changed the rules applied to various religious groups, while in India, reform efforts remained focused on Hindu law, and the changes in minority law were limited especially until the 1970s. Moreover, various indigenous customs with uncertain relations to classical Islamic discourse were incorporated into Islamic law in Indonesia, increasing women's rights in the process, but not in India. If governing elites had engaged more with minority initiatives and drawn their understandings of the nation from the norms of various religious groups, the minority laws could have been changed earlier and more extensively in India. Under these circumstances, the Indian state would also have been more likely to accommodate autonomist movements among the religious minorities effectively, and to have applied preferential policies and special civil-rights laws to Muslim and Christian lower-caste individuals, not only those that followed religions of South Asian origin.

VIII. VISIONS OF MODERNITY, AUTHENTICITY, RELIGIOUS NORMS, AND THE FAMILY IN INDIA

When projects for postcolonial state building and state-led social change were sharply outlined in India in the 1940s and 1950s, modernist nationalists who favored culturally grounded reform planned changes in personal law. B. R. Ambedkar, India's first postcolonial Law Minister (1947–51), developed proposals for personal-law reform by building on the suggestions of the bureaucrats who manned the Hindu Law Commissions of the 1940s, and Nehru underwrote the path the Law Ministry sketched. Such modernists framed their plans in view of the preferences of the less conservative Gandhian traditionalists, with whom they were closely allied. The Gandhians wished to conserve many precolonial Indian traditions, which they envisioned in ways that justified moderate reductions in deep inequalities along caste and gender lines. Conservatives inclined to retain many more forms of social dominance also occupied important positions in the political elite and the Congress Party. Prominent among them was Rajendra Prasad, India's first President (1950–62).

The majority of the modernists wished to consolidate a competitive multiparty democracy, build a developmental state, promote industrialization, gradually redistribute life chances, and consolidate the Congress Party's dominance. They gave these goals priority over changes in religious norms and family life. These priorities induced them to pursue economic redistribution and social reform in ways that did not alienate dominant groups. They thus sought to change personal law to signal the family norms that the state favored without rapidly restricting contrary practices, particularly until the 1970s.

The majority of the traditionalists shared certain goals of the modernists (to consolidate democracy, build broad social coalitions, introduce changes (albeit not extensive) in status hierarchies and economic relations based on indigenous traditions rather than solely on post-Enlightenment outlooks and Western precedents, and (with the exception of a few Gandhians) promote industrialization), enabling these groups to compromise over multiculturalism, social reform, and personal law. The modernists and traditionalists therefore readily agreed that they should not rapidly homogenize or secularize family law, or systematically change personal law based on egalitarian liberal principles. As a result, the Constituent Assembly placed an article that called for the introduction of a Uniform Civil Code (UCC) in the Directive Principles of State Policy, which could not be enforced through judicial mandate; and no branch of government vetted the personal laws systematically with reference to the Fundamental Rights recognized in the Indian Constitution. Rather, political elites agreed that they should maintain distinct personal laws, and change them gradually based on group traditions and initiatives.

The orientations of the majority of modernist and traditionalist political elites toward family law were similar in other respects too, as were those of the cultural pluralists and proponents of Hindu hegemony, especially until the 1970s. These elites primarily engaged Hindu initiatives, and conceived projects to form the Indian nation and to reduce deep inequalities mainly in light of such initiatives. As a result, their discourses about the Indian nation and the Hindu community overlapped significantly, and led them to focus on Hindu law reform, which they framed as the basis for a future UCC. These discourses also influenced the ways in which they sought to change Hindu law. By way of contrast, most political elites sought to base minority laws on group culture and opinion, and did not see the making of minority laws as a means to form the Indian nation. Most Muslim political elites opposed changes in Muslim law that lacked a basis in Islamic norms, and the majority of Hindu political elites were inclined to accommodate this preference. Moreover, at least until the 1970s, most Hindu political elites misunderstood minority opinion, taking it to oppose reform, and were in any case wary of changing Muslim law based on alternative Islamic norms that they understood poorly. As a result, no changes were attempted in the minority laws until the 1970s.

The major participants in the personal-law debates of the 1940s and 1950s relied on many of the same sources to argue that their proposals promoted practices appropriate for India and enjoyed support in widely valued traditions. Regarding Hindu law, they based their arguments on the schools of Hindu law as colonial officials had constructed them, and also drew on the *shastras*, commentaries on the *shastras* that served as sources of colonial Hindu law, and customs specific to region and caste, particularly those the colonial courts had recognized. Some of them also relied on the model of the monogamous nuclear family as the main unit of domestic life and intimacy, which Western law provided at that time.

The modernists, particularly those like Ambedkar and Nehru who were trained as lawyers, mainly based their Hindu law proposals on reconstructions of colonial Hindu law, with which they were most familiar. They understood the *shastras* and commentaries on them far less, but claimed support in certain selections from these texts to convince more conservative political elites and civil-society actors that their proposals had a sound basis in the traditions these groups valued. For instance, Ambedkar proposed to give daughters greater rights to ancestral property by modifying the inheritance shares prescribed by the *Dayabhaga* school of Hindu law, and to give all Hindu men and women divorce rights by incorporating in Hindu law the divorce customs of various middle castes and lower castes, practices for which he sought support in particular *shastras*. Conservative traditionalists, including certain Hindu religious elites, resisted these proposals based on similar sources. They gave priority to the inheritance rules of the *Mitakshara* school, which gave coparcenaries (collective entities composed of male lineage members), rather than individuals, control over ancestral property; to the colonial understanding that the *shastric* view of marriage as a *samskara* (life cycle ritual / sacred purifying ceremony / process of self-realization) gave marriage the same status as the Judeo-Christian sacrament; and to the upper-caste norm of marriage indissolubility.

Muslim mobilizers addressed the content of Muslim law based on their aim to build community solidarity, as well as with reference to certain religious traditions interpreted in view of contemporary circumstances and the relationship of personal laws to the major nationalist projects of the time. However, they made greater efforts than most Hindu elites to maintain continuity with earlier forms of religious jurisprudence, placed less rhetorical emphasis on modernity, were less inclined to follow Western precedents, and were open to the influence of Islamic discourse in other societies. Moreover, Muslim mobilizers were more uncertain than Hindus were of the relationship their religious group would have with emergent nations and states, since the nature of Muslim representation and recognition in India and the contours of the Pakistani political project remained uncertain.

Various Muslim elites proposed changes in Muslim law from the late nineteenth century onward, and changed some of its features starting in the 1910s. The major changes enabled the maintenance of family trusts and increased women's divorce rights. Professional elites and religious elites cooperated to consolidate Muslim law through the passage of the Shariat Act in 1937. Professional elites attached greater value to the symbolic consolidation of the Muslim community in the process, while what religious elites found most important was the application of Islamic norms, rather than customs shared with members of other religious groups, to Muslim family life.

The disengagement of policy makers from Muslim law reform after independence, the periodic assertion of political elites and judges that a UCC was needed, and legislative initiatives to introduce uniformly applicable adoption and alimony laws in the 1970s led Muslim mobilizers to focus more on maintaining distinct Muslim personal laws than on changing these laws. The more conservative among them, represented in the All India Muslim Personal Law

Board (AIMPLB) formed in 1972, also rallied in favor of various judicial precedents. A number of reformist organizations and women's organizations grew among Indian Muslims especially from the 1980s onward; they articulated alternative Islamic discourses that envisioned greater rights for women and nuclear family members. Many Muslims were disappointed with the response of conservative mobilizers to Muslim socioeconomic decline since independence, which helped the reformers challenge the conservatives more effectively.

Christian mobilizers reconstructed some features of religious discourse and reconciled other aspects of church doctrine with the changes they demanded in Christian law from the 1950s. In demanding increased divorce rights, for instance, Christian lay organizations highlighted the increased acceptance of divorce in various global churches and the growth of marital separation among Indian Christians. Recognizing that this demand was in tension with the predominant clerical view that marriage should be indissoluble, they emphasized that churches would not be required to recognize civil divorces. Some of them supported a UCC that would offer Christians adoption rights and increased divorce rights. However, because various Muslim organizations opposed a UCC and some Christians feared that a UCC would delink their religious vision from the regulation of their family lives, they reframed their demands as part of a changed Christian personal law. This linked their legal mobilization more closely to religious visions, and helped them overcome the resistance of church leaders to greater divorce rights.

IX. POSTCOLONIAL REFORM IN INDIA

Policy makers changed personal law less extensively than they did certain other colonial multicultural legacies, such as preferential policies, language policy, and patterns of devolution of authority. Preferential policies based primarily on caste and tribal identity were made more uniform across the country and the constitution was framed to permit such preferences for some time. Moreover, various vernaculars were given official status and significant power was extended to states formed mainly along the lines of language use after independence. The lower priority they accorded changes in family life led the modernists to a compromise with the conservatives over Hindu law reform in the 1950s. The compromise gave women greater conjugal autonomy (by accepting intercaste marriages within Hindu law, reducing restrictions on kin endogamy, and enabling divorce) than it gave them access to property, as kin coparcenaries retained control over ancestral property, in much of which women could not demand shares. Of the most contentious proposals, divorce rights were introduced based on the arguments that some Hindu texts justified divorce under specific circumstances, and that the provision of divorce rights solely based on spousal fault and only two years after judicial separation made a rapid rise in divorce seem unlikely. By contrast, the attempt to give daughters substantial shares in ancestral property did not succeed because neither school of Hindu law provided for it and it seemed to pose a greater threat to patrilineal authority than divorce did, making many modernists wary of this change and conservative traditionalists particularly opposed to it.

These changes gave the majority of Hindu women new rights—for example, to divorces and to a share equal to that of their brothers in their parents' self-acquired intestate property. But the promotion of the monogamous nuclear family also reduced certain rights of women engaged in alternative practices—for example, of women in some matrilineal groups to control property, and of later wives to inherit property from their polygamous husbands. This was a particular way in which the promotion of modernist visions of the normative family constricted the space for alternative forms of family and intimacy. The accommodation of certain Hindu traditions that conservative elites particularly valued deprived remarried widows of their rights in their deceased husbands' property. Although only Hindu law was changed in the 1950s, these Hindu law reforms had such mixed implications for women's rights that Muslim law gave women greater rights than Hindu law in certain respects even after these reforms. Crucially, Muslim law gave women greater access to ancestral property and quicker divorces.[108]

The unimplemented modernist proposals of the first postcolonial decade did not disappear from the agenda. For instance, Ambedkar's proposal to give Hindu women the right to inherit shares of jointly owned ancestral property was reconsidered more readily when women's organizations pressed this claim from the 1970s onward, because lineage authority had declined in the meantime and it was already a part of important modernist visions of the family. This change was introduced initially between the 1970s and 1990s in five southern and western states, in which the prevalence of bilateral and matrilineal customs weakened the defense of patrilineal authority, and in 2005 in the rest of India. Group norms remained a basis of debate over this reform during the past decade. Proponents of the reform overcame the objection that the tradition of sons performing their deceased fathers' *pinda* (memorial ceremony) justified giving them greater rights in ancestral property, by highlighting alternative Hindu customs that allowed daughters to perform this ceremony.

Divorce was enabled on more extensive grounds among Hindus in 1976, based on mutual consent and without the necessity of prior judicial separation. This became possible because political elites valued conjugal autonomy more by then, and the provision of divorce rights in the 1950s had not led to a flood of divorces. This value change also made policy makers more willing to increase Christian divorce rights once the major Christian organizations agreed on this change in the 1990s. Proposals to enable no-fault divorce even in the absence of mutual consent did not succeed, however, because the aim of maintaining the nuclear family, particularly strong among traditionalists, coalesced with feminist concerns that this change would disadvantage most women in the absence of stronger provisions for alimony and sharing matrimonial property. The latter concerns carried weight because women's organizations had gained greater influence over gendered social policies by then.

Minority laws were changed starting in the 1970s, as policy makers began to engage more with reformist minority traditions and initiatives. Even then, it was visions of group culture, rather than projects to form the Indian nation, that shaped these changes. Thus, judges extended alimony rights and limited unilateral male repudiation among Muslims based on particular interpretations of Islamic traditions—the construction of *mata* (provision), one of the forms of support from husbands to ex-wives mentioned in the Qur'an, as mandatory, and of unilateral male repudiation as valid only if the husband provides good reasons for repudiating his wife and spousal reconciliation is attempted. Similarly, Parsi and Christian divorce rights were increased only when mobilization grew among these groups for these changes based on reconstructing aspects of their religious traditions.

Even after the onset of minority-law reform, many policy makers understood minority traditions poorly and considered the religious minorities marginal to the Indian nation. This prevented the accommodation of certain culturally grounded demands for minority law reform—for instance, to give Muslim women throughout India the right to inherit agricultural land and to give Christians adoption rights. Concerns to consolidate Hindu hegemony especially motivated political elites and bureaucrats to resist the extension of adoption rights to Christians because they feared that this would lead to a surge in the Christian population. The minority-law reforms of the last generation thus did not optimally use the room that mobilized group opinion and group traditions provided to promote equality and liberties. The conception of the nation, its constituent groups and cultures, and its deepest inequalities through asymmetric engagement with the major religious groups continued to limit efforts to reduce gender inequality, promote individual autonomy, and build interreligious understanding while recognizing valued traditions.

CHAPTER 3

OFFICIAL NATIONALISM, MULTICULTURALISM, AND MAJORITARIAN CITIZEN MAKING
The Formation of the Postcolonial Policy Frame

THE OUTLINES OF POSTCOLONIAL FAMILY-law policy were formed in the first postcolonial decade, and many policy changes since the 1970s fitted within this frame. The state continued to apply distinct personal laws to the major religious groups and tribal groups; it presented this decision as a way to maintain the relevance of religious norms and religious identities for certain social and cultural rights while secularizing public life in various ways. Policy makers changed personal law less extensively soon after independence than they did other aspects of multiculturalism, such as language policy, federalism, and preferential policies. They did so because political elites wished to maintain broad social coalitions, their preferences about personal law varied considerably, and the modernists among them attached lower priority to reforming personal life than to changing various other features of social and economic life.

Personal-law reform soon after independence was less extensive in another way. It applied only to Hindu law even though initiatives to change personal law based on the concerned group's norms and practices were of comparable strength among Hindus and Muslims, and such initiatives had emerged among Christians too. The fact that most political elites were far more engaged with the initiatives and traditions of the Hindus than with those of the religious minorities reinforced the predominant emphasis that Indian nationalist discourses placed on Hindu norms and the Hindu community, and led policy makers to focus their efforts to promote modern and culturally Indian forms of family life on Hindu law. These circumstances, and the prior stereotypes that most Hindu political elites entertained of Muslims as backward, led these elites to misunderstand the reform initiatives among Muslims that were largely cast in religious discourse as efforts to maintain Muslim law in its existing form. As Muslims emphasized personal law far more than other minority mobilizers, political elites based their approach to the minority laws on their view of Muslims, and were reluctant to change them.

Legislators indicated that they might change personal law further in the future, and the Constitution urged that these laws be replaced with a homogeneous and secular family-law system. Couples were given easier access to the civil laws specified in the Special Marriage Act (SMA) in the first postcolonial decade, and this was presented as a step toward a future UCC. However, various constraints were placed on those choosing to be governed by the SMA, because policy makers feared that if many used this option, this might provoke widespread alarm about the impending secularization of public life.

The changes in Hindu law were framed as based on Hindu cultural repertoires, both older sources and norms that had emerged in recent decades in the imagination and sometimes in the practice of social reformers. Policy makers tailored these changes to make rapid and widely unpopular social changes unlikely. Despite the reliance on Hindu norms, these reforms were said to indicate the forms of family life that the state valued and wished to promote among all citizens. This suggested that a UCC, formed partly in terms of certain Hindu norms, might be applied later to the religious minorities. Some members of these groups were wary that this might be part of a project to gradually assimilate them into an emergent Indian national culture drawn primarily from Hindu mores. Tensions between majoritarian citizen making and minority accommodation would be a recurrent feature of the formation of postcolonial family law.

This chapter explains the formation of the outlines of postcolonial personal law in the first postcolonial decade. It explores the factors and processes which shaped this policy frame—the outlooks and demands of mobilizers, the priorities and proposals of policy makers, the forms of resistance to the proposed reforms and the visions that underlay them, and the considerations that drove the resort to compromise and shaped the terms of the compromise. It highlights how the analytical approach of this study aids a fuller understanding of these processes and their outcomes.

I. THE BACKGROUND TO POSTCOLONIAL POLICY MAKING

A. Initiatives for Legal and Social Change

Various initiatives emerged to promote changes in cultural and religious practice, family relations, and the laws regulating personal life in response to the social and ideational changes of the colonial period. Scholars identify these initiatives with groups that gained Western education,[1] educated women,[2] and urban professional and commercial groups that became somewhat independent of lineages.[3] Western education provided exposure to post-Enlightenment ideas and to accounts of modern social changes in the West, and aroused aspirations to reform or defend indigenous cultural traditions, primarily as they were conceived in colonial knowledge. The ambitions of social reformers extended to many areas of familial life. Certain members of professional and commercial groups aimed to consolidate the autonomy they had gained from rural lineages, so that they could pursue alternative lifestyles, retain more of their earnings, and face fewer constraints in investment decisions, even if lineage property had enabled their professional training and lineage-based networks aided their commercial activities. This aim directed their attention toward the personal law systems of the colonial period, which underwrote the authority of lineages and their control over property in various ways. (The *Mitakshara* school of Hindu law—which applied to most Hindus in the colonial period—and many of the region-specific customary law systems especially upheld lineage authority).

While the men who dominated the professional and commercial elite mainly aimed to choose their spouses, organize their households, and determine their heirs as they wished, some women wished to build their conjugal relationships on less unequal terms, gain easier redress from intimate abuse, and inherit and control greater shares of family property. Women's organizations were formed in the interwar period, notably the Women's Indian Association (WIA), the National Council of Women in India (NCWI), and the All India Women's Conference (AIWC), and mobilized to increase women's rights in various arenas, including family law. As these organizations engaged only in limited mass mobilization, their influence on policy depended largely on their ability to exert judicious pressure and build alliances with favorably disposed male leaders of mass organizations, particularly the Congress Party.

These groups were at the forefront of efforts to reduce constraints on spousal choice, make nuclear families more autonomous, promote companionate marriage, individuate rights to inheritance and property, increase the inheritance rights of nuclear-family members, and in some cases to increase the rights of women to enjoy family property, gain economic sustenance from kin, and lead autonomous conjugal lives. Visions of nations, of revitalized religious, regional, and linguistic communities, and of indigenous forms of modernity framed projects to reform social practice and personal law. Lawyers often based their understandings of the relevant cultural traditions on colonial personal law, but some of them also relied on certain precolonial religious norms. Demands to partially replace colonial personal law with classical religious law, and to increase the powers and recognition accorded to religious courts, were strong among Muslims. Many who raised such demands revived forms of reasoning that colonial law had marginalized, particularly *fiqh* (Islamic jurisprudence that involved seeking reflective equilibrium between classical texts, the contexts of these texts, and contemporary social contexts), *takhayyur* (selective borrowing from other Islamic legal schools), and *ijtihad* (innovative methods of legal interpretation with a long history in Islamic practice). Some Hindus also grounded their demands on precolonial *smrti* texts, like the Manu *Smrti* (dated between 200 BCE and

200 CE) and the Yajnavalkya *Smrti* (between the third and fifth centuries CE), and more often on authoritative commentaries on these texts, especially the *Mitakshara* (circa eleventh or twelfth century) and the *Dayabhaga* (circa twelfth century*)*, that were important sources of colonial Hindu law.

Certain cultural mobilizers promoted the cultural and political solidarity of particular religious groups by consolidating the personal laws that governed them, overriding prescriptions specific to schools of law, sect, region, and caste that the colonial courts recognized. Various Muslim religious and political elites mobilized through the 1920s and 1930s to apply Islamic law rather than South Asian customs to all Muslims in family matters, leading to the passage of the Shariat Act in 1937. This act did not specify the version of Muslim law that would be authoritative, and the courts generally followed colonial judicial precedent. Efforts to consolidate Hindu law began later, partly in response to the consolidation of Muslim law and the Pakistan movement, and influenced the committees that proposed Hindu law reforms in the 1940s.

Still others wished to change and increase the scope of civil and criminal laws pertinent to family life that applied to all Indians, such as those concerning child marriage, spousal violence, and the maintenance of female and minor kin. A few wished to homogenize and secularize family law soon, or to provide citizens the option of being governed entirely by secular family laws. Many more felt that the introduction of a UCC would be unpopular for some time, and so wanted the state to commit itself to this change without setting a time horizon for it or specifying the UCC's content. There was no correspondence between whether groups relied mainly on religious or secular reasoning and the extent to which they sought to maintain or reduce gender and generational inequality. Thus, alliances often formed between groups guided significantly by religious reasoning and those with more secularized outlooks, both to change and to maintain the existing personal laws.

B. Late Colonial Policies

The colonial state claimed it would not interfere in religious practice after the Great Rebellion of 1857, in a posture that was in some tension with its ongoing interpretation and adjudication of personal laws partly based on religious traditions. The courts attempted to resolve this tension by relying on what they took to be the authoritative understandings of religious scholars regarding Hindu, Muslim, Parsi, and Jewish law, while vetting these understandings according to standards of "justice, equity and good conscience" that they conceived and applied inconsistently. The statutes of Christian law were largely drawn from English and Scottish family law of the mid-nineteenth century, and the courts often interpreted them in the light of subsequent changes in British matrimonial legislation. The posture of noninterference made colonial bureaucrats reluctant to change personal law. But reformist mobilization sometimes overcame such reluctance, especially once institutions of self-government grew in the early twentieth century and gave some Indian political elites influence over legislation.

Some changes were introduced as a result in criminal law, Hindu law, and Muslim law. For instance, the state specified and later increased an age of consent, established a minimum marriage age, and made men responsible to support their minor children and indigent wives. Moreover, Muslims were allowed to make bequests of a portion of their property that did not need to conform to Islamic inheritance rules, a provision that they typically used to increase the shares of nuclear family members. The *Mitakshara* school of Hindu law, as it was imagined in colonial law, recognized property jointly held by coparcenaries, typically composed of male kin. Upon the death of a member, shares in such property passed to the other members (who were considered "survivors"), rather than passing to individual heirs based on wills or the rules of intestate inheritance of property owned by individuals. The rules concerning joint property limited the ways in which it could be sold or its proceeds invested. Reform empowered individual Hindus to retain the income they earned as a result of their education, rather than being obliged to share such earnings with the other coparceners whose joint property had supported their education. Hindu widows gained the right to remarry, and later to enjoy (though not bequeath) a part of their ex-husbands' property; Muslim women gained divorce rights under specific circumstances.[4] Further personal-law reforms and uniform family laws were introduced in particular presidencies (administrative units) of British India, and in certain princely states governed by hereditary Indian rulers under indirect British rule. They provided divorce rights or changed the inheritance rules for various groups.

The mobilization that led to these legal changes and the debates to which these reforms gave rise influenced how policy makers considered the course of postcolonial family law.

II. POLICY FORMATION AFTER DECOLONIZATION

A. Understandings of Aims, Processes, and Outcomes

i. Focus on Hindu Law Reform. Scholars offer different understandings of the reasons for the personal-law policies adopted in the first postcolonial decade—specifically, for the focus on changing Hindu law, and for the particular changes introduced. Many consider the exclusive attention to Hindu law a result of the special interest in minority accommodation. They ignore the possibility that minority accommodation could have been reconciled with culturally grounded changes in the minority laws. Moreover, some of them readily accept policy makers' views that Muslims opposed changes in their personal laws.[5] However, this view of Muslim and minority opinion was inaccurate, as many critics indicated at the time.

Even among Muslims, assumptions about whose opinions most influenced the decision not to change the minority laws, some mobilizers were open to reforms in their personal laws based on the group's norms, practices, and opinions. Various *ulama* such as Maulana Hussain Ahmad Madani of the Darul Uloom Deoband (DUD), Muslim elites educated in secular institutions such as the lawyer-jurists Badruddin Tyabji and Asaf Ali Fyzee, Muslim women's organizations like the Anjuman-i-Khavatin-i-Islam (All India Muslim Ladies' Conference), and certain Muslim leaders of the AIWC wished to proceed further with the reforms begun in Muslim law in the 1930s.[6] Such reformist currents influenced the positions that some Muslim leaders took in the Constituent Assembly debates on family law. Most Muslim leaders wished to retain distinct personal laws, but remained open to changes in these laws if they had the relevant group's consent. Some like Naziruddin Ahmad and Hussain Imam were willing to envisage the future introduction of a UCC if all religious groups accepted this.[7] Although Christian reformers did not focus as much on personal law, some Christians had begun to demand increased divorce rights by the 1950s.[8]

The above analyses do not take account of these reformist currents or explain the failure of policy makers to engage with them to change the minority laws. Moreover, minority accommodation was not connected to the choice to focus on changing Hindu law, rather than the optional civil laws. The more influential political elites adopted this emphasis because they did not wish to rapidly secularize family law and saw the reform of Hindu society as central to making the Indian citizen, even if they were cultural pluralists.

Opinions differ about the relationship between the vision of the Constitution and the decision not to change minority law. The unequal rights that all the personal-law systems accorded the genders in various respects and the differential treatment that these systems gave similarly positioned members of different religious groups were contrary to some of the fundamental rights enumerated in the Constitution—especially those contained in Articles 14 (equality before the law and equal protection), 15 (nondiscrimination on grounds only of religion, race, caste, sex, or place of birth) and 21 (protection of life and personal liberty; construed by the Supreme Court to protect privacy and human dignity as well).[9] The failure to change the minority laws to promote the rights upheld by these articles thus seems contrary to Article 13, which declares void all laws in force prior to the adoption of the Constitution that are inconsistent with the fundamental rights. Archana Parashar made this argument most fully.[10] Article 25, which ensures freedom of religious practice, contains a qualification enabling social welfare and reform legislation with implications for religious practice. This was meant precisely to make possible reforms in religious practice, such as in access to places of worship and in the rights granted by the personal laws. The defeat of the efforts of some Muslim members of the Constituent Assembly to protect the personal laws made it entirely clear that the Constitution did not bar personal law reform.

However, this does not clarify the implications of the Constitution, if any, for the pace of personal-law reform. There was some unclarity about which laws should be vetted for consistency with the fundamental rights, pursuant to Article 13. The Constituent Assembly also served as the national parliament, called the Constituent Assembly (Legislative), from the adoption of the Constitution in 1950 until the first postcolonial national elections were called in 1952. This body chose to retain various features of Hindu law contrary to Articles 14, 15, and 21, introduced other such laws (such as the "conjugal right" to the company of a spouse who prefers to live on her own; although the colonial courts had recognized this right from the late nineteenth century and the colonial state had it made a part of statutory Christian law, it was only incorporated in statutory Hindu law by the postcolonial state), did not accept certain changes proposed in Hindu law despite the modest scale of the proposals, and did not consider changes in the minority laws.[11] This suggested that it did not have the personal laws in mind when it formulated Article 13, although the various personal laws were in operation when it adopted the Constitution. This was the Bombay High Court's interpretation of Article 13 when it rejected a challenge to the recognition of different rights for individuals based on their religious identities in *Narasu Appa Mali v. State of Bombay* (1952), setting the precedent for the succeeding decades.[12] Even if the Constituent Assembly did not wish to immediately void personal laws considered contrary to certain fundamental rights, Article 13 might be taken to require the future interpretation and revision of the personal laws in light of the fundamental rights. We will see later in this chapter and in Chapters 4 and 5 that neither the Hindu law legislation of the 1950s nor the personal-law reforms introduced thereafter were systematically driven by constitutional rights. Although policy makers claimed justification for some of the changes introduced in personal law partly in constitutional rights, they changed the minority laws only if they also found grounds for reform in the traditions, initiatives, and practices of group members; they approached Hindu law similarly in most instances.

It could be argued that the classification of individuals according to gender and religious identity in the personal laws was reasonable inasmuch as it was based on differences in gendered socialization, social roles, and resource allocation and in attitudes to social reform among the religious groups, rather than only on religion and sex (the forms of discrimination that Article 15 forbade). Policy makers offered this argument in their defense of the reform of Hindu law alone, and of the retention of various gender-differentiated rights.[13] Furthermore, they repeatedly claimed in parliament that their Hindu law reform proposals promoted constitutional rights, especially those to equality before the law and equal protection.[14] This led some scholars to accept policy makers' claims that early postcolonial personal-law policy was aligned with the Constitution. Jacobsohn did so most elaborately, adding that the ameliorative nature of Indian secularism balanced the commitments to social reform and to maintenance of the integrity of religious life by placing many of the articles calling for egalitarian reform, including the call for a UCC, in the nonjusticiable Directive Principles of State Policy.[15] This left the pace of egalitarian reform to the judgment of political representatives. While the postponement of the introduction of a UCC was an appropriate exercise of the space the Constitution gave legislators to judge the pace of social reform, the same cannot be said of the postponement of minority-law reform due to the vigor of minority reformist initiative.

ii. Nature of Changes in Hindu Law.   Scholars also understand the extent of the changes introduced in Hindu law and the reasons for the specific nature of these changes in varied ways. Werner Menski characterized these changes, whether initiated by the legislature or the judiciary, as modernist until the 1970s.[16] By that, he referred to the adoption of Western precedents, at times to liberalize matrimonial law and at other times to intensify state regulation of family life, with inadequate attention to indigenous norms and the socioeconomic dimensions of conjugal relations in India. Menski claimed that judges became sensitive to the resulting disjunction of statutory personal law from litigants' dispositions and concerns after the passage of a generation, and adjusted adjudication in a postmodern fashion to the social context of marital disputes starting in the 1980s. This understanding is inaccurate in various ways. First, the personal-law reforms were less extensive than Menski suggests when the Indian experience, particularly before the 1970s, is viewed in the comparative perspective adopted in Chapters 1 and 2. Second, the state did not assume a monopoly over the regulation of family life; rather, it chose to accept the continued intervention of community courts in matrimonial disputes, although without making a commitment that state courts would either validate the decisions of the community courts or direct the bureaucracy and the police to implement these decisions. Third, Menski's characterization of personal-law policy through the first three postcolonial decades is in tension with his own observation that elements of classical Hindu moral discourse and classical and customary Hindu law retained a presence in the legal system, including in Hindu law. Fourth, various visions of Hindu and

Indian culture inspired the early Hindu law initiatives, both those of reformers and conservatives—visions drawn from colonial Hindu law, precolonial texts and traditions, and emergent visions of reformed Hinduism and a distinctively Indian modernity. They influenced the particular personal laws adopted in India, and this was a reason why elements of classical and customary Hindu law were retained, though not as extensively as Menski claims. Fifth, although certain matrimonial laws adopted in the 1950s bore some resemblance to laws operating in various Western countries at the time or a little earlier, the particular forms these laws took in India cannot be understood with reference to Western precedents, such as the conditions under which divorce was made available. Moreover, other statutes adopted then bore no resemblance to Western precedents. For instance, this was the case with the incorporation of joint property ownership by male kin in the Hindu Succession Act (HSA). Such legislation resulted from compromises between alternative interpretations of indigenous norms. Sixth, the terms of the compromise were determined by the concern of political elites to retain broad social coalitions, and the inclination of the modernists to signal the practices they valued—but not to press citizens to adopt them soon, since such pressure seemed likely to be widely unpopular. Seventh, subsequent adjudication was sensitive to various features of the social context beginning in the 1960s, as we will see in Chapter 4.

Parashar, Lotika Sarkar, Reba Som, Flavia Agnes, Eleanor Newbigin, and Rochona Majumdar pointed out that the changes were far more limited than what many expected based on the achievement of independence and the nature of the Constitution.[17] Agnes inaccurately claimed that the Hindu-law reforms reduced women's rights in all respects, and Som that the changes were largely symbolic, although these reforms provided most Hindu women with various new rights. For instance, they enabled most Hindu women to inherit a share equal to that of their brothers in their parents' separate property, though not in the property the parents owned jointly with kin, in intestate cases (the potential benefit was especially great for women from patrilineal groups, which account for the majority of Hindus); to get divorces, though only two years after judicial separation in most cases (not available to most upper- and upper-middle-caste Hindus until then); to prevent their husbands from practicing polygyny; to live separately while getting material support from their polygamous husbands; to will the property they inherited from their deceased husbands, provided they did not remarry and were deemed to have remained "chaste"; and to marry some extended kin. Crucially, most of them gained the right to inherit their parents' property for the first time; previously, they had been able to inherit property only in the absence of four generations of agnatic male kin, and that too only as "limited estate" (that is, the right to enjoy but not bequeath property) under *Mitakshara* law, or to inherit only moveable goods (usually dower) as absolute estate (including the right to bequeath) under *Dayabagha* law.[18]

Sarkar traced the limited nature of personal-law reform to the constitutional guarantee of free religious practice in Article 25, although Clause 2(b) of this article enabled the state to intervene in religious practice to effect social reform. Agnes attributed it to the fact that policy makers attached higher priority to the consolidation of Hindu law and to nation building than to the promotion of gender equality.[19] While policy makers' priorities were indeed as Agnes claimed, this does not explain the limits within which Hindu law reform empowered women, because different norms could have been promoted in the course of Hindu-law consolidation and Indian nation building. Newbigin claimed that the main agents of reform, professional and commercial elites, wished to transfer the authority that colonial Hindu law (especially *Mitakshara* law) gave to lineage leaders over jointly owned family property to individual men who would independently own property.[20] She took these agents, even though they used a rhetoric of women's empowerment, to value property rights for individuals only as a means to control their earnings more fully, face fewer constraints in investing their income, and become authors of a postcolonial patriarchy organized around the nuclear family under the husband's tutelage. She and Sreenivas believed that the changes in economic structure and family forms through the late nineteenth and early twentieth centuries loaded the dice in favor of these new forms of patriarchy.[21] While recognizing initiatives to partition family joint property, Majumdar noted the simultaneous salience of visions of the joint family as the primary family unit. She argued that public opinion and the majority of political elites did not favor either the retention of "traditional" patrlineages or the empowerment of the individual to autonomously forge conjugal links and control property. Rather, she described the emergence of modernized forms of marriage, in which joint families arranged marital partnerships using new media and novel standards of desirable and compatible mates, and of preferences that the joint family should remain the main property-owning unit but use its property for the new purpose of promoting national economic development.

The arguments of Newbigin and Sreenivas would have been accurate had postcolonial rulers given individual men absolute property rights, confined their wives to coverture, and given their daughters only a right to maintenance from family resources. However, the modernist Indian nationalists who framed the initial Hindu law reform proposals wished to extend the right to claim shares in family joint property to female kin, and to give daughters shares equal to those of sons in their parents' separate intestate property. These were among the proposals that Ambedkar presented to the first postcolonial parliament, with the support of a minority of Congress Party legislators. The first proposal largely failed, since it enjoyed only limited support even among the modernists (for some of the reasons that Sreenivas and Newbigin identify), and faced considerable resistance among traditionalists who valued patrilineal authority. The strength of such resistance was greater than Sreenivas's and Newbigin's understanding of ongoing socioeconomic change would lead us to expect, especially considering that professional and commercial groups dominated the early postcolonial political elite and parliaments. It forced a compromise that left parents much space to convert the property they earned into family coparcenaries with solely male members to limit their daughters' shares in such property, or to bequeath both their separate property and their shares of joint property to their sons alone. Majumdar and Madhu Kishwar more accurately recognized that while wishing to free investment of the constraints imposed by joint ownership, Indian commercial and industrial elites also wanted to limit the fragmentation of landholdings and business enterprises; these elites found the retention of joint property and the control of male kin over property the most reliable means to this end.[22] Majumdar and Kishwar thus took steps toward a better understanding of the limits to Hindu succession law reform in the 1950s.

The lines of battle over these reforms did not conform to class and occupational status as much as Sreenivas and Newbigin suggest, because religious and ethnic traditions influenced preferences regarding family life in ways that social status does not predict. It was easier to make joint-family property accessible to women among Muslims and among Hindus to whom *Dayabhaga* law had been applied until the 1950s than among Hindus governed by *Mitakshara* law. Islamic law applied the same rules to the inheritance of ancestral property and of property accumulated by the deceased, and gave women definite shares in both kinds of property; *Dayabhaga* law prescribed that individuals inherit and control property, and many Muslims and Dayabhaga-governed Hindus connected these rules with their identities. The lack of correspondence between occupation and positions on gendered personal law is even clearer if one compares the occupational background and positions on personal law taken by the parliamentarians of the 1950s with those of the 2000s, when the inheritance rights of Hindu daughters were increased much further and women gained rights in the matrimonial home upon separation and divorce. The shares of the groups that Sreenivas, Newbigin, and Agarwal considered most averse to reforms that empower women ("agriculturists") increased from 22.4 percent to 49.1 percent and those of the groups considered favorable to such reforms (lawyers, traders, industrialists and businessmen, educators, writers and journalists, doctors, and engineers) declined from 72.7 percent to 25.1 percent between 1952 and 2004.[23] Nevertheless, more political representatives supported or did not oppose the extensive reforms of the past decade than supported or did not oppose the more modest changes introduced in the 1950s. Chapter 4 explores why the positions of legislators changed. It indicates that they changed in response to changes in the structure of ownership and control of property (particularly agricultural property), in household and family forms, in civil society mobilization, in gendered visions of the Indian nation, its religious communities, and its families, and in the links people made between community identity and particular features of personal law.

Agarwal more fully recognized the potential advantages that the Hindu inheritance law reforms of the 1950s offered women, but also described the various barriers that they faced in benefiting from these legal rights in considerable detail. She showed that kinship practices—specifically, group customs regarding inheritance, marital networks, and postmarital residence—influenced attitudes to family law. Groups that practiced patrilineal inheritance; village, regional, and kin exogamy; and virilocal residence offered most resistance to the division of joint-family property (especially landed property) and the control of women (especially married women, who were taken to leave their natal patrilineages on marriage) over such property. Such groups were predominant in northern and western India, and political elites from these groups were the leading defenders of joint-family control over property. Agarwal showed that the predominance and widespread valuation of patrilineal practices blocked efforts to abolish joint-family coparcenaries and to enable daughters to claim shares in the properties controlled by these entities in national-level legislation; it also enabled the passage of land tenure laws (exempted by Article 31b of the Constitution from the need to be compatible with the fundamental rights) that limited women's property rights most in northern and western states, while posing less of a constraint to giving daughters shares in the property that their parents had accumulated. Her analysis also shed light on why the southern states, in which practices of bilateral and matrilineal inheritance, village and kin endogamy, and uxorilocal or nuclearized residence were more widespread, led the way from the 1970s in either abolishing joint property (as happened in Kerala) or giving daughters the right to claim shares in such property (as happened in Andhra Pradesh, Tamil Nadu, Karnataka, and Maharashtra).[24]

Agarwal's explanation of legal change with reference to the bargaining power of coalitions that favor or oppose "gender progressive" legislation, however, ignored some ways in which her own nuanced understanding of kinship practices could inform our understanding of legislative preferences. For instance, the openness of certain defenders of patrilineal norms to giving daughters (especially unmarried daughters) access to their parents' separate property, reducing the constraints on mate choice, and offering women divorce rights under conditions of spousal fault—even while they strenuously opposed giving women shares of joint property—do not clearly fit the "gender progressive" and "gender regressive" categories. Moreover, Agarwal is mistaken to believe that strong and cohesive women's organizations are necessary for the enhancement of women's rights. We saw that women's rights were increased in the absence of these conditions in early republican Turkey and early postcolonial Tunisia, as a concomitant of the efforts of centralizing states to contain the authority of lineages and religious elites. While women's organizations had been the most active advocates of women's empowerment in India since the 1920s, their influence was too limited for them to have a major say in legislation in the 1950s or even over the 2000s, when they had grown stronger. Various lawyers, political elites, and bureaucrats, most of whom were men disengaged from women's organizations, initiated proposals for personal-law reform in the 1940s and 1950s. They responded more to mainstream visions of national and community revitalization, legal rationalization, and democratization than to agendas of women's empowerment. Their efforts nevertheless provided women's organizations the occasion and space to form and press their more ambitious agendas. I give more central attention to the formation of the visions of these agents, which contributed most to the initial reform proposals of the executive, and attend to how discourses of nation and community framed that vision, than does Agarwal who sees "social perceptions" and "social norms" only as constraints to reform.

Agarwal, Newbigin, Parashar, and Everett gave inadequate attention to the formation of views on conjugality; Agarwal, Parashar, and Som traced preferences regarding the formation and dissolution of marriages and the consequences of marriage dissolution too readily to practices and preferences regarding property control. Thus, Parashar and Som inaccurately assumed that all political elites gave questions of property control priority over the regulation of conjugality, and claimed on this basis that conservatives opposed the proposed changes in succession law more than those in marriage law. This led them to characterize the eventual compromise as a defeat for modernism as it provided individuals, especially women, greater conjugal autonomy than property access. The analysis of parliamentary debates later in this chapter shows that conservative resistance to divorce rights was stronger than that to giving daughters shares in their parents' separate property, though weaker than that to giving them claims to ancestral property; and that the reformists were eager to demonstrate their valuation of companionate marriage by providing room for divorce under conditions in which the woman was clearly an unwilling party to a marriage. The reformists introduced divorce rights despite strong conservative resistance, but shaped them in ways suggested by their visions of a reformed and culturally indigenous nation—available only when spousal fault was demonstrated, two years after marital separation to maximize chances for spousal reconciliation. They believed that this was the best way to promote stable and companionate marriages, and thereby disprove conservative allegations that Hindu women's newly gained property rights would undermine the nuclear family.

B. Options Considered, Choices Made

The political elites and bureaucrats that planned postcolonial policy in the 1940s and 1950s gave the following options close consideration: the retention of various colonial personal laws, including variations by sect, caste, and region; the consolidation of Hindu law; the reform of Hindu law; and the provision of an option to have one's personal life governed entirely by civil laws. Many proposed both the consolidation and the reform of Hindu law, and most reform proposals involved the retention of various colonial-era provisions. Policy bureaucrats did not consider reforms in the minority laws because they believed group opinion was unfavorable; they did not consider consolidation because these legal systems had fewer internal variations than Hindu law. Neither did they consider the introduction of further uniform laws pertinent to family life, the expansion of the scope of religious law, an increase in the powers of community courts, or the introduction of a UCC.

The piecemeal Hindu law reforms and more extensive changes in Muslim law in the 1930s triggered demands to change and consolidate Hindu law further. This prompted the colonial government to form two Hindu Law Committees composed of retired judges and bureaucrats in the 1940s, and the postcolonial parliament to form a Select Committee in 1947–48 to consider the second Hindu Law Committee's recommendations. The Hindu law reform proposals were modified several times between 1941, when the first Hindu Law Committee submitted its report, and 1955–56, when parliament passed four acts—the Hindu Marriage Act (HMA), the HSA, the Hindu Minority and Guardianship Act, and the Hindu Adoptions and Maintenance Act (HAMA). The revisions were particularly extensive after the first postcolonial parliament accepted only one aspect of the Hindu Code Bill (HCB), the recognition of intercaste marriages in Hindu law, after debating it over three years. The option of a civil law was initially proposed as a part of the Hindu Marriage and Divorce Bill of 1952, and such legislation would have made it available to those governed by Hindu law. It was recast in 1953 as an amendment to the SMA, to make it available to all Indians. The reports of the two Hindu Law Committees and the parliamentary Select Committee, along with the debates in the first postcolonial parliament from 1948 to 1951, indicate the bases of the initial proposals.

i. Considerations that Influenced Policy Proposals. Policy makers claimed at times that the reforms they proposed would promote rights recognized in the constitution adopted in 1950.[25] But constitutional rights did not shape the changes they proposed, the relative priority they accorded these proposals, the relative value they gave these changes and other ends such as the consolidation of regime support, and thus the compromise they eventually reached. Other considerations that influenced policy making included legal uniformity, the social solidarity of Hindus or all Indians, conformity with classical or colonial Hindu law, and the recognition of valued customs. Policy makers acknowledged the influence of all these goals.

The law ministers who presented the proposals to parliament argued that the postcolonial state should pursue legal uniformity far more than the predecessor regime had, because it valued national cohesion and administrative rationality more, and took greater pride in the legal system's aesthetic qualities. They and other reform proponents argued that the colonial state had inhibited legal change by treating religious traditions and customs as common-law precedents; this was a reprise of critiques offered by colonial officials such as Henry Sumner Maine and James Fitzjames Stephen of how local traditions had been recognized. The postcolonial state, these reformers believed, could more effectively change personal law because its decision makers were better aware of the more gender-equal features of religious traditions and ethnic customs ignored by colonial law.[26] They considered Hindu law consolidation a step toward a UCC, but varied in whether they wanted the reformed Hindu laws to become the core of the UCC. Ambedkar argued that the UCC should take as its starting point the SMA rather than Hindu law because the former was a civil law and more progressive than Hindu law. He nevertheless believed that Hindu law homogenization would aid the eventual introduction of a UCC. Hari Vinayak Pataskar and Charu Chandra Biswas, the law ministers who piloted the Hindu law reforms and the SMA through parliament in the mid-1950s, suggested that the reformed Hindu laws would be extended to other groups once they were ready for this, to the extent that these laws had beneficial consequences.[27] Although the government did not commit itself to either approach, the statements of the latter ministers especially aroused fears among some minority representatives that Hindu law reform was a step toward the stealthy assimilation of their groups into Hindu norms.

The goal of legal uniformity influenced Hindu law reform at different points from the nineteenth century. The utilitarians led the call for codification everywhere. Even many proponents of historical jurisprudence, who had opposed codification in Britain and Germany, believed that it was necessary in the colonies because the shallow training of some judges in common-law jurisprudence and the limited understanding of local practices among others would otherwise lead to excessive variation in adjudication, and thus uncertainty. They also believed that the colonial state could overawe opposition to codification. The first colonial Law Commission of 1833 sketched plans to codify the Indian legal system, leading to the codification of civil law, penal law and criminal law in 1860, 1861, and 1862 respectively, and a consideration of Hindu law codification at different points through the last decades of the nineteenth century.[28] Colonial officials abandoned Hindu law codification because of considerable resistance. But this plan was revived in the 1940s, as decolonization appeared imminent.

By the 1930s, some political elites believed that a postcolonial state could more effectively codify Hindu law because it would continue the Indian nationalist movement's efforts to build a popular national culture, command considerable support, and have officials aware of local cultures.[29] The proponents of legal homogenization believed it would enable administrative rationalization; the consolidation of state control; a limitation in the range of judicial interpretation; a reduction in the roles of custom, uncodified legal traditions, and colonial judicial precedent; the promotion of national unity; and the cohesion of religious communities. Women's organizations, which demanded a Hindu code from 1934, and some modernist male leaders expected such a code to aid women's empowerment too.[30]

The modernist lawyers who framed the Hindu law proposals of the 1940s especially valued the goals associated with codification. This was particularly the case with Ambedkar, who chaired the joint committee of the first postcolonial parliament that devised the bill initially presented to parliament. Ambedkar wished to limit room for judicial interpretation so that law would be more certain and more tightly tethered to the intention of a popularly elected legislature, and to restrict the choice available to individuals regarding the laws that govern them. His preference for legal consolidation and for the Hindu code to be complete was also shaped by aesthetic considerations: "our law . . . should not altogether be unaesthetic: It must be good to look at."[31] Ambedkar's enthusiastic equation of Hindu law homogenization with "slum clearance" reflected the tensions between legal rationalization and accountability, as well as between Ambedkar's concerns to promote national unity and to gain greater recognition for the lower castes and poor, who tend to be concentrated in slums.[32] Ambedkar resisted the recognition of customs, suggested that only customs that were more progressive than Hindu law should be recognized (without systematically incorporating this in his proposals), and was particularly averse to recognizing new practices not incorporated in statutes.[33] Judicial disinclination to recognize new practices would prove a predicament for those of his Mahar caste who followed his lead and converted to Buddhism, but could not induce the courts to recognize their novel wedding ceremonies from the 1950s to the 1980s.

The jurisprudential visions of some other crucial policy makers were less sharply defined than Ambedkar's, and this made them more flexible about policy. Nehru and Pataskar were more open to the recognition of customs—especially those of tribal groups whose norms were very different from Hindu laws—valued legal uniformity only to the extent that it promoted national cohesion, and accepted the ongoing judicial interpretation of statutes.[34] The legislation of 1955–56 bore signs of Ambedkar's vision even though he had resigned from the government and the Congress Party a few years earlier. But Nehru's approach had greater influence over these acts, for instance on the decision not to apply Hindu law to tribal groups—in keeping with the unanimous preference of legislators from these groups.[35]

Pataskar shared aspects of the Hindu nationalist vision, and wished to promote Hindu solidarity through legal change. He said that "bring[ing] together what are now termed Hindus" was central to the "ideology underlying the [Hindu Marriage] bill."[36] The concern with Hindu consolidation influenced aspects of the HMA; for example, it provided for divorce immediately after the conversion of a spouse to a religion originating outside South Asia, while desertion, cruelty, and adultery were only grounds for judicial separation, which could lead to divorce two years later, until 1976. This was justified by claims that spousal reconciliation was less likely and perhaps less desirable after religious conversion than after desertion or cruelty.[37] Limiting the recognition of custom also served Hindu consolidation. The aim to maintain Hindu hegemony over national culture influenced adoption law. Anxieties that the population share of non-Hindu groups might grow rapidly through the adoption of foundlings of unknown ancestry led policy makers to prevent Muslims and Christians from having adoption rights even if they registered their marriages under the SMA, and to resist demands that emerged later to include adoption rights in Christian law. In contrast, they allowed Hindu couples to retain the adoption rights that Hindu law gave them if they chose to be governed by the SMA. Parashar, Agnes, and Menski do not address the different approaches of key policy makers to legal consolidation.

While some of the policy preferences of Ambedkar, Nehru, and Pataskar were different, their visions converged in other ways. This was the case, for instance, regarding the application of Hindu law to Sikhs, Jains, and Buddhists. Ambedkar wished to apply Hindu law to these groups despite associating Hinduism with caste discrimination because he believed Hinduism was the only religion of South Asian origin associated with a legal framework. He made this claim although (a) Buddhist legal traditions existed in Burma, Thailand, and Japan, (b) distinct Buddhist laws were recognized in Burma and Thailand in the mid-twentieth century, and (c) the personal lives of the majority of Sikhs were governed by Punjabi customary law, which also regulated personal law and aspects of land ownership among various Muslim and Hindu landholding castes in the Punjab.[38] Pataskar shared Ambedkar's preference to apply Hindu law to Sikhs, Buddhists, and Jains, but unlike Ambedkar he wished to promote Hindu hegemony thereby.

Both the proponents of Hindu law reform and their critics sometimes defended their positions based on the need to conform to particular classical Hindu norms or certain customs recognized in colonial law. The two Hindu Law Committees of the 1940s (which presented their reports in 1941 and 1947) and the Joint Committees of the Central Legislative Assembly (1943) and the first postcolonial parliament (1948) took the provisions of the two schools of colonial Hindu law as their points of departure. They sought to change these provisions in ways that bore some relationship to the visions of kinship and right underlying colonial Hindu law, while modestly advancing ends such as economic enterprise, fairness, and equity. For instance, these committees preferred the inheritance rules of the *Dayabhaga* school to those of the *Mitakshara* school because they believed that the former's reliance on the same rules for the inheritance of separate and joint property would enable the growth of individual property, which would be conducive to economic enterprise, and because *Dayabhaga*'s emphasis on the inheritance rights of heirs rather than of survivors was favorable to nuclear family members. Moreover, they proposed to modify the *Dayabhaga* rules to (a) place daughters, widows, and sons' widows on a par with sons and give mothers priority over fathers in the lexical ordering of a man's intestate successors, (b) make the daughter's share half that of a son's without regard to her marital status, and (c) make dowry the bride's property, basing themselves partly on the support that some *smrtis* provided for women's property rights. While these measures were meant to reduce gender inequalities, the committees felt the need to match them by giving sons a corresponding share in their mother's property—half that of daughters.

Policy makers later accommodated their critics by maintaining the *Mitakshara* joint family and the associated colonial construction that much of Hindu family property is jointly owned. However, they gave daughters minor shares in joint property upon a parent's death, justifying this modification of *Mitakshara* rules with reference to popular lore that Yajnavalkya, the author of the text on which both the *Mitakshara* and the *Dayabhaga* were commentaries, divided his property between his two wives when he abandoned worldly life.[39] In a similar vein, the Hindu Law Committees proposed to maintain kin exogamy, but in a less stringent form—recognizing the marriage of partners without shared ancestors or descendants within five generations on the paternal side and three generations on the maternal side; the *Mitakshara* rule prohibited marriages to kin who share ancestors or descendants within seven generations on the paternal side and five generations on the maternal side. They also wished to recognize marriages across caste boundaries and within the same *gotra / pravara* (imagined megalineage), as well as those celebrated without religious rituals in Hindu law, while banning polygamy and enabling delayed divorce if there was spousal fault.[40]

The parliamentary debates on these proposals delved further into the sources of Hindu law and various customary practices, and reforms that seemed to be based on such sources had higher prospects of success. The Hindu nationalist parties (the Hindu Mahasabha, the Bharatiya Jan Sangh, and the Ram Rajya Parishad) were unanimous and most vociferous in opposing reform in parliament and on the streets, although some policy makers argued that the reforms would promote Hindu solidarity. They resisted Hindu law homogenization mainly because many of the proposed changes were contrary to the norms of their main support groups, the twice-born castes of northern and western India. Hindu nationalists like Shyama Prasad Mookerjee (the founding leader of the Bharatiya Jan Sangh), N. C. Chatterjee and V. G. Deshpande (of the Hindu Mahasabha), and Nand Lal Sharma (Ram Rajya Parishad) resisted divorce rights, arguing that, in describing marriage as a *samskara*, the *shastras* gave marriage the indissoluble status of the Judeo-Christian "sacrament."[41] While they were willing to continue the recognition of the divorce customs of many middle and lower castes, they did not wish the state to recognize divorce rights as the Hindu norm or place them within easy reach of groups without divorce customs.[42] Moreover, they made no effort to hide their disdain for the customs of south Indians, the lower castes, the middle castes, and tribes. For instance, S. P. Mookerjee said: "I say good luck to South India! Let South India proceed from progress to progress, from divorce to divorce . . . but why force it on others who do not want it?"[43] As a result, the Hindu nationalists preferred that a uniform Hindu law, based on the customs of their core support groups, govern all Hindus and eventually others too, once public opinion was appropriately shaped.[44]

In response to these conservative interpretations of Hindu tradition that had been incorporated in colonial law, divorce proponents like Nehru and Ambedkar emphasized certain cultural grounds for divorce rights more than the Hindu Law Committees had. They argued that Orientalists had misinterpreted the *shastras* to regard marriage as a sacrament, pointed to the support in some *shastras* for divorce under specific circumstances, and claimed that divorce rights would ensure that men respect the sanctity that the *shastras* associated with marriage by calling it a *samskara*. On this basis, they said that customary divorce was no further removed from the *shastras* than were upper-caste norms.[45] Moreover, Ambedkar argued that the customs of most of the lower and middle castes, groups that account for the majority of Hindus, recognized divorce, and that statutory Hindu law should be based on the customs of most Hindus unless such customs were undesirable. The idea of incorporating certain lower caste and middle-caste customs into Hindu law addressed some of Ambedkar's abiding political concerns, and attracted greater support for divorce rights in the context of growing demands for the recognition of these groups.[46] It harkened back to the acceptance of diverse forms of *achara* in the *shastras*, in contrast with the view in the colonial courts that Hindu law prescribed specific practices and that alternative customs were exceptions to Hindu law.[47] Moreover, it reinforced the arguments of the Hindu Law Committees that the inclusion of divorce rights in Hindu law was unlikely to trigger a divorce explosion, since divorce rates were low among the groups whose divorce customs already enjoyed judicial recognition.[48] It was such interpretations of Hindu norms that led modernist political elites to propose only limited divorce rights, not the precedents of English law (which had not yet accepted no-fault divorces), as Menski claimed.[49]

Differing constructions of cultural traditions also entered the debates over inheritance law. The focus in this case was more on normative and current group practice, but some reformists also claimed support in certain *smrtis* and their commentaries. Ambedkar pointed out that giving daughters shares in parental property involved a return to the *Manusmrti* and the *Yajnavalkyasmrti*, which had prescribed that a daughter get a quarter of a son's share (a prescription that custom had erased and colonial law had not considered), and that a share for married daughters was recognized in the *Dayabhaga* (which gave them priority over unmarried daughters). The Hindu Law Committees of the 1940s increased the daughter's share to half of the son's; a Joint Committee of parliament placed it on a par with the son's in 1953, justifying this with reference to the dynamic character of Hindu norms and the committee's inclination to incorporate what it considered the best emergent Hindu social practices into Hindu law. Similarly, these committees found it appropriate to extend the recognition of *stridhanam* (woman's property, which primarily comprised dower) as absolute estate in classical Hindu law to widows' shares in their deceased husbands' property. They considered such changes in tune with the ongoing nuclearization of families and partition of jointly owned family property into individual holdings.[50] Proponents of succession law reform such as Ambedkar, Pataskar, Biswas, S. V. L. Narasimham, Hansa Mehta, Renu Chakravartty, Parvathi Krishnan, and Debeshwar Sarma reassured those concerned to maintain the joint family that the changes proposed in the property shares of kin would not make the fragmentation of family property more likely. They argued that male coparceners already had the right to partition joint property, and that the dissolution of joint property, changes in who controlled such property, and the nuclearization of residential arrangements would not necessarily weaken the solidarity of extended families. Moreover, they pointed out that state-specific legislation meant to prevent the fragmentation of landholdings had priority over the inheritance rules of Hindu law.[51] These statements overcame the resistance of some defenders of lineage authority, but also indicated that their authors were more intent to signal the practices that the state valued than to ensure that many would adopt them soon.

When the parliamentary Joint Committee and the Law Ministry decided to retain the *Mitakshara* coparcenary in 1955, some reformers like R. Venkataraman, Jayashri Raiji, Narendrabhai Nathwani, Rajeshvar Prasad Narain Sinha, W. S. Barlingay, R. Seshagiri Rao, Krishna Chandra, Upendranath Barman and Sushama Sen of the Congress Party, Shankar Shantaram More of the Peasants and Workers Party, Renu Chakravartty and Parvathi Krishnan of the Communist Party of India (CPI), and the independents Rajendra Pratap Sinha and S.V.L. Narasimham expressed their concern that this would constrain the individuation of property rights and limit the inheritance rights extended to women. They preferred to increase the daughter's share in intestate joint property, to restrict testamentary rights in joint property to prevent parents from denying their daughters a part of such property, to make daughters coparceners at birth so that they could claim their shares of their parents' interest in joint property at any point as their brothers already could, or to dissolve *Mitakshara* coparcenaries and give daughters shares in all parental property equal to those of sons.[52]

Conservatives such as Pandit Thakur Das Bhargava, Pattabhi Sitaramayya, Sardar Hukam Singh, Seth Govind Das, Ganesh Sadashiv Altekar, C. D. Pande, Mulchand Dubey and U. R. Bogawat of the Congress Party, and the Hindu nationalists V. G. Deshpande, N. C. Chatterjee, and U. M. Trivedi demanded the retention of the *Mitakshara* coparcenary and resisted efforts to make daughters coparceners on birth in joint property and to give them significant shares of such property intestate, based on the prevalence and presumed value of patrilineal and virilocal practices. Because their focus was more on these practices than on *smrti* prescriptions and the rules of colonial personal law, some of them were willing to accept women's rights that they did not feel seriously threatened patrilineal authority (such as the right of unmarried daughters to a share of their parents' separate property and of women to a share in their husband's and their in-laws' property), as well as certain changes that valorized monogamy and conjugal autonomy (for example, a ban on bigamy and the recognition of intercaste marriages). These preferences were based on the patrilineal assumption that women became a part of their husband's joint families on marriage, making their inheritance of shares of their parents' property a diminution of the property of their natal patrilineages. In addition, Thakur Das Bhargava, Sardar Hukam Singh, Bhopinder Singh Mann, and Ranbir Singh underlined their emphasis on regionally specific practices by demanding the continued recognition of Punjabi customary law that authorized lineage control over property, levirate marriages that kept widows within their deceased husbands' patrilineages, and the extension of all the rights of sons to adopted sons.[53]

While the majority of participants in the family-law debates based their arguments on particular understandings of Hindu traditions and the norms of particular Hindu groups, some of them also wanted Hindu law to catch up with or borrow from India's other personal-law systems and the legal traditions on which these personal laws were based, in certain respects. Hindu law was considered some steps behind Muslim law and Christian law in the extent of its consolidation, and in its provisions for divorce and women's property. For instance, Begum Aizaz Rasul, Raj Bahadur, Jayashri Raiji, and Shivrajwati Nehru welcomed the HCB for reducing the gap between Hindu law and Muslim law (or *sharia*) in the rights they provided women.[54] Ambedkar urged that Hindu law should borrow the extension of shares in family property to daughters, the construction of marriage as a contract, and the associated provision of divorce rights from Islamic, Parsi, and contemporary Western law.[55] R. Venkataraman added that India's Christian law provided women more inheritance rights than Hindu law, and argued that Hindu law should be brought on a par with the other personal laws before the inheritance rights of men and women could be equalized and a UCC framed.[56] Renu Chakravartty indicated that the restriction of testamentary rights could be drawn from Islamic legal traditions, which limit wills to a third of all forms of property to protect the shares of heirs.[57] R. N. Singh Deo believed that the provision of a minimum waiting period between divorce and remarriage was based loosely on the stipulation in Islamic law that one could remarry only after the passage of *iddat* (a waiting period of three menstrual cycles after the man pronounces divorce).[58] Proposals for Hindu law to borrow from the other personal laws and legal traditions only had minor influence in the early postcolonial policy debates, but became more important from the 1980s onward.

ii. Policy Making: Motivating Ambitions, Resistance, and Compromise. The opposition to many initial proposals was sufficiently strong to prevent the HCB's passage. The Congress Party's decisive victory in the first postcolonial elections of 1952, in which the conservative opposition had made the proposed Hindu law reforms an important issue, was presented as a mandate for these reforms. Moreover, Nehru's popularity and strong support made it easier for the second parliament to change Hindu law. But the modernists in the Congress Party realized that the HCB had to be modified, in view of the resistance it encountered, to limit defection from the party. The focus of opposition and the priorities of policy makers influenced how the proposals were changed. The resistance was strongest to proposals that threatened patrilineal authority—specifically to women's rights to inherit natal family property (particularly the rights of married daughters and rights to joint property)— and those that did not favor the continuity of the nuclear family, especially divorce rights. These proposals were changed most. Since more legislators accepted divorce rights than accepted granting daughters shares equal to those of sons in joint property, and since many felt that suitably restricted divorce rights would not undermine the nuclear family, policy makers changed the proposals regarding the inheritance of joint property more than those concerning divorce.

a. Hindu Marriage Law. The main changes proposed in Hindu marriage law were to recognize intercaste, intra-*gotra / pravara,* and some kinds of intrakin marriage (such as marriages to one's mother's cousins' children), to ban bigamy, and to extend divorce rights based mainly on spousal fault. Divorce rights and the recognition of intercaste and intralineage marriages aided conjugal autonomy; the recognition of intrakin marriages had an ambiguous effect on freedom in mate choice, since elder kin arrange most such marriages; and the ban on bigamy strengthened the autonomy of first wives while weakening the recognition and economic implications of other conjugal relationships that men formed. Intercaste and intrakin marriages were readily accepted, because building solidarity across caste boundaries was central to Hindu reformist as well as Hindu nationalist ideas and the forms of intrakin marriage recognized were widespread in some regions. There was some resistance to a ban on bigamy because many Hindus practiced bigamy (a survey conducted as part of the 1961 census estimated the Hindu bigamy rate to be 5.8 percent), and some *smrtis* and other Hindu texts permitted a man who did not have children with his first wife to marry another woman to beget a son who could perform his *pinda* (memorial ceremony). Various conservatives cited this second reason to explain their preference to recognize bigamy at least under some circumstances.[59] Many more parliamentarians opposed divorce rights than the ban on bigamy, and the Anti-HCB Committee, which spearheaded street protest against the HCB from 1948 until the 1952 elections, made divorce rights the focus of its ire. As a result, the antibigamy clause of the HMA passed without modification on a voice vote, but the divorce proposals were modified significantly and passed only after a vote in which 20 of the 170 Lok Sabha (lower house of parliament) members voted against them. Many other parliamentarians also opposed divorce rights but desisted from voting against that clause.

Legal precedent was not a reason for which antibigamy legislation faced less resistance than divorce rights. While the majority of Indians, as well as the majority of Hindus, had divorce rights under some circumstances, bigamy was prohibited for a little under a third of India's Hindus and just over a quarter of all Indians before the 1950s. Parsis gained divorce rights in 1865, converts to Christianity and their spouses in 1866, and other Christians in 1869. While Muslim men could always initiate divorce, Muslim women were able to do so in the state courts from 1939. Muslim community courts considered women-initiated divorce pleas even earlier. A majority of Hindus—many middle and lower castes—had customs of nonjudicial divorce that the colonial courts recognized. Moreover, five states (Kolhapur, Baroda, Bombay, Madras, and Saurashtra) provided divorce rights to all Hindus between the 1930s and the early 1950s. Antibigamy provisions had been introduced in Christian, Parsi and Jewish law throughout India, as well as in Hindu law in four states (Bombay, Madras, Saurashtra, and Madhya Pradesh). Ambedkar was thus accurate in saying that divorce provisions were less innovative than the bigamy ban in Hindu law.[60]

Hindu norms, public opinion, and reformist mobilization influenced the experiences with bigamy and divorce legislation. Although Hindu law permitted bigamy until the 1950s, Hindu texts indicated that men who did not have sons with their first wives could adopt a son to ensure the performance of their *pinda*, and reformers highlighted this possibility. Besides, Christian missionaries had brought bigamy into some disrepute, leading many Hindu reformers to promote monogamy. This reduced the opposition to banning bigamy, especially once policy makers clarified that they meant to deter the practice and protect first wives more than to punish bigamists.[61]

Considerable stigma attached to divorcées, especially among the upper and upper-middle castes that dominated the legal and political elite. This stigma was much greater among India's upper strata in the 1950s than it was among the social elite of Western Europe when comparably extensive divorce rights were introduced there.[62] It remained strong enough in India thereafter that the courts often denied divorce petitions for this reason. Moreover, reformers could only find stray *smrti* references in support of divorce under very specific circumstances. However, the value that many Hindu reformers gave companionate marriage urged them to offer couples in irretrievably impaired marriages the option of divorce, although their inclination to promote stable nuclear families led them not to make divorce readily available. Thus, reformers pressed for divorce rights despite considerable opposition, but framed divorce law to encourage spousal reconciliation. The Law Ministry, a Joint Committee of parliament and the Rajya Sabha (upper house) changed the divorce proposals along these lines between 1952 and 1955. Judicial separation was made more easily available than divorce. For instance, one could claim judicial separation if one's spouse engaged in adultery once, but could petition for divorce without prior judicial separation only if one's spouse "lived in adultery." The minimum time after judicial separation when divorce petitions could be considered was raised from one year to two years; the minimum time after the wedding when divorce petitions could be considered on grounds that did not require prior judicial separation (such as the spouse's conversion to another religion, renunciation of the world by entering a religious order, and engagement in bigamy, rape, sodomy, or bestiality) was raised to three years; and the minimum period after divorce when remarriage was possible was raised from six months to a year. (The SMA, which became available to all Indian couples but which only a few couples were considered likely to choose, did not place these restrictions on access to divorce). Other changes, such as the reduction of the minimum marriage age from twenty-one to eighteen for men and from sixteen to fifteen for women and the recognition of distinctive marriage and divorce customs, also eased the HMA's passage.[63]

Conservative resistance did not lead policy makers to reduce divorce rights in all respects. The Hindu Women's Right to Divorce Bill of 1938 and the Hindu Law Committee Report of 1941 proposed divorce rights only for couples that had civil marriages. Only a small minority of Indian couples had such marriages and their numbers were not expected to rise rapidly. Official proposals made divorce available to couples that had religious wedding ceremonies too, starting with the report of the second Hindu Law Committee, of 1947. Policy makers persisted with this provision because they wished to indicate that they supported conjugal autonomy for all citizens, not just for the unconventional. The extent of resistance to divorce rights, the ways these provisions were modified to ensure their acceptance, and the persistence of reformers despite the opposition show that political elites of all inclinations attached crucial importance to how the divorce question was resolved, contrary to the claims of Everett, Parashar, Som, and Newbigin.

b. Hindu Inheritance Law. The main changes that the HCB of 1948 proposed in inheritance law were to: dissolve jointly owned family property; give individual male and female kin shares of such property; place daughters, widows, and sons' widows on a par with sons among the first tier of heirs; give women half the share of their brothers in their father's separate property and men half the share of their sisters in their mother's separate property; make dowry the bride's property; and place cognates on a par with agnates in the order of heirs and the property shares due to them. These changes were presented as a version of *Dayabhaga* rules that gave priority to "blood relationship" and "propinquity and love," taken to be based mainly on nuclear family bonds rather than to patrilineal norms and sons' imputed ritual roles. Moreover, they were portrayed as ways to increase women's property rights and social autonomy, orient Hindu law to contemporary practices, and spark enterprise.[64]

Reformers varied in their attachment to these proclaimed ends. While all of them wanted to revive the dynamism of religious law and increase women's property rights, they constructed family identity in different ways—as the patrilineal or bilateral joint family or the nuclear family. These differing conceptions influenced the changes they desired in inheritance rights and their relative prioritization of these changes, and thus their responses to opposition. Agarwal highlighted the impact of kinship practices on women's access to land, but not on family identity and lawmaking. Majumdar addressed the influence of kinship practices on the Hindu inheritance law reforms of the 1950s, and my analysis is similar to hers in some respects.[65]

The majority of Indian political elites were attached to patrilineal visions of the family, crucially because most Indians and most Hindus were embedded in patrilineal practices and patrilocal residential arrangements. This induced them to value joint property to maintain the joint family as a unit of identification and social support, and limited their inclination to increase women's inheritance rights. It specifically made them disinclined to give married daughters inheritance rights in natal family property or to give daughters (whatever their marital status) rights to absolute ownership of the two forms of property considered crucial to the family's status and resources—agricultural land and the ancestral residence. Pataskar largely fitted this profile and opposed the dissolution of *Mitakshara* coparcenaries, but unlike many other defenders of patriliny he was inclined to give daughters a minor share in joint property. He said that "a daughter does go out of [the] family on marriage" and that he did not wish to make daughters and their heirs coparceners in joint property because he believed this would undermine the continuity of the family.[66]

Ambedkar favored the dissolution of joint property and the prioritization of the rights of nuclear family members over those of extended kin, and the HCB of 1948 included these changes. But he indicated even then that he was open to the retention of joint-family control or primogeniture regarding agricultural land if most parliamentarians preferred this.[67] Thus, even the Law Ministers of the first postcolonial decade were less determined to pass all the initial proposals regarding inheritance than regarding divorce, particularly as the permissive nature of divorce law (in contrast with the mandatory character of inheritance law in the absence of wills) made it the politically easier terrain on which to demonstrate modernist values. We saw that resistance was strongest to (a) dissolving family coparcenaries, (b) making daughters coparceners on birth, (c) giving daughters intestate shares equal to those of sons in joint property and in agricultural land, (d) giving married daughters shares of natal family property, and (e) limiting testamentary rights; there was less resistance to giving women absolute estate in some forms of property and making their shares equal to those of their brothers in separate property and moveable property.[68] These priorities of the reformers and the conservatives and their inclination toward compromise loaded the dice in favor of aspects of the eventual legislation—maintaining joint property and giving women absolute rights to some forms of natal family property while limiting their rights in coparcenaries and agricultural land.

The Hindu Succession Bill that the Law Ministry presented to parliament in May 1954 took steps toward such a solution. It excluded the *Mitakshara* coparcenary from its purview, and Pataskar argued that making daughters coparceners in such property would make the joint family unviable.[69] Many members of the parliamentary Joint Committee that considered this bill (Rajeshvar Prasad Narain Sinha, R. Seshagiri Rao, S. S. More, R. P. Sinha, Renu Chakravartty, Parvathi Krishnan, and S. V. L. Narasimham) argued that this would deny most women access to much of their natal family property, leading the Committee to apply the bill to *Mitakshara* joint property and to give daughters minor shares in such property. The Committee's bill continued to restrict membership in these coparcenaries to male kin, who thus alone would have the right to claim shares in such property at any time as survivors. But it gave daughters a share in joint property if there was intestate succession; this share would have been the same as that of their brothers who remained part of the coparcenary until the succession opened, and a little less than that of brothers who partitioned their shares earlier.[70] Moreover, it increased the daughter's share in the father's separate intestate property from half of the son's share to the same as the son's share, and the son's share in the mother's separate intestate property from half of the daughter's share to the same as the daughter's share. Conservatives did not pay much attention to separate property, and so did not resist the equalization of shares in such property strenuously.

The Committee's bill offset the increase in the daughter's shares by increasing the coparcener's testamentary powers in joint property; giving family members the preemptive right to purchase shares of such property from another member; preventing daughters from partitioning the family residence; and giving state laws meant to promote agricultural production and limit the fragmentation of agricultural land (many of which limited women's shares) priority over the bill's provisions. These changes addressed the concern of the defenders of the patrilineage to prevent the fragmentation of lineage property and land holdings, as well as their concern over the control of daughters-in-law over parts of lineage property (including the ancestral residence) and the entitlement of women to considerable property. Pataskar claimed that the added testamentary rights were meant to enable parents to compensate for the increased property that the rules gave sons who partition their shares during the parent's lifetime and to adjust the property allocated to an heir according to the person's needs; but he clearly indicated to conservatives that the rules would restrict the property that passed into the daughter's control in most cases.[71]

Parliament amended the Committee's bill so that the daughter's share in intestate joint property was computed based on her parent's share alone. This meant that the HSA gave daughters much lower shares than sons in such property, because sons got shares qua coparceners as well as portions of their parent's share (upon the parent's demise) qua heirs. For instance, in a family with a daughter and a son, there would be two coparceners (father and son) and the father would have three heirs if he predeceased his wife (son, daughter, and widow). On birth, the son would get a one-half share of the interest the father inherited in the property, which he could claim before the father's death or upon it as a survivor. If the father did not write a will, the son, daughter, and widow would each get one-third of the father's one-half share—that is, one sixth of the father's inherited interest in the joint property—making the net shares of the son, daughter, and widow two thirds, one sixth, and one sixth respectively. Clause 6 of the HSA, which specified these rules, crucially reduced conservative resistance to the bill. It became the focus of much litigation and reformist mobilization over the subsequent decades, leading to its amendment in 2005 to make daughters coparceners.

The bill of 1948 had excluded the nontribal groups of Kerala and Karnataka with matrilineal customary laws (the Marumakkattayam, Aliyasantana and Nambudri laws) from its purview, on the urging of representatives of these groups, because their customary laws gave women greater control over property than the HCB. (The HCB, along with the acts of the 1950s, did not apply to any tribal groups). However, when the Joint Committee applied the bill to these groups, thereby reducing the property rights of their women, it encountered little resistance from group representatives. This reflected a decline in support for matrilineal practices, especially among younger men. The entry of many group members into the professional elite—particularly among the Nairs, but also among the Bunts, the Ezhavas, and the Namboodiri and Thiyya subgroups whose customary laws were recognized under colonial rule—and the conversion of significant chunks of these groups to Christianity increased their aspirations toward integration into the largely patrilineal norms valued by most upper caste Hindus, Christian missionaries, and Hindu nationalists. The only features of these customary laws that were accommodated in the bill were the inclusion of mothers among the Class I heirs, and the equation of the rights of agnates and cognates.[72]

Majumdar attributed the retention of considerable patrilineal control over property to the visions of economic development most influential at the time and to the tendency of most political elites who favored increased property rights for women to give higher priority to the requirements of efficient production as they saw them.[73] She highlighted two concerns of certain key architects of economic policy: the need to limit the fragmentation of agricultural holdings and to accommodate the value that peasants attached to a male monopoly over land ownership; she took their implications for women's property to coincide with the preference of most industrialists to remove the constraints that coparcenaries placed on investment decisions, while limiting women's property control. These orientations are said to have led to the continued authorization of the control of male kin over joint property.

While planners did not consider women's independent land rights, as Agarwal demonstrated amply, Majumdar did not accurately depict the views of most agrarian planners at the time about the desirable size of landholdings. These policy elites believed that to increase the incentives to invest in agrarian infrastructure and optimize production, very large landholdings should be divided, the land owned by particular families should be consolidated into continuous plots, and larger farmers should be allowed to take over very small plots that they considered uneconomical.[74] Partitioning very large agrarian plots, the majority of which were controlled by joint families, would have coincided with how they saw the preconditions of economic growth.

Moreover, leaders of women's organizations such as Hansa Mehta, Sucheta Kriplani, Jayashri Raiji, Sushama Sen, Renu Chakravartty, and Parvathi Krishnan, as well as male parliamentarians who valued women's property rights such as S. S. More and S. V. L. Narasimham, repeatedly argued that women's inheritance rights would not increase land fragmentation or undermine agrarian management. Many other male parliamentarians, including R. Venkataraman, C. C. Shah, Rajeshvar Prasad Narain Sinha, R. Seshagiri Rao, Krishna Chandra, C. R. Chowdary, K. Kelappan, K. K. Basu, and N. P. Nathwani, argued that to stimulate economic growth, one needed to reduce the constraints that both men and women faced in their ownership and transfer of property. In the eyes of such reformers, considerations of economic efficiency only reinforced justice-driven arguments to increase women's rights to most forms of family property and to dismantle joint property. Some of them expressed these views in notes of dissent from the Report of the Joint Committee,[75] and others tried without success to amend the bill to dissolve coparcenaries, increase women's shares in joint property, limit testamentary rights, or maintain widows' rights in their deceased husbands' property after remarriage.[76] They did not vote against the HSA only because they realized that parliament would give women no further inheritance rights at that point. But the presence of such opinion among a significant minority of the political elite provided a base on which later efforts to change inheritance law built.

The majority of defenders of patrilineal property control prioritized it over growth optimization. The retention of joint property, restriction of female kin's access to such property, and increase in testamentary rights conciliated them because they felt it ensured that female kin, and married daughters in particular, would not gain much property.

c. The Special Marriage Act. Visions of indigenous forms of modernity gained fuller influence over the SMA than over Hindu law. The SMA was introduced in 1872 as a first step to provide for civil marriage, in response to demands to recognize the emergent rituals of many members of the reformist Brahmo Samaj sect, formed earlier in the nineteenth century. It was more modernist in many respects than the personal laws; for example, it set a higher minimum marriage age than any of the personal laws did, and required monogamy, which only Christian law also did at that point. This act enabled individuals to contract marriages that crossed caste or religious boundaries, were solemnized through unorthodox wedding ceremonies, or had legal consequences that differed from those of the marriages of most of their coreligionists.

Conservatives had succeeded in limiting the conditions under which couples could register their marriages under this act in the 1870s. The act was applicable only to couples that renounced their affiliation with India's major religions until 1923, after which it was made available to couples in which both members were Hindu, Sikh, Jain, or Brahmo Samaj members. It required such couples to give a month's notice of their wedding plans, during which time others could contest the validity of the planned marriage. No such advance notification was required for weddings governed by the religious laws. Colonial law severed couples that made this choice from their joint families and separated any shares they might have in family coparcenaries. This granted these couples control over their shares of joint property, but also made their continued economic cooperation with their kin less likely, and was in fact meant to induce them to forego their rights to ancestral property. These restrictions deterred individuals from contracting marriages that only the SMA would recognize and from claiming the provisions of the act; they enabled the couple's kinsfolk to prevent such marriages. The legislation also underlined the liminal status of those who contracted such marriages by giving couples whose only living son registered his marriage under the SMA the right to adopt a son to perform their *pinda*, on the assumption that it would be inappropriate for a biological son whose marriage broke social norms to do so.[77] The restrictive conditions under which one could resort to the SMA ensured that very few couples were governed by this act under colonial rule—mostly couples whose marriages the various personal laws did not recognize (such as couples belonging to different religious groups or castes, or to the same *gotra* or *pravara*), or whose wedding ceremonies were unlikely to be recognized in the courts otherwise. The major religious laws did not govern marriages that crossed religious boundaries (other than between groups practicing Indic religions); Hindu law did not recognize intra-*gotra/pravara* marriages until 1946 and most intercaste marriages until 1949.

Because the SMA did not draw explicitly from religious norms and did not pertain to a specific religious group, certain postcolonial policy makers felt that its wider application would enable the secularization and homogenization of family law. Indeed, C. C. Biswas, the Union Minister of State for Law, said when he introduced a revised SMA in the Rajya Sabha that it was a "first attempt of Government to secure for the citizens a Uniform Civil Code in one branch of the law," and that it would help build a homogeneous society.[78] The new SMA passed in 1954 was more modernist in various respects than the HMA—for example, it offered women more extensive inheritance rights and couples easier access to divorce. All couples were allowed to opt for this act, and couples whose marriages were initially governed by their personal laws were permitted to change the terms of their marriages by registering them under the SMA later. This act was framed mainly in terms of universalist values—for instance, as shaped by the dictates of eugenics—in contrast with Hindu law reform, which was framed significantly in terms of Hindu tradition and regional and caste customs.[79] These features of the SMA suggested that the act would initially apply modernist norms to a social vanguard that preferred such rules to their personal laws, and to all others once public opinion was appropriately shaped. Some SMA proponents said that the act should govern all citizens soon.[80] These suggestions, however, were contrary to the act's name and its preamble, which said that it provided "a special form of marriage," as well as with Biswas's statement that he expected only a few couples to choose the SMA for a long time, primarily those belonging to different religious groups.[81] Moreover, policy makers portrayed Hindu law reform, not just the new SMA, as a step toward a UCC, and gave the SMA much less attention than Hindu law.

While committees had drafted plans for a Hindu code since 1941, a new Special Marriage Bill accessible to all citizens was framed only when the second parliament met in 1952. (Separate rules to govern civil marriages were proposed earlier as part of the HCB of 1948, and they would have been unavailable to Muslims, Christians, Parsis, and Jews in this form). This bill was hastily drafted, and included many features of the act of 1872 that were less modernist than the reformed Hindu law proposals then under consideration. This was particularly the case regarding its divorce provisions, since the initial bill retained the rule that the Indian Divorce Act (IDA) of 1869 would govern couples that registered their marriages under the SMA. The IDA, which applied mainly to Christians, provided extremely limited divorce rights that differed for men and women. It enabled men to seek divorce only on the ground of adultery, and allowed women to do so only if they could demonstrate adultery as well as another spousal fault. This made divorces very difficult for Christians to gain, and various Christian representatives had already approached the Law Ministry to amend these provisions.[82] The initial bill also denied adoption rights to couples that would be governed by it, basing itself on the act of 1872. This meant that Hindu couples that opted for the SMA would have lost the adoption rights that Hindu law gave them.

Ambedkar, who now sat in the opposition benches, criticized the excessive borrowing from colonial legislation, called the initial divorce proposals retrograde, and argued that the provision to sever SMA couples from joint property, initially introduced on the insistence of conservatives to penalize those who contracted unorthodox marriages, should be dropped.[83] Two parliamentary committees subsequently included divorce provisions in the bill that were more extensive than those in the HMA (including a provision for mutual-consent divorce that faced some opposition in parliament), and deleted the clause that prevented adoption. The path to these outcomes shows that the policy elite did not clearly direct its ambitions to promote modern family practices toward the conception of the SMA as it had with its Hindu law proposals.

Many features of the eventual legislation made it unlikely that large numbers would choose to be governed by it soon. First, religious personal law remained the default choice for couples belonging to the same religious group. This seemed to place those choosing the SMA on the margins of their religious group, although they no longer needed to renounce their religious identities. This was particularly the case as the Indian Succession Act (ISA), which governs Christians, also applied to the inheritance of the property of SMA couples, appearing to impute a Christian identity to non-Christians who opted for the SMA.[84] Second, policy makers removed only a few of the obstacles to the registration of marriages under the act. Couples registering under the act still had to give a month's notice of their weddings; until 1976, Hindu couples doing so were legally separated from their joint families; couples belonging to different religious groups continue to face this consequence; and Hindu couples whose only living son chooses the SMA could adopt a son to perform their *pinda*. SMA couples were penalized in these ways despite the opposition of many parliamentarians.[85] Third, couples choosing the SMA had no adoption rights, because most courts interpreted the SMA's silence regarding adoption to mean that Hindu couples choosing the SMA could not adopt children rather than retaining the adoption rights that Hindu law gave them. Fourth, as the Hindu Marriage Disabilities Removal Act had accepted intra-*gotra* and intra-*pravara* marriages and the Hindu Marriages Validity Act had accepted intercaste marriages in Hindu law in 1946 and 1949 respectively, it was no longer necessary for such couples to register their marriages under the SMA. Fifth, only a minority of citizens preferred the more modernist provisions of the SMA to those of the various personal laws, making it more unlikely that many couples would choose the SMA.

Hindu conservatives resisted the SMA much less than they did the changes in Hindu law, because the former act seemed very likely to apply only to a small number for the foreseeable future. This enabled the SMA's quick passage and its formulation along more modernist lines. While fifteen years passed between the presentation of the first Hindu Law Committee report and the passage of three of the four major acts of Hindu law, the SMA was passed within two years of its presentation to parliament. Its inheritance and divorce provisions especially gave women more rights and individuals more autonomy than the major personal laws. The ISA, which governed the inheritance of the property of all couples choosing the SMA until 1976 and still governs non-Hindu couples making this choice, gave daughters a greater share in ancestral property and easier access to such property than Hindu law (insofar as it did not provide for joint property in which women's shares were limited) or Muslim law (equal to, rather than half of, the share of sons). The SMA enabled divorce on the same grounds as those for judicial separation (including mutual consent), and these grounds were more extensive than those under Hindu law. It did not require judicial separation before petitioning for divorce on most grounds. Moreover, it set a higher minimum marriage age for women (eighteen rather than sixteen) and placed fewer restrictions on intrakin marriage (disallowing marriages to those sharing ancestors or descendants within three generations, in contrast with the five generations on the paternal side and three generations on the maternal side required by Hindu law since 1955). Policy makers did not feel the need to introduce the special provisions they had retained or added in Hindu law to maintain joint property and discourage divorce in the SMA; they assumed that the social vanguard choosing the SMA would be more independent of family support and would have the maturity to manage their shares of family property effectively and to resist any urge to resort to quick divorces. Although the SMA granted individuals various new rights, the many constraints on accessing its provisions meant that the act only partly circumvented the control of communities and families, contrary to Perveez Mody's understanding.[86]

Conservative Muslims resisted the SMA far more than conservative Hindus did; they especially opposed the application of non-Islamic inheritance laws to Muslims. B. Pocker Sahib and Kazi Ahmad Hussain of the Muslim League argued accurately that Muslims who opt for the SMA could inherit property from agnates who would lack the reciprocal right to inherit their property; and wrongly that the SMA would reduce the inheritance and divorce rights of Muslim women. Since they could not muster much parliamentary support and the SMA was optional, parliament ignored their objections. The Muslim League registered its opposition to Muslims having access to the SMA, but conservative Muslim organizations ended their opposition to the act later.[87]

III. THE POLICY OUTCOMES AND THEIR CONSEQUENCES

Approaches to family law were shaped by the state's association with secularism in a multireligious country in which religion plays major public roles; by official commitments to recognize cultural specificity and, at the same time, promote national consolidation; by the inclinations of policy makers to gradually promote forms of modernity based in indigenous cultures; and by the inclination of political elites to build broad coalitions. The choices made based on these concerns in the first postcolonial decade set the framework for subsequent policy.

Visions of indigenous forms of modern family life focused on Hindu law; no significant changes were made in the minority laws until the 1970s, although opinion and mobilization did not favor personal-law reform significantly more among Hindus than among Muslims. The changes made in Hindu law were based both on visions of authentically Indian forms of modern family life and on specifically Hindu norms, both enduring and emergent. Although they drew heavily on Hindu norms, these changes were presented as a step toward a UCC. The association of Hindu law reform with the formation of future civil laws was part of a majoritarian approach to forming nation and citizen. The SMA was changed to give a small social vanguard a slightly wider path to civil family laws, and policy makers claimed that this would also pave the way to a UCC. However, the much lesser attention that political elites gave the SMA than Hindu law and the constraints placed on couples governed by the SMA suggested that a UCC might draw mainly from Hindu law.

Although Hindu law was changed and the minority laws were not in the first postcolonial decade, Hindu law did not provide women more rights or individuals greater liberties after these reforms than the other personal laws did in various respects. For instance, Christian law, Muslim law, and the customary laws of various matrilineal tribes gave women greater rights to ancestral property, and Muslim law gave them more divorce rights, than Hindu law did. There were many reasons for the mismatch between the focus of early postcolonial reform and the extent to which the various personal laws recognized women's rights and individual autonomy. First, some of the minority laws favored these ends more in certain respects than Hindu law did before the reforms of the 1950s. Since it was codified in the 1860s and 1870s, Christian law gave women greater inheritance rights than Hindu law. Muslim law provided women more rights to inheritance and divorce than Hindu law, especially after it was changed in the 1930s.[88]

Second, the visions of family life that motivated the reform proposals did not favor women's rights and individual autonomy in all respects. For instance, many reform proponents valued the stability of the nuclear family, rights to the spouse's conjugal company, widows remaining a part of their dead husbands' enduring social personality by not entering other conjugal relationships, and patrilineal or bilateral constructions of family identity. As a result, even the initial Hindu law proposals included only limited divorce rights, underlined rights to the company of one's spouse even if she preferred to live on her own, made the widow's claim on her dead husband's property contingent on her "chastity," and did not draw from the matrilineal norms of some Hindu groups that especially favored women's conjugal autonomy and access to property.

Third, modernist policy makers aimed to signal their family values more than to promote rapid and potentially unpopular social changes, to limit the political costs of reform. Thus, they indicated that women were equally worthy of owning property by giving them rights to shares equal to those of their brothers in their parents' separate intestate property, but did not ensure women's empowerment by limiting testamentary rights. Fourth, modernist political elites abandoned some of their initial proposals to avoid an erosion of conservative support and maintain the Congress Party's dominance. The resistance was strongest to giving women (especially married daughters) substantial shares in their natal family's ancestral property, which was contrary to the widely shared patrilineal constructions of family identity. As a result, the legislation retained joint property that could not be readily decomposed into individual shares, limited women's shares in such property, provided testamentary freedom with regard to such property, and gave state agrarian legislation priority over Hindu inheritance rules.

Agnes and Som highlighted how the legislation of the 1950s failed to promote women's rights effectively.[89] They indicated that divorce rights and antibigamy law had ambiguous implications for women because of their limited economic autonomy, that bigamy law had loopholes that judicial interpretation widened to seriously limit the punishment of bigamists, and that the proposal most valuable to women—giving women equal access to ancestral property—was not adopted. Various studies show that the majority of Hindu parents used two features of inheritance law to avoid giving their daughters their intestate shares of family property.[90] First, they used their freedom in testamentary rights, which they had even earlier in separate property but gained in joint property through the reforms, to bequeath most of their property to their sons. Second, some of them placed parts of their property in coparcenaries jointly owned with their sons. This limited their daughters' shares in such property even in the absence of wills, and restricted their access to these notional shares. Srimati Basu demonstrated the inaccuracy of claims often made in support of the grant of much family property to sons— that daughters get a commensurate share in the form of marital expenses, dowry, and dower, and further property or at least maintenance from their husbands' natal families.[91] She found that parents direct fewer resources to their daughters' weddings than to their sons' inheritance; daughters do not benefit from such expenses after their weddings; their husbands and in-laws invariably control their dowries; dowries tend to be much higher than dowers; and women often do not control their dower either, although they had the right to do so even before independence. The serious limits to women's control over property and the inadequate implementation of decrees for the maintenance of separated and divorced women further restricted women's gains from divorce and antibigamy law.

Thus, Agnes and Som accurately depict some consequences of Hindu law reform, but partly misunderstand legislative intention. Legislators introduced some laws mainly to underwrite particular values, rather than to make all citizens adhere to these rules soon. They did not believe that the ban on Hindu bigamy ought to lead to the rapid imprisonment of bigamists, because many citizens tolerated the practice and many women in bigamous relationships wished to retain the economic support they gained as a result. Judges followed legislative intention in finding bigamy much more often when women demanded maintenance payments and a separate residence from their husbands than in criminal cases against bigamists, as we will see in Chapter 4.

Legislators introduced other legal changes (such as the provision of divorce rights on limited grounds) partly because they were confident that they would not thereby generate rapid social change. Judges urged most couples seeking divorce to initially attempt reconciliation, and followed legislative intention in this regard as well.

Parashar and Som closely associated the limits to women's empowerment with a retreat from Ambedkar's vision. However, the legislation of 1955–56 favored women more in some ways than Ambedkar's vision would have, particularly in the significant room it left for judicial interpretation and in its retention of certain tribal customary laws. Chapter 4 shows that the higher courts used their interpretive powers from the 1970s onward to provide women easier access to divorce by setting lower standards of proof of spousal faults; they also granted women the right to reside in the matrimonial home on separation or divorce especially if they found spousal cruelty. The retention of tribal customary laws had ambiguous effects on women's rights because these laws were rather differently gendered. Among matrilineal tribal groups such as the Khasis, Garos, Jaintias, Lalungs, and Rabhas of Meghalaya, Tripura, Assam, Nagaland, and West Bengal, the Kurichiyas of Kerala and Tamil Nadu, and the Koyas and Malmis of Lakshadweep, customary law gave women greater access to property and more conjugal autonomy than Hindu law, at least until certain recent changes in Hindu law.[92]

The strategy adopted toward family law in the first postcolonial decade and the proposals and debates that led to its formation influenced subsequent litigation, adjudication, legal mobilization, and legislation in many ways. For instance, both legislators and judges continued to feel freer to change Hindu law than the minority laws. They considered evidence of support in the norms, practices, and initiatives of the relevant group a binding precondition of minority-law reform. This limited changes in the minority laws to a few minor judicial initiatives until the 1970s. A growth in reformist mobilization among Muslims and Christians and the engagement of some policy makers with these initiatives contributed to the onset of cautious minority-law reform thereafter. But majoritarian constructions of the nation continued to limit changes in minority law.

Certain modernist proposals that were not accepted in the 1950s remained a part of public debate, and some of them were adopted once conditions became favorable. More legal and political elites came to value conjugal autonomy, and they attempted to increase divorce rights starting in the 1970s. Women's organizations and other rights organizations, which grew from the 1970s as well, initiated efforts to increase women's rights to alimony, redress from intimate abuse, and inheritance. They resorted to litigation and popular mobilization to oppose certain features of the policy compromise of the 1950s—the limits placed on divorce rights and on women's rights to joint property but not on testamentary rights in joint property. In the process, they revived some arguments made in the policy debates of the 1940s and 1950s: that divorce rights do not strengthen conjugal autonomy if economic support is not ensured for the economically weaker partner; that *Dayabhaga* law, which does not recognize joint property, represents Hindu tradition no less than *Mitakshara* law; that the joint family may remain a viable basis of identity even if joint property is decomposed into individual shares; and, drawing greater support from subsequent social changes, that joint-family residential arrangements were in decline. Chapter 4 explores how these initiatives led to an increase in the grounds on which Hindus could claim divorce, a reduction and then the elimination of the required waiting time between judicial separation and divorce, and the inclusion of daughters among the coparceners in joint property. The call to increase women's access to property by restricting testamentary rights, which has yet to be heeded, revived the argument of a few legislators in the first postcolonial decade that the limitation of testamentary rights to a third of one's property in the Islamic legal tradition should be incorporated in Hindu law.

Early postcolonial policy discourse also influenced aspects of later Hindu nationalist legal mobilization. Its slippage between the formation of Hindu law and a UCC made it easier for Hindu nationalists to present themselves as the advocates of secular and more gender-equal family laws, once their political fortunes rose in the 1980s and public support for certain women's rights increased. Although Hindu nationalists had resisted Hindu law reform in the 1950s, they argued in the 1980s that minority accommodation had prevented the introduction of a UCC and thus the promotion of modern values, and that they alone would take the long-overdue step of homogenizing family law, since they would not give the religious minorities undue recognition. Such rhetoric was not accompanied by efforts to specify the content of the UCC they aimed to introduce. This led some to infer that a UCC introduced by these forces would be based on some version of Hindu law, following the preferences that many Hindu nationalist leaders had voiced in the 1950s.

CHAPTER 4

RECASTING THE NORMATIVE NATIONAL FAMILY

Changes in Hindu Law and Commonly Applicable Matrimonial Laws Since the 1960s

MODERNIST POLITICAL ELITES HAD INDICATED the patterns of family life they wished to promote among Indian citizens through the changes they made in Hindu law in the first postcolonial decade. They valued the family as a monogamous nuclear unit, formed and maintained through the autonomous choices of partners, in which women enjoyed a measure of economic independence. This vision was in tension with their wish to encourage the maintenance of nuclear families even in face of serious marital problems, and with the preference of many of them to recognize the patrilineal joint family as a residential unit, basis of family identity, and property-owning entity. Chapter 3 showed that an inclination to consolidate broad social coalitions influenced how modernist policy makers resolved these tensions in the 1950s. The modernists signaled the value of conjugal autonomy by extending divorce rights while limiting the space to dissolve marriages, and expressed their commitment to women's economic independence by giving them rights to inherit separate intestate property. But, because their conservative allies attached greater value to the patrilineage and various forms of gendered familial authority, they also maintained lineage authority and aligned lineage identity largely with its male members by retaining jointly owned family property, devolving such property patrilineally, and restricting women's access to such property.

From the 1970s, changes were made in Hindu and commonly applicable matrimonial laws that made membership in nuclear families a more important basis of familial rights and responsibilities, departed from primarily patrilineal constructions of kinship and inheritance, and promoted conjugal autonomy and women's economic entitlements in various respects. The main changes in Hindu law increased divorce rights based on mutual consent or on a wider range of spousal faults without the need for an initial period of judicial separation, and provided women easier access to family joint property and greater shares of such property. Changes in commonly applicable laws that provide alimony to the indigent, offer security and economic support to women and children facing domestic violence, and punish the practice of dowry reinforced the effects of the Hindu law reforms. Proposals are also currently being considered to enable no-fault divorce under conditions of irretrievable marital breakdown even if the respondent resists the divorce petition, along with giving women greater rights to alimony, child support, and custody, and enabling courts to give them shares of matrimonial property.

These reforms were introduced although regimes continued to value broad coalitions and did not abandon the rural groups that had defended patrilineal authority soon after independence. Indeed, the intensification of political competition and the decline of the Congress Party starting in the late 1970s made the retention of support a greater concern for parties, and agrarian groups gained greater political representation even while their share of the population gradually declined. Moreover, political elites did not prioritize personal-law reform any more than they had in the first postcolonial decade. Nevertheless, changes in the following variables enabled the earlier-mentioned family-law reforms: forms of social, economic, and residential organization; salient discourses about the nation, its religious and other cultural traditions, and indigenous forms of modern family life; patterns of political competition and social and political mobilization; and the composition of policy bureaucracies.

Urbanization and industrialization reduced the importance of landed property, especially for men, who shifted to nonagrarian occupations more than women did. This reduced resistance among rural men to giving women access to land and weakened lineages, whose power rested primarily on land control. The increase in first generation rural-urban migrants and tendencies toward circular migration between rural and urban areas blurred the boundaries between urban and rural experiences and mentalities. Moreover, joint-family residential arrangements gradually declined, particularly among urban and professional groups, leading to a shift from the lineage to the nuclear family as the primary social unit with which many members of these groups felt an affective tie.[1] Many political elites changed their understanding of the forms of family life appropriate for India accordingly, and became more willing to empower the nuclear family, divide joint property (including agricultural land) into separate shares, require the bilateral devolution of family property, and increase women's property rights.

Majoritarian visions of the Indian nation gained popularity, especially starting in the 1980s. Hindu nationalists demanded the rapid adoption of a UCC especially after *Shah Bano*, but did not gain sufficient support to introduce this change. Although the Bharatiya Janata Party (BJP) led national coalition governments from 1998 to 2004, some of its allies had significant support among the religious minorities that they were unwilling to lose by supporting a UCC. Moreover, when Hindu nationalists became the most vocal champions of a UCC from the 1980s, many of their opponents shifted their attention from a UCC to the reform of the existing personal laws. This was true of women's organizations, other rights organizations, and the communist parties.

Pluralistic visions of the nation assumed new forms through closer engagement with various cultural traditions, both durable and emergent. Pluralist nationalists changed personal law more than the Hindu nationalists did, and selectively appropriated cultural repertoires in favor of reform. While claiming continuity with the social visions underpinning traditions of religious law, they also became more willing to adopt Western legal precedents. They relied on such sources to promote conjugal autonomy and women's economic entitlements because changes in social practice, civil society mobilization, and the public ethos led them to value these ends more.

Until the 1960s, ruling elites focused on determining the basic features of the polity, building state institutions, and pursuing ambitious strategies of economic development and social change. The consolidation of democracy and the postcolonial state's authority led policy makers to shift their attention thereafter to addressing demands pressed by a more mobilized civil society, the pressure to do which became stronger as party competition intensified. An aspect of this revised approach to governance was a shift from the wide-ranging personal-law reforms proposed in the 1940s and the 1950s to periodic changes in specific legal provisions that mobilizers, patterns of litigation, and emergent values and social practices suggested were urgently needed. Such focused legal changes seemed unlikely to cost parties much electoral support; this seemed particularly so regarding Hindu law because conservative Hindu elites devoted less attention to family law after the 1950s. Modernist political elites became more willing to introduce such changes as a result.

Rights organizations proliferated and grew larger, became more autonomous of political parties, and addressed a wider range of policies, especially after India's brief authoritarian "emergency" of the mid-1970s. They included women's organizations and other organizations that addressed women's rights, religious and other cultural norms, and family law. Various civil-society organizations built networks with legislators, judges, and bureaucrats. Some of their intellectuals and leaders became members of policy bureaucracies, such as the Law Commission and the Minorities Commission, that addressed personal law at times. Many of them were members of commissions engaged with gender-relevant policy, such as the Committee on the Status of Women in India (CSWI), formed by the Ministry of Education and Social Welfare in 1971; the Department of Women and Child Development, established in 1985 as part of the Ministry of Human Resource Development and turned into an independent ministry with access to greater resources in 2006; and the National Commission for Women (NCW), formed in 1992. The CSWI assessed women's condition and the impact of policies meant to improve their circumstances, and many later initiatives to promote women's rights and status drew on its report.[2] The functions of the Department of Women and Child Development and the NCW included the assessment and promotion of women's legal and constitutional rights. The proposals of these institutions contributed to certain changes in personal law over the past two decades.

Women's organizations and rights organizations gained some influence over the deliberations in certain parties regarding gender-relevant policies. Moreover, their growth contributed to the emergence of a public ethos favoring greater women's rights in various social arenas. This made many parties wary of advocating policies clearly contrary to women's interests. For instance, it led Hindu nationalists, who had steadfastly resisted Hindu law reform in the first postcolonial decade, to support certain initiatives to empower women. Thus, over the last decade, the BJP supported giving Hindu women greater access to their parents' shares in joint property and opposed enabling no-fault divorce because it seemed this bill would not safeguard the interests of women and children adequately. The changes in the public ethos also tempered the opposition of parties based among the middle castes and lower castes of northern India (the Samajwadi Party (SP), the Rashtriya Janata Dal (RJD), the Janata Dal (United), and the Bahujan Samaj Party (BSP)) to giving married daughters shares in joint property and rights to live in and partition the ancestral home, and to a quota for women in political representation.[3]

The growth in civil society mobilization, the increased attention of rights organizations to litigation and legal policy, and the experience of the emergency led certain judges in the higher courts to support the rights of weaker groups sporadically. The onset of economic liberalization in the 1990s reduced the support that judges gave poorer groups, but did not change the inclination, albeit inconsistent, of some judges to support women in certain ways in family disputes. These individuals were not a majority of the judiciary (among whom a survey showed the presence of very gender-unequal values in the 1990s) or the legal policy bureaucracy, but nevertheless were important to legal change.[4] They played crucial roles in increasing personal-law reform from the 1970s onward.

Even while these changes occurred in Hindu law and commonly applicable matrimonial laws, there were certain continuities with the policy logic of the first postcolonial decade. First, Hindu law remained the focus of personal-law initiatives, and Hindu law reform was framed significantly in light of how policy makers wished to shape the Indian nation. The changes in the minority laws were less extensive and more closely tied to visions of group culture rather than to discourses about the nation, as we will see in Chapter 5. Second, even the more extensive changes in Hindu law were framed partly in terms of indigenous culture. For instance, views that the Hindu marriage was meant to be sacramental and the Indian family durable led legislators and judges to prioritize the maintenance of marriages, even while they made divorces more accessible if efforts to resolve marital problems failed. They dissuaded legislators from making divorce available in the absence of spousal fault or mutual consent up to the present day, but the Rajya Sabha passed a bill that does so in August 2013. (The bill needs the Lok Sabha's assent for it to take effect). Similarly, views that the joint family is a widely valued and durable aspect of Hindu and Indian culture made legislators reluctant to decompose family joint property into separate shares or restrict the testation of such property, even while they gave women greater shares of such property and required its bilateral devolution in cases of intestate succession.

I. INITIATIVES TO CHANGE HINDU LAW: DIVORCE

The main changes made in Hindu law since the 1960s concerned its divorce and inheritance provisions. The courts played major roles in the changes in divorce, marriage, and alimony law, prompting some of the major legislative initiatives. The reforms in divorce law began in the 1960s and became more significant in the 1970s. Divorce legislation was introduced at the federal level.[5] The changes in inheritance law began later, in the 1970s. As the courts felt more constrained in interpreting inheritance statutes, it was the legislature alone that changed these provisions. Resistance remained stronger to increasing women's inheritance rights than to increasing divorce rights until the last decade. As a result, inheritance law was initially changed, from the mid-1970s to the mid-1990s, only in five states in southern and western India, where the salience of bilateral and matrilineal inheritance practices made resistance weaker to women's access to ancestral property. Parliament extended these changes to the rest of India only in 2005, a generation after the initial reforms. While being hesitant to change daughters' inheritance rights, the courts did grant women greater rights to their dower and wedding gifts, and to reside in and perhaps partly own their matrimonial homes if they lived apart from their spouses or got divorced. These reforms belie Parashar's claim that "since the enactment of the Hindu Law Acts, not much legislative activity has taken place with regard to Hindu personal law."[6]

The divorce provisions introduced in Hindu law in the 1950s represented a compromise between aims to maintain the nuclear family and promote conjugal autonomy, and between understandings of Hindu marriage as a sacrament and as a contract. They allowed divorce if one's spouse was guilty of the following matrimonial faults: (a) "living in adultery" (rather than specific instances of adultery); (b) nonresumption of cohabitation for at least two years since a decree of judicial separation or restitution of conjugal rights; (c) (grounds available for women only) having another living spouse, rape, sodomy, and bestiality; (d) conversion to another religion; (e) affliction with a venereal disease, leprosy or mental illness for at least three years; (f) renunciation of the world and joining a religious order; or (g) not being known to have been alive for at least seven years. Desertion without cause, adultery and "such cruelty that the petitioner cannot reasonably be expected to live with the respondent" were made grounds for judicial separation, but not for divorce, unless the party petitioning for divorce had obtained judicial separation on these grounds at least two years earlier, and her spouse had not resumed cohabitation since then.

Litigation made policy makers aware that this compromise did not adequately address the growing problem presented by dysfunctional marriages. Ongoing changes in Western law suggested that this problem could be addressed by providing a wider and swifter path to divorce based on spousal fault, as well as by enabling no-fault divorce. Colonial law became a less significant basis on which policy elites understood desirable forms of Hindu and Indian family life, making it easier to consider increasing divorce rights. This led legislators, through a private member's bill of Diwan Chand Sharma (Congress Party) in 1964, to make individuals eligible for divorce if they had not resumed cohabitation for two years after decrees of judicial separation or restitution of conjugal rights, even if they had refused to live with the spouse who had gained the earlier decree. Unlike the initial introduction of divorce rights in 1955, this change evoked little opposition.[7] It took a step toward delinking eligibility for divorce from spousal fault and connecting it to the state of marital relations, while letting such eligibility depend on an earlier decree of judicial separation based on spousal fault or a failure to comply with a decree restoring conjugal rights.

A bigger change was made in divorce law in 1976; it made cruelty, desertion for two years, and adultery grounds for divorce; enabled divorce based on mutual consent; and reduced the period of nonresumption of cohabitation after decrees of judicial separation or restitution of conjugality that would entitle one to a divorce from two years to one year both under the HMA and the SMA.[8] However, an initiative of the Law Commission in 1978 to make divorce available in a case of irretrievable marital breakdown, even if one's spouse resisted, this did not succeed. Menski provided the most comprehensive understanding to date of the approaches to divorce law reform from the 1970s to the early 2000s.[9] He claimed that modernist inclinations to liberalize matrimonial law and intensify state regulation of family life drove legislation until the 1970s and influenced adjudication until the 1980s. Even though women's organizations increased the modernist ranks from the 1970s, he argued, a growing awareness of a mismatch between modernist aims and various features of social norms and matrimonial relations in India restrained legislative initiative, and led judges to construct a postmodern Hindu law that was better attuned to Indian society, drew less readily from Western precedents, and maintained or revived features of classical Hindu law, though often expressed in a secular idiom.

Regarding divorce and nullification of marriages, Menski said that judges had interpreted statutes conservatively to maintain social stability in the 1960s, but that modernist ambitions, particularly as expressed in the Report of the CSWI, led the legislature to make divorce more readily available in 1976.[10] In a context in which divorce brought women greater stigma, women were the economically weaker partners in most marriages, alimony rarely compensated them adequately for the loss of access to the resources they had shared with their husbands, and the state did not provide effective legal aid for the poor, ensure alimony payments, or give women access to matrimonial property, the easier availability of divorce impaired the interests of many women, especially poorer women. Menski argued that as ongoing intervention in matrimonial disputes made them aware that easier divorce had weakened women's circumstances as well as social stability, judges in the higher courts interpreted Hindu divorce law to encourage spousal reconciliation. They are said to have become especially selective from the late 1980s in handing down divorces based on cruelty, requiring stricter proof of adultery, rejecting men's divorce pleas based on the nonresumption of cohabitation after decrees of judicial separation or restitution of conjugal rights if the petitioners had prevented cohabitation, and paying greater attention to whether both parties continued to favor mutual consent divorce petitions.[11]

Various features of policy proposals, legislation, and adjudication do not fit well with Menski's interpretation. We saw in Chapter 3 that the reforms of the 1950s drew not just on Western precedents but also on understandings of colonial Hindu law, reformed Hindu discourse, and the distinctive future of Indian society. This was a crucial reason why the resulting statutes retained various indigenous norms, albeit in a modified form. The architects of the divorce law reforms of the 1970s also framed their proposals partly with reference to indigenous norms. Justice P. B. Gajendragadkar, who chaired the Law Commission that recommended these reforms, had earlier in his career coauthored *Narasu Appa Mali* (1952), which refused to vet personal law systematically with reference to constitutional rights. A scholar of the Hindu classics, he drew inspiration from the dynamism of Hindu law, and presented his proposals as promoting constitutional egalitarianism while adhering to Hindu jurisprudence, much as the modernist legislators of the 1950s had. The Law Commission's *Fifty-Ninth Report* adopted such an approach, recommending that individuals whose marriages have irretrievably broken down be given easier access to divorce; however, it also tried to promote the stability of marriages by requiring judges to attempt spousal reconciliation before they pronounced divorce and enabling them to grant judicial separation in response to divorce petitions. While urging that the nonresumption of cohabitation after a maintenance order in favor of the wife also be made a ground on which she could get a divorce, the report cautioned that a man should not be allowed to get a divorce decree by virtue of the passage of time since he ceased to provide his wife maintenance; further, it urged that those who were minors when they got married be allowed to repudiate their marriages once they become adults. Gajendragadkar believed that this approach would maintain the vision of marriage underlying classical Hindu law although marriage had ceased to be a sacrament, yet urged the application of his proposals to both the HMA and the SMA.[12] The Commission's approach thus differed considerably from modernism as Menski understood it. The Law Ministry largely pursued the path the Law Commission recommended, and parliament readily accepted most of the proposed reforms.[13] Thus, the attempts of judges to limit room for divorce to give reconciliation the fullest chance and to prevent parties from taking advantage of their "own wrong," as detailed by Menski, were in keeping with the vision underlying the legislation of 1976. This amendment expanded the divorce provisions of both the HMA and the SMA in light of visions of Hindu/Indian modernity, and effected a convergence in the divorce rights of couples governed by the two acts.

Women's organizations were even further from adopting a modernist perspective, as Menski understood it, than the majority of policy elites. Rather than urge the liberalization of divorce in all respects, they recommended that policy proceed cautiously in this regard as long as alimony provisions remained weak, decrees to provide alimony and child support were ineffectively implemented, and women did not enjoy rights in matrimonial property. Thus, the CSWI recommended that irretrievable marital breakdown be made a ground for divorce only if women were granted at least a third of their husbands' property on divorce.[14] When the Law Commission recommended the introduction of this ground for divorce without giving women rights in matrimonial property in 1978 (based on the suggestion of certain courts), and the Law Ministry presented a bill along these lines in 1981, women's organizations, reflecting the interests of women of different strata, opposed this course because they believed it would undermine the economic position of many women.[15] The executive abandoned this proposal precisely because many legislators were persuaded by the concerns of the women's organizations, rather than because it was "clearly unwilling to be steered by elitist feminist lobbying."[16]

Women's organizations did sometimes equate legal uniformity too readily with women's entitlement, and misunderstood the lack of legislative change in Muslim law after independence to mean both that Muslim law recognized fewer rights for women than other personal laws and that Muslims especially resisted personal law reform. Some of the CSWI's proposals regarding personal law reflected this—for example, its emphasis on curbing polygamy and unilateral male repudiation among Muslims and on introducing a UCC.

Even these positions resulted not from the elitism of women's organizations but from their inadequate engagement with certain social implications of matrimonial law, minority opinion, and minority mobilization. It was only when many women's organizations changed these stances from the 1980s that they gained greater influence over policy, as Mazumdar, a CSWI member, indicated.[17]

A. Divorce Based on Irretrievable Marital Breakdown

Various judges felt that the liberalization of divorce would be preferable to maintaining marriages beset by serious and irresoluble problems, although they were aware of the potential high cost for women. In a few cases, courts granted divorces to couples facing long-lasting and particularly intractable marital problems although none of the statutory divorce grounds applied, while clarifying that these cases could not serve as precedents.[18] In other cases, they deemed the irretrievable breakdown of marriage a reason to grant divorce while also taking certain spousal faults to exist, or considered the state of the marriage relevant in assessing alleged faults;[19] in still others, they felt they lacked the statutory powers to decree divorce even though they considered the marriages irretrievably impaired.[20] The Supreme Court granted divorce on these grounds in some cases, using its special powers under Article 142(1) of the Constitution to render "complete justice," and in a couple of cases urged legislation making irretrievable breakdown a ground for divorce.[21] Based on these judicial suggestions, the Law Commission once again proposed such legislation in 2009.[22] Concerns about the implications for women's economic situation did not prevent the reconsideration of divorce liberalization, because women's organizations did not unconditionally oppose liberalization; rather, they made their acceptance contingent on the simultaneous reinforcement of women's and children's interests. As a result, a bill to effect this change in both the HMA and the SMA was presented to parliament in 2010.[23]

The main safeguard the government's bill provided women was to enable them to oppose their husband's divorce petition based on irretrievable marital breakdown if divorce would cause them "grave financial hardship," without giving men a similar right. Various women's organizations felt that this did not protect the rights of women and children adequately, for the same reasons they cited when a similar bill was briefly considered in 1981, and suggested amendments. Since more political elites had become inclined to increase women's economic rights over the intervening decades, a Parliamentary Standing Committee accepted some of these suggestions. It made the first official proposal to give women a share in their matrimonial property (though without specifying the share), instructed courts to decide about this share in considering divorce petitions, and recommended especially that women be given a share in property to whose acquisition they contributed. The proposed changes could effect a major change in matrimonial relations.[24] The BJP and the Communist Party of India-Marxist (CPI-M) also demanded changes in the current bill to protect the interests of women and children, based on the opinions of the women's organizations.[25] In response to the committee's suggestions, the cabinet required that women be given a share in matrimonial property on divorce, but left the precise share to the court's discretion. While various women's organizations were dissatisfied that women's share was left to the courts to determine and that maintenance rights had not been reinforced, the limits to the economic entitlements extended divorcées weakened conservative resistance.[26] Based on the debate in the Rajya Sabha, the Law Ministry amended the bill further to give divorcées a share in their husband's residential property, even if it was inherited, inheritable, or bought before the couple's marriage, although the Ministry of Women and Child Development voiced reservations about this.[27] The parliamentary debates suggest that divorcées are likely to be entitled to an unspecified share in matrimonial property soon. But the Ministry of Women and Child Development's reservations and the reluctance of conservative legislators to enhance the entitlements of divorcées considerably led the Law Ministry to abandon the proposal to grant divorcées a share in the husband's inherited or inheritable property, while leaving room for courts to take the value of such property into account in determining alimony. This is the form in which, in August 2013, the Rajya Sabha passed the bill, which remained to be considered by the Lok Sabha when the book went to press.[28]

B. Cruelty

Cruelty is the ground on which most petitions for divorce and judicial separation are presented. Agnes claimed that until the legislation of 1976, "cruelty was defined within the narrow confines of conduct which would be harmful or injurious to the petitioner. Hence it was necessary to base the allegation of cruelty upon acts of physical violence."[29] Both she and Kusum noted that the courts have construed "cruelty" more expansively since then, but Menski added the qualification that the courts declared findings of spousal cruelty more selectively from the 1990s.[30] My exploration of case law indicates that some courts did not consider physical violence necessary to find spousal cruelty even in the 1950s and 1960s, and the predominant though not consistent trend in the higher courts has been to rely on broader understandings of cruelty since the 1970s.

While cruelty *simpliciter* became a divorce ground only in 1976 in Hindu law, the courts granted judicial separation in many cases earlier based on findings of "mental cruelty" even in the absence of proof of physical violence. Moreover, cruelty *simpliciter* had been a ground for divorce in Muslim law since 1939, and a few courts had granted Muslim women divorces on this basis well before the 1970s. For instance, as early as 1950, the Allahabad High Court upheld the divorce decree that the lower courts had granted a Muslim woman on the ground of cruelty because her husband had made false adultery charges against her, leading the police to issue warrants for her arrest in *Abbas Ali v. Mt. Rabia Bibi* (1951). Courts later applied similar standards to assess cruelty in responding to pleas for judicial separation among Hindus.

In 1955, the same court pointed out that legal cruelty need not involve physical violence, while granting a woman a separate residence after her husband assaulted her, evicted her from their home, and married another woman, in *Sm. Pancho v. Ram Prasad* (1956). It declared:

When a husband habitually insults his wife and behaves towards her with neglect and un-kindness so as to impair her health, he must be held to be guilty of cruelty. Where evidence of physical violence is not per se sufficient to warrant a finding of cruelty the Court is bound to take into consideration the general conduct of the husband towards the wife and if this is of a character tending to degrade the wife, and subjecting her to a course of intense indignity injurious to her health, the Court is at liberty to pronounce the cruelty proved.[31]

In *Shri Gurcharan Singh v. Shrimati Waryam Kaur* (1960), the Punjab High Court held that claims of cruelty should be assessed based on emergent norms and the effect of the impugned actions on the individual concerned, and that such an approach could lead to findings of cruelty even if there had been only isolated acts of violence. It granted a Sikh woman judicial separation, rather than accommodate her husband's plea to restore his conjugal rights, because he had ejected her from their home, failed to provide her and their child support even after a maintenance decree, and made unproven adultery allegations.[32]

The Patna High Court expanded further on the meaning of mental cruelty in 1963, declaring that factors such as "environment, status in society, education, cultural development, local custom, social convention, physical and mental condition of the parties, etc." should be considered in assessing which acts amount to mental cruelty; in this case, however, it accepted the lower court's view that "occasional thrashings" need not constitute cruelty.[33] Reasoning similarly, Justice Mirza Hameedullah Beg, who later became Chief Justice of India, elaborated the concept of cruelty found in the HMA in 1964 as one "based on mutual regard and consideration by each spouse for the other. It excludes . . . selfish brutality or disregard for the health, needs, desires, and feelings of the other by either spouse."[34] A few courts decreed judicial separation based on similar constructions of cruelty in the 1960s and early 1970s, prior to the legislative amendment of 1976.[35] But the majority of judges even in the higher courts did not share such an understanding then, and most decrees of judicial separation on grounds of cruelty were based on evidence of significant physical violence.

The Supreme Court handed down the most consequential of these early cruelty-based judicial separation decrees, *Dr. Narayan Ganesh Dastane v. Mrs. Sucheta Narayan Dastane* (1975). Justice Y. V. Chandrachud, who later became Chief Justice of India and gained wider attention for authoring *Mohammad Ahmed Khan v. Shah Bano Begum* (*Shah Bano*)(1985), indicated that in matrimonial cases, evidence should be assessed based on "on a preponderance of probabilities" rather than proof beyond reasonable doubt, which is appropriate only for criminal and quasi-criminal cases. This preponderance standard, borrowed from English and Australian law, was applied thereafter to the majority of matrimonial cases of all kinds.[36] Rather than cruelty having to be of "such a character as to cause danger to life, limb or health, bodily or mental," a standard used in English law until a little earlier, the court relied on Section 10(1)(b) of the HMA to decide that it would be adequate if the specified behavior would "cause a reasonable apprehension in the mind of the petitioner that it will be harmful or injurious to him or her to live with her spouse," and that the actions that might cause such apprehension would depend on the impact on the litigant. Moreover, it pointed out that the petitioner may be taken to have condoned certain of his spouse's matrimonial offenses; that the spouses continuing to live together was an inadequate proof of condonation, but that their maintaining intimate relations and having children was; and that future matrimonial offenses could revive an offense that had earlier been condoned. *Dastane* exercised far greater influence over subsequent adjudication than the earlier judicial separation decrees based on mental cruelty had, because it was the first such Supreme Court decree, it was more fully argued, it was reinforced within a year by legislative reforms in divorce law, and more judges had become sensitive by the mid-1970s to the complex determinants of serious marital problems and were inclined to provide spouses facing such difficulties an exit. Cited in at least 298 reported cases, it influenced the standards by which many courts construed spousal cruelty thereafter, although its reference to a reasonable apprehension of harm ceased to be relevant after this criterion was omitted from the HMA in 1976.[37]

There was greater continuity than Menski suggested in the higher courts' approach to divorce petitions on the ground of cruelty since the legislative reforms of 1976. In the first half of the 1980s a few courts, starting with *Madan Lal Sharma v. Smt. Santosh Sharma* (1980), interpreted the Marriage Laws (Amendment) Act of 1976 to have undone *Dastane*'s liberalization of judicial separation based on cruelty. Taking the act to apply equally to cruelty-based divorce provisions, they tried to reinstate what had been the predominant judicial trend until the 1970s, equating spousal cruelty with behavior that poses a threat to the partner's life, limb or health. They did this even though the Statement of Objects and Reasons of the act identified the liberalization of divorce as its main aim.[38] However, the majority of courts did not follow this approach even in the late 1970s and early 1980s, preferring to follow the interpretation of cruelty offered in *Dastane* while taking into account the deletion of the reference to a reasonable apprehension of harm in 1976. *Ashwini Kumar Sehgal v. Smt. Swatantar Sehgal* (1979) was an elaborately argued judgment along these lines, which declared that "cruelty in such cases has to be of the type which should satisfy the conscience of the court to believe that the relations between the parties had deteriorated to such an extent due to the conduct of one of the spouses that it has become impossible for them to live together without mental agony, torture or distress."[39] In the 1980s, certain courts countered the equation of cruelty with physical violence and actions inimical to the spouse's health in *Madan Lal Sharma. Keshaorao Krishnaji Londhe v. Nisha Londhe* (1984) deduced from the Law Commission's *Fifty-Ninth Report* as well as the Marriage Laws (Amendment) Act's Statement of Objects and Reasons that the intention behind this legislation was to enable divorce when a couple no longer shared emotional bonds and to give courts considerable flexibility to understand spousal cruelty in light of the circumstances and sentiments of particular couples. It reinforced the understanding that conduct that makes cohabitation a source of "mental agony, torture or distress" constitutes cruelty, and shaped the subsequent judicial approach.[40]

The Supreme Court lent such interpretations its authority in *Shobha Rani v. Madhukar Reddi* (1988), *V. Bhagat v. Mrs. D. Bhagat* (1994), and *G.V.N. Kameshwara Rao v. G. Jabilli* (2002). In *Bhagat*, the most widely cited of these judgments (in 227 reported cases), it declared that spousal cruelty could be inferred when "the wronged party cannot reasonably be asked to put up with such conduct and continue to live with the other party" even if the matrimonial offenses did not affect the petitioner's health, and that the deletion of the qualification that cruel conduct should cause "reasonable apprehension in the mind of the petitioner that it will be harmful or injurious for the petitioner to live with the other party" was meant to enable courts to adjudicate in light of diverse and changing social mores.[41] The higher courts have used such an understanding of cruelty since then in the majority of petitions for divorce and judicial separation.[42]

The adoption of such a liberal understanding of cruelty as a ground for divorce had different effects on how readily courts decreed divorces when coupled with an inclination to effect spousal reconciliation if possible. There were variations even in the cases in which the Supreme Court signaled its approach to cruelty. It provided the woman a divorce based on evidence of violence related to dowry demands in *Shobha Rani*. However, it found that a woman's complaint to the police that her husband and mother-in-law had attacked her was an act of cruelty toward her husband, and granted him a divorce in *G.V.N. Kameswara Rao*, rejecting the woman's argument that her husband was thus taking advantage of his "own wrong" (a problem which Section 23(1)(a) of the HMA alerts judges to consider). In *Bhagat*, it granted the man's divorce petition because it believed that the woman had been cruel to her husband when she argued, in the very court in which he practiced as a lawyer, that he, his parents and grandparents were insane.

The high courts varied even more in their approaches to cruelty-based divorce petitions. Many declared findings of cruelty when men, and sometimes their parents harassed their wives over dowry payments (a problem that had become pervasive with the ongoing spread of the practice of dowry down the caste and class spectrum), granting the wives either divorce or judicial separation.[43] Others denied men's divorce petitions based on desertion or cruelty in view of evidence that the pressure these men had exerted on their wives for dowry had caused the estrangement.[44] But some declared that women who lodged police complaints about spousal abuse to extract dowry or responded to harassment for dowry with threats to commit suicide had been cruel toward their husbands and granted the latter's divorce petitions.[45] They also varied in their attitudes toward women demanding that the couple live apart from their in-laws; until the 1980s, the majority considered it cruelty toward their husbands that entitled the latter to divorce, but since then many judges have regarded it as legitimate since they no longer wished to limit family nuclearization.[46]

C. Adultery

From the mid-1950s until 1976, litigants could petition under both the HMA and the SMA for judicial separation based on their spouse's adultery and for divorce based on the spouse's "living in adultery," which courts had interpreted since 1907 to mean having a continuing extramarital relationship.[47] Courts already allowed Muslim women and Christian men to seek divorce on the ground of adultery and recognized many forms of extrajudicial unilateral repudiation by Muslim men, but granted Christian women divorces only if they could demonstrate both adultery and another matrimonial fault. Moreover, Section 125(4) of the Criminal Procedure Code (which was Section

488(4) until 1973) disentitled a woman living in adultery to maintenance from her husband, even if she had valid reasons to live apart from her husband and had no property or income.

Agnes claimed that the Indian courts did not require men to provide their wives and ex-wives maintenance if these women had committed a matrimonial fault such as adultery, but shifted from the 1980s onward to a more compassionate approach that made the eligibility of women living apart from their husbands and ex-husbands for maintenance dependent only on their economic circumstances.[48] Once they made this shift, she said, the courts required spousal maintenance for women guilty of "occasional lapses of virtue," but not to those living in adultery. Contrary to these claims, the majority of courts held since the early twentieth century that women who committed adultery, but did not live in adultery, were entitled to their husband's support; these courts took living in adultery to be a more serious violation of a woman's matrimonial obligations, and assumed that women who did so were likely to have their lover's material support. In *Honamma v. Timannabhat* (1877) and *Parami Ramayya v. Mahadevi Shankarappa* (1909), the Bombay High Court decreed that adulterous women should receive bare maintenance from their husbands while living in the latter's houses—but not maintenance in a separate residence, a right that it gave women whom their husbands superseded to marry someone else, not due to any matrimonial fault on their part. In the latter case, it interpreted classical Hindu law to hold that "a Hindu wife cannot be absolutely abandoned. If she is living an unchaste life, he [her husband] is bound to keep her in the house under restraint and provide her with food and raiment just sufficient to support life."[49] The same court interpreted the relevant provisions of criminal law similarly in *Fulchand Maganlal v. Unknown* (1928): "A single act of adultery does not necessarily amount to 'living in adultery' within the meaning of Clause (4) of Section 488 and will not justify a Magistrate in refusing maintenance."[50] The majority of courts followed this interpretation thereafter.[51] Courts drew support for such decrees from *shastras* such as the *Yajnavalkya Smrti*, which recommended that the adulteress be "deprived of authority, unadorned, living on food barely sufficient to sustain herself, rebuked, sleeping on the floor, thus [her husband] shall make the unfaithful wife dwell in his house," commentaries that expanded on such an understanding, and certain British legal precedents.[52] It was only in a few cases in the first decades of the twentieth century that courts indicated special circumstances in which women who commit adultery, but are not living in adultery, could be denied maintenance from their husbands.[53]

In considering petitions for judicial separation, divorce, and maintenance under the HMA and the SMA involving allegations of adultery, the courts did not require direct evidence "by way of photographs or of eye-witnesses who have seen actual adultery or . . . of detectives peeping through key-holes and deposing about adulterous intercourse," as such evidence "is generally discredited when it is produced."[54] Rather, since the early twentieth century, they inferred adultery from circumstantial evidence, such as the birth of children despite lack of contact between the spouses and hotel rooms shared or letters exchanged by the alleged lovers.[55] While adhering to these standards, courts became more reluctant from the 1970s onward to arrive at the conclusion that adultery had occurred based merely on evidence of closer interaction across gender lines, in response to the lowering of social barriers to interaction between men and women among various groups.

In some cases in the 1950s and the early 1960s, courts declared adultery if there was evidence that the parties had an "adulterous disposition" and the opportunity to engage in sexual intercourse. For instance, in *Mahalingam Pillai v. Amsavalli* (1956), the Madras High Court declared: "when . . . adulterous disposition is shown to exist between the parties at the time of the alleged act, then mere opportunity, together with comparatively slight circumstances showing guilt, may be sufficient to justify the inference that criminal intercourse has actually taken place."[56] Similarly, courts concluded that a woman had committed adultery based on evidence that she had shared a hotel room with her alleged lover in *Bhagwan Singh Sher Singh Arora v. Amar Kaur* (1962), and that a man and the woman from whom he was renting a room were living in adultery because they "had reasonable opportunity of having sexual intercourse" in *Devyani Kantilal Shroff v. Kantilal Gamanlal Shroff* (1963).

By the 1990s, courts declared that they do not "as a general rule infer adultery from evidence of opportunity alone," but look for more persuasive evidence of adultery, such as of someone other than the husband having impregnated the woman.[57] Thus, while the Supreme Court annulled a marriage in

1964 because the woman delivered a baby less than nine months after her marriage and did not seem to have had premarital sexual contact with her husband, in the 1990s High Courts set aside three lower-court divorce decrees that had been based on evidence that the women respondents had given birth to children over a year after they had last had sexual contact with their husbands because they did not find definite evidence of extra-marital impregnation either.[58] In the last of these cases, *Smt. Leela Pande v. Shri Sachendra Kumar Pande* (1994), the court highlighted the possibility that the pregnancy was the result of rape rather than of voluntary sexual intercourse and criticized the trial court for having failed to attempt reconciliation. The courts tended not to support adultery claims when the evidence did not clearly suggest anything more than a friendship between a man and a woman, but did not urge the reconciliation of estranged couples if their marriages seemed to have irretrievably broken down. This was clear in *Smt. Swayamprabha v. A.S. Chandrasekhar* (1982), in which the court did not find a woman riding on a scooter with a man, traveling with him to another city, and getting "improper" letters from him signs that they were lovers, and said that evidence of the two spending a night together in a hotel room would not have shown that they were lovers either. Rather than attempt spousal reconciliation, it granted the woman a divorce based on the husband's cruelty in making unfounded adultery allegations.[59] Courts were also reluctant to find adultery based only on the testimony of interested parties (for example, husbands of the women accused of adultery, domestic servants who were on poor terms with these women, or estranged wives of the alleged lovers).[60]

However, courts accepted adultery claims that rested on persuasive evidence, especially if the marriages whose dissolution was being sought seemed dysfunctional. For instance, in *Tai v. Harishchandra* (1984), the court upheld the lower court's divorce decree in the man's favor based on his wife's adultery, although the man had also started another relationship; the man's relationship had started later and the marital problems appeared incapable of resolution. In a similar vein, in *Gita Masand v. Narain Dass* (1985), the trial court had granted the man a divorce because it took the woman to have made a false adultery charge; but the Delhi High Court set this decree aside because it took the woman's charge of adultery to have been proven by her husband having married his lover in the meantime. The high court felt the man had rushed into another marriage to deter the full consideration of any appeal his first wife might file, and it did not wish to permit him to thus take advantage of his own "extreme wrong."

Courts assessed charges of women living in adultery particularly carefully because they were aware that men often used them to end their maintenance obligations toward their wives; the courts' approach did not change significantly in recent decades. The Bombay High Court declared that a woman had committed adultery, but was not living in adultery in *Rajani Prabhakar Lokur v. Prabhakar Raghavendra Lokur* (1958), even though the woman had a relationship with her lover even before she entered her marriage unwillingly, and continued that relationship for over a year after she got married, because it found no evidence that she was still involved with her lover when the divorce petition was filed. It therefore granted the man judicial separation rather than divorce, and did not absolve him of his maintenance obligations. Various other high courts responded similarly in cases of the 1950s and 1960s, in which they found that the woman committed adultery, but was not living in adultery.[61] Since the 1950s, courts have declared that women were living in adultery only when there was clear evidence of them sharing a house with their lovers, as in *Devyani Kantilal Shroff* (1963) and *Sanjukta Padhan v. Laxminarayan Padhan* (1991),[62] or had long-lasting relationships with them, as in *M. Kanniappan v. Akilandammal* (1954) and *S.S. Manickam v. Arputha Bhavani Rajam* (1980). The evidence was comparably strong in cases in which courts found women to be living in adultery over the past two decades.[63] Thus, there has been no significant change in the standards by which most courts assess claims of living in adultery.

However, some courts began to separate the eligibility of divorcées for alimony from whether they were considered to have failed in their matrimonial responsibilities, starting in the 1980s. The Calcutta High Court upheld a maintenance order in favor of a woman against whom a divorce decree had been passed earlier on the ground of desertion in *Sukumar Dhibar v. Smt. Anjali Dasi* (1983), while noting that the husband had made the woman unwelcome in their matrimonial home and might be in another relationship. However, it said that divorcées would not be eligible for maintenance from their husbands if they did not remain chaste, and perhaps also if they were unwilling to live with their ex-husbands without sufficient cause. In *Smt.*

Vanamala v. Shri H.M. Ranganatha Bhatta (1995), the Supreme Court awarded maintenance for a divorcée, but held that the rule that men should not be required to provide maintenance for wives who were either living in adultery or refusing to live with their husbands for no valid reason, or if the couple were living apart by mutual consent, does not apply to divorcées, as adultery is conceivable only when one is in a matrimonial relationship and divorced couples cannot be expected to live together. It followed *Vanamala* while awarding maintenance for a divorcée held to have deserted her husband in *Rohtash Singh v. Smt. Ramendri & Ors* (2000).[64] Some high courts relied on these Supreme Court precedents over the past decade to uphold maintenance orders in favor of divorcées who were living with other men either during their marriages or after the dissolution of their marriages, or who were found to have other matrimonial faults.[65] These courts moved toward making divorcées' eligibility for maintenance independent of their earlier matrimonial behavior and current conjugal behavior. However, this process is incomplete because some high courts, apparently unaware of the Supreme Court opinions in this regard, continued to deny maintenance to divorcées whom they took to be living in adultery.[66]

D. Desertion

Individuals whose spouses deserted them for at least three consecutive years were made eligible for judicial separation in 1955, and for divorce in 1976. This was meant to enable them to change their marital status if they abandoned their hopes of resolving their matrimonial problems, provided they had until then shown an inclination to resume their conjugal relationships. Patrilocality is the predominant pattern of postmarital residence in India and men typically exercise greater influence than their wives even over nuclearized households, an influence they sometimes use to evict their wives from the matrimonial home. As it is the woman who leaves the matrimonial home in these situations, the man then often proceeds to claim on this basis that the woman has deserted him in a petition for judicial separation or divorce. Legislators guarded against this possibility by stipulating in Section 23(1)(a) of the HMA that individuals could not take advantage of their "own wrong" or disability to claim judicial separation or divorce. Menski explored the increased attention of courts to such situations from the late 1960s.[67] The case law on desertion was limited in India until independence, and the Indian courts drew significantly from understandings of desertion in British law from the 1950s.[68] They borrowed the notion of "constructive desertion" to reject many petitions of men to change their matrimonial status after they or their parents had evicted their wives or induced them to leave by making life difficult for them, as well as to grant the divorce, separation, and maintenance pleas of women whose husbands or in-laws had made them leave their matrimonial homes.[69] Some of them derived justification for this from the HMA's equation of the "willful neglect" of one's spouse with desertion.

Agnes identified *Bipin Chander Jaisinghbhai Shah v. Prabhawati* (1956) as an important case, which shaped how courts used the notion of constructive desertion.[70] In it, the Bombay High Court rejected the man's divorce petition because it took him to have resisted the woman's efforts to resume their matrimonial relationship.[71] The Supreme Court disagreed with the lower court's finding that the man had engaged in constructive desertion, insofar as it believed that the woman left the matrimonial home of her own accord because she could not face her husband and her in-laws, who suspected her of infidelity for good reason, a feature of the case Agnes did not note. It indicated thereby that a finding of constructive desertion is appropriate only when the deserted spouse does not initiate the change in the marital relationship. The Supreme Court nevertheless concurred with the high court's decree because the man resisted the woman's later efforts to resume cohabitation, signaling that a finding of desertion is appropriate only if the deserter remains disinclined to resume the relationship and the deserted individual does not consent to the spouses living apart at any point.

Many courts rejected men's desertion petitions from the 1950s onward if they found that the man had given his wife good reasons to leave the matrimonial home. They did so, for instance, in *Kuppanna Goundan v. Palani Ammal* (1955) because a bigamist, whose second marriage predated the ban on Hindu bigamy, refused to provide his first wife a separate residence and maintenance, to which bigamists' first wives became eligible in 1946, and in *Sirigiri Pullaiah v. Sirigiri Bushings Amma* (1962) because another bigamist contracted his second marriage after Hindu bigamy was banned. Courts also rejected men's claims of desertion by their wives because they had rejected their wives' efforts to resume living with them in *Perumal Naicker v. Sithalakshmi Ammal* (1955) and *Shyam Chand v. Janki* (1966); the man had acted similarly and got remarried while the woman could still appeal the lower court's divorce decree in *Snehlata Seth v. Kewal Krishan Seth* (1986); the man made unfounded accusations of adultery in *Lachman Utamchand Kiriplani v. Meena alias Mota* (1964); the man beat and otherwise mistreated his wife to extract dowry, and refused to make a commitment that he would end his violence and provide her a separate room in his house in *Shri Kishan Chand v. Smt. Munni Devi* (2003); the man ended his sexual relationship with his wife in *Jyotish Chandra Guha v. Meera Guha* (1969) and *Lt. Col. Mohinder Pal Singh v. Kulwant Kaur* (1975); the man started an informal relationship with another woman in *Renganayaki v. Arunagiri* (1993); the man rejected his wife's demand that they live apart from his sexually predatory father in *Ram Sarup Aggarwal v. Shrimati Dev Kumari* (1950) and from his abusive parents in *Teerth Ram v. Parvati Devi* (1995) and *Rekha v. B. Susheelendra* (2010); and the man's parents had killed another daughter-in-law of theirs in *Kamala Sharma v. Suresh Kumar Sharma* (2001). The man's resort to extreme physical and mental torture to extract dowry led the Delhi High Court to refuse to recognize an *ex parte* divorce the man had secured from an American court, and to order him to provide his wife maintenance in *Smt. Anubha v. Vikas Aggarwal* (2002). Courts also granted a woman a divorce based on desertion because her husband had forced her out of her matrimonial home through frequent physical violence and refused to secure her the medical attention she needed in *Smt. Asha Handa v. Baldev Raj Handa* (1984), and granted another woman maintenance from her husband while she lived separately because the husband had married someone else in *A. Bhagavathi Ammal v. Sethu* (1986).

By using the notion of constructive desertion along these lines, courts limited the ability of men to use their influence in the matrimonial home to unilaterally gain judicial separation or divorce, and enabled women to gain maintenance, as well as judicial separation or divorce, after the actions of their husbands and their in-laws had led them to move out of the matrimonial homes. As a result, they gave women greater autonomy in deciding the terms and duration of their matrimonial relationships.

E. Customary Divorces

The legislature had indicated its willingness to accept the variety of ways in which marriages were solemnized and dissolved in Indian society in Sections 7(1) and 29(2) of the HMA, which indicated that "a Hindu marriage may be solemnized in accordance with the customary rites and ceremonies of either party thereto" and that the HMA would not "affect any right recognized by custom or any special enactment to obtain the dissolution of a Hindu marriage, whether solemnized before or after the commencement of this Act." This continued the approach of the colonial courts, which had recognized the divorce customs of a variety of castes and lineages, the majority of which were of lower or middling status. Hindus could only get divorces based on the customs of their caste or lineage in much of India until the HMA extended them this right under the rubric of Hindu law. Courts based their acceptance of specific divorce customs until then on the claim that, although Hindu law did not recognize divorce, divorce under certain conditions was not repugnant to its principles.[72]

Litigants called on state courts to assess the validity of customary divorces that *panchayats* (assemblies) of subcastes, lineages, or villages had earlier pronounced, in connection with the contestation of the validity of marriages, matrimonial rights, the eligibility of individuals to get remarried, maintenance obligations and rights, bigamy claims, the legitimacy of children, and inheritance rights, as well as to consider divorce petitions based on the customs of the relevant group rather than the general principles of Hindu law, statutory and otherwise. The wide variety of divorce practices recognized in community courts are beyond our scope, but this section addresses how state courts assessed the validity of such divorces and considered divorce petitions framed with reference to custom. J. D. M. Derrett initiated the exploration of this question, which Livia Holden pursued in much greater detail.[73]

Under colonial rule, courts made the recognition of customs contingent on a demonstration that they were ancient and continuously followed, and that they were compatible with public policy and morality. Only a custom followed "for such a long period and with such invariability as to show that it has, by common consent, been submitted to as the established governing rule" was considered worthy of recognition.⁷⁴ The HMA (Section 3(a)) defined custom accordingly, as "any rule which, having been continuously and uniformly observed for a long time, has obtained the force of law among Hindus in any local area, tribe, community, group or family." Courts continued to expect customs to be of long duration, but construed this expectation flexibly from the 1980s onward, especially if the recognition of a custom would provide a litigant support they felt inclined to offer, although not if it would enable conviction for bigamy. Courts have looked for evidence that the divorce customs under consideration were prevalent in the caste, lineage, tribe, family, or ancestral territory of the couple since colonial times. Since the 1950s, courts recognized specific divorce customs among various groups, including Sikh Jats in the Malerkotla and Jullundar regions of Punjab; Patwas, Khatis, and Gonds of Madhya Pradesh; Ezhavas of Kerala; Chetti potters and Ambalakkarar of Tamil Nadu; Pakhalis of Gujarat; Gollas of Andhra Pradesh; Kolis of Rajasthan; and the Maratha Patils of Maharashtra. By contrast, they concluded that such customs did not exist among Koravas of Andhra Pradesh, Arora Khatris of Punjab, Kongu Vellala Gounder of Tamil Nadu, or Marwari Shwetambar Jains of Rajasthan.⁷⁵

While accommodating a variety of prevalent divorce practices, courts employed certain standards, though not consistently, to assess the compatibility of these customs with public policy. These standards changed over the past three decades, reflecting the changing values that governed the adjudication of divorce with reference to statute as well. Among the cases that Derrett and Holden discussed, as well as others that I examined of the colonial and early postcolonial periods, *Keshav Hargovan v. Bai Gandhi* (1915), *Jina Magan Pakhali v. Bai Jethi* (1941), *Sitaram v. Demai* (1949), and *Shivalingiah v. Chowdamma* (1956) indicated that courts should accept only customs that made divorce contingent on the respondent's consent; and *Mt. Subhani v. Nawab* (1941) showed that courts were unlikely to recognize practices that adversely affect the interests of women who are not given the chance to represent themselves. *Karumpa Kochappi v. Sirkar* (1911) suggested that if a caste tribunal accepted a man's divorce petition, the man provided his wife with either a lump-sum payment or a share of his property, and the proceedings were publicized, the woman's consent would not be necessary. More recently, *Tara Singh v. Shakuntala* (1974) indicated that caste tribunals should have attempted reconciliation and gained the couple's consent to the divorce after these attempts failed, if courts are to validate the divorces they granted; at the same time it invalidated customs that enabled women to desert their husbands and remarry on the payment of quit money to the caste council. The consent of the respondent in a customary divorce was inferred from his accepting a compensatory payment from the woman's subsequent husband in *Shamlal v. Rajkumar* (1958) and *Rewaram Balwant Khati v. Ramratan Khati* (1963). Other courts recognized customs by which individuals could unilaterally abandon their spouses without the mediation of a caste tribunal, in *Lachu v. Dal Singh* (1896), *Velayudhan Kochappi v. Sirkar* (1915) and *Gopi Krishna Kasaudhan v. Musammat Jaggo* (1936); by which divorce could be based on the consent of minors in *Smt. Premanbai v. Channoolal* (1963); and by which women could remarry after desertion by their husbands in *Virasangappa v. Rudrappa* (1885) and *Pritam Singh v. Nasib Kaur* (1956). Yet other courts failed to recognize some of the same customs later, in *Laxmansingh v. Kasharbai* (1965) and *Laserbai v. Jugribai* (1978). Courts thus varied more in how they assessed the validity of customary divorces than in their approaches to divorce on statutory grounds. Amid these variations, they granted divorce far more liberally based on custom than when they applied statutory Hindu law, until the latter laws were liberalized in the 1970s.

Holden highlighted the reluctance of courts to recognize woman-initiated customary divorces until recently. Courts considered such divorces contrary to public policy in *Keshav Hargovan* (1915) and *Kishenlal v. Prabhu* (1963), and incompatible with Hindu law when the man did not consent to them in *Reg. v. Karsan Goja and Reg. v. Bai Rupa* (1864), *Uji v. Hathi Lalu* (1870), and *Narayan Bharthi v. Laving Bharthi* (1877). But courts had recognized such divorces as early as 1915 among the Ezhavas of Kerala in *Velayudhan Kochappi v. Sirkar*.[76] It is only from the 1980s that Holden found courts much more willing to accept woman-initiated customary divorces, notably in the Supreme Court decree in *Govindaraju v. Munisami Gounder* (1997). This judgment was remarkable in another respect. It took customs of unilateral common law divorce to exist among all Shudras, the castes that occupy the fourth rung of the *varna* (megacaste) hierarchy and account for a large share of the Indian population: "Hindu law is clear on the subject that if a Shudra woman is turned out of the house by her husband, or she willfully abandons him and is not pursued to be brought back as wife, a divorce in fact takes place, sometimes regulated by custom, and then each spouse is entitled to re-arrange his/her life in marriage with other marrying partners."[77] It sought no proof of the prevalence of this custom among the concerned group, contrary to the predominant judicial practice. If this precedent had been followed, it could have enabled the recognition of unilateral common law divorces among a large number of Indians. However, no other reported judgment appears to have cited it. Even the Supreme Court continued to seek proof of the prevalence of the specific divorce customs in the concerned group thereafter, in various cases including *Yamanji H. Jadhav v. Nirmala* (2002), which was followed in many subsequent decrees, and *Subramani v. Chandralekha* (2004). In the latter case, it did not take divorce customs to have been shown to exist among Kongu Vellala Gounders, the caste of the couple in *Govindaraju*, but another court declared otherwise. In *Asha Rani v. Gulshan Kumar* (1995), the Punjab and Haryana High Court clearly stated that litigants should show divorce customs to exist in their caste, rather than inferring their existence from the customs of another group.[78]

Holden found that courts became far more willing in recent decades to recognize customary divorces and the subsequent marriages of the spouses, and to infer the validity of these practices from the earlier husband's consent, his acceptance of compensation payments from the subsequent husband, or the recognition of the later marriages in the relevant communities.[79] But they also became more wary of claims meant to deprive women of maintenance from the 1980s onward.[80] The validation of customary divorces deprived women of maintenance claims on their former husbands only until 1973, after which ex-wives were also made eligible for maintenance.[81] But some men living apart from their wives attempted to get their wives' divorces from their earlier husbands invalidated so that their own marriages would be declared void and they would thereby avoid maintenance obligations, and courts were more inclined to accept customary divorces in such contexts. They did so in *Rita Rani v. Ramesh Kumar* (1996) and *P. Mariammal v. Padmanabhan* (2001), making the woman eligible for maintenance from her later husband in the first case and eligible to inherit his property in the second. Even while rejecting a man's customary divorce from an earlier wife and thus deeming his later marriage void, the Bombay High Court gave his later wife maintenance from him, in her capacity as his mistress, in *Rajeshbai v. Shantabai* (1981); but the Andhra Pradesh High Court made the children from the later marriage ineligible to inherit jointly owned ancestral property as a result in *Edla Neelaya v. Edla Ramada alias Ramadas* (1995).[82] The Bombay and Punjab and Haryana High Courts rejected men's claims to have divorced their wives according to custom and recognized the women's maintenance claims in *Jairam Somaji More v. Sindhubai* (1999) and *Rajesh Kumar Madaan v. Mrs. Mamta alias Veena* (2005) respectively. Moreover, the Kerala High Court specifically opined that divorce deeds in which women relinquish their maintenance claims are contrary to public policy in *Sadasivan Pillai v. Vijayalakshmi* (1986), and this rule was followed in various cases, including some involving customary divorce.[83] But the dependence of a woman's maintenance claim on the validity of the dissolution of her earlier marriage did not incline the court to accept that a divorce custom existed among Arora Khatris in *Asha Rani* (1995); nor did a woman's conjugal rights depending on her earlier marriage having ended lead another court to recognize such a custom among Marwari Shwetambar Jains in *Virendra Kumar v. Preeta* (2009). Thus, the increased inclination of judges to grant women maintenance and conjugal rights (discussed later in this chapter) did not usually override their concern to recognize only divorce customs prevalent in the relevant group.

II. CONJUGAL RIGHTS

Churches and later states recognized individuals' rights to their spouses' conjugal company, initially to return women to their husbands' authority and later to encourage the reconciliation of estranged spouses. In England, ecclesiastical courts initially enforced this right using the sanction of excommunication and state courts did so later with sanctions of imprisonment, fines, or attachment of property, until this practice was abandoned in 1970. Although neither Hindu nor Islamic legal traditions had recognized this right, the colonial courts enforced it among all Indians from the 1860s, initially with threats of imprisonment. This right was incorporated in the IDA (applied to Christians) in 1869, in the Parsi Marriage and Divorce Act in 1936, and in the SMA and the HMA in the 1950s. It was in tension with concerns to promote conjugal autonomy, particularly when restitution decrees ordered people back into abusive relationships. Courts could either imprison or fine those who refused to obey restitution decrees or attach their property, and after independence usually attached their property or fined them. Poorer women were frequently unable to pay the price of disobeying restitution decrees.

Two women contested their husbands' right to gain their conjugal company through judicial intervention, the first in the 1880s and the second nearly a century later. High courts initially accepted the responses of these women to restitution petitions, partly in the first case and completely in the second. However, both victories proved short-lived. In *Dadaji Bhikaji v. Rukhmabai* (1885–6), the Bombay High Court initially rejected the man's petition to order his wife, to whom he had been married when she was a child, to begin a matrimonial life with him.[84] It did so because restitution of conjugal rights had no foundation in Hindu law, which according to the woman's lawyer saw marital functions as duties of imperfect obligation to be enforced only by religious sanction, and because the couple had never shared a home. But on appeal, a different bench of the same court granted a restitution decree and affirmed that courts should recognize the right of Hindus to such decrees.[85] The courts interpreted Islamic law to consider men eligible for restitution decrees only if they had paid their wives their prompt dower.[86] Many came to see restoration of conjugal rights as an expression of Hindu as well as Islamic conjugal norms thereafter—although in the vigorous debate over the *Rukhmabai* case, certain lawyers and publicists had highlighted that it was an English import that fit poorly with the widespread Indian practice of child marriages, which could not involve the parties' considered consent. As a result, the Hindu Law Committee of 1941 foresaw no objections to its incorporation into statutory Hindu law; the parliamentarians who opposed this incorporation in the 1950s said they were advocating the replacement of a "barbaric relic of the [presumably Indian] past" with laws reflecting emergent visions of companionate marriage, but failed partly because they neglected to ground their positions in indigenous norms.[87]

Litigants resisted restitution petitions for a century after *Dadaji Bhikaji* by offering reasons for withdrawing from their spouse's company, rather than by challenging the state's authority to enforce cohabitation.[88] Until 1976, their success depended on their showing that their spouses exhibited matrimonial faults that would warrant divorce or judicial separation. Courts occasionally noted the discord between restoring conjugal rights and Hindu legal traditions, for instance in *Bai Jiva v. Narsingh Lalbhai* (1927) and *Rukmani Ammal v. T.R.S. Chari* (1935). But neither these courts nor any others refused restitution decrees for this reason until the 1980s, when a high court decided *T. Sareetha v. T. Venkata Subbiah* (1983).[89]

In 1981, Sareetha, an important film actress, resisted the efforts of her husband, who had objected to her career and stopped living and dealing with her for this reason a few months after they got married, to share in the wealth and prestige she had acquired in the meantime by regaining her conjugal company. She did so by challenging the constitutionality of Section 9 of the HMA, concerning restitution of conjugal rights. A single-judge bench of the Andhra Pradesh High Court upheld her challenge because it found restitution of conjugal rights contrary to the constitutional rights to personal liberty, privacy, and human dignity. It declared that forcing a woman to return to her husband's company when she might be contemplating divorce would deprive her of "her choice over when and by whom the various parts of her body should be allowed to be sensed." In so far as a return to a conjugal relationship might lead to sexual intercourse and pregnancy, Justice P. A. Choudary said that it could change a woman's mind, body, and life, and thus become the "starkest form of governmental invasion of personal identity" and "zone of intimate decisions." Moreover, he found a right to regain conjugal company incompatible with equality and equal treatment, since the remedy was sought almost exclusively by men but could more seriously affect women's lives by leading to pregnancy. Aside from constitutional rights as amplified by prior judicial construction and American and English legal precedents, this judgment relied on the absence of indigenous cultural grounds for restitution of conjugality. It pointed out, as Rukmabai's lawyers had much earlier, that ancient Hindu law had treated the wife's duty "to abide by her husband as an imperfect obligation, incapable of being enforced against her will" and "refused to recognize any state interests in forcing unwilling sexual cohabitation between the husband and wife." Thus, the judgment concluded that restitution of conjugal rights was a recent and "wholly illegitimate" import, which "promotes no legitimate public purpose."[90] While Martha Nussbaum succinctly captured the major features of this judgment, Menski misunderstood it as an instance of "elite law-making."[91] Restitution decrees were more of a burden for poorer women who could not afford the fines for disobeying them.[92]

This verdict was ahead of its time, as shown by the speed with which a few high courts dissented from it and the Supreme Court overruled it. In amending personal law in light of constitutional rights, *Sareetha* departed from the predominant judicial practice since *Narasu Appa Mali* (1952). A few courts invalidated personal-law provisions by invoking constitutional rights, but only when legislatures had ignored the recommendations of courts or other policy elites to change them for many years. For instance, courts amended Christian divorce law only after the legislature had failed to heed their calls and those of several law commissions and Christian organizations for such reform for over three decades, as Chapter 5 indicates. To take another example, they dissolved marriages in the absence of spousal fault and mutual consent only after a law commission had recommended that irretrievable marital breakdown be made a ground for divorce, and a bill to this effect had been presented to parliament. By way of contrast, there had been no mobilization to abandon the restitution of conjugality, courts had not recommended this move, and no law commission had explored this possibility prior to *Sareetha*. The indigenous cultural sources that Justice Choudary highlighted for his judgment did not secure the acceptance of other judges.

Within a year, various litigants relied on *Sareetha* to resist restitution, but the courts upheld the constitutionality of restoring conjugal rights. The Delhi High Court responded in greatest detail to *Sareetha* in *Smt. Harvinder Kaur v. Harmander Singh Choudhry* (1984), and the Supreme Court relied largely on this judgment to overrule *Sareetha* in *Smt. Saroj Rani v. Sudarshan Kumar Chadha* (1984). *Harvinder Kaur* misrepresented *Sareetha* to have taken restitution decrees to aim solely to compel women to "have sex with their husband(s)," and cited English case law and legal texts of the late eighteenth to early twentieth centuries that defended restitution as enforcing cohabitation but not sexual intercourse. This ignored *Sareetha*'s concerns that sexual intercourse often accompanies spousal cohabitation and that a man to whom his wife returns unwillingly following a restitution decree may force himself on her, leading to her pregnancy. Justice Avadh Behari Rohatgi, author of *Harvinder Kaur*, asserted that restitution of conjugality serves the legitimate purpose of facilitating spousal reconciliation—although other provisions of the various personal laws address this concern more directly, such as Section 23(2) of the HMA and Section 34(2) of the SMA, which require courts to attempt reconciliation before they decree divorce or judicial separation. He held that it was not contrary to personal liberty and privacy, because individuals could respond to restitution petitions by indicating valid reasons to live on their own, or disobey restitution decrees and pay the resulting fines. Moreover, he considered restitution compatible with equal treatment, since both women and men petition for restitution—although men file such petitions far more frequently, often in response to their wives' maintenance petitions.[93] He did not address another reason why the earlier judgment held that restitution provided unequal treatment—only women may as a result experience pregnancy and attendant life changes.

While holding that restitution decrees were compatible with constitutional rights, *Harvinder Kaur* also asserted that basing family law on these principles would violate the privacy of the home, cause spousal dissension and unlimited matrimonial litigation, and destroy the institution of marriage. It argued that courts should follow legislative intention, shown in the balance struck between the liberalism of the HMA's divorce provisions and the conservatism of its restitution provisions. The court claimed that provisions for restitution and for divorce if cohabitation does not follow a restitution decree are necessary parts of a fault-based divorce regime, and could be abandoned only if irretrievable marital breakdown is made the sole ground of divorce. While leaving it to the legislature to consider such moves, it cautioned that no law commission had suggested abandoning the restoration of conjugality, and that legislators had not accepted a law commission's recommendation to make irretrievable marital breakdown a ground for divorce. Thus, *Harvinder Kaur*, unlike *Sareetha*, took its cues partly from current policy initiatives. At least two litigants attempted without success to use the *Sareetha* precedent in other high courts before the Supreme Court overturned it.[94] The Supreme Court largely relied on *Harvinder Kaur* to uphold the constitutionality of Section 9 of the HMA and by implication the corresponding sections of other matrimonial acts, adding that the right to the conjugal company of one's spouse is inherent to the institution of marriage in India, rather than a product of statute alone.[95] *Saroj Rani* did not address the problems that restitution decrees pose for poorer women reluctant to return to their husbands, and maintained judicial mechanisms to pressure individuals to return to their spouses.

Judges could exercise their discretion about the conditions under which to grant restitution decrees after the Supreme Court validated restitution provisions. Courts tended to reject men's restitution petitions that followed their wives' maintenance petitions or decrees even in the 1960s, especially if there was evidence that they had abused their wives, since such petitions were usually meant to avoid maintenance orders. They were also attentive to whether both men and women were using restitution petitions to pave the way for divorce in the absence of demonstrable spousal fault, by not resuming cohabitation after restitution decrees. For instance, the Madhya Pradesh High Court did so as the man had petitioned to restore conjugality soon after he was ordered to support his wife, who had left him because of his frequent violence, in *Baburao v. Mst. Sushila Bai* (1964). So did the Madras High Court in *Solomon Devasahayam Selvaraj v. Chandirah Mary* (1968), when the man demanded his wife's company after her maintenance was increased, although he had made it impossible for her to live with him and had shown no signs of wishing to live with her for almost a decade. The same court also rejected a bigamist's effort to resist his first wife's maintenance petition by regaining her company even though she preferred to live apart from him and his second wife, in *A. Annamalai Mudaliar v. Perumayee Ammal* (1965). Courts responded similarly to restitution petitions under such circumstances through the succeeding decades.[96]

Until the 1970s, the majority of courts assumed that men had the right to determine the location of their matrimonial home, since they were usually the main breadwinners and patrilocality was the predominant norm particularly among the upper and upper-middle castes that were most litigious. Indeed, they sometimes made this assumption even when the woman was making a major contribution to family income. In such cases, they often cited a quotation from Mulla's *Hindu Law*, a major reference book in the courts, to the effect that "under the Hindu law a wife's duty to her husband is to submit herself obediently to his authority, and to remain under his roof and protection."[97] In *Smt. Tirath Kaur v. Kirpal Singh* (1964), the Punjab High Court ordered the woman to give up her job and move back with her husband because it took her father-in-law's offer of land to compensate her for her loss of income as a sign that the husband's family did not depend on the woman's income. The same court recognized that the man had no steady income in *Smt. Surrinder Kaur v. Mohinder Singh* (1967), yet considered this and the couple's likely unhappiness if they lived together inadequate reasons for the woman to live apart, because it found no evidence of cruelty on the man's part. Other high courts held that Hindu law required women to live wherever their husbands may choose to in *Ram Parkash v. Shrimati Savitri Devi* (1957), *Vuyyuri Potharaju v. Vuyyuri Radha* (1965), *A.E. Thirumal Naidu v. Rajammal* (1968), *Surinder Kaur v. Gardeep Singh* (1973), and *Kailash Wati v. Ayodhia Parkash* (1977). Several litigants challenged *Kailash Wati* with reference to the constitutional rights to equality and equal treatment, drawing different responses from the courts, for instance in *Mrs. Swaraj Garg v. K.M. Garg* (1978) and *Pritam Kaur v. Surjit Singh* (1984), which are discussed below.

A. Annamalai Mudaliar (1965), the earlier-mentioned case of a Hindu bigamist who unsuccessfully resisted his first wife's maintenance petition, showed how far courts believed that women needed to accept the way their husbands arranged their matrimonial lives. While recognizing a woman's right to live apart from her husband and get maintenance payments from him so long as he lived with his other wife, the court held that if he abandoned his second wife, he would be entitled to require his first wife to live with him as "he can at his option live with any wife."[98] Indeed, while bigamy was accepted among Hindus, many courts held that polygamous husbands could claim the company of their first wives while living with their second wives as well, in cases such as *Jeebo Dhon Banyah v. Mt. Sundhoo* (1872) and *Mt. Kishan Devi v. Mangal Sen* (1935).

Other courts responded differently starting in the 1960s to men's petitions for their wife's company, which they rejected in *Smt. Alopbai v. Ramphal Kunjilal* (1962) and the earlier mentioned *Baburao* (1964) with a view to the woman's happiness, even if the man's behavior did not amount to cruelty.[99] In *Sadhu Singh v. Jagdish Kaur* (1969), the court similarly refused to order the woman back to her husband because it found that her in-laws had ejected her from their home, her husband had made no effort to build a relationship with her initially or resume their relationship after she was sent away, he had made unfounded adultery allegations, and he was clearly seeking a restitution decree as a means to a divorce. Moreover, it found the woman's refusal to comply with her husband's demand that she live with his parents, rather than with him, entirely reasonable.

Agnes highlighted the greater responsiveness of courts since the 1970s to the need of women in well-paying jobs to live close to their place of work.[100] *Mrs. Swaraj Garg v. K.M. Garg* (1978) provided strong support for the right of women to live apart from their husbands if their husbands did not accept their choice of location for the matrimonial home, based on the constitutional right to equality, differing in this regard from *Kailash Wati*. Justice V. S. Deshpande held that the woman should not be expected to give up her steadier and higher-paying job, especially as the couple had not agreed on the location of their matrimonial home before they got married. He argued that the earlier understanding in Hindu law that the husband has a monopoly over this decision had to be revised in light of the growth in women's workforce participation. Other features of the case reinforced his decision: the man had taken a big dowry, kept his wife's marriage gifts, did not arrange medical treatment for his wife when she was sick, and threatened to control her income and her movements. Aside from refusing conjugal restitution, the judge said the marriage had broken down in a way that warranted divorce.

A few courts reasoned as did *Swaraj Garg,* recognizing that women might need to live near their places of work in restitution and divorce cases. Even before *Swaraj Garg,* the Madras High Court had refused to order women to give up their jobs to join their husbands in *Sulochana v. Selva Madhavan* (1974) and *N.R. Radhakrishnan v. N. Dhanalakshmi* (1975). Justice Maharajan noted the need to amend Hindu law in light of changes in matrimonial relations in these cases, which drew less attention than *Swaraj Garg* because they did not rely on constitutional law. *Dhanalakshmi* was influenced by the court's finding that it was the man who had denied the woman his conjugal company: he had got himself transferred to another town when the couple had marital problems and did not try to get transferred back to the location of his matrimonial home, although his company operated in both towns unlike the city corporation that employed his wife. In both cases, the woman earned more than her husband and had supported their child while living on her own. In *L. Mallya Naika v. Somli Bai* (1978), the Karnataka High Court dismissed the petitions of two brothers for the sisters whom they married to live with them, because the brothers' choice to live away from their father-in-law's home was contrary to the custom of *illatom* adoption prevalent among certain southern Indian castes. This custom involves a man without a son adopting a man as his son-in-law and giving him a son's share in his property, in return for the latter marrying one of the adopter's daughters, living in his father-in-law's home, and helping manage his property. The court recognized this custom because the HMA did not specify contrary rules for the location of the matrimonial home, but also pointed out that its decree was in keeping with the recent trend of deciding restitution cases in light of the spouses' relative economic status. In *Smt. A. v. Sri B.* (1990), the woman had given up jobs a few times and found other jobs in the towns to which her husband's company transferred him, but had become reluctant to repeat the process to live with her husband near his current place of work. The Bombay High Court found her attitude reasonable, as the parties were "equal partners having independent earnings" and dismissed her husband's divorce petition based on desertion and cruelty.

The above cases indicate a change in the attitudes of judges regarding the authority of spouses in determining the location of the matrimonial home, but the judiciary remains more divided on this question than Agnes suggested. Some courts continued to follow the earlier patterns. This was especially true of the Punjab and Haryana High Court, which rejected constitutional challenges to *Kailash Wati* in the 1980s and 1990s that attempted to use the *Swaraj Garg* precedent, and ordered women with jobs in other towns to live with their husbands in *Pritam Kaur v. Surjit Singh* (1984), *Smt. Sumitra Devi v. Narender Singh* (1993) and *Sundari Devi v. Ram Lal* (1995) although the spouses had not agreed on the location of the matrimonial home in these cases. This court granted the man a divorce on the ground of cruelty in *Sundari Devi* although the couple lived in nearby towns where they had jobs even before they got married. Its approach might reflect the predominance of virilocality and village exogamy in northwestern India. The Supreme Court has not had the occasion to adopt a definitive approach to the location of the matrimonial home.

III. MAINTENANCE RIGHTS AND OBLIGATIONS

Claims to maintenance often arise in connection with divorce and judicial separation cases, for support both during and after the consideration of these cases. The majority of successful claimants are women and children, but courts also order support for young adults without income whose parents are engaged in matrimonial disputes, and occasionally for the men involved in these disputes. We earlier considered how courts responded to maintenance claims associated with petitions for divorce and to restore conjugal rights. This section places that discussion in the context of the ongoing formation of maintenance law.

The *shastras* and precolonial commentaries on these texts placed obligations on Hindu men to provide their wives maintenance through the latter's lives, obligations that they transferred to the men's heirs after their death. In return, they expected women not to have other sexual partners, both during and after their husbands' lives. These norms usually went hand in hand with the prohibition of divorce and widow remarriage, and especially governed the upper castes. The maintenance rights of women could assume the form of an entitlement to a share in the husband's property, including his share in ancestral property. *Shastric* traditions also recognized the maintenance claims of women in nonmarital conjugal relationships, especially those accorded the status of *avurudha stree* (permanent concubine), but these claims were typically weaker than those of wives. *Shastric* norms coexisted with the extensive practice of divorce and remarriage, as we saw. Among groups with these customs, the obligation to support divorcées was usually placed on their natal families or later husbands, the responsibility of the former husbands being restricted to a reimbursement of the woman's wedding expenses. Aside from the maintenance provided by their husbands, their husbands' families, and their natal families, divorced, separated, and widowed women could draw on their *stridhanam* (woman's property), which primarily comprised the dower and gifts that they received when they got married, but in some Hindu traditions also included a specific share of family property.[101]

Rules regarding the maintenance of wives and children were made more uniform and codified under colonial rule, and the claims of divorcées and the scope of *stridhanam* were restricted. When a Code of Criminal Procedure applicable to all religious groups was adopted in 1872, it required men to support their wives and children, both legitimate and illegitimate.[102] Women could live apart from their husbands while they derived such maintenance under various circumstances. As these provisions did not apply to divorced women, Muslim men could end their wives' economic claims on them by divorcing them, and many Hindu men belonging to groups with recognized divorce customs could limit such claims similarly.[103] Moreover, various forms of women's property were recast as "limited estate," which women had the right to enjoy during their lifetimes, but not to sell (other than in special circumstances), donate, or devolve to their heirs. Colonial courts transferred much of the property that women inherited to the heirs of the people from whom they had inherited such property.[104] These changes were partly offset by the reinforcement of widows' rights to inherit nonagricultural property as limited estate in the Hindu Women's Right to Property Act of 1937, as well as the maintenance rights of women who live separately from their husbands due to the latter's matrimonial faults in the Hindu Married Women's Right to Separate Residence and Maintenance Act (HMWRSRMA) of 1946.

The Hindu law reform initiatives of the 1940s and 1950s focused on divorce and inheritance, rather than maintenance, and contestation was limited in parliament over the maintenance provisions of the HMA and the HAMA. Nevertheless, these acts departed from predominant colonial case law in certain ways. The HMA gave all Hindus divorce rights, and extended certain maintenance provisions of Hindu law to divorcées. Section 18 of the HAMA incorporated the entitlements to maintenance that the HMWRSRMA gave women if they lived apart from their husbands for a range of reasons. Moreover, Section 14 of the HSA made Hindu women full owners of the property they possessed, including property they received instead of maintenance payments, rather than the limited owners they had been in colonial law. Furthermore, the HMA gave women and men maintenance while they were in the midst of matrimonial litigation. The right to maintenance under both the HMA and the HAMA was contingent on the beneficiary not having other sexual partners, reflecting *shastric* understandings of reciprocal spousal responsibilities. The HAMA denied women this right if they had converted to a religion originating outside South Asia, adding to the disincentives that other policies provided for such conversion (which was, for instance, also a ground for divorce or for a woman to live apart from her husband while claiming maintenance from him in Hindu law). The maintenance rights that wives enjoyed under the Code of Criminal Procedure were extended to divorced wives as well in 1973, to supplement the support available to divorcées in both Muslim law and Hindu law.[105] Finally, the Protection of Women from Domestic Violence Act (PWDVA), adopted in 2005, extended these rights to women in informal relationships, polygamous relationships, and marriages whose validity could not be proved.

The provision of divorce rights in 1955 and their further liberalization in 1976 made lawyers and legal mobilizers focus at least as much thereafter on the consequences of divorce as on the conditions under which divorce would be available, much as had happened a little earlier in most Western societies.[106] In a reflection of this trend, Agnes gave case law about maintenance fuller attention than divorce law in a recent textbook for law students.[107]

All the changes made in maintenance law after independence, except the most recent change effected by the PWDVA, were meant to reinforce the economic support available to individuals, primarily women, who were in monogamous marriages at some point, even if these relationships became attenuated or the marriages were dissolved. Since they promoted such relationships as the postcolonial conjugal norm, they did not focus on providing support to women who forged alternative conjugal bonds, and left it uncertain whether these women would retain the support that colonial Hindu law and precolonial traditions offered them. The maintenance that would be decreed for women in polygamous relationships and informal relationships, or the validity of whose marriages was uncertain for other reasons, was a focus of litigation since the 1950s. The rest of this section explores the relevant case law.[108]

So long as polygamy was recognized among Hindus, later wives in polygamous relationships could claim maintenance from their husbands who failed to support them or treated them in ways that made courts consider it appropriate for them to live separately. Until the 1930s, courts generally did not consider a man living with another woman a sufficient reason for his wife to be allowed to live separately and claim maintenance from him if he was willing to also have her live with him.[109] From the 1930s, some courts exempted women from the obligation to live with husbands from whom they got economic support if their husbands were living with another woman.[110] But others continued to follow the earlier practice. The passage of the HMWRSRMA in 1946 and the incorporation of its clauses into the HAMA in 1956 clearly gave the first wives of polygamists the right to maintenance while living apart from their husbands if their husbands lived with one or more of their later wives; but courts varied in whether they recognized this right if the man's later marriages predated the HMWRSRMA.[111] It was not clear that legislators meant the HMWRSRMA and the HAMA to give later wives this right if their husbands lived with other women, but some courts gave such women separate residence and maintenance.[112]

Judges in the higher courts unanimously recognized that the criminal-law provisions regarding spousal maintenance did not apply to later concurrent wives between 1955, when polygamy lost recognition among Hindus, and the passage of the PWDVA in 2005.[113] However, the HMA, the HAMA, and the SMA were ambiguous regarding the maintenance rights of women in such situations, and many courts interpreted the references to "wives" in the maintenance clauses of these acts to also apply to such women. Menski highlighted the relief sometimes made available to these women under the Hindu law statutes, though not under the secular criminal law.[114] Recognizing this, certain courts sympathetic to the maintenance claims of later concurrent wives denied them because they had been pressed with reference to criminal law, but urged these women to seek relief under Hindu law.[115]

Menski and Agnes claimed that courts began to interpret Hindu law statutes to provide support to the later wives of polygamists in the mid-1970s, with *C. Obula Konda Reddy v. C. Pedda Venkata Lakshmamma* (1976) and *Govindrao Ranoji Musale v. Sou. Anandibai* (1976).[116] Menski considered this part of a new trend of judicial activism to make the husbands and ex-husbands of women facing destitution responsible for their continued economic support, and Agnes regarded it as a sign of increased (albeit inconsistent) judicial ingenuity to uphold the rights of women whose conjugal relationships did not fit the model of marital monogamy. But the stage was set to strengthen the maintenance claims of the later wives of polygamists as early as the early 1960s, soon after Hindu polygamy was banned, when certain courts interpreted Hindu maintenance provisions to require men to support their ex-wives after their marriages were annulled. This enabled women in polygamous marriages to gain maintenance from their former husbands once they got their marriages annulled due to the polygamous nature of their marriages. The Gujarat High Court affirmed the need to construe the HMA and the HAMA in light of the legislative intention to ameliorate Hindu women's disabilities, and held that women could get maintenance under Section 25 of the HMA after a nullity decree in *Kadia Harilal Purshottam v. Kadia Lilavati Gokaldas* (1961), as did the Calcutta High Court in *Arya Kumar Bal v. Smt. Ila Bal* (1968). In a similar vein, the Punjab High Court held that the HAMA's maintenance provisions should be liberally construed to increase women's rights to maintenance and property in *Jal Kaur v. Pala Singh* (1961).

Although these cases did not involve bigamy, they provided the bases for the Punjab High Court to grant a bigamist's second wife maintenance after her marriage was annulled because of her husband's bigamy, in *Dayal Singh v. Bhajan Kaur* (1973), a few years before *Obula Konda Reddy* and *Govindrao Ranoji Musale*. In *Kadia Harilal Purshottam*, *Arya Kumar Bal* and *Dayal Singh*, the courts based themselves on older Hindu understandings of conjugal relationships and responsibilities to enable emergent alternatives to marital monogamy, but also demonstrated that they considered monogamous marriage the norm. This was particularly clear in *Dayal Singh*, in which the court deprecated the man's second marriage as a "mock marriage" and the wedding as a "sham ceremony," and felt that it was particularly appropriate to grant the woman alimony since she had been "robbed of her maidenhood" when she was lured into a bigamous situation, thus making it more difficult for her to get remarried after the annulment of this marriage. Following *Dayal Singh*, the Andhra Pradesh High Court argued that the reference to a "legally wedded wife" in Section 18 of the HAMA encompasses later concurrent wives whose marriages had been solemnized, since this clause required maintenance if the husband had other living wives in *Obula Konda Reddy*. The Bombay High Court concurred with *Dayal Singh* when it decreed alimony under the HMA in *Govindrao Ranoji Musale*. The latter two courts felt that these statutes were meant to support women beguiled into marrying men who already had other wives. Some courts followed these precedents to grant the later wives of polygamists maintenance.[117] This supplemented the tendency of various courts since the nineteenth century to presume that marriages that could not be clearly proven were valid for the purposes of the women's maintenance and inheritance rights and the legitimacy of children from these marriages if there had been prolonged cohabitation.[118]

While such decisions reinforced the maintenance rights of later concurrent wives and women in nonmarital conjugal relationships, other courts resisted granting such women maintenance. Larger benches of the Andhra Pradesh and Bombay High Courts specifically overruled *Obula Konda Reddy* and *Govindrao Ranoji Musale* in *Abbayolla M. Subba Reddy v. Padmamma* (1998) and *Bhausaheb alias Sandu Magar v. Leelabai* (2004) because they believed that the broad interpretation of "wife" in the earlier cases was contrary to legislative intention. *Bhausaheb* also rejected such a construction because it believed this would encourage bigamy. Other courts also refused to grant later concurrent wives maintenance under the rubric of Hindu law, for example, *Khemchand Om Prakash Sharma v. State of Gujarat* (2000), *Malti v. State of U.P.* (2001) and *Ms. Suresh Khullar v. Mr. Vijay Khullar* (2002).[119] Thus, judges shared the disposition of legislators to uphold marital monogamy as the norm, but this inclination led some judges to deny later wives maintenance while others reconciled it with requiring support for women whose relationships departed from this norm.

In response to the judgments that denied the maintenance claims of later wives under Hindu law, as well as the continued rejection of these claims under criminal law, some reformist lawyers' groups and women's organizations mobilized for legislation to strengthen the maintenance rights of women in polygamous and nonmarital relationships. This demand was accommodated in the PWDVA, which made it unnecessary for women to prove that their conjugal relationships were valid marriages to be eligible for maintenance or police protection from their violent partners. The Supreme Court rejected a challenge to the resulting equalization of the maintenance claims of first wives and those of later wives and mistresses in *Aruna Parmod Shah v. Union of India* (2008), holding that this did not violate the sanctity of marriage. Moreover, in *Chanmuniya v. Virendra Kumar Singh Kushwaha* (2010), it held that the PWDVA's provisions should be applied to all maintenance cases under criminal law, to reinforce the rights of women the validity of whose marriages was uncertain as well as women in nonmarital relationships, because this statute reflected recent value changes regarding conjugality. The PWDVA and cases that succeeded it such as *Aruna Parmod Shah* and *Chanmuniya* demonstrated novel forms of legal reasoning and more open visions of the kind of conjugal relationships that can be given direct or indirect judicial support. (The cases of the 1970s and 1980s in which courts awarded maintenance to later wives did not, contrary to Menski's understanding). As this trend is recent, it remains to be seen if it will be sustained. The two-judge bench of the Supreme Court that considered *Chanmuniya* referred the question of the maintenance rights of women in nonmarital relationships and women the validity of whose marriages is uncertain to a larger bench. The response of the latter bench is difficult to predict since judges' views vary on this question, as shown by some high courts' continuing to deny women in such circumstances maintenance in the meantime (for example, in *Vineeta Devi v. Bablu Thakur & State of Jharkhand* (2011)).[120] As the majority of judges value marital monogamy, the maintenance rights of women who do not adhere to this norm remain uncertain.

IV. SUCCESSION

We saw that fewer reform proposals regarding succession were adopted in the 1950s, due to the opposition of the defenders of lineages. But lineage power declined and rural elites became more open to giving women rights in joint property and devolving such property bilaterally through the subsequent decades. Along with the growth of civil society mobilization to promote women's rights and the increased attention to gender equity in public discourse, these developments enabled considerable change in succession law from the 1970s. Indeed, inheritance was the area of personal law in which the most consequential reforms occurred over the past decade. Legislation accounted for the major changes in succession law since the 1970s, unlike the changes in matrimonial law, which were significantly due to novel judicial interpretation as well. Bina Agarwal comprehensively discussed the changes in succession law, particularly with regard to agricultural land, and also influenced the major amendments introduced in 2005. The following analysis builds on her work and B. Sivaramayya's, but differs from these accounts in certain respects and discusses the policymaking process more fully.[121]

A. Consequences of the Hindu Succession Act, 1956

The compromise of the 1950s provided equal shares to daughters and sons in separate property passing by intestacy, but only minor shares in joint property, as we saw in Chapter 3. Sons were coparceners in the family's joint property on birth, along with their fathers, and this gave them shares in such property to which they had a right through survivorship. They could gain control over their shares by demanding the partition of such property even during their fathers' lifetimes, and could not be deprived of them through bequest. In addition, they could get a share in their father's interest in such property through succession, and wills did not usually deny them these shares either. Female kin were not coparceners, and were entitled to no share in joint property through survivorship; daughters could only get shares in their father's interest in such property, which was far less than what sons gained through survivorship and succession. In much of India, widows enjoyed a larger share in joint property than daughters did. The versions of *Mitakshara* law applied in western, central and northern, India (the Maharashtra School applied in the former Bombay Presidency and other parts of western India, the Mithila School applied in Uttar Pradesh and neighboring regions of northern India, and the Banaras School applied in Orissa and Bihar) gave widows a share of such property when it was partitioned, though not the right to effect such partitions, in addition to giving them a share in their husbands' interest in such property. Widows were given larger shares than daughters based on the patrilineal understanding that women leave their natal lineages and join their husbands' lineages on marriage, a view particularly strong in these regions. However, the Dravida subschool of *Mitakshara* law, applied in much of southern India (Tamil Nadu, Pondicherry, Kerala, Andhra Pradesh, and the regions of Karnataka that were not part of the Bombay Presidency), gave widows no share in joint property on partition. This reflected the greater prevalence of bilateral kinship practices in this region, and made the shares that widows enjoyed in joint property as meager as those of daughters.[122] Moreover, widows were entitled to shares in their husbands' property, both separate and joint, only if they remained "chaste" and did not get remarried. Female kin could get their modest shares of family property only on the death of the property holder, and only if he did not will his interest in the property to someone else. The HSA gave men testamentary freedom for the first time regarding their interest in joint property, of which their sons, daughters, widows, and mothers were eligible to receive equal shares in the absence of wills. Wills usually gave sons at least their intestate shares in all forms of family property, but often denied female kin their intestate shares in both separate and joint property. Men were also free to renounce or gift their shares of joint property, which they did at times to benefit their sons. Moreover, they could convert their separate property into joint property, and thereby limit the shares accruing to their female kin in the absence of a will.

Men and women had unequal succession rights in other ways too until the past decade. The heirs of an intestate man included kin two generations down the male line of descent, but only one generation down the female line; daughters-in-law and granddaughters-in-law were Class I heirs who were given first priority in succession, but not sons-in-law or grandsons-in-law; and agnates had priority over cognates. The rules for succession to a woman's property also limited the shares of the woman's heirs. If a woman had no children and had been predeceased by her husband, her property devolved, in descending order of priority, on her husband's heirs, her parents, her father's heirs, and her mother's heirs. However, property she inherited from her parents devolved on her father's heirs and property she inherited from her husband or her father-in-law on her husband's heirs, reflecting the persistence of colonial constructions of women's property as limited estate, to be inherited by the heirs of the last full owners of such property.[123] The Bombay High Court upheld these rules of devolution of women's property because it considered them based on propinquity and the rules of Mitakshara law in *Sonubai Yeshwant Jadhav v. Bala Govind Yadav* (1983).

Besides, Section 4(2) of the HSA exempted the provisions of state-specific laws to prevent the fragmentation of agricultural holdings, for the fixation of land ceilings, and for the devolution of tenancy rights in agricultural land from the succession rules of the HSA. It was meant to prevent the patriarchs of major landholding families from nominally devolving family land to various individuals to circumvent land ceilings. But it also served to restrict women's rights to inherit agricultural land in six states in northern and northwestern India (Delhi, Haryana, Himachal Pradesh, Punjab, Uttar Pradesh, and Jammu and Kashmir), in which strong patrilineages shaped land reform legislation to give women very limited land rights. (Lineages enjoyed greater scope to do so, because Article 31b of the Indian constitution exempted land tenure laws from the need to be compatible with the fundamental rights). In Punjab in 1969 and in Haryana in 1979, the legislatures considered bills to exclude daughters entirely from inheriting agricultural land, supposedly to prevent the fragmentation of family land. The Haryana legislature passed this bill, but the President of India denied it his assent, needed for state legislation on matters under the concurrent jurisdiction of the national government to take effect.[124]

In the other states, land tenure laws specified that the relevant personal law or the HSA would apply to the devolution of agricultural land (in Madhya Pradesh and Rajasthan), or specified no rules for devolution, resulting in the HSA's succession rules being applied to Hindus (in much of Andhra Pradesh, as well as Tamil Nadu, Kerala, Karnataka, Maharashtra, Gujarat, Bihar, Orissa, and West Bengal).[125] Finally, a man's daughters, wives and mothers were given the right to reside in his ancestral home, considered the seat of the patrilineage, but not to have the house partitioned to claim their shares if male kin lived in the home; and married daughters were denied the right to live there unless they were widowed, separated, or deserted by their husbands.

Although daughters had the smallest shares in joint property among the nuclear family members, the courts decided that Section 6 of the HSA offered them little room to increase their shares. Moreover, they upheld unequal rights in the ancestral home, except for giving daughters the right to partition them if their male kin rented out their shares.[126] However, some of them found justification in the Explanation to Section 6 for giving widows the same shares as sons in family joint property when the man died. In cases in which widows claimed shares of joint property although their sons did not partition it, some high courts understood the notional partition effected to determine the interest of the deceased in joint property to not give the widow a share in this property. Some of them drew support for this interpretation in the view, predating the HSA, that the widow's share in joint property was only a substitute for maintenance.[127] However, the majority of high courts understood such notional partition to give the widow a coparcener's share in the joint property even if the coparceners did not choose to partition this property, starting with *Rangubai v. Laxman Lalji Patil* (1965).[128] The Supreme Court made this interpretation definitive in *Gurupad Khandappa Magdum v. Hirabai Khandappa Magdum* (1978).

The limited rights that the HSA gave women in joint property led Parashar and Newbigin to connect the act's continued recognition of the joint family's control over property to the limits on women's rights.[129] However, women's inheritance rights were limited not so much because the HSA recognized the joint family as because of its primarily patrilineal construction of inheritance. Indeed, the amendments made in the HSA, initially in certain states and then at the national level, increased daughters' inheritance rights not by dissolving family joint property, but by requiring that such property be devolved bilaterally and equally to sons and daughters rather than patrilineally and primarily to male kin. This partly reconciled the ownership of property by kin collectives with the promotion of women's inheritance rights.

B. Early Reform Initiatives

The judicial enhancement of widows' rights in joint property did not bring these rights on a par with those of sons, since they did not make widows coparceners able to claim their shares in such property while their husbands were alive, and did not reduce testamentary rights (usually used to disadvantage female kin, including widows). Moreover, courts did not reduce the most glaring gender inequalities in Hindu succession law, which concerned daughters' rights in joint property, the order of succession to separate property, and rights in the ancestral home. Furthermore, the Marriage Laws (Amendment) Act (1976) reduced the inheritance rights of the daughters of Hindu, Sikh, Buddhist, and Jain couples that had registered their marriages under the SMA, because it applied the rules of the HSA to such women (and their siblings), rules which limited their access to joint property and shares in such property, rather than those of the ISA, which had governed them until then and had given them rights equal to those of their brothers in all family property.[130]

In response to these inequalities enshrined in the HSA, women's organizations and other civil society organizations demanded changes in these provisions from the 1970s onward. But they emphasized these concerns less than those to amend laws concerning domestic violence, dowry, rape, and workplace harassment—because women brought the latter concerns to their legal aid centers more frequently, and these organizations connected women's well-being more closely to employment and income than to property ownership. (Agarwal highlighted the limitations of this approach in various writings). Official committees concerned with women's well-being nevertheless discussed inheritance law reform. The CSWI's report of 1974 demanded the equalization of sons' and daughters' rights to inheritance and in the ancestral home, and indicated a preference for dissolving *Mitakshara* coparcenaries. In 1995, the NCW recommended that daughters be made coparceners on birth in *Mitakshara* joint property without decomposing the property into separate shares, and that rules for succession to women's property be made the same as those to men's property; and in 1998 the Committee for Gender Equality in Land Devolution in Tenurial Laws specifically recommended the equalization of the land tenure rights of men and women.[131] Some of these recommendations were adopted, initially in the southern and western Indian states of Kerala (in 1976), Andhra Pradesh (in 1986), Tamil Nadu (in 1989), Karnataka (in 1994), and Maharashtra (in 1994), and later through national government legislation (in 2005). All these reforms were presented as meant to improve women's condition, curtail dowry, and realize constitutional equality. However, they varied in crucial ways.

The Kerala Joint Hindu Family System (Abolition) Act ended the legal recognition of the joint family, and converted coparceners in joint property into tenants in common whose shares in such property it took to have been partitioned, as the CSWI had recommended. Although it pertained to all of the state's residents, it was significantly based on the Hindu Code Bill that the Parliamentary Select Committee had presented to parliament in 1948. But while the Hindu Code Bill had envisioned the partition of joint property equally among all members of the Hindu Undivided Family that owned this property, the Kerala act made a crucial distinction. In families that had been governed by *Mitakshara* law, it partitioned the property only among the former coparceners (that is, certain male kin), but in families governed by other laws (including the majority of the state's families to whom various matrilineal laws, such as the Marumakkathayam, Aliyasanta, and Nambudiri systems, had applied until then), it partitioned the property among all members.[132]

Thus, after the passage of this act, the Kerala High Court recognized the rights of women to shares in their Marumukkathayam *tharavad*'s (matrilineage) property in *C. Vathsalan v. Kotta Madathil Narayanankutty* (2007) and *Shanta v. Sahadevan* (2011) (as had the Supreme Court in *C.T. Radhakrishnan v. C.T. Viswanathan Nair* (2006)), but rejected the claims of women who had been governed by *Mitakshara* law to shares in their natal families' joint property in *Puthiyadath Jayamathy Avva and Others v. K.J. Naga Kumar* (2000) and *Dharmambal v. S.Lakshmi Ammal* (2002). Not having examined the relevant case law, Sivaramayya believed that the act did not benefit daughters and Agarwal that it gave all daughters the same rights in joint property as sons.[133]

In Andhra Pradesh, Tamil Nadu, Karnataka, and Maharashtra, daughters who were unmarried when the HSA was amended in the state were made coparceners in joint property, and the NCW recommended that the rest of India follow this approach. Legislators provided two reasons to exclude already married daughters from coparcener status—daughters leave their natal patrilineages on marriage, and parents spend considerable amounts on their daughters' wedding expenses and dowry. The differential treatment of married and unmarried daughters showed that patrilineal visions of family identity, as reflected in the *shastras*, were relevant in these regions too, making other states less resistant to these reforms.[134] These amendments were prospective; courts gave daughters increased shares in joint property only if the property had not been partitioned before their passage.[135] They rejected the pleas of women litigants to make these provisions retrospective[136] and to treat daughters married before these amendments were passed as coparceners, based on legislative intent to ameliorate women's circumstances.[137] These reforms reduced the shares that sons could get through survivorship if they had not partitioned their shares of joint property before the amendments took effect, because they increased the number of coparceners. They also reduced the amount of property accruing to widows and mothers through succession, because they diminished the interest of the deceased in such property. The entitlements of widows declined more in Andhra Pradesh, Tamil Nadu, and much of Karnataka, where they were not given shares of joint property on partition based on the Dravida school of *Mitakshara* law, and less in Maharashtra and the parts of northern Karnataka that had been part of the Bombay Presidency, where they were given such shares on partition based on the Maharashtra school. Testamentary rights were not restricted in either Kerala or the states in which unmarried daughters were made coparceners.[138]

Agarwal highlighted the influence of kinship practices over the location of the earliest reforms in southern India, where the prevalence of bilateral and matrilineal inheritance and lineage formation, the frequency of intravillage and intrakin marriages, and varied patterns of postmarital residence reduced support for patrilineal authority and limited resistance to giving women rights in family property.[139] In Kerala, where succession law was changed earliest and most extensively, a high proportion of the population was matrilineal and women's standards of living were by far the highest in India.[140] The prevalence of matriliny and the high levels of women's education aided the growth of strong women's organizations, which exerted extensive pressure to increase women's inheritance rights, preferably by dissolving joint property. The ongoing gradual erosion of matriliny made many men accept the dissolution of joint property for reasons unrelated to women's rights. In the abolition of the joint family system, various men saw a means to symbolically end the association of their castes with matriliny, which was linked to "tribal" status by many Christian missionaries who had long been active in Kerala and by certain Hindu and Christian elites who wished to associate themselves with the emergent national mainstream. These inclinations reinforced the demands of women's organizations to dissolve joint property. In Andhra Pradesh, Tamil Nadu, and Karnataka, bilateral kinship practices were widespread, certain smaller groups were matrilineal, and village and kin endogamy were common. These factors also reduced resistance to the reforms in these states.

Patterns of party and civil society mobilization also influenced the location of the early reforms in ways that Agarwal did not discuss. In Kerala, women's organizations were strong, and some of them were associated with the Communist Party of India, which led the alliance that ruled the state when joint property was abolished. The Congress Party, the other partner in that alliance, was also eager to associate itself with this change passed during the authoritarian "emergency" that the party oversaw and justified as a means to promote the interests of the underprivileged. Somewhat different political alignments proved conducive to Hindu succession-law reform in Andhra

Pradesh, Tamil Nadu, Karnataka, and Maharashtra. The Telugu Desam in Andhra Pradesh and the Congress Party in Karnataka and Maharashtra had considerable support among women, which they tried to consolidate by amending the HSA. In Tamil Nadu, the All India Anna Dravida Munnetra Kazhagam (AIADMK), which had lost power a little before the passage of the legislation, had comparable support among women. The leaders of the Dravida Munnetra Kazhagam (DMK), which had replaced the AIADMK in power, saw an opportunity to rebuild their party's female support in the recent demise of the AIADMK's founding leader, and followed the Andhra Pradesh precedent for this reason.[141] Women's organizations reinforced the calculations of the ruling parties, particularly in Kerala and Maharashtra where they were strong and had contributed to a public ethos that dissuaded other parties from resisting this measure. Thus, the enhancement of women's rights in joint property faced little legislative opposition, even from the BJP whose predecessor organization (the Bharatiya Jan Sangh) had stoutly resisted more modest reform proposals in the 1950s.[142] Resistance to women's inheritance rights declined for this reason even in states where it had been strong until the 1970s. As a result, widows (but not daughters) were placed on a par with sons as heirs of tenure in agricultural land in 1982 in Uttar Pradesh, in northern India, in a change that was in keeping with the patrilineal understanding that men's wives and widows become part of their lineages, while their daughters leave these lineages on marriage.[143]

C. *The Process of National Reform*

Women's organizations grew rapidly, and various other institutions and individuals oriented to women's rights acquired greater policy influence through the 1980s and the 1990s; they advocated national legislation to advance women's inheritance rights. Based on the NCW's recommendation that daughters be made coparceners in joint property, the Department of Women and Child Development urged other state governments to consider the adoption of the reforms initially introduced in Andhra Pradesh. This led the Law Commission to consider national legislation along these lines, inasmuch as succession is under the concurrent jurisdiction of the national government and the state governments.[144]

The Law Commission engaged in public consultation much as the Hindu Law Committee had in the 1940s, but approached a group more favorable to women's rights, composed predominantly of lawyers, civil society leaders, and academics. A definite majority of its respondents favored reforms even more extensive than those adopted earlier in Kerala—the dissolution of *Mitakshara* coparcenaries, the denial of testamentary rights over a half or a third of all forms of property, the invalidation of land tenure laws that discriminate against women, and the extension of equal rights to daughters in the ancestral home.[145] The Law Commission was divided in its approach and this was reflected in its report, which was far more radical in its analysis of the problems with the existing laws than in its recommendations.[146]

Although it noted that the reforms in Andhra Pradesh discriminated against daughters married before their passage, and that the Supreme Court had ruled against married daughters being denied benefits which unmarried daughters could get (in *Savita Samvedi v. Union of India* (1985), which concerned retirement benefits), the commission recommended that *Mitakshara* coparcenaries be retained and that only daughters who were not married before the legislation be made coparceners, as had been done in Andhra Pradesh. It justified the retention of joint property with the inaccurate claim that the dissolution of such property in Kerala had given daughters no shares in such property; it grounded the exclusion of daughters married before the reform from coparcener status in claims that parents were likely to have given substantial wedding gifts to these daughters, but not to those married after the reform, in view of the latter having been made coparceners. While acknowledging that testamentary rights were often used to limit women's property control, the report did not recommend their restriction. It suggested only one step that would have empowered women more than had been done in Andhra Pradesh—giving daughters the same rights as sons to partition and live in the ancestral home—and accepted only a minor feature of the Kerala legislation—the abandonment of the "doctrine of pious obligation" that required sons to repay debts that their fathers had accumulated and perform their *pinda* in return for coparcenary membership. The Law Commission's recommendations were out of tune with its assessment that the *Mitakshara* coparcenary needed radical reform.[147]

The Law Ministry based the bill it presented to parliament in December 2004 entirely on the Law Commission's recommendations.[148] However, various civil-society groups contributed to significant changes in this bill before parliament passed it in August 2005. The eventual legislation increased women's shares in family property and promoted the bilateral devolution of such property more than the initial proposals did, unlike the pattern in the 1950s when the initial proposals regarding succession were scaled down in the face of resistance. The major changes made in the bill were the inclusion of married daughters as coparceners, the prioritization of the HSA's rules over state-specific land tenure laws, the extension of rights to daughters equal to those of sons to partition and live in the ancestral home, the entitlement of remarried widows to shares in the property of their husbands and their husbands' families, and the entitlement of women's heirs to inherit property that the women had themselves inherited.

Certain developments helped make reform more extensive. Political elites resisted women's rights less and attached less value to patrilineal property transmission than their forebears had in the 1950s. Moreover, the multiparty United Progressive Alliance (UPA) that ruled India then was open to enhancing certain civil and economic rights, it included parties (the CPI-M and the Communist Party of India) that vigorously promoted these changes, and the women's organizations affiliated with these parties (the All India Democratic Women's Association [AIDWA] and the National Federation of Indian Women [NFIW] respectively) specifically advocated women's inheritance rights. Finally, civil society organizations mobilized to shape the legislation, networked effectively with crucial political elites, and presented their proposals as both compatible with indigenous traditions and the stability of the family; and conducive to gender equity, human development, and the alignment of personal law with constitutional rights and transnational human rights standards. Particular political elites and bureaucrats expressed misgivings about certain civil society proposals in public consultations and behind the scenes, and prevented the dissolution of coparcenaries, the restriction of testamentary rights, and the protection of the inheritance shares of widows and mothers. This in turn contained resistance.

After the bill was presented to the Rajya Sabha in December 2004, the Human Rights Law Network and the Housing and Land Rights Network launched a campaign to amend the bill, and gained the support of various women's organizations, other rights organizations, and organizations focused on livelihood concerns and land reform. Bina Agarwal used her extensive knowledge of succession law and gendered agrarian laws and practices to direct some of these efforts.[149] Forty-seven organizations, of which the AIWC was by far the oldest and largest, agreed in January 2005 on a memorandum outlining the changes they sought—the abolition of coparcenaries, the application of the amended HSA rules to agricultural land, the denial of testamentary rights over half or a third of a person's property, and the invalidation of deeds women sign under duress relinquishing their inheritance entitlements—and sent it to all parliamentarians and Sonia Gandhi, the President of the Congress Party and the UPA's Convenor.[150] Five other organizations, including the AIDWA and the NFIW, sent the same elites a memorandum that differed from the first only in demanding the invalidation of wills that discriminate against female kin rather than the restriction of testamentary rights.[151] The Indian government invited these organizations to present their recommendations to the Parliamentary Standing Committee on Personnel, Public Grievances, Law and Justice, which considered the bill.

The discussions of this committee, continued civil society lobbying, and the interventions of the Law Commission, the Law Ministry, and Sonia Gandhi gave the legislation its final shape. In an account enriched by the author's role in the process, Agarwal attributed the inclusion of more provisions favorable to women to support from members of the UPA, the concerted efforts of rights organizations, the choice of these organizations to frame their arguments in terms of social rights and livelihood concerns, the lack of attention of conservatives to the implications of applying the HSA to land inheritance, and the speed with which the bill was altered, which gave opponents little time to plot resistance.[152] She believed that these circumstances counteracted two unfavorable conditions—the increased representation of agrarian groups since the 1960s, and the persistence of social norms contrary to women's property rights, particularly in agricultural land. Agarwal did not attend to two other relevant factors—the lower importance that many political elites, including those from agrarian groups, gave patrilineal inheritance than they had before the 1960s (which became evident during policy discussions), and the manner in which key lobbyists (including her) framed their proposals as compatible with indigenous traditions.

Various Parliamentary Standing Committee members with differing attitudes about women's rights felt that the legislation should be compatible with Hindu and Indian traditions regarding the joint family. Justice N. Y. Hanumanthappa and S. K. Kaarvendhan of the Congress Party argued that Hindu joint family traditions required the retention of coparcenaries and the doctrine of pious obligation, and were incompatible with making married daughters coparceners. Moreover, they felt the application of national inheritance legislation to land tenure would infringe excessively on state government autonomy. The Law Ministry supported their preferences by arguing that the dissolution of joint property had given daughters no property in Kerala, and that making married daughters coparceners would lead their in-laws to cause family tensions by pressing these women to claim their new entitlements.[153]

Many wished to increase women's inheritance rights while continuing to recognize the joint family as a primary social unit. They included E. M. Sudarsana Natchiappan, the Chair of the Parliamentary Standing Committee whose support women's rights activists considered important to their success, Radhakant Nayak, and P. C. Alexander of the Congress Party, in which policy preferences varied as they had in the 1950s. Natchiappan indicated that the

> joint family . . . is a unique feature of the Indian society. It does have its own negative aspects, but, at the same time, it is a redeeming feature of the Indian culture, which has been in existence for thousands of years and is still continuing. We might not be in a position to think of discontinuing the joint family system, but, at the same time, we want to give equal rights to women.

He accepted the connections seen in Hindu traditions between property inheritance, the continuity of the family, spirituality, and ritual obligations, but felt justified in including daughters as coparceners if they assumed the traditional obligations that accompanied this status. Natchiappan pointed out that dowry and wedding gifts did not justify the exclusion of married daughters, since dowry was illegal and wedding gifts were usually far less valuable than potential inheritance shares, and that the prioritization of the HSA's rules over state land tenure laws was not contrary to constitutional federalism. He did not wish legislation to hasten family nuclearization, and preferred to retain coparcenaries for this reason, while making daughters, and perhaps widows too, equal members of coparcenaries.[154] His acceptance of certain premises of conservative committee members, especially his preference to retain coparcenaries, helped him contain opposition to reform and shape crucial features of the committee's report.

The civil society representatives who testified before the committee systematically countered objections to their proposals, and the committee drew on some of their arguments. Bina Agarwal argued (a) that increasing women's property entitlements would promote family stability by dissuading men from leaving their wives, reduce domestic violence, and improve the quality of life of children (claims supported by studies of the effects of women's property control and the earlier state-level reforms), (b) that the dissolution of joint property would not affect the viability of the joint family, (c) that it was crucial to entitle women to agricultural land because men were shifting to nonagrarian occupations more than women were, and (d) that as testamentary rights were transplants from British law, a restriction of these rights would return to indigenous traditions to strengthen women's entitlements.[155] She indicated that the inadvertent reduction of widow's shares in joint property in the process of increasing the rights of daughters was contrary to *Mitakshara* traditions, which prioritized widows' claims over those of daughters, and that daughters would consider it a privilege to perform their parents' *pinda* and assume other obligations that accompany coparcener status. The AIDWA representatives, Kirti Singh and Subhashini Ali, added that if dissolving coparcenaries had not given daughters property in Kerala, or would not do so if it were applied to groups in which female kin did not have rights in ancestral property earlier, female kin could be specifically given an equal share of joint property when it was decomposed. They also demanded that state agrarian legislation be required to give daughters and wives the same rights as sons.

The CPI-M's representative on the committee, V. Radhakrishnan, alone supported the dissolution of joint property, and legislators from this party

(Susmita Bauri and C. S. Sujatha) pressed this demand in parliamentary debates over the revised bill. However, since this approach was contrary to the concern of most committee members—including many proponents of daughters' inheritance rights—to continue to recognize the joint family as a property-owning entity, the committee's report did not endorse it.[156] However, the proposal to restrict testamentary rights, which had as much potential effect on the shares of female kin in family property, faced no resistance insofar as it was seen to support Hindu traditions linking family identity to inheritance. Indeed, Ram Jethmalani of the BJP (who was the Law Minister from 1998 to 2000) welcomed this proposal, as well as one to give the HSA priority over state agrarian laws. However, other BJP legislators voiced concerns about these proposals.[157]

Based on these deliberations, the committee recommended (a) that married daughters be made coparceners or otherwise given shares in family property, (b) that the succession rights of cognates be brought on a par with those of agnates, (c) that female kin be given equal rights in the ancestral home, (d) that the HSA be given priority over state land legislation, and (e) that the inheritance rights of widows should not change if they remarried. It framed these recommendations as ways to recognize the joint family as a unique, enduring, and widely valued Indian institution, while remolding it so that it would not be patriarchal and patrilineal. The committee found further justification for making daughters coparceners in evidence that they often performed *pinda* in Bengal. It also suggested that the government explore ways to protect widows' inheritance shares and restrict testamentary rights, while leaving these measures to the government's discretion.[158]

Sonia Gandhi influenced the way the Law Ministry framed the bill that parliament passed. Her intervention encouraged the committee to accept many civil-society proposals, and led the Law Ministry to incorporate most of the committee's recommendations in the amended bill, although this was not the preference of the Law Minister, Hans Raj Bharadwaj. The sharp divisions among its members limited the influence of the Law Commission, although it was consulted. The bill made married daughters coparceners, but did not restrict testamentary rights or increase widows' shares.[159] The failure to restrict testamentary rights meant that wills could deprive women of the shares they had gained in intestate property. Nevertheless, the extension of coparcener status to daughters and the adoption of bilateral rules to devolve family property that passed through intestacy were important advances in women's rights.

The amended bill faced little resistance in parliament. Some legislators wished the reforms to proceed further, by dissolving joint property, limiting testamentary rights, invalidating deeds in which women sign away their property rights under duress, and requiring agrarian legislation to give daughters and wives the same rights as sons. D. Purandeswari (Congress Party), Susmita Bauri and C. S. Sujatha (CPI-M), Bhartruhari Mahtab (Biju Janata Dal), and M. Ramadass (Paattaali Makkal Katchi—PMK) raised these demands, but lacked sufficient support to change legislation accordingly.[160] Others had misgivings about making married daughters coparceners and devolving family property bilaterally, but they did not express their objections forcefully or vote against the bill, because their parties had decided to support it.[161] The failure to restrict testamentary rights might have made parties that resisted other women's rights initiatives around the same time (such as the SP, the RJD, the Janata Dal (United), and the BSP, which opposed the Women's Reservation Bill) and other conservative legislators more willing to allow the act's passage.

Only a minority of the legislators enthusiastically supported the HSA amendment, the most ambitious personal-law reform of the past generation, and many of them had reservations about it. This limited the scope of the reform, and showed that proposals to increase women's inheritance rights further (such as through the dissolution of joint property or the restriction of testamentary rights) did not enjoy extensive support among the political elite. If the legislation passed nevertheless, this was crucially because its proponents grounded it in emergent visions of indigenous tradition that had some appeal.

In the limited case law that has accumulated since this reform, courts applied its provisions to pending cases.[162] However, they did not give it retrospective effect or enhance women's shares in family property more than the act required, for instance by compensating widows for the amendment's reduction of their shares in view of the act's presumed aim to increase women's access to property.[163]

V. THE MODIFIED NORMATIVE NATIONAL FAMILY

The changes made since the 1970s in Hindu law and in criminal laws about maintenance and domestic violence made nuclear family membership more consequential, promoted bilateral inheritance, and enhanced conjugal autonomy and women's economic entitlements. Ongoing changes in social practice and civil-society mobilization reduced the value that various actors attached to patriliny, created a public ethos more favorable to women's entitlements, and thereby enabled such legal changes—although disagreements persisted about these policies among the political elite, who did not give personal law any more importance or value broad coalitions any less than they had soon after independence.

The shifts in personal law in these directions were far from complete, because prior traditions of law and kinship remained important considerations. For instance, legislators and judges enabled individuals to gain divorces without much delay if they could prove spousal fault or their divorce petitions had their spouse's consent, but not otherwise, and judges continued to attempt reconciliation, especially in the absence of mutual consent. This sometimes prevented the decline in the economic circumstances of the spouse with lower income and less property (usually the woman) that often followed divorce because alimony obligations were limited, alimony decrees were not effectively enforced, and rights in matrimonial property were not recognized. But it also restricted the ability of individuals to leave unsatisfactory and abusive relationships, especially if courts restored the respondent's conjugal rights rather than grant the petitioner's plea for divorce or judicial separation. Courts declared findings of cruelty more often when provided evidence of harassment short of physical violence, especially if it was meant to extract dowry, and took greater account of the effects of litigants' actions on their partners. But they varied in how they construed cruelty, sometimes taking women's responses to the harassment of spouses and in-laws to amount to cruelty. Judges more often made the conjugal behavior of divorcées and widows irrelevant to their claims to maintenance from their ex-husbands or to derive maintenance from their property, but were not unanimous in this regard. Courts more often recognized women's rights to participate in determining the location of their matrimonial homes. They especially considered it legitimate for women to reside close to their places of work, and did not allow their husbands to divorce them or compel women to live with their husbands if they lived separately for this reason, but some courts ruled differently. While the courts largely enabled conjugal autonomy in these respects, the Supreme Court's support for the judicial restoration of conjugal rights, after a high court judgment that deemed it unconstitutional, had the opposite effect.

Other changes in adjudication were unambiguous. Courts became more selective in finding adultery, in view of the decline in social barriers to interaction across gender lines. Moreover, they usually took the maintenance claims of spouses into account in their responses to allegations of matrimonial fault in petitions for divorce and judicial separation and petitions to restore conjugal rights; in addition, they resisted restitution petitions that seemed to be meant only to enable divorce later. Legislators reinforced the effects of these judicial practices by increasing women's rights to alimony, protection from domestic violence, and rights in the matrimonial home if they faced such abuse.

Legislators (a) gave daughters rights equal to those of sons in family joint property and over the ancestral home, (b) placed the inheritance rights of cognates on a par with those of agnates, (c) made the rules to inherit women's property the same as those to inherit men's property, (d) made the inheritance rights of widows in their deceased husbands' property independent of their current civil status, and (e) gave these modified inheritance rules of Hindu law priority over state-specific agrarian legislation in determining the devolution of agricultural land. However, they did not give widows rights in joint property similar to those of daughters, and indeed reduced their shares in such property. Moreover, they retained the joint ownership of property by kin rather than equalize the inheritance rights of nuclear family members by dissolving joint property into separate shares, and did not protect the inheritance shares of female kin by restricting testamentary rights. This helped them contain resistance to giving daughters equal rights in intestate joint property, but also made it likely that the majority of women will not gain control over much family joint property soon. Thus, these changes in Hindu law and commonly applicable matrimonial law did not reconstitute the family in entirely novel ways. Rather, they followed the pattern set in the first postcolonial decade of introducing culturally grounded reforms that underwrote certain emergent practices without requiring their rapid adoption, as the latter course seemed likely to generate considerable conflict or seriously erode support for the parties promoting the changes.

The judiciary was not united in deciding cases in new ways, even in the higher courts. Besides, the most far-reaching legislative changes were based on the enthusiastic support of only a minority of legislators, backed by certain rights organizations. The initiatives of a small number of actors gave married daughters coparcener status in joint property, extended increased protection and access to the matrimonial home to women facing domestic violence, and recently led the executive to propose enabling courts to apportion shares of matrimonial property on divorce. The first two changes were introduced because crucial actors in the ruling UPA were favorably disposed, and various legislators and parties with misgivings about them were reluctant to openly resist women's rights, to which the public ethos had become favorable. The narrow support for the most extensive reforms suggests that ambitious proposals currently being pressed by civil-society organizations are unlikely to be adopted soon—specifically those to limit testamentary rights and dissolve joint property in Hindu law.

CHAPTER 5

MINORITY ACCOMMODATION, CULTURAL MOBILIZATION, AND LEGAL PRACTICE
The Experiences of Muslim Law and Christian Law

PERSONAL LAW WAS AN IMPORTANT SPACE where Indian political elites developed their approaches to recognize, regulate, and form the religious minorities. The discourses they articulated about the nation and its cultural groups influenced their strategies regarding the minorities. This chapter explores how these discourses impinged on the personal laws of India's two largest religious minorities, the Muslims and the Christians. It also considers how alternative discourses of nation and community may have suggested other ways to make minorities and accommodate them in the core of the nation, rather than relegate them to its margins.

We saw in Chapter 2 that centralizing state elites that uphold homogeneous and formally inclusive visions of nations, as is the pattern in France, Turkey, and China, characterize the nation implicitly in terms of the practices and traditions of the majority and seek minority assimilation in many respects. Those that understand national culture largely with explicit reference to the ethnic, religious, or racial majority, as in Israel, Pakistan, Bangladesh, Thailand, and Malaysia, even while acknowledging cultural diversity, are likely to be unaware of sources of dynamism and variations in the traditions and practices of minorities, particularly those that are stereotyped as backward. This leads such majoritarian nationalists to (a) mainly accommodate dominant interpretations of minority cultures, (b) privilege conservative minority elites as the voices of group opinion, (c) adopt forms of recognition that are insensitive to emergent practices, ideas, and initiatives, and (d) not promote the same practices among these groups as they do among the majority. However, these actors sometimes promote reform and empower its agents more among minorities that they consider attuned to modernity, as happened at times in Egypt and Malaysia. State elites that incorporate the cultures of various identity groups into their understandings of the nation tend to adopt multicultural institutions, and mobilizers that do so support such institutions. If they emphasize cultural maintenance and the distinctness of group cultures, they are disposed to retain existing forms of recognition and limit cultural exchange, as happened in Lebanon. If instead they prioritize the transformation of indigenous cultures and highlight the overlap in group cultures, they are likely to (a) change the ways they accommodate both the minorities and the majority, (b) value the repertoires of different groups, (c) promote similar practices among various groups, and thus (d) build synthetic, inclusive, and dynamic national cultures. Such elites are more likely to engage with different currents among various groups and thus recognize initiatives for reform even among some groups stereotyped as backward. These patterns were seen in Indonesia.

The kinds of social coalitions that regimes aim to assemble also shape approaches to accommodation. Regimes that prioritize broad coalitions tend to limit the scope of reform, especially of practices about which mobilized opinion varies significantly. They are especially reluctant to change forms of minority accommodation if official narratives portray national culture largely in terms of majority mores and stereotype the concerned minorities as backward. Under such conditions, the personal laws of various minorities were barely changed: consider those of the Berber groups of Morocco and Algeria, the Muslims and Druze of Israel, the Hindus and Christians of Pakistan, the

Hindus and Buddhists of Bangladesh, and the Muslims of Thailand and the Philippines. However, some regimes that aimed for broad coalitions made moderate changes in the laws of minorities that they considered progressive (for example, the Egyptian government did so regarding the Copts, though the desire for broad support discouraged reform after a point), included minority representatives that favored reform (as the parties representing predominantly non-Muslim groups in Malaysia's ruling alliances did), or could base reform on aspects of the relevant group's norms of which they were aware (as happened with several of Indonesia's ethnic groups). The focus of Egyptian regimes on an Arab identity shared by the country's Christians, and of Indonesian regimes on a nondenominational monotheism in which all the country's citizens were taken to believe, also made these ruling elites more open to changing certain minority laws. Regimes that prioritized modernist social reform over broad support were willing to apply new laws to their minorities as well, especially if they did not value cultural diversity, as in Turkey.

How did ruling elites' discourses of nation and community and their coalition-building ambitions impinge on minority accommodation in Indian personal law? The majority of Indian nationalists considered the nation diverse and claimed that various religious and ethnic groups and regions belonged equally in the nation. The aspect of official discourse most relevant to personal law was the view of the Indian nation as a composite of religious (and ethnic) cultures. Proponents of this view varied in whether they presented the nation as an aggregate of distinct religious cultures or emphasized cultural overlap. While the aggregate view encouraged the recognition of distinct religious norms, the cultural-overlap view urged the promotion of similar norms among various religious groups. Indian policy makers recognized distinct personal-law systems, but also introduced similar rules in some of these systems.

While acknowledging the nation's diverse and composite character, we saw that the narratives of most Indian nationalists drew predominantly from the cultures of the Hindu groups with which they were most closely engaged. Moreover, many of them equated the Hindu and the culturally indigenous, and took groups practicing religions of foreign advent—Muslims, Christians, Zoroastrians, and Jews—to have stronger links to their transnational religious communities and traditions than to groups practicing religions originating in South Asia, or to the Indian cultural soil. They emphasized the pride that Indian Muslims were said to take in memories of Muslim dynasties of Central Asian origin and their affinity with the Islamic normative and jurisprudential traditions that emerged from the Arab world as signs of their uncertain relationship to the Indian nation. In a similar vein, they took Indian Christians to have a close affinity with European colonizers, churches, and missionaries. This made such apparently pluralist Indian nationalists uncertain about the role of these minorities in initiatives to give the nation a cohesive and indigenous cultural identity. It inclined them to consider the mobilization of the minorities as religious communities in tension with building national solidarity, although many Muslims and Christians participated in cross-religious initiatives against colonial rule. As a result, some of them believed that these groups needed to be specially accommodated to ensure their commitment to the nation. But others felt that such commitment was unlikely and so were predisposed to limit the public influence of these groups, as were the Hindu nationalists who more openly promoted Hindu hegemony.

Perceptions of the postcolonial roles of Muslims and Christians were similar in these ways, but differed in certain other respects. Muslims were not only much more numerous and politically influential, efforts to mobilize a national-level religious community had also proceeded further among them and created stronger demands to maintain the separate electorates through which minority political identity was recognized in the early twentieth century. Moreover, a movement to form a separate country for the group grew among Muslims, and was eventually successful. These were among the reasons why Hindu mobilizers came into conflict much more frequently with Muslims than with Christians. As a result, various Hindu political elites were more concerned about the political trajectories of Muslims, leading some of them to attend more to accommodating them and others to focus more on marginalizing them.

The majority of colonial intellectuals understood Islamic traditions to have taken shape through prolonged involution that rendered Muslims particularly resistant to post-Enlightenment modernity. The call of various *ulama* to resist Western education and maintain connections to Islamic learning and *shari'a* lent these discourses greater credibility with various Indian nationalists, who nevertheless drew different conclusions from them. Influenced by such claims as well as by certain secularist narratives that devalued religious norms, pluralist Indian nationalists such as Nehru felt that attachment to Islamic law was an aspect of Indian Muslim backwardness that needed to be temporarily accommodated. But their secularized outlook made them unreceptive to most distinctly Muslim cultural forms, and they believed that a UCC based on universalistic reasoning could be introduced once the postcolonial state promoted the socioeconomic status of Muslims and inculcated in them and others the virtues of modern national citizenship. The predominant colonial discourse about Muslims encouraged Hindu majoritarian Indian nationalists to associate the defense of Islamic law with a propensity to polygamy and unrestrained fertility, and to nurse fears about the Muslim demographic presence and its imminent growth. These impressions impelled them to quickly impose a UCC, drawn largely from Hindu norms, on Muslims and other minorities as part of an enforced assimilation into Indian modernity.[1]

Muslim Indian nationalists, such as Maulana Abul Kalam Muhiuddin Ahmed (popularly called Abul Kalam Azad), had rather different preferences about the roles of Muslims in the Indian nation and the course of Muslim law. They wished to retain a distinct Muslim law indefinitely and continue the pattern of Muslim law reform of the early twentieth century, which relied on widely recognized Islamic norms and interpretive methods to respond to various contemporary predicaments. They believed that Indian Muslims could thereby develop a distinctive approach to modernity and contribute to the ongoing development of a composite Indian national culture. Other Muslim leaders had played more central roles in initiating the Muslim law reforms of the 1930s, such as Maulana Husain Ahmad Madani of the Jamiyat Ulama-i-Hind (Association of Indian *Ulama*), or wished to promote more extensive culturally grounded changes in Muslim law after independence, like the jurist Asaf Ali Fyzee. While relying on the support of such leaders to counter the Pakistan movement, policy makers did not involve them in shaping postcolonial Muslim law or designing other forms of Muslim accommodation.[2]

Colonial narratives presented Christians rather differently, as a group with a special affinity with modern values. The emergence of the most powerful models of modernity in predominantly Christian societies, the promotion of Western education by Christian missionaries, and the leading roles of certain Indian Christians in social reform encouraged most Indian nationalists to internalize these narratives. The application of statutory laws based on British precedents to Christian personal life and the limited attention of late colonial Christian mobilizers to personal law led postcolonial policy makers to consider Christians likely partners in their efforts to promote modern family forms and introduce a UCC. Such orientations toward Christians were, however, in tension with the paternalistic attitude among most of these political elites toward the lower castes and tribes, the groups that converted to Christianity most extensively. Indeed, Indian nationalists such as Gandhi, who uneasily combined advocacy of a syncretic public spirituality with an inclination to protect Hindu community boundaries, came into conflict with Christian missionaries over their conversion of the lower castes. Moreover, the image of Christians as agents of modernization only reinforced the concerns of some Hindus that Christian elites might continue to link themselves to various Western forces and the extensive resources at their disposal, aid further Hindu conversion to Christianity, gain greater public prominence, and weaken indigenous cultural forms.

The impressions of the nation and its religious groups among the majority of policy makers urged them to accommodate the minorities, including in personal law. Their vision of Muslims and Christians suggested that they would promote reform and its agents more extensively among Christians. However, state elites considered Muslim accommodation more of a priority and found that Muslims gave personal law far more attention. This led them to base their approaches to the other minority laws mainly on their strategy regarding Muslim law soon after independence. Their limited engagement with minority initiatives and traditions, their inclination to build broad coalitions, and their stereotypes of Muslim backwardness led them not to change the minority laws in the first postcolonial generation, although reformist opinion was no weaker among the minorities than among Hindus. Moreover, they informally suggested that these laws would be changed only as a result of group initiative, and usually took conservative religious and political elites to be the voice of the minorities, particularly regarding personal law. Such a pattern of policy consultation seemed to make minority law reform unlikely.

However, the minority laws underwent some change starting in the 1970s. The growth of reformist mobilization among the religious minorities and the engagement of more Hindu activists, intellectuals, and policy makers with such initiatives made policy elites more aware that the traditions, practices, and initiatives of these groups offered bases for personal law reform. As a result, judges changed Muslim law to give divorcées alimony or a share of their ex-husbands' property and to restrict men's right to unilaterally repudiate their wives, and struck down statutory Christian law provisions that provided men and women the right to claim divorce on limited and dissimilar grounds. Moreover, in some states they also granted Muslim women divorces from their bigamous husbands and gave Christian couples the right to adopt children rather than to act only as their guardians.

Legislators continued to be influenced by the view that Muslims favor reform less than other groups; at times they accommodated the suggestions of reformist mobilizers and judges regarding Christian and Parsi law, but not with regard to Muslim law, especially as greater support emerged among Christians and Parsis than among Muslims for specific personal law reforms. They equalized the divorce rights of Christian men and women and provided Christians and Parsis divorce rights on new grounds including mutual consent. But they did not accommodate the demands of Muslim organizations, both conservative and reformist, to give Muslim women throughout India the right to inherit the shares of agricultural land that Islamic law prescribes. Nor did they clearly support judicial initiatives to increase the economic support that divorcées could get from their ex-husbands or to limit unilateral male repudiation among Muslims. Most legislators remained inadequately aware of the support that Islamic norms offered for these changes. Even while they introduced certain changes in Christian law, legislators resisted demands to make Christians eligible to adopt children, because they feared this would enable a growth in the Christian share of the population. The growth of Hindu nationalism as well as of conversion to Christianity since the 1980s had added to the fears among many political elites that Christians might use their transnational links to weaken Hindu hegemony and Indian national cohesion.

Both judges and legislators attended to cultural accommodation while they changed the minority laws. For instance, certain courts provided alimony to Muslim divorcées by taking the criminal law provisions concerning alimony to apply to Muslims (in opposition to the contrary interpretations of other courts), by interpreting statutes concerning economic support for divorced Muslim women to require alimony, and by alluding to commentaries that took some verses of the Qur'an to require men to support their ex-wives for the rest of their lives. Judges and legislators changed Christian divorce law with reference to the more extensive practice and acceptance of divorce in mainline Protestant churches and among Christian laity, and the mobilization of many important Christian clerical and lay organizations in favor of increased divorce rights. While the courts also grounded these reforms on the constitutional rights to equality, equal protection, life, and personal liberty, policy makers changed the minority laws only when group laws, norms, or initiatives offered justification for the specific changes.

We now examine the processes through which Muslim law and Christian law were formed and changed in postcolonial India, with greater attention to Muslim law.

I. CULTURAL AND LEGAL CURRENTS OF THE LATE COLONIAL PERIOD

A. Approaches to Muslim Law: Mobilization and Legislation

Religious mobilization addressed personal law most consistently through the colonial period among Muslims. Various Muslim elites, particularly in North India, felt that the decline of the Mughal empire, the defeat of the Great Rebellion of 1857, the attendant consolidation of colonial rule, the formation of partly secularized public arenas, and the sharpening of religious boundaries in a society in which they were a minority were signposts of community decline. To respond to these changes, many of them adopted somewhat novel approaches to Islamic reasoning, and built new religious and political institutions. Both *ulama* and Western-educated professional elites drew in innovative ways on earlier discursive traditions to change Islamic law in response to contemporary circumstances. These initiatives changed the ways in which disputes were resolved in the state courts as well as in the *ulama*-run community courts, made Islamic law more uniform, abridged the role of customs that did not have a definite basis in classical Islamic traditions and were often shared with the members of other religious groups, and increased the rights of women and nuclear family members in certain respects. They were framed as ways to purify Islamic practices and revitalize the Muslim community. Concerns to build broad coalitions for various projects and maintain religious boundaries inflected these initiatives, limited the abridgement of custom, and shaped and restricted the promotion of women's rights.

Paul Brass claimed that *ulama* educated in *madrassas* (Islamic schools) and Muslim professional elites educated in institutions run by the colonial government or Christian churches responded very differently to the changes under colonial rule.[3] He argued that the "traditionalist" *ulama* defended precolonial Islamic law, at least in the sphere of personal life to which the colonial state restricted it, while the "modernist" Western-educated professional elite fully accepted the incorporation of Islamic jurisprudence within a common law-framework and interpreted the contemporary meaning of Islam more innovatively. More careful analyses show that both groups approached religious texts and Islamic law in novel ways from the eighteenth century, although the *ulama* more often claimed to continue earlier religious traditions.

Various prominent *ulama* resorted with greater frequency to legal innovation from the eighteenth century onward, specifically employing *takhayyur* (selective borrowing from other *madhhabs*) and *ijtihad* (innovative legal interpretation) in a departure from the emphasis of most Sunni *ulama* until then on authoritative commentaries, *taqlid* (following interpretive precedent) and *qiyas* (reasoning by analogy). Shah Waliullah Dehlavi, a Delhi-based scholar of the eighteenth century, was an important forerunner of this trend, whose ideas influenced the major Islamic religious institutions thereafter. Western-educated Muslim elites also resorted to *ijtihad*, but in a somewhat different way. The orthodox view among the Sunni *ulama* was that only the founding figures of the major *madhhabs* and certain other major scholars who lived in the early Islamic centuries had the competence and authority to independently interpret the founding texts of Islam and its *madhhabs*. This led them, even over the last two centuries, to employ *takhayyur* and *ijtihad* only as a collective body, in response to major questions to which they found no satisfactory answer in the current approaches of their *madhhab*, with copious reference to authoritative commentaries, and after considerable dialogue.

Some Western-educated Muslims felt freer to engage in *ijtihad* in their individual capacity, referred more often to recent reformist commentaries, and oriented their legal reasoning to arrive at rules conducive to greater professional and material success, and to wresting from the *ulama* the authority to interpret the call of Islam. The educational reformer Sir Sayyid Ahmed Khan, the early Indian nationalist and jurist Badruddin Tyabji, the poet Mohammad Iqbal, and the legal scholar Asaf Ali Fyzee were among the prominent professional elites who engaged in or called for *ijtihad* along these lines. Most of them relied, however, on much the same interpretive methods and sources as the *ulama*, and some of them were closely allied with particular *ulama*. This was because some of them were trained by *ulama* in addition to attending Western educational institutions. This was true of Sir Sayyid Ahmed Khan and many other members of the Mughal service gentry, Sayyid Mumtaz Ali (who interpreted Islamic law to provide women extensive rights in the late nineteenth century), and Abul Kalam Azad. As a result, many professionals and *ulama* jointly piloted various reform initiatives, although members of these groups also criticized each other sharply in other contexts.

From the mid-nineteenth century, the *ulama* built larger religious institutions, notably the Darul Uloom Deoband (DUD), the Ahle Sunnat wal Jama'at and its Darul Uloom Manzar-e-Islam (DUMI) of Bareilly, the Darul Uloom Nadwatul Ulama of Lucknow, and the Jama'at Ahl-e-Hadith, to develop understandings of the normative Islamic practices appropriate for the times, urge Muslims to adopt such practices, and build groups of similarly trained scholars. They initially resisted the colonial state's restriction of the application of Islamic law to personal life, but shifted from the late nineteenth century to a defense of Muslim personal law as it operated in the state courts. Some *ulama* trained in the DUD also built institutionalized religious court systems and urged Muslims to take their disputes to these courts, in which the judges reasoned primarily based on Islamic jurisprudence—in which they were well trained, unlike the judges in the state courts. The largest of these was the Imarat-e-Shariah, headquartered in Phulwari Sharif in Bihar, northern India. Some *ulama* demanded that the government establish such a system of sharia courts.[4]

Many *ulama* sought to build a more certain religious-law system, perhaps in response to such expectations emerging from the colonial legal system. They promoted a return to authoritative religious texts and texts of religious law, and a reduction in the recognition of customs that did not enjoy clear support in these texts. This was a move away from the extensive reliance of *qadis,* through Islamic history in many regions, on customs not clearly contrary to Islamic legal traditions in their adjudication. Some texts of the seventeenth and eighteenth centuries that advocated such a reliance on custom, notably the work of the Arab scholar ibn Abidin, influenced many adherents of the Hanafi school in the Arab world, Central Asia, and South Asia. Although ibn Abidin's work remained influential among the *ulama*, the majority of them, including those belonging to the networks centered around the DUD and the DUMI, came to consider it crucial to distinguish the laws governing India's Muslims from the laws of non-Muslims, and reduce the prevalence of customs shared with Hindus, purify Islamic practice, build Muslim solidarity, and sharpen religious boundaries.[5] Many influential *ulama* supported certain customs that found direct support only in Hindu texts, but were also widely practiced by South Asian Muslims—even while they framed their efforts as abridging such customs. But they felt pressed to find support for these practices in classical Islamic texts, as Maulana Ashraf Ali Thanawi did for caste endogamy in the *hadith*.[6]

The majority of the Jamiyat Ulama-i-Hind's members supported Indian nationalism after the organization was formed in 1919, and a minority supported the Pakistan movement in the last colonial decade. Engaging such visions of territorially rooted political communities did not make them any more receptive, however, to South Asian customs not based in classical Islamic norms. By way of contrast, many *ulama* in various Muslim-majority societies in the Arab world and Southeast Asia incorporated more local customs not clearly supported by authoritative Islamic texts in Islamic law, to give Islamic traditions stronger indigenous roots.

Certain groups that account for the majority of Indian Muslims, the *ajlaf* and *arzal* (plebeian/lower-middle caste and lower-caste Muslims), did not claim ancestry in West and Central Asia, as the *ashraf* (elite/upper-caste Muslims) did. Their movements, such as the Momin Tehreek, focused on the experiences of caste-based subordination that these groups shared with castes of similar status among the Hindus, Christians, and Sikhs. This created the potential for them to imagine Indian Muslim law to include South Asian practices that cross religious boundaries and do not have clear roots in classical Islamic norms. This potential was not realized, because these movements did not articulate distinct religious discourses or address personal law, and gained much less support than the organizations of similarly ranked castes affiliated with India's other religions.[7]

Many Muslim professional elites aimed to abridge regional customs too, but unlike the *ulama* they thereby sought to promote Muslim political solidarity more than to purify Islamic practice. They joined forces with the *ulama* to demand a reduction in the recognition of such customs, which the colonial courts especially applied to inheritance in many regions. These efforts resulted in the passage in 1937 of the Shariat Act, which made Islamic law rather than local custom the basis on which to regulate the personal lives of Muslims. Support for this goal extended across the emerging divide between the supporters of Indian nationalism and the Pakistan movement. Indeed, although Mohammad Ali Jinnah was by then the main leader of the Pakistan movement, his piloting the act through the Central Assembly did not reduce its support among Muslim Indian nationalists. Despite the act's abridgement of the recognition of regional customs, it was framed through a compromise with the powerful votaries of particular customs. Landholding elites ensured that customs that gave patrilineages control over property would continue to govern the inheritance of agricultural land among Muslims in much of India, rather than individual kin being allowed to inherit such land following the prescriptions of Islamic law. The political elites that piloted the act claimed that the inheritance of agricultural land was exempted from the purview of Islamic law because the provincial legislatures had authority over this subject, whereas it was the Central Assembly that passed the Shariat Act. However, the path to the compromise was paved in the Punjab earlier, where the large landholders who led the ruling Unionist Party had blocked the efforts of the Jamiyat Ulama-i-Hind and the Muslim League to end the application of Punjabi customary law to land inheritance a few years earlier.[8]

Muslim political elites prioritized broad coalitions more once the demand for Pakistan emerged, whether they supported or opposed it. This inclined those that proposed the Shariat Act to accommodate the preference of landed elites, who were their important supporters. While *ulama* were less concerned with coalition building, they too were influenced by their dependence on the patronage of landed groups. Thus, when Islamic law was applied to the inheritance of agricultural land in various regions (in Bengal, Assam, and Bombay Presidency in the 1900s, in the Northwest Frontier Province and the princely state of Hyderabad in the 1930s, in Madras Presidency in 1949, and in Kerala in 1963), neither major *ulama* nor most Muslim political elites pressed for this change. Moreover, *ulama* remained reluctant to press vigorously for this reform even later. The main organization that organized their personal law initiatives since its formation in 1972, the All India Muslim Personal Law Board (AIMPLB), supported the Shariat Act's application to agricultural land from the outset, but did not demand this change of the government until 2006 and did not mobilize much for this goal at any point.

Both professional elites and *ulama* supported the Mussulman Wakf Validating Act (MWVA) in 1913 and the Dissolution of Muslim Marriages Act (DMMA) in 1939. The MWVA approved bequests to family members, which parents sometimes used to give property to their daughters rather than to extended kin. The DMMA increased women's divorce rights by borrowing certain rules from Maliki law, which governed virtually no Indian Muslims. It declared that a marriage would not be annulled by the apostasy of a party to the marriage (contrary to the predominant view in Hanafi law, which governs the vast majority of Indian Muslims), and enabled women to obtain divorces on other grounds at a time when Hindu law did not provide divorce rights.[9] While women gained new rights thereby, the main motive of this act's sponsors was to ensure that Muslim women would not feel pressed to resort to apostasy to gain divorces, as they feared this would reduce the Muslim community's numerical strength and blur its boundaries.

The engagement of certain *ulama* in increasing women's rights through the legislation of the 1930s, albeit only in very specific circumstances and with a view to enabling group consolidation, contrasted with the opposition of major Hindu religious leaders at the time to proposals to reform Hindu law. These initiatives strengthened the conviction of many Muslims that a body of authoritative *ulama* could derive effective responses to contemporary predicaments from Islamic traditions through collective *ijtihad*. Despite the *ulama*'s success in influencing legislation, their demand that Muslim judges alone should consider Muslim divorce cases was not accommodated. This reinforced their inclination to urge their followers to seek community courts.

Some Muslims, particularly the increasing numbers of women active in public life, called for more extensive Muslim law reforms in the last colonial decades. Muslim women's organizations such as the Anjuman-i-Khavatin-i-Islam, Muslim women's journals such as *Tahzib un-Niswan, Sharif Bibi, Khatun* and *Avaz-i-Niswan,* and Muslim leaders of the All India Women's Conference (AIWC) particularly voiced these demands. The Anjuman-i-Khavatin-i-Islam demanded that polygamy and unilateral male repudiation no longer be recognized and that the minimum marriage age be increased from fourteen to sixteen; it drew support from various male Muslim public intellectuals. While she was president of the AIWC in the 1930s, Begum Sharifa Hamid Ali prepared a model *nikahnama* (marriage contract) that gave women the *talaq-i-tafwid* (delegated divorce right) if their husbands married other women without their consent or failed to fulfill other conditions stipulated in the contract, without requiring these women to forfeit their *mahr* (dower), as Hanafi law required if women initiated divorce petitions. Baji Rashida Latif, Begum Hafeezuddin, and Begum Qudsia Aizaz Rasul, leaders of the Muslim League (the last of whom joined the Congress Party after independence), demanded the application of Islamic law to the inheritance of agricultural land too.[10] These demands gained greater support once organizations representing women, and Muslim women in particular, became stronger from the 1970s.

Early postcolonial policy did not engage with these vigorous initiatives for Muslim law reform. The involvement of many Muslims in the Congress Party could have lent the party's Muslim leaders a greater voice in shaping the ways in which Muslims were accommodated. The likes of Azad wanted to maintain the momentum behind Muslim law reform, give Muslim cultural practices greater representation in official nationalist discourses, and perhaps incorporate features of Islamic legal tradition in a future UCC if it were left optional. However, the party's most influential leaders, particularly Nehru, understood these concerns poorly. They accommodated the preference of the Congress Party's Muslim leaders to retain a distinct Muslim law, but missed the opportunity to involve them in framing further culturally grounded changes in these laws and promoting Muslim support for these reforms.

B. Christian Mobilization

Christian groups did not address personal law in the late colonial decades, but some differences between Christian and Muslim mobilization through these years influenced the approaches these groups took to personal law later. Although Christians were much smaller in number than the Muslims (these groups accounted for 2.0 percent and 24.3 percent respectively of the Indian population in the last colonial census of 1941), the Christians were more diverse than the Muslims in their religious organization and forms of worship. Many Christian denominations were present in India, and the evangelical churches had especially grown rapidly since the late nineteenth century, increasing the Christian share of the population from 0.7 percent in 1881 to 2 percent in 1941.[11] There were significant differences in religious practice, social organization, and social status between the Orthodox, Catholic, and Protestant churches, between groups that converted to Christianity during British rule and those that had become Christian several centuries earlier, and between different castes. The earlier converts, especially those belonging to the Orthodox churches, belonged predominantly to the upper and upper-middle castes, and recent converts and evangelicals belonged more to the lower castes and tribal groups. Groups that had became Christian well before British rule had developed distinct indigenous religious practices and indigenous clergies, and were mostly Orthodox and Catholic. The groups that converted during British rule and later were predominantly Protestant, and their largely European and American episcopal hierarchies initially transplanted the religious practices of their churches from Europe and the United States. But the Catholics among these groups retained many pre-Christian practices. The many lower and lower-middle castes that had converted to Islam aligned themselves with the upper-caste-led Muslim religious organizations formed in the nineteenth century. In contrast, most lower caste and tribal Christians belonged to distinct churches, and did not support the efforts of Christian elites to mobilize a national Christian community, for instance behind the

All India Conference of Indian Christians.[12] Moreover, the Indian nationalist movement mobilized only a minority of Christians because of the affinity that some Christians felt with the colonial state, the opposition of many Indian nationalist leaders (particularly Gandhi) to the conversion of lower caste and tribal groups to Christianity, and the limited mobilization of lower caste and tribal groups that were particularly numerous among the Christians.[13] The low levels of mobilization of Christians as a national community led Hindu hegemonists to see them as less of a threat than Muslims; but their lower support for Indian nationalism and greater recent success in converting Hindus contributed to Hindu fears of their transnational links and public influence.

The reform initiatives of the European clergy, like those of the major *ulama*, were based on models of religious behavior that emerged among their coreligionists outside South Asia. They urged the abandonment of certain indigenous practices, such as polytheism, animism, polygyny, and child marriage. Some Indian Christians, particularly recent Protestant converts from the upper and middle castes, discouraged the above practices but promoted indigenization and the adoption of certain Hindu practices concerning worship, religious organization, and spiritual understanding much more than Muslim mobilizers did. They also pressed without much success for the greater inclusion of Indians in episcopal hierarchies.[14] Christian cultural indigenization did not address personal law in the colonial period, but the revaluation of certain indigenous practices enabled later personal-law reform initiatives to base themselves on emergent local Christian practices. It also made Christians more open than Muslims at times to a UCC. Moreover, the codification and reform of the canon laws of the world's major churches since the early twentieth century made Christians more receptive to personal law reform.

C. *The Courts and Contentious Questions in the Minority Laws*

Litigants contested the rules according to which certain kinds of personal disputes were resolved in Muslim law and Christian law, and the courts changed how they resolved them in certain respects over the last generation. Muslims especially contested the validity of unilateral male repudiation and the conditions under which it would be valid, the economic consequences of divorce, the validity of polygamy, bequests to family members, and the implications of apostasy for the status of marriages; Christians litigated the conditions under which divorce would be accessible and the possibility of adoption. Of these questions, colonial-era legislation only resolved the validity of family bequests and the implications of apostasy among Muslims. Colonial judicial precedents were the points of departure for postcolonial litigation on the other questions.

i. Muslim Law. The colonial state's rhetoric of noninterference in religious practices, the judges' limited knowledge of Islamic traditions, the uncertainty of Sunni orthodoxy about contemporary *ijtihad,* and the resistance of most Muslim mobilizers to novel interpretations of Islamic law by non-Muslims and nonexperts in Islamic law shaped the basic posture of the colonial courts toward Muslim law. The courts were reluctant to interpret the founding texts of Islam and its major *madhhabs* independently, and generally followed what they understood to be the verdicts favored by the *ulama* of the litigants' *madhhab.* They sometimes applied the predominant interpretation in Hanafi jurisprudence to all Muslims, but applied the rules of the litigants' *madhhab* in other contexts. The courts recognized the rules of the non-Hanafi schools, for instance the Shia rules regarding inheritance and the right to *mahr* (dower) on divorce, and, for the minority of Indian Sunnis governed by Shafi'i law, a bar on women retrospectively repudiating marital alliances contracted when they were minors or to which they did not consent. The Ithna Ashari, the Nizari Ismaili, and the Musta'lian Ismaili schools, which together govern most Indian Shias, apportion inheritance rights equally to agnates and cognates and give women the right to retain their dower after divorces they initiate, in contrast with the various Sunni schools that prioritize the inheritance rights of agnates and require women to forego their dower after divorces they initiate. Shafi'i law does not allow women to repudiate marital alliances retrospectively, while Hanafi law permits this until the consummation of the marriage or until the woman turns eighteen.

The most common form in which divorces occur among Indian Muslims is the *talaq ul-ba'in* (unilateral and immediately irrevocable male repudiation), pronounced by the husband in a verbal or written statement that he is immediately ending the marriage. It typically involves the man repeating thrice that he is divorcing his wife ("*talaq, talaq, talaq*," called the triple *talaq*), thereby giving the divorce immediate effect. If the man makes the statement just once, he is taken to indicate his plan to divorce his wife, but his pronouncement of divorce remains open to reconsideration during *iddat* (period of waiting, lasting three menstrual cycles of usual duration, three months, or until the end of the woman's pregnancy if she was pregnant when the husband announced his intention to divorce her). If the spouses do not resume their relationship, the divorce takes effect at the end of *iddat*. The early Islamic community recognized only the revocable mode of pronouncement of divorce, which alone left space for the man to reconsider his plan to end his marriage and for the couple to attempt reconciliation, as recommended in the Qur'an 4:35. All *madhhabs* consider irrevocable repudiation irregular, and prefer that the husband's initial pronouncement of divorce be revocable through *iddat*, during which they recommend efforts at spousal reconciliation. Of the major schools in India, the Hanafi and Shafi'i schools recognize divorces pronounced irrevocably as taking immediate effect; but the Ithna Ashari, Musta'lian Isma'ili, and Ahl-i-Hadith schools consider even such pronouncements initially revocable.

The majority of colonial courts considered immediately irrevocable divorces valid, following the predominant Hanafi interpretation, even among Muslims belonging to *madhhabs* that consider such divorces open to reconsideration during *iddat*. They did so although this did not comport with the judges' preference for durable marital bonds or the practices valued in the early Islamic community and in all *madhhabs*. A judgment of the Bombay High Court in 1905 standardized the rationale for this position, saying that immediately irrevocable unilateral male repudiation was "good in law, though bad in theology."[15] The courts followed this precedent until 1978, varying only on whether the divorce might be pronounced in the wife's absence and on the standards of proof for the pronouncement of divorce (from none to oral or written evidence).[16] Some judges expressed misgivings about the insecurity that the ready availability of unilateral male repudiation caused Muslim women, but claimed that Islamic tradition required them to recognize such divorces.[17]

The courts required Muslim men to provide for their ex-wives only through *iddat*. In addition, some required these men to give the women any gifts the women might have received. They required Shias to pay or return the women's dower—which the man's natal family typically controlled while the couple was married—requiring Sunnis to return it as well unless the woman initiated the divorce petition. Maintenance was decreed for longer periods only in the exceptional cases in which marriage contracts required it.[18] The period through which the man was obliged to support his ex-wife depended on when the courts took the divorce to have taken effect: when witnesses attested that the man orally pronounced divorce (even in the wife's absence); when the man wrote a divorce statement; when the woman learned of the divorce; or when the man stated in court that he had repudiated the woman. Men were required to provide maintenance from when they stopped supporting their wives until three months after the date on which the divorce took effect. These judicial verdicts were based on the assumption that only one of the forms of support from husbands to ex-wives mentioned in the Qur'an was mandatory—*nafaqa* (maintenance during *iddat*, mentioned in Qu'ran 4:34) and not *mata* (usually translated as provision, mentioned in Qur'an 2:236, 240, and 241). All Islamic jurists considered *nafaqa* mandatory if the wife had submitted to her husband's authority. But most Hanafi jurists gave the ex-husband discretion over whether to grant *mata* and how much support it would provide. The other *madhhabs* in India consider *mata* obligatory, but *qazis* of these schools do not appear to have systematically required such transactions. Various litigants contested colonial precedents regarding unilateral repudiation and the economic consequences of divorce, leading to reforms from the 1970s onward.

ii. Christian Law. Colonial Christian law applied to both European Christians living in India and Indian Christians, although the colonial state governed these groups differently in other respects. The major Christian-law statutes, adopted in the 1860s and 1870s, were drawn from the British matrimonial legislation of the time. Some of these acts bore the "Indian" rather than the "Christian" label (such as the Indian Divorce Act (IDA) and the Indian Succession Act (ISA)) even if they applied only to Christians.[19] The greater codification of Christian law than of Muslim law (whose first statutes were introduced only in the twentieth century) divested Christian law of an appearance of association with divinity. If Christians felt that their laws had transcendent moral value, this feeling pertained to church canon rather than the Christian laws operative in the courts. This was in contrast with many Muslims, who attributed divine significance not only to *shari'a* but sometimes also to Muslim personal law. These circumstances made the Christians feel that their personal laws and their religious identities were less intimately linked.

Some features of Christian law were meant to influence the interactions between European Christians and other groups. For instance, couples in which only one of the partners was a Christian were allowed to register their marriages under the Indian Christian Marriage Act (ICMA) to encourage Europeans who had non-Christian partners to marry them, thereby legitimize their children, and raise them as Christians. This was in contrast with the application of the other personal laws only to couples in which both parties belonged to the relevant religious group. While wishing to urge more conjugal partners to marry, colonial administrators and judges were reluctant to enable non-Europeans to inherit property in Britain. As a result, they did not give Christians the right to adopt children, preventing propertied Britons from adopting Indian children and thus making them eligible to inherit shares of their property in Britain. Christian couples could be guardians of children, but their wards did not have the rights either to receive maintenance from their parents once they attained adulthood or to inherit family property. A few courts, however, recognized the adoption customs of particular Indian Christian groups. Moreover, the ICMA enabled only ministers of the Anglican, Scottish Presbyterian, and Catholic churches, which had closer links to the colonial state, to solemnize marriages, and required government certification before ministers of other churches could do so.[20]

Litigants contested the somewhat restricted room for divorce that the IDA provided and, to a lesser extent, the absence of adoption rights. The IDA enabled men to seek divorce on the sole ground of adultery, but allowed women to do so only if (a) they could demonstrate adultery as well as another spousal fault (bigamy, such cruelty as would entitle them to judicial separation, or desertion without a reasonable excuse for at least two years), (b) their husband had engaged in incestuous adultery, rape, sodomy, or bestiality, or (c) their husband had converted to another religion and married another woman.[21]

Moreover, it required a three-judge bench of the relevant High Court to ratify the divorce decrees of district courts; if the case hinged on a claim of adultery, the adulterer had to be made a corespondent. This act was based largely on the English Matrimonial Causes Act of 1857, and directed the courts to base their judgments on current English matrimonial law. The majority of colonial courts considered Christian divorce cases on the more extensive divorce grounds made available in England after the IDA's passage, but some abided by the rules mentioned in the IDA. The tendency of many courts to consider Christian law cases in the light of current British law attenuated Christian concerns about the growing gap between the IDA's rules and Indian Christian opinion and practice. However, most courts ruled after independence that British legislation was no longer relevant to adjudication, and relied on the nineteenth-century Indian statutes until Christian divorce statutes were changed in 2001.[22] Under these circumstances, Christians found that access to divorce was difficult, and in most instances required demonstration of adultery.[23] The divorce rights of Christians were far more limited than those of other religious groups after the HMA's passage, and Christian divorce procedures were also more cumbersome. This made an increase in divorce rights the main Christian demand regarding personal law for almost six decades. It was the focus of an unsuccessful private member's bill in the Central Legislature in 1941, and of other such bills from the 1950s onward.

II. THE FORMATION OF EARLY POSTCOLONIAL POLICY

We saw in Chapter 3 that the Constituent Assembly and the courts considered the future course of minority law soon after independence. All Muslim members of the Constituent Assembly wished to retain distinct personal laws, but were open to changing personal law based on the concerned community's consent. Mohammad Ismail, B. Pocker Sahib, and Mahboob Ali Baig of the Muslim League argued that the right to religious freedom required that religious groups with distinct personal laws be allowed to retain these laws. The links they claimed between religious practice and personal law suggested that distinct personal laws should be indefinitely retained. They tried without success to add to the clause of the Constitution about a UCC the qualification that "any group, section or community of people shall not be obliged to give up its own personal law in case it has such a law."[24]

Naziruddin Ahmad and Hussain Imam, also of the Muslim League, rested their case for the retention of distinct personal laws on current social conditions rather than on personal law being based on religious jurisprudence. Unlike Mohammad Ismail, Pocker Sahib, and Mahboob Ali Baig, they supported the future introduction of a UCC. Hussain Imam clearly said: "I feel that it is all right and a very desirable thing to have a uniform law, but at a very distant date." Given the earlier history of British noninterference in the personal laws, he and Naziruddin Ahmad argued, the state needed to secure the consent of the concerned group before changing its personal laws or introducing a UCC. They believed that current opinion required that such changes be gradual, and that an increase in the literacy and social power of the majority of members of all the religious groups was necessary before such reforms would enjoy considerable support. Naziruddin Ahmad suggested mechanisms to consult community representatives through elections in which the political representatives would commit themselves to a particular position on their group's personal law, but could not get the Constituent Assembly to agree that "the personal law of any community which has been guaranteed by the statute shall not be changed except with the previous approval of the community."[25] Hussain Imam even seemed open to the application of Hindu law to Muslims if Hindu law had been reformed so that it was more egalitarian than Muslim law, but opposed such a course in 1951 because the reforms then being proposed would not, in his judgment, have made Hindu law sufficiently egalitarian.[26]

As the Muslim community was in some disarray amid the violence and population movements that accompanied Pakistan's formation, even the Muslim representatives who were open to changes in Muslim law did not propose specific reforms along these lines at that time. The positions of the Muslim representatives, the disengagement of most policy makers from Muslim initiatives, and the failure to involve Muslim leaders of the Congress Party in designing Muslim accommodation resulted in no changes being made in Muslim law. Some Christians approached the Law Ministry in the early 1950s to expand the grounds on which Christians could gain divorces.[27] But, policy makers did not address this demand then. They presented their decision not to change the minority laws as a matter of noninterference. But it was a result of their disengagement from minority mobilization and their failure to base their visions of the modern Indian family on the perspectives and cultures of the religious minorities. However, they made an informal commitment that minority-law reforms would be possible only based on the concerned group's initiative. In choosing not to change personal law based on constitutional principles, the courts reinforced these executive decisions.

III. POSTCOLONIAL INITIATIVES FOR CULTURAL AND LEGAL CHANGE

Changes gradually occurred in the practices, opinions, and initiatives of the religious minorities regarding personal life; in the patterns of mobilization of women's organizations and other rights organizations; in the vision of the national family that policy makers sought to promote; in policy makers' understandings of minority norms and initiatives; and in the conditions under which judges and legislators were willing to change the rules regulating family life. They revived public debate about minority-law reform especially from the 1970s onward, and enabled changes in Muslim, Parsi and, Christian law. Policy makers changed the minority laws only if they were convinced that the reforms enjoyed support in the concerned group's norms and initiatives. They thus reconciled minority-law reform with recognition in personal law.

A. Cultural and Legal Mobilization

As we saw in Chapter 4, women's organizations and other rights organizations increased in strength, engaged in more mass mobilization, became more autonomous of political parties, built networks with legislators, judges, and bureaucrats, and gained more direct roles in policy making from the 1970s onward.[28] They increased their engagement in mobilization and litigation regarding personal law, and so did community organizations. The major conservative Muslim religious and community institutions formed the AIMPLB in 1972 to defend judicial precedent in Muslim law, prevent a UCC, and block the uniform adoption law that parliament was then considering (inasmuch as they did not believe that Islamic norms supported adoption). In response to the growth of a public ethos that favored certain rights for women, Hindu nationalists increased their criticisms of gender-unequal practices among Muslims and the support that Muslim law offered for some such practices, and called for the rapid introduction of a UCC to effect national consolidation behind their cultural vision. They especially did so after *Shah Bano* (1985). Their failure to offer specific proposals regarding the UCC's content or to begin a public debate about it suggested that their rhetoric about a UCC was meant to isolate Muslims rather than to enable legal change.[29]

The growth of Hindu nationalism, the attendant increase in attacks on non-Hindus, and the increased emphasis of Hindu nationalists on a UCC led various women's organizations, other rights organizations, and reformist lawyers' associations to value cultural accommodation more, and focus their attention on personal law reform rather than a UCC. Some of their activists explored Islamic and Christian traditions, to rebut Hindu nationalist criticisms of these traditions and incorporate their more gender-equal features in family law. Their reliance on group norms favorable to women helped them build alliances with reformist community organizations, and reduced the ability of conservatives to oppose their proposals as attacks on group identity.[30]

i. Mobilization Regarding Muslim Law.   Conservative Muslim elites faced more direct and extensive challenges from the 1980s onward. Associations of Muslim women and liberal Muslims grew and promoted various changes in gendered practices and Muslim law. Most of them were based in major cities, but had activists in smaller towns. They included the All India Muslim Women's Rights Network, *Awaaz-e-Niswan*, the Muslim Women's Forum, the Committee for the Protection of the Rights of Muslim Women, STEPS, *Bazm-i Shama-i Niswaan*, the Bharatiya Muslim Mahila Andolan, the Progressive Muslim Association, the Hindustani Muslim Forum, and the Muslim Satyashodhak Samaj.[31]

These organizations advocated the reforms that the state courts later introduced in Muslim alimony and divorce law. But their demands were more ambitious, including the invalidation and perhaps the criminalization of polygamous marriages, an end to the recognition of unilateral male repudiation or the inclusion of *talaq-i-tafwid* in all marital contracts, the extension of inheritance rights in agricultural land to women in all Indian states, the abandonment of the requirement that Sunni women forego their dower if they petition for divorce in community courts, a substantial increase in dower amounts, giving women rather than their husbands' natal families control over their dower after their marriages, an end to the practice of dowry, enabling women to reject marital alliances forged by family patriarchs against their will or when they were minors, greater openness on the part of community courts to women's pleas for divorce with or without the husband's consent (*khul'* and *faskh-i-nikah* respectively), and the inclusion of women in prayer groups and thus in mosque councils, or the establishment of separate mosques for women. Some of these proposals were incorporated into model marital contracts, which were revised versions of Begum Sharifa Hamid Ali's draft of the 1930s. The Women's Research and Action Group in Mumbai proposed such a model contract in 1993, and began a debate about the norms on which Muslim marriages should be based.

Four new organizations were formed in 2005 to offer perspectives different from the AIMPLB's regarding Muslim law. In response to the dominance of representatives of the DUD over the AIMPLB, two alternative boards emerged, which claimed to represent Shias (the All India Shia Personal Law Board) and the followers of the DUMI (the All India Muslim (Jadeed) Personal Law Board). The Shia Board has significant support and the Jadeed Board some support in northern India, especially in Uttar Pradesh. Moreover, two other boards emerged to represent the concerns of Muslim women. The Muslim Women's Personal Law Board has been active in parts of Uttar Pradesh and Delhi, and established a women's court that considered some matrimonial cases.[32] The new organizations weakened the AIMPLB's claim to represent Muslim opinion, although the AIMPLB remained much stronger.

The growth of reformist mobilization among Muslims and the increased influence of Hindu nationalism pressed conservative Muslim elites to engage with community reformists, to retain their influence among Muslims and counter perceptions of Muslim backwardness. These developments reinforced the inclination of various prominent *ulama* to interpret Islamic texts innovatively. In 1989 they prompted some of them to form the Islamic *Fiqh* Academy, an institution that promotes discussion among major religious scholars, in order to devise responses to the new questions that social changes raise about appropriate social practices and approaches to adjudication in the religious courts. The leadership of Maulana Mujahidul Islam Qasmi (the former chief *qazi* of the Imarat-e-Shariah, the largest network of Islamic courts in India, who became the President of the AIMPLB towards the end of his life) and his efforts to build a loose consensus among the more imaginative *ulama* gained the academy greater acceptance among conservative Muslims, particularly among followers of the Deoband-centered *madrassas*. In departures from the positions of conservative *ulama* until then, the *Fiqh* Academy advocated that Muslim women be allowed to reject spouses chosen by family patriarchs, that dower be specified in gold or silver to protect its value in the face of inflation, and that provisions in marital contracts allowing dowry or absolving husbands of economic obligations toward their ex-wives be deemed invalid.[33]

In response to the same sociopolitical pressures, the DUD and the DUMI launched a social reform movement in the 1990s in which they highlighted their opposition to dowry, caste endogamy, and other practices that they did not consider rooted in Islamic tradition. The AIMPLB published a compendium of the forms of family life and adjudication it favored in 1999, to guide lawyers and judges in the state courts as well as the judges in the religious courts. The booklet did not support major changes in adjudication. For instance, it expressed the preference that unilateral male repudiation be initially revocable, but did not support the denial of recognition to immediately irrevocable unilateral divorces.[34] Moreover, the AIMPLB formally consulted reformist Muslim women activists for the first time in 2002. Although the board failed to sustain such consultation,[35] it drafted its preferred model *nikahnama* in 2005, in response to the versions of the Women's Research and Action Group and other Muslim women's organizations. To respond credibly to the greater rights that women were given in the marital contracts of the reformist women's organizations, the initial draft of the AIMPLB's version gave women the delegated right to unilateral repudiation, divorce rights on new grounds in community courts, the right to a separate residence if their husbands contracted concurrent marriages and the right to retain on divorce all gifts they received while they were married; in addition, it required men considering a second concurrent marriage to seek a community court's prior approval. However, more conservative *ulama* ensured the deletion of these clauses in the final draft. Moreover, the Board's model *nikahnama* did not influence adjudication in the courts of the Imarat-e-Shariah, although major AIMPLB officials led the Imarat-e-Shariah. This reflected the fact that the conservative *ulama's* minor reformist gestures were meant to respond to the criticisms of reformers, whose influence is primarily in larger cities, while the litigants in the Imarat-e-Shariah's *darul qazas* (religious court) are largely poor and from villages and smaller towns.[36] Although it did not bring its limited reformism to bear on adjudication, the AIMPLB did approach the government of Uttar Pradesh, and then the Indian government, in 2006 to give all Muslim women the rights to inherit agricultural land and to a share in family agricultural income. However, it did not mobilize to press these demands.

Some conservative Muslim organizations supported more extensive reforms than the AIMPLB did. For instance, the Shia Personal Law Board stipulated in its model *nikahnama* that divorcées should be given alimony until they become self-sufficient, that women could seek divorces if their husbands restricted their education or employment or had misrepresented their personal situation when they contracted their marriages, that women should be able to effect delegated divorces without losing their dower, and that spousal reconciliation should be attempted after men indicate their intention to repudiate their wives. It also supported quotas for women in the state assemblies and the national parliament. The Muslim Majlis-e-Mushawarat (a political organization) and the Jamaat Ahl-i-Hadith (a minor religious school) highlighted their opposition to immediately irrevocable male repudiation. Due to the lack of consensus among its constituent organizations about unilateral repudiation, the AIMPLB did not intervene in the crucial case, *Shamim Ara v. the State of U.P.* (2002), in which the Supreme Court declared the *talaq-ul-ba'in* invalid, contrary to its usual defense of conservative precedent.[37]

Hindu nationalist growth also prompted conservative Muslim leaders to shift their attention from defending Muslim law precedent to responding to Hindu nationalist violence against Muslims (particularly in Gujarat in 2002) and their places of worship (notably the Babri Masjid in Ayodhya, destroyed in 1992). Even the AIMPLB, which was formed to address personal law, focused from the early 1990s on preventing the construction of a Hindu temple at the Babri Masjid's former site.[38]

ii. Mobilization Regarding Christian Law.   Scholars have explored Christian social reform initiatives far more in the colonial period than after independence, although it was over the past three decades that the Christian presence in India became more significant due to extensive conversion. Christian mobilizers gave personal law more attention starting in the 1980s.[39]

Many Christian leaders were concerned as far back as the 1950s about the restricted access to divorce and the lack of adoption rights for Christians, and the need for ministers of churches other than the Anglican, the Scottish Presbyterian, and the Catholic churches to gain government certification to solemnize marriages. Some Christian leaders presented demands to the Law Ministry in the early 1950s, and Christian parliamentarians presented private member bills in 1956, 1958, and 1973 to permit judicially separated couples that had not resumed cohabitation for two years to seek divorce, as was possible in Hindu law. Three Law Commission reports suggested this change, in 1960, 1961, and 1983, and the second led the government to introduce a bill in parliament in 1962, prepared in consultation with the leaders of the major churches. But parliament only discussed this bill briefly and passed no legislation because the Catholic Church and certain Orthodox churches opposed an expansion of divorce rights.[40]

Christian mobilization for personal-law reform began in the late 1970s, and was led by the professional elite, in which Christians were much better represented than Muslims. The Joint Women's Program (JWP) led these efforts after it was formed in 1978, and was joined in the 1990s by two other lay organizations, the All India Catholic Union (AICU) and the Young Women's Christian Association (YWCA), as well as two clerical organizations, the Catholic Bishops Conference of India (CBCI) and the National Council of Churches of India (NCCI). (Twenty-seven mainline Protestant and Orthodox churches are members of the NCCI). Two evangelical organizations, the Indian Pentecostal Church of God and the members of the Evangelical Fellowship of India (EFI), also supported these efforts from the late 1990s. The main demands of these organizations were to provide Christians more extensive and accessible divorce rights, to equalize the divorce rights of Christian men and women, to extend Christians adoption rights, and to give the ministers of all churches the right to solemnize marriages.

The JWP's leaders belonged to the Church of North India (CNI), which had been formed in 1970 through a merger of the Anglican, Congregationalist, Presbyterian, British Baptist, and British and Australian Methodist Churches, along with the Church of the Brethren and the Disciples of Christ. The JWP worked closely with two older institutions, the William Carey Study and Research Center and the Christian Institute for the Study of Religion and Society. These organizations initially demanded a UCC that would incorporate Hindu marriage and adoption law, so that the minorities could gain the divorce and adoption rights that Hindus already had, and the rules of the ISA (applied to Christians and non-Hindus who opt for the SMA), which gave women greater rights in ancestral property than Hindu law did until 2005. The proposal to introduce a UCC including the features of different personal-law systems most favorable to women's rights and individual autonomy appeared rather different from most Muslim perspectives on personal law, which were rooted in interpretations of particular religious traditions. However, the Christian organizations' orientations toward personal law were formed through the development of religious perspectives in light of various contemporary social predicaments and the major changes introduced through the twentieth century in the theology and canon of the global churches.

The JWP's leaders developed their vision of matrimonial life through dialogue with members of the YWCA and the Women's Fellowships, church-affiliated groups in which women study the Bible, share their understandings of social changes that affect their lives, and offer their members counsel. The feminine interpretations of Christian texts that emerged through these discussions in the 1980s accepted the Biblical understanding of marriage as a sacrament, but also emphasized the importance of love and companionship in marital relations, urged women to cultivate greater spousal understanding and support, and suggested that separation and divorce might be appropriate if such bonds were absent between spouses. They also encouraged women to participate actively in the workforce and public life. Jyotsna Chatterji, the JWP's founding president, offered such interpretations in six booklets published between the late 1970s and late 1980s, and many others who participated in these discussions had similar perspectives.[41] The JWP's policy proposals emerged from these feminine religious visions, particularly once the stout resistance of Muslim organizations such as the AIMPLB to a UCC, as well as the preference of many Christians to maintain explicit connections between religious vision and personal law, led the JWP to abandon aspirations for a UCC in the mid-1980s and instead demand changes in Christian law.

It was in the CNI that the clergy became initially involved in promoting personal-law reform, because of the JWP's close links with this church. The church's Commission on Religion and Life and the JWP drafted three proposed bills, the Christian Marriage and Matrimonial Causes Bill, the Indian Succession (Amendment) Bill and the Christian Adoption and Maintenance Bill, in 1982; they obtained the signatures of about ten thousand Christians on a memorandum summarizing the changes demanded. These proposals were the bases of discussions with the Law Commission and the Prime Minister's office, in response to which the Law Commission recommended increases in Christian divorce rights once again.[42] However, the prime minister's office wished to ascertain clerical opinion before considering Christian law reform. This induced the lay organizations to engage in sustained discussions with the mainline churches between 1984 and 1994, which led to a partial convergence in the perspectives of the lay and clerical organizations, brought the reform demands the support of the lay AICU and the clerical CBCI and NCCI, as well as greater popular support, and led policy elites to consider these demands representative of broad Christian opinion.

The leaders of the JWP, the AICU, the CBCI, the NCCI, and certain canon law experts and civil lawyers formed the Ecumenical Committee for Changes in Christian Personal Laws, which drafted revised proposals that were presented to the government. They included (a) an increase in divorce rights and their equalization for men and women through adoption of the relevant provisions of the SMA, (b) the extension of adoption rights, (c) equal shares for the spouses in matrimonial property, (d) an increase in alimony, (e) the elimination of the right to the spouse's conjugal company, (f) the closing of loopholes that enabled child marriage, (g) the prioritization of widows over other kin in inheriting their husbands' property if the couple had no children, (h) the invalidation of prenuptial contracts that deprived widows of their husbands' property, (i) the state's automatic acceptance of marriage annulment by churches, (j) the elimination of the need for high courts to confirm lower-court divorce decrees, (k) the extension of the right to solemnize marriages without government certification to the ministers of all churches, and (l) the application of the ISA to Christians in the former princely states of Travancore and Cochin, whose customary laws had denied women rights in ancestral property. (The Supreme Court had indicated, in *Mary Roy v. State of Kerala* (1986), that the last change had come into effect in 1951, but the Christian organizations wished the ISA to reiterate this). Moreover, the churches that accepted these proposals agreed to require couples whose marriages they solemnized not to give or receive dowry in connection with their weddings, and to allow their priests to remarry divorced individuals.[43]

The initial resistance of the hierarchies of certain churches to some of these proposals was overcome through dialogue with lay organizations and church members. The leaders of the Catholic Church and some evangelical churches felt that an increase in divorce rights would be contrary to their view that marriage was sacramental, and the former had demanded from the 1960s to the 1980s that any new divorce rights not be applied to Catholics. However, the AICU's leaders argued with the Catholic hierarchy that changes in the civil effects of marriage would not undermine the institution's sacramental character, that these reforms were necessary to help Christians in dysfunctional marriages, and that increased civil divorce rights would not oblige the churches either to recognize civil divorces or to remarry individuals who had obtained such divorces. Moreover, the reformers agreed to replace the word "divorce" with the expression "dissolution of the civil effects of marriage" in their proposals, to allay the qualms of some priests. These arguments and compromises secured the Catholic hierarchy's agreement to increased divorce rights, and Father Alan de Lastic, who was the President of the CBCI and the Catholic Archbishop of Delhi in the late 1990s, was crucial in ensuring this. The resistance of the evangelical churches that were members of the EFI to an increase in divorce rights was in tension with their members being primarily from the lower castes and tribes, among which divorce customs had long existed. Church leaders had considered the inculcation of greater marital commitment important to their mission among these groups. However, a survey they conducted confirmed the claims of reformers that marital separation was widespread and increasing among their members, leading them to reconcile their insistence on marital commitment to an acceptance of greater divorce rights. But most evangelical and Catholic clergy continued to refuse to remarry divorced people even after Christian divorce rights were increased.

The Malankara Orthodox Syrian Church and the Syro-Malabar Catholic Church were reluctant to discourage dowry, as they gained shares of their members' dowries. Although the laws against dowry made it difficult for them to argue their position forcefully, the considerable influence of these churches in Kerala, a state with a high Christian population (19 percent according to the census's low estimate) and a high proportion of India's Christian professional elite, made the lay reformers eager to secure their support. The lay organizations dropped two of their initial demands to ensure the agreement of these churches to discourage dowry: to give divorcées a share of matrimonial property, and to eliminate the right to the spouse's conjugal company. Other churches were likely to have opposed these demands if the Malankara Orthodox Syrian and Syro-Malabar churches had not, and legislators were unlikely to have accommodated them, since none of India's personal laws recognize rights in matrimonial property[44] and a right to the spouse's conjugal company is recognized among all citizens.[45] The consensus built among major Christian mobilizers over personal-law reform enabled increases in divorce rights and widows' rights in their husbands' property, the equalization of the divorce rights of men and women, and a simplification of divorce procedures, but did not secure the other changes.

Major Christian and Muslim religious leaders responded rather differently to demands for reform because of the extent of recent change and flexibility in their social and religious visions, and the nature of their relationships with their followers and reformist mobilizers. First, the global churches to which the Christian clergy belonged had changed their doctrines considerably and codified and liberalized their canon laws over the past century, making the doctrinal orientations of certain Indian church leaders more flexible. The major Muslim religious institutions of India were not branches of global institutions. Many of their leaders had links with religious institutions in the Arab world and Central Asia, particularly in Egypt, Saudi Arabia, Iraq, and Iran, but religious reasoning had changed far less in these institutions than in the Christian churches, because sociocultural change, secularization, and popular mobilization had been more limited in these societies than in Europe and Latin America where the changes in Christian theology and canon had largely emerged. Moreover, only some Indian Muslim leaders were influenced by transnational reformist currents, and most of them considered the extensive changes in Islamic state law in countries such as Tunisia, Morocco, and Indonesia irrelevant to India.

Second, the Christian clergy was more receptive to the concerns of their church members than most *ulama* were to their supporters. Some church members aired their concerns about Christian law with their ministers, who responded by recognizing some emergent practices. The *ulama*'s reformist initiatives were more minor in scope, and many Muslims felt that they addressed their concerns ineffectively. Third, the main reformist mobilizers and the religious leaders differed less in perspective and had less antagonistic relations among Christians. Most Christian reformists belonged to churches, and some crucial reformist organizations organized the members of particular churches for example, the AICU of the Catholic churches and the JWP largely of the CNI. The reformists had ongoing contact with their church leaders, built alliances with the more liberal ministers, and maintained contact with some conservative ones. This enabled dialogue between the lay reformers and religious leaders, and an eventual convergence in their views on personal law. By way of contrast, the major *ulama* considered the reformist organizations havens of dissent, and many Muslim reformers challenged their religious leaders more directly. Women were not members of the major Islamic religious institutions, and some *ulama* were uncomfortable about dialogue with reformist women. Muslim religious leaders changed their tactics in response to reform demands to prevent an erosion of their support and prestige, rather than because they accepted many of the reformers' views. This hindered agreement among Muslim mobilizers about changes in social practice and personal law.

B. Changes in Policy Makers' Outlook

The formation of legal policy tends to be particularly autonomous of public opinion, social practice, and social mobilization, because law is often viewed as an arena where expertise may legitimately trump popular demands. This is all the more the case regarding laws that pertain to minorities, that account for a small proportion of voters, mobilized citizens, and state officials. In recognition of the autonomy of policy elites, intentionalist analyses highlighted the significance of the ideas familiar to policy elites and the ends these elites value. Alan Watson and Donald Horowitz have emphasized the influence of these factors over legal change, and Jürgen Habermas, Dieter Rueschemeyer, and Theda Skocpol have stressed their relevance to a wider variety of policies.⁴⁶ The growth in some policy makers' knowledge of minority traditions, the changes in the family norms they valued, and the increased inclination of some judges to change family law influenced changes in the minority laws.

Legislators, judges, and bureaucrats continued to feel that the minority laws should especially recognize group norms and be based on group demands, and therefore changes in these laws depended on their understanding of the relevant group's norms and initiatives. Their understanding of Islamic traditions was particularly limited until recently. The increased emphasis of reformist mobilizers and lawyers on minority traditions and the growth of transnational legal networks made some policy elites more aware of reformist interpretations of these traditions, particularly those that other governments had recognized. These policy makers based minority law reform partly on such interpretations.

The judges who changed the minority laws included both reformists of the relevant religious group who felt that the social climate gave them more space to draw on their understandings of their religious tradition, and Hindus whose knowledge of Islamic and Christian norms had grown through their careers. Justice Baharul Islam, who provided the first high court judgments that unilateral male repudiation did not necessarily end a Muslim marriage and who later became a Supreme Court justice, was the former kind of reformist judge. Justices V. R. Krishna Iyer and A. M. Bhattacharjee belonged in the latter category. From a bench of the Kerala High Court, Krishna Iyer was the first judge to observe, in an *obiter dictum*, that early Islamic traditions considered unilateral repudiation revocable when men initially pronounced it; he later authored the first two Supreme Court verdicts in favor of alimony for Muslim women. He also called for more extensive judicial reforms in the various personal laws in his writings.⁴⁷ Bhattacharjee demonstrated his understanding of Islamic and Hindu traditions in two books on personal law to which the Indian legal elite often refer, and observed that the divorce provisions of Christian law were contrary to constitutional rights in an *obiter dictum* in *Swapna Ghosh v. Sadananda Ghosh* (1989).[48] He and Baharul Islam had developed their reformist interpretations of authoritative Islamic texts through their extensive reading of the relevant scholarship. Krishna Iyer was a widely known forerunner of judicial activism, whose judgments advanced the rights of various underprivileged groups, including prisoners, urban squatters, and tribal forest dwellers. He developed considerable knowledge of transnational law and some awareness of Islamic tradition through his long judicial career, during which he had extensive contact with rights activists. Other central figures in landmark Muslim law cases, like Justice S. Rajendra Babu, who authored *Danial Latifi v. Union of India* (2001), the authoritative Supreme Court judgment on alimony, were neither consistent reformists nor particularly knowledgeable about Islamic traditions. However, they carefully crafted culturally grounded verdicts, drawing from the record of pertinent judicial reform. The judges who changed Christian law, such as Justices T. V. Ramakrishnan, Ashok Agarwal, B. Sreedevi and K. P. Balachandran, similarly relied on the information they gleaned from litigants' briefs in crucial cases—about the prevalence of marital separation and the wish to adopt children among Indian Christians, the presence of adoption customs among particular Christian groups, and the acceptance of divorce in the canon of various Protestant churches and of adoption in the Vatican canon.[49]

The sources cited in some recent landmark judgments indicate the growth of understanding of Islamic legal and normative traditions among the legal elite. Reformist interpretations of Islamic law find more extensive mention in recently authored textbooks of Indian Muslim law than in those that the state courts most often used in Muslim law cases through much of the twentieth century.[50] The benches of the higher courts referred with some frequency to the more recent textbooks and consulted the authors of some of these books in Muslim law cases.[51]

Hindu nationalism's influence has been significant among the legal elite for at least two decades.[52] Although those with Hindu nationalist sympathies were inattentive to non-Hindu norms, some of them enabled minority-law reform, which they sometimes claimed was a step toward a UCC. The most prominent Hindu nationalist who helped introduce minority-law reform was

Arun Jaitley, who was the Law Minister from 2000 to 2004. He oversaw the changes in Christian law that significantly increased divorce rights and equalized them across gender in 2001, and gave demands for Christian adoption rights sympathetic consideration. The Hindu nationalist sympathies of some judges urged them toward reformist judgments in the course of which they attacked Muslim practices and called for a UCC. This was particularly true of the Allahabad High Court's treatment of unilateral male repudiation as invalid if it was not followed by reconciliation efforts in *Rahmat Ullah v. State of U.P. and Khatoon Nisa v. State of U.P.* (1994).[53] However, similar inclinations led other policy makers to block Muslim law reform to reinforce their critique of Muslims. The attorney general is said to have acknowledged that this was a reason why the Law Minister instructed him to oppose granting Muslim women alimony rights in *Danial Latifi*, which the Supreme Court considered while the BJP led the national government.[54]

Many policy elites (Hindu nationalist and otherwise) continued to believe that Muslims opposed changes in their personal laws, and this limited their recognition of reformist Muslim initiatives. This is an important reason why they ignored the demands of the conservative AIMPLB and some reformist Muslim organizations to give Muslim women rights in family agricultural land throughout India. Muslim women currently enjoy this right only in Bengal, the northeastern states, Maharashtra, Gujarat, Andhra Pradesh, Kerala, Tamil Nadu, and parts of Karnataka, where Islamic law is applied to the inheritance of agricultural land.

Understandings of religious tradition influenced Christian law less than Muslim law since Christian law was more codified, policy elites regarded legislation and current Christian practices and initiatives as their main points of reference, and explored religious norms in Christian cases only if litigants claimed support in church canons. Moreover, policy elites were less wary of changing Christian law than Muslim law because they considered Christians more liberal; this premise was reinforced by the consensus that emerged among the major group mobilizers by the 1990s in favor of personal-law reform among Christians but not among Muslims. Thus, the demands of certain Christian elites and the private member bills presented in parliament in 1956 and 1958 to increase Christian divorce rights led the Law Commission to suggest such a change in two reports of 1960 and 1961, and the Law Ministry to incorporate some of the Law Commission's suggestions in a bill that the parliament briefly considered in 1962, well before Christian legal mobilization gathered steam. Many judges were receptive to concerns about the limited access Christians had to divorce, and called for legislative change in the IDA without introducing judicial reform, from 1968 to the 1990s. Once various Christian organizations agreed on increasing divorce rights in the 1990s, the executive soon drafted legislation to address this demand. Similarly, the Law Ministry proposed an Adoption of Children Bill applicable to all Indians in 1972 and another that pertained to non-Muslims in 1980, in response to the early demands for Christian adoption rights. (The first proposal was abandoned due to strong opposition from conservative Muslim organizations, which believed that Islamic traditions did not provide for adoption, and the second was given up because of Parsi opposition for similar reasons). This makes for a contrast with the limited policy initiatives regarding Muslim law. No Law Commission explored changes in these laws, and the only legislative change in Muslim law (the Muslim Women (Protection of Rights on Divorce) Act (MWPRDA)) after independence seemed to be meant to preserve conservative precedent. Judges did not suggest legislative reforms in Muslim law either.

Many policy makers with majoritarian inclinations did not want to enable a growth in the religious minorities' share of the population, anxieties about which were fed by ongoing increases in the Christian share of the population through conversion (from 2.0 percent in 1941 to 6.7 percent in 2005) and in the Muslim share of the population due to higher fertility rates and perhaps migration from Bangladesh (from 9.9 percent in 1951 to 14.6 percent in 2011).[55] This led two Union Law Ministers (Hans Raj Bharadwaj, who occupied this post from 1991 to 1996 and from 2004 to 2009, and Ram Jethmalani, who did so from 1998 to 2000), certain bureaucrats in the Law Ministry, and some ruling parties to resist giving Christians unlimited adoption rights. Both the governments led by the BJP and by the Congress Party (which includes many with a Hindu majoritarian outlook) were willing to give Christian couples the right to adopt children of known Christian parentage, but not children of non-Christian biological parents or foundlings of unknown parentage. They took this position although the adoption rights of Hindus were not similarly limited, to address fears that the Christian population might grow if Christian couples had unlimited adoption rights. Since the Christian organizations opposed the proposed restrictions, Christians have yet to gain adoption rights other than through high court decisions recognizing canons and customs that accept adoption and pertain to particular Christian groups.

Similar concerns about the growth of the Muslim and Christian populations led certain courts to resist validating the bigamous practices of men whose religious behavior did not back their claims to have converted from Hinduism to Islam, in *Sarla Mudgal v. Union of India* (1995). They also influenced an attempt made while the BJP led the national government to restrict the application of the ICMA to Christian couples, rather than to couples in which one partner was a Christian as well, as has been possible since the act was adopted in 1872. This proposal was meant to discourage couples in which one partner was a Christian and the other a Hindu from raising their children as Christians, or at least to avoid ascribing the children from such marriages a Christian identity by default. It was not presented to parliament due to the opposition of the churches.[56]

We saw in Chapter 4 that judges and legislators became more inclined starting in the 1970s to promote conjugal autonomy while maintaining the stability of the nuclear family, and to reduce inequalities in matrimonial relations by reinforcing economic support for the indigent after marital separation and divorce. This led them to accommodate certain demands for minority-law reform that favored these ends while being grounded in the concerned group's norms and orientations as they saw them.

IV. CHANGES IN MUSLIM LAW

Many scholars have misunderstood the course of Muslim law in the Indian courts. Parashar, Ratna Kapur and Brenda Cossman, and Rajeswari Sunder Rajan claimed that the courts interpreted legislation to increase women's rights in Muslim law in certain respects in the 1970s and 1980s. But they believed that the majority of mobilized Muslims opposed these reforms, which they took to undermine the recognition of their religious identity, leading the legislature to abandon Muslim law reform and reinstate precedent.[57] Vrinda Narain added that constitutional rights shaped these judicial reforms.[58] These claims referred to the requirement of alimony among Muslims and the effects of the MWPRDA, and are inaccurate in various ways. We will see that even many conservative Muslims viewed only some of the judicial reforms in Muslim law as threats to their religious freedom, and they rallied only against these reforms. Some conservative Muslims welcomed certain reformist Muslim law judgments, which prompted them to understand Islamic traditions differently. Although the MWPRDA was intended to limit the obligation of Muslim men to maintain their ex-wives, certain courts interpreted the act in ways that left Muslim men responsible to provide for these women until their remarriage or death, in the form of alimony or a share of their property. They faced limited Muslim resistance when they interpreted Muslim law based on Islamic legal traditions, rather than prioritizing criminal law over Muslim law or overruling aspects of Muslim law based on constitutional rights. The legal changes introduced by such judgments were therefore not overturned. Moreover, the courts also restricted the conditions under which a Muslim man's unilateral repudiation of his wife ended their marriage, and enabled women to get divorces or judicial separation if their husbands were bigamous. They justified the latter reforms with reference to Islamic norms and Muslim-law statutes, not constitutional rights. The following discussion demonstrates these trends by exploring pertinent legislation, case law, and the forms of reasoning used by the litigants, judges, and legal mobilizers who intervened in crucial cases. It elaborates on the trends outlined by Basu, Agnes, Sylvia Vatuk, and Gopika Solanki.[59]

A. Economic Support after Divorce: Shah Bano and Its Aftermath

Legislators required men to support their indigent ex-wives in Section 125 of the new Criminal Procedure Code adopted in 1974, in response to concerns that the various personal laws provided inadequate or delayed support for indigent divorcées. This appeared to extend the obligation of Muslim men to maintain their ex-wives beyond *iddat*, the period to which the courts had so far restricted this obligation, until they gained independent economic support through employment or remarriage.[60] The resistance of conservative Muslim legislators led the government to add a qualification in Section 127(3)(b) of the Code that a magistrate may cancel an alimony decree under Section 125 if the husband has paid the amount due to his ex-wife under their personal law. It was not entirely clear whether Section 127(3)(b) exempted Muslim husbands from providing support to their ex-wives beyond *iddat* or merely deducted the maintenance they provided based on their personal law from the amount that would be decreed under Section 125. While the wording of Section 127(3)(b) suggested the former interpretation, the adoption of the section in response to the demand of certain conservative Muslim legislators to deduct dower payments from the husbands' obligations suggested the latter construction.[61] Various litigants argued the alternative interpretations in cases that were considered between 1974 and 1985, and most *ulama* supported the restriction of husbands' obligations to the *iddat* period.

The high courts varied in their responses to the maintenance claims of Muslim divorcées between 1974 and 1985. The husbands were required to pay permanent maintenance in more of these cases until 1985, and three judgments of the Supreme Court from 1979 to 1985, including one by a Constitution Bench in *Mohammad Ahmed Khan v. Shah Bano Begum* (1985), lent this interpretation authority.[62] The courts required Hindu and Christian husbands to pay alimony in all postdivorce maintenance cases after 1974, in contrast with their varying responses in such cases involving Muslims.

The verdicts granting Muslim women alimony between 1974 and 1985 relied on one or more of the following arguments: that Section 125 applied to all Indians, insofar as the legislators meant Section 127(3)(b) to only deduct amounts that the man provided his ex-wife following his personal law from the obligations that Section 125 imposed; that Section 125 should supplement Muslim law if Muslim law is taken to require husbands to provide maintenance only through *iddat*, since the latter law did not consider the possibility of vagrancy among divorcées; and that the Qur'anic verses about *mata* required husbands to provide permanent maintenance.[63] The first two arguments took criminal law to supplement the rules of Muslim law in some contexts. The third justified permanent alimony with reference to Islamic norms and accepted certain reformist interpretations of Islam's founding text, breaking with the predominant judicial practice of reliance on authoritative commentaries, textbooks of Muslim law, and case precedent. *Bai Tahira v. Ali Hussain Fisalli Chothia* (1979) and *Fuzlunbi v. Khader Vali* (1980), the Supreme Court's first two alimony verdicts, made the first argument, interpreting Sections 125 and 127(3)(b) of the Code with reference to Article 15(3) of the Constitution, which stipulates that nondiscrimination based on ascriptive identity does not preclude special provisions for women and children. *Shah Bano*, the most publicized personal-law judgment, supplemented the first two arguments with the third, relying on an unusual translation of *mata-un bil-maroof* (usually rendered as "fair provision" or "customary provision") as "maintenance on a reasonable scale," and interpreted the relevant Qur'anic verses to require husbands to provide for their ex-wives until their death or remarriage.

As a broad Muslim coalition opposed *Shah Bano*, Parashar and Sunder Rajan assumed that this coalition was united in its resistance to the requirement of alimony. Contrary to this assumption, the majority of *ulama* and the political elites allied with them did not protest the first two Supreme Court alimony decrees that interpreted criminal law statutes with reference to the Constitution. These decrees could be considered compatible with the view in some schools of Islamic law (of which the Ithna Ashari and the Shafi'i are present in India) that *mata* was mandatory. Although the predominant Hanafi interpretation was that *mata* was optional and most *ulama* believed that it was meant to be a lump sum (rather than a periodic) payment that need not provide for the divorcee's material requirements until her death, five years before *Shah Bano* some Hanafi *ulama* supported a proposal for legislation that would give the courts the discretion to require *mata* and determine its amount.[64] They did so in response to *Bai Tahira* and the widespread sense that the growth of indigence among divorcées needed to be addressed.[65] Danial Latifi, a prominent reformist lawyer, responded similarly to *Bai Tahira*, and declared that it was consistent with the Qur'anic verses regarding *mata*.[66] The early judgments in favor of alimony among Muslims thus led to a convergence of opinion among certain major Muslim reformers and conservatives on the courts' right to decree *mata*. However, *Shah Bano* brought these actors into conflict with one another, and particular features of this judgment pressed most *ulama* to oppose changes in alimony law.

Various individuals and organizations long engaged with Muslim law were involved in *Shah Bano* when the case reached the Supreme Court. Some conservative Muslim organizations, including the AIMPLB, intervened in the Supreme Court on behalf of the husband, who claimed that his obligations towards his ex-wife ended with *iddat*. They argued that Section 127(3)(b) of the Code excluded Muslims from the purview of Section 125, that *mata* was a requirement only for the virtuous rather than for all Muslim men, and that it was meant to be a lump-sum payment that need not sustain the woman for long. Although some *ulama* were prepared to consider *mata* mandatory a few years earlier, the majority of them were unwilling to concede now that the courts might legitimately declare it to be so. Danial Latifi brought a familial tradition of advocacy of Muslim law reform and an extensive knowledge of Islamic traditions to bear on his representation of the woman. His grandfather, Badruddin Tyabji, and his uncle, Asaf Ali Fyzee, were authors of major textbooks of Muslim personal law and advocates of innovative Islamic legal reasoning; his aunt, Begum Sharifa Hamid Ali, had pressed successfully to ban child marriage and attempted to amplify Muslim women's matrimonial rights. Latifi had earlier defended communist insurgents and trade unionists, and appeared in cases to clarify minority cultural and educational rights.[67] He framed his petition within Islamic legal traditions, and argued that alimony was in keeping with the Qur'anic verses regarding *mata*, as interpreted by Imam Shaf'i and Imam Ja'far al-Sadiq, the founders of the Shafi'i and Ithna Ashari schools. Recognizing that he was advocating the application of non-Hanafi interpretations to Hanafis, he presented this as a legitimate exercise in *takhayyur*, which followed the precedent that Indian *ulama* had set when they imported Maliki provisions to increase Muslim women's divorce rights in the 1930s.[68]

Shah Bano incorporated Latifi's arguments, as well as the claims of earlier Supreme Court decisions that maintenance rights should be understood in light of the growth of indigence among divorcées. But Justice Y. V. Chandrachud, the main author of the judgment, went well beyond these arguments and rejected important Islamic understandings of postdivorce maintenance. He suggested that the Qur'anic verses were self-explanatory and that the alternative Hanafi interpretation merited no consideration, and found in Section 125(3) of the Code a justification for the whole section to take priority over Muslim law if the latter did not require alimony.[69] By referring early on to the view that the "fatal point in Islam is the degradation of woman," though without endorsing it, he indicated the larger problem of religious norms upholding gender inequality. (The reference just before that to the statement in the *Manu Smrti* that woman does not deserve independence was perhaps meant to establish that this entirely Hindu bench was equally critical of all of India's various religious traditions). Moreover, Justice Chandrachud argued for a UCC, citing Tahir Mahmood, a prominent scholar of Indian Muslim law, who called for the formation of a UCC through a confluence of the major personal law traditions, much as certain Muslim leaders had imagined around the time India became independent.[70]

Conservative Muslims, including the strongest Muslim religious and political organizations, responded to *Shah Bano* with the most extensive mobilization concerning personal law in India since the 1950s, because they objected to the court independently interpreting the Qur'an rather than following the commentaries that the Indian courts had recognized since the nineteenth century; prioritizing commonly applicable criminal laws over provisions of the personal laws; recommending that the legislature introduce a UCC; and suggesting that Islam degrades women. These features of *Shah Bano* led Latifi himself to call them "exuberances of expression offensive to Muslim sentiment," and Tahir Mahmood, whose call for a syncretic UCC *Shah Bano* had quoted approvingly, to abandon this position once the Hindu nationalists appropriated it.[71] It was opposition to these features of the judgment, rather than to the requirement of alimony, that united the coalition against *Shah Bano*, as Rina Verma Williams noted.[72] The *ulama* who considered the adoption of the interpretation that *mata* was obligatory, as well as various Muslims who favored more extensive reform, felt compelled to oppose such an argument when an entirely Hindu Supreme Court bench offered it, added the suggestion that Islam might be inimical to women's dignity, and pointed toward a UCC. Some reformist Muslims supported the judgment (although some like Latifi had their misgivings about it), and many Muslim women did so too. But opposition to the judgment was much more widespread among Muslims.

The breadth of the coalition against *Shah Bano* and community pressures induced Shah Bano herself to renounce the alimony that the court had decreed in her favor. It temporarily reduced the influence of the reformist Muslims and rights activists who favored the verdict, and led a national government facing erosion in its support to introduce the MWPRDA in 1986 to contain conservative Muslim mobilization. The act was an alternative to a private member's bill introduced by G. M. Banatwala of the Indian Union

Muslim League, which would have exempted Muslims from Section 125 of the Code. The act's incorporation of certain phrases in Banatwala's bill, the consultation of AIMPLB leaders in framing the act, and the parliamentary and public debate prior to the legislation suggested that it was meant to overturn *Shah Bano*. When presenting the bill, the Union Law Minister, Ashoke Kumar Sen, said that *Shah Bano*'s interpretation that Muslim law requires men to provide their ex-wives maintenance beyond *iddat* did not reflect the predominant view among Indian Muslims or the nature of Islamic law in most Muslim-majority countries, and that its call for a UCC ignored Ambedkar's assurance to the Constituent Assembly that such a code would be introduced only based on the consensus of the various concerned communities. He pointed out that the bill was meant to clarify that it was the natal kin of indigent Muslim women or community *waqf* (trusts), rather than the former husbands, who would be expected to provide these women economic support beyond *iddat*.[73] A large number opposed the act in parliament, through signature campaigns and public demonstrations, based on the same understanding of its consequences.[74]

Nevertheless, some of the MWPRDA's provisions did not clearly imply that Muslim men would not be required to support their ex-wives beyond *iddat*. While Section 3 restricted the man's maintenance obligations to *iddat*, Sections 3(1)(a) and 4 called for the man to pay for his ex-wife's "fair and reasonable provision" (perhaps in addition to maintenance) for an unspecified length of time "within the *iddat* period." The latter sections lent themselves to the interpretation that the man should make a lump-sum payment to support his ex-wife for an indefinite period within three months of pronouncing divorce. AIMPLB officials expressed their concerns about the bill's ambiguities to Rajiv Gandhi, the prime minister, as did some legislators critical of the bill's possible restriction of alimony.[75] The law minister nevertheless had parliament pass the bill without amendment, with the aid a Congress Party whip. Because of its ambiguous drafting, the passage of the act did not end litigation over Muslim alimony law.

Lawyers contested the MWPRDA's possible restriction of the husband's maintenance obligations to *iddat* in a number of maintenance cases filed on behalf of Muslim divorcées between 1986 and 2001. They did so with reference to (a) the wording of the MWPRDA that they took to dictate alimony,

(b) the alleged incompatibility of inadequate provision for indigent women with the constitutional rights to life and dignity (Article 21), (c) the presumed incompatibility of authorizing different alimony rights according to religious group membership with the rights to equality and nondiscrimination (Articles 14 and 15 of the Constitution), and (d) the putative legislative intent to apply Section 125 of the Code to all Indians.

The high courts responded differently to these alimony plaints, much as they had before the MWPRDA was passed. Minimalist courts interpreted the MWPRDA to require nothing of the ex-husband but maintenance during *iddat* and the payment of dower, resisted interpreting the Qur'an otherwise, and left it to legislators to resolve tensions between such alimony guidelines and the Constitution.[76] Some of them drew more from interpretations that *mata* is optional to restrict alimony rights than from the MWPRDA;[77] others granted maintenance for just three months even if the marriages began before the MWPRDA's passage,[78] though not if lower courts had ruled in favor of alimony before the MWPRDA was passed.[79] In most of these cases, the courts did not direct natal kin or *waqf* boards to support the divorcee, although the MWPRDA called for the one or the other to assume maintenance responsibilities after *iddat*. In the few cases in which they required this, the courts did not ensure that this responsibility was fulfilled.[80]

Other courts ruled in favor of more generous provision for Muslim divorcées. The majority of them found justification for their verdicts in the MWPRDA's call for "fair and reasonable provision," which they took to apply to the period until the divorcée's remarriage or death, the claims to protect Muslim women's rights in the act's preamble, and by reading the act in light of the constitutional rights to life, dignity, and equality.[81] Some courts considered such provision compatible with the Qur'an,[82] and others took the MWPRDA to override uncodified Muslim law in this regard if the latter indeed restricted maintenance rights to *iddat*.[83] Yet other courts grounded alimony decrees on the argument that the mandate of Section 125 of the Code for the husband to provide permanent maintenance overrode the MWPRDA.[84] In some cases in which women were given maintenance beyond *iddat*, the maintenance payments were well in excess of 500 rupees per month, which was the maximum that could be decreed under Section 125 until this ceiling was removed in 2001.

The Supreme Court resolved the differing signals given by high courts in *Danial Latifi* (2001), in which the lead lawyers who had represented Shah Bano earlier successfully argued that Muslim men owed their ex-wives permanent alimony even after the MWPRDA's passage. The legal team led by Latifi argued for the confirmation of *Shah Bano* based on the preamble and Sections 3(1)(a) and 4 of the MWPRDA, and the understanding of *mata* its members had offered in the earlier case, not basing their argument on constitutional rights or criminal law alone. The NCW and some women's organizations intervened on behalf of the petitioners, arguing that the constitutional rights to liberty, equality, equal protection, and nondiscrimination required the court to give the commonly applicable alimony law (Section 125 of the Code) priority over both the MWPRDA and uncodified Muslim law. and to overrule Sections 3(2), 4, and 5 of the MWPRDA, which they felt discriminated against Muslim women, while also claiming that Qur'anic *mata* authorized alimony.[85] The AIMPLB argued that *Shah Bano* had misinterpreted *mata*, which was required only of the virtuous and need not sustain the woman for the rest of her life, and that the MWPRDA had overturned *Shah Bano*. The Indian government, then led by the BJP, also argued for restricting Muslim men's maintenance obligations because this was the intention behind the MWPRDA, and it felt this would aid its efforts to portray Muslim law and the Muslim community as incapable of reform.

The entirely Hindu *Danial Latifi* court aimed to provide a fair verdict, while avoiding the protest that had followed *Shah Bano*, and its members were forthcoming about their approach to the case.[86] It navigated the conceptual and political difficulties posed by the case primarily along the lines that Latifi suggested, not feeling bound by the legislative intent behind the MWPRDA (the focus of the Indian government's intervention) or the predominant interpretation of *ulama* (the AIMPLB team's emphasis), while resisting the pleas of the NCW and the women's organizations to give criminal law priority over Muslim law and to overrule certain sections of the MWPRDA. Justice Rajendra Babu, who led the bench, and Justice Shivaraj Patil wished to bring a sense of "justice, equity and good conscience" to bear on the case, following an established standard of judicial construction since colonial times. This made them disinclined to deny Muslim women alimony even though this was the legislative intent behind Section 127(3)(b) of the Criminal Procedure Code and the MWPRDA. Justice Babu especially felt compelled to support alimony because the Muslim women to whom he had spoken after the MWPRDA's passage shared his sense that a denial of support to indigent divorcées was unjust. Both he and Justice Patil felt it would be unwise to give Section 125 of the Code priority over Muslim law, offer an independent interpretation of the relevant Qur'anic verses, accept a particular interpretation of *mata*, or call for a UCC, as they feared that such approaches would lead to a reprise of *Shah Bano*'s aftermath—widespread conservative Muslim protest, followed by legislative overturn of Muslim alimony rights. They were the more disinclined to rely heavily on criminal law because this would have only provided support to women facing the prospect of indigence, rather than giving all Muslim divorcées alimony. Justice G. B. Pattanaik, who voiced many Hindu nationalist stereotypes about Muslims, felt uncertain about whether to promote women's rights in Muslim law or consider Muslim law incapable of reform. Justice Babu convinced him and the other members of the Court to follow the course that he had plotted.

Danial Latifi interpreted matrimonial law in view of the fact that most Indian women focused on their domestic roles to the detriment of their professional careers, which made them economically dependent on their husbands. It assumed that this made divorce more damaging to women, making monetary compensation necessary.[87] The bench said that the introduction of the MWPRDA in *Shah Bano*'s aftermath made it appropriate to interpret the act's usage of the words "maintenance" and "provision" in light of how they were used in *Shah Bano*—maintenance to refer to *nafaqa* (support during *iddat*), and provision to *mata* (other support). The Court preferred this interpretation to overruling *Shah Bano,* as the act aimed to do because it was the only construction of the act consistent with both the criminal law regarding alimony and constitutional rights. This interpretation also made it unnecessary for the Court to overrule any of the act's provisions.[88] Justice Babu felt comfortable construing statutory law in light of the Constitution, since he felt this was the judiciary's mission, but would not have been at ease interpreting the Qur'an and other Islamic texts similarly. The incorporation of Islamic norms about the economic consequences of divorce in a statute thus made judges more willing to adopt a reformist interpretation of this aspect of

Muslim law, contrary to the fears of many when the MWPRDA was passed that it would close the door to Muslim alimony.

Understanding conjugality as an important source of economic obligations, and stepping beyond the predominant view in Islamic traditions that natal bonds are more consequential, *Danial Latifi* found it "difficult to perceive that Muslim law" would place the responsibility to compensate a divorcee entirely on people unconnected to the matrimonial relationship, such as the woman's natal kin and *waqfs*, which the MWPRDA deemed responsible for the woman's maintenance beyond *iddat*.[89] It thereby justified its understanding that the act obliged the man to offer his ex-wife provision until her remarriage or death, while holding natal kin and community trusts responsible to support divorcées if their former husbands failed to do so. The Court did not venture to interpret the Qur'an, but found support for its verdict in the way *Shah Bano* had interpreted *mata*. It felt comfortable directing husbands to provide *mata* on a monthly basis if they found this more feasible, although *mata* was meant to be a lump-sum payment.[90]

Thus, *Danial Latifi* interpreted legislation meant to end the requirement of alimony among Muslims in a way that recognized this obligation without departing from personal law. In fact, it made the alimony claims of Muslim women potentially stronger than those of non-Muslim women insofar as the judgment, unlike Section 125 of the Code, did not place a ceiling on maintenance payments or make alimony available only for women facing imminent vagrancy. (The legislature removed the ceiling that criminal law had placed on maintenance amounts later in 2001). Its interpretation of the MWPRDA became authoritative in the lower courts thereafter. Thus, Sunder Rajan's assessment that the MWPRDA was "regressive" and the act's ironic appellation by Okin as the "The Protection of Muslim Husbands' Rights on Divorce Bill" did not accord with the act's consequences.[91] However, many lower courts did not grasp the consequences of *Danial Latifi* and continued to restrict Muslim divorcées' maintenance to a three-month period, requiring the Supreme Court to reiterate the status of Muslim alimony law eight years after this verdict.[92] The Supreme Court also clarified in 2007 that Muslim divorcées retained the right to seek maintenance under criminal law, but could gain their ex-husband's economic support through the usually faster route of the family courts only if they pleaded under the MWPRDA.[93]

Cultural accommodation could serve to advance Muslim women's alimony rights further. The role that the Qur'an gives *maroof* (custom) in determining the extent of *mata* could be used to include in Indian Muslim law the customs of matrilineal Indian Muslim groups that give divorcées significant property rights, much as customs that give women shares in matrimonial property were incorporated into Islamic law in Indonesia.⁹⁴ The MWPRDA's requirement that men provide "fair and reasonable provision" to their ex-wives could also be interpreted to give divorcées shares of matrimonial property. The *Danial Latifi* court did not consider these possibilities since the petitions did not raise them, but courts may do so in the future given that the language of the MWPRDA and the Qur'an's *mata* verses lend themselves to such an interpretation whereas Section 125 of the Code does not. The considerable sums that the courts awarded a few Muslim divorcées with wealthy ex-husbands suggest that this might be possible.

Danial Latifi's provision of alimony without overruling aspects of Muslim law or independently interpreting Islamic traditions limited the room for resistance. The changed political context since *Shah Bano* also deterred protest. The Hindu nationalists had grown much stronger partly by criticizing Muslim resistance to personal-law reform, violence against Muslims had increased, and the national government provided greater tacit support for antiminority violence under the BJP's leadership from 1998 to 2004. They had also cultivated greater international tolerance of their attacks against Muslims in the post–September 11 context by presenting the violence as meant to counter terrorism and ensure security. Moreover, modernist and feminine interpretations of Islamic traditions and Islamic law had gained greater support, and the influence of conservative Muslim elites had declined. As they were concerned not to provide the Hindu nationalists an excuse to launch further violence against Muslims and wished to retain what they could of their status as reputable interpreters of the call of Islam in the eyes of Indian Muslims, conservative Muslim elites muted their opposition to *Danial Latifi*. This rendered a legislative overturn of Muslim alimony rights unlikely.

B. Unilateral Male Repudiation

The courts often assessed the validity of unilateral male repudiation when considering the claims of Muslim women for maintenance from their husbands.

This was because until 1973 all courts recognized such maintenance rights only during the course of a marriage or during *iddat* if they took the marriage to have ended, and many courts took that position even thereafter, especially between 1986 and 2001. The man often responded to the woman's maintenance claims by declaring that he had already divorced the woman or that he was divorcing her right then, to minimize his obligations to her. The desire to minimize economic obligations increased the tendency of Muslim men to repudiate their wives irrevocably and with immediate effect. Judges considered immediately irrevocable *talaq* valid in colonial times and followed this precedent until the 1970s, when they introduced some conditions for the validity of unilateral repudiation. There was no legislation about repudiation, and adjudication on this issue was based on Islamic legal traditions, the Qur'an, and colonial precedent.

Some judges in the 1970s said that the *talaq-ul ba'in* was incompatible with Islamic traditions and should be considered revocable, drawing from the mode of repudiation that the Qur'an recommends, *hadith* that report the Prophet Muhammad to have treated the triple *talaq* as revocable, and various reputable commentaries. Justice Krishna Iyer said so in an *obiter dictum* in *A. Yousuf Rawther v. Sowramma* (1971), in which he added that repudiation required judicial approval with reference to the grounds the man cited, as did Justice Khalid in *Mohammed Hanifa v. Pathummal Beevi* (1972). Justice Baharul Islam proceeded further in *Jiauddin Ahmed v. Anwar Begum* (1978) to declare repudiation revocable when initially pronounced, even if it is declared in an irrevocable form. The latter judgment cited Qur'an 4: 35 and some recent commentators to conclude that "the correct law of talaq as ordained by the Holy Qur'an is that talaq must be for a reasonable cause and be preceded by attempts at reconciliation between the husband and the wife by two arbiters—one from the wife's family and the other from the husband's. If the attempts fail, talaq may be effected."[95] It thus established two conditions for the validity of unilateral repudiation—the husband pleading a reasonable cause (without specifying how judges should assess the cause) and reconciliation having been tried. The judgment rendered the contested divorce invalid, making the man liable to provide his wife maintenance from the point when he ceased to do so.

The verdict that the *talaq-ul ba'in* was revocable was followed by similar verdicts from some other high courts and declarations of support from a conservative religious institution (the Jamaat Ahl-i-Hadith) whose legal doctrine treated the *talaq-ul ba'in* as revocable and a conservative political organization (the Muslim Majlis-e-Mushawarat) that included the adherents of *madhhabs* that varied in their views of such repudiation. Conservative Muslims were more divided in their response to the introduction of conditions for the validity of unilateral repudiation than to the requirement of alimony because reputable commentators, while having different interpretations of *mata*, agreed that the Qur'an recommended that repudiation should be initially revocable and followed by efforts at reconciliation. Moreover, the *darul qazas* of some *madhhabs* in India (the Ithna Ashari, Musta'lian Isma'ili and Ahl-i-Hadith) do not recognize the *talaq-ul ba'in*, while none seem to require men to provide their ex-wives *mata*.[96] As its constituent organizations disagreed on the status of this mode of repudiation, the AIMPLB did not intervene in the cases in which its validity was contested. Smaller associations of Muslim religious elites or lawyers defended precedent in some of these cases, but had fewer resources at their disposal.[97] The support of some conservative Muslim elites and the lack of resistance from major conservative organizations made it easier to consolidate Muslim divorce law reform.

The high courts responded differently to cases regarding the validity of repudiation pronounced in an irrevocable form from 1978 until the Supreme Court delivered its definitive verdict in *Shamim Ara v. State of U.P.* (2002).[98] The first two judgments placing conditions for the validity of unilateral repudiation were not widely noticed, and the next one was delivered over a decade later. Even after the recent growth of judicial knowledge about Islamic traditions, judges remained far more aware of legislation and were more comfortable independently interpreting statutes than religious traditions. As a result, more of them were willing to decree post-*iddat* maintenance based primarily on the MWPRDA or Section 125 of the Code than to invalidate irrevocable repudiation. Thus, the high courts deemed the *talaq-ul ba'in* revocable only in a minority (ten) of the reported cases in which the practice was challenged in the twenty-four years between the first such high court decree and the definitive Supreme Court judgment of 2002; by contrast, they decreed permanent maintenance in a little over a half (twenty-two) of the reported cases in which Muslim divorcées petitioned for it in the fifteen years between the passage of the MWPRDA and the definitive Supreme Court judgment of 2001. (Moreover, a number of the reformist judgments based themselves on the Constitution in maintenance cases, but only one (*Rahmat Ullah*) did so regarding repudiation). This was true even though conservatives resisted the reform of repudiation law much less than they did the changes in maintenance law.

Shamim Ara settled the question for the formal courts, but drew far less attention than *Danial Latifi* because major social organizations and activist lawyers were not involved in it, the litigants did not challenge statutes or base their arguments on constitutional rights, and only a two-judge panel considered the case. Justice Ramesh Chandra Lahoti, who led the court, highlighted his inclination to reconsider precedent based on contemporary social circumstances and a "sense of justice, equity and good conscience." As he believed that the postcolonial constitution gave the standard of "justice, equity and good conscience" a new form, he brought constitutional principles to bear implicitly on the case, and indicated when I interviewed him that he would have been willing to rule on constitutional grounds if the litigants had referred to them. At the same time, he wished to avoid conservative Muslim protest, much as the *Danial Latifi* Court did; this made him avoid invalidating all forms of unilateral repudiation even though he believed this would be desirable, because he did not find a basis for such a decree in Islamic traditions. It also led him to avoid reference to a UCC.

Justice Lahoti drew confidence from the presence of *hadith* and major Islamic commentaries that treated the *talaq-ul ba'in* as revocable, and the precedents authored by Muslim judges knowledgeable about Islamic tradition. He highlighted these precedents, and not *Rahmat Ullah*, which had aroused controversy by basing itself explicitly on constitutional principles and Hindu-majoritarian assumptions. The judgment repeated the conditions specified in *Jiauddin Ahmed* for the validity of male repudiation, and added others—that the claim of repudiation must be clearly made in the initial petition rather than being added as the case proceeds, and that it should be corroborated by eyewitnesses or documentary evidence. This closed the door to men pronouncing divorce in the midst of cases in which their wives seek maintenance or the restitution of conjugal rights. It did not require the judicial approval of unilateral repudiation, as the Islamic laws of Tunisia and Jordan do, but made the validity of repudiation open to judicial consideration. This judgment also aroused no protest.

Neither *Shamim Ara* nor its precedents specified the standards by which courts should assess the reasons men provide for repudiating their wives. Justice Lahoti wished these standards to be different from the divorce grounds recognized in the various personal-law statutes and in Islamic legal traditions. For instance, he wanted the breakdown of marriage to be an acceptable ground even in the absence of spousal fault or mutual consent, although this was not the case in Indian statutes, and he did not believe that a woman's disobedience of her husband would be an appropriate reason, although Islamic traditions recognize it as such. But the judgment did not specify any standards. *Masroor Ahmed v. State of Delhi* (2007), a subsequent high court judgment, clarified that the *talaq-ul-ba'in* would be considered revocable even among Hanafis and Shafi'is, whose schools predominantly take such pronouncements of divorce to end marriages. It added that a man's pronouncement of divorce needs to be communicated to his wife for it to take effect; and that if *talaq* is pronounced in revocable form, reconciliation was possible before the divorce takes effect at the end of *iddat*.[99]

C. Patterns of Change in Muslim Law

The courts justified the changes that they introduced over the last generation in Muslim law with reference to features of statutory Muslim law and Islamic legal and normative traditions. They also alluded to constitutional rights, but departed from precedent only when they felt that group law and group norms also offered plausible support. Policy makers' visions of group norms and the implications of group recognition shaped and limited legal change. These considerations constrained the Supreme Court from overruling sections of the MWPRDA, as the petitioner demanded in *Maharshi Avadhesh v. Union of India* (1994), and from invalidating unilateral male repudiation, banning polygamy, and providing daughters shares of family property equal to those of sons, as the petitioners demanded in *Ahmedabad Women's Action Group (AWAG) v. Union of India* (1997). The Court believed that such changes lay solely in the legislature's jurisdiction and that it could not assess personal laws based on constitutional rights alone.[100] Legislators did not adopt these changes either, or require judicial approval of male repudiation, allow either woman-initiated no-fault divorce through judicial mediation or unilateral female repudiation, extend rights to inherit agricultural land to women in all states, give separated and divorced women shares in matrimonial property, recognize the matrilineal customs of certain Muslim groups, or extend Muslim couples adoption rights, although activists highlighted the bases many of these proposals had in reformist interpretations of Islamic tradition. Policy makers did not introduce these reforms because there had been limited mobilization and litigation in their favor, these rules did not seem to them a part of the sense of group tradition shared by many Indian Muslims, and their vision of the normative family did not suggest that these changes were imperative.

In response to their losses in the state courts, conservative Muslim institutions underlined their suggestion that Muslims take matrimonial disputes to the *darul qazas* over which they had influence. The AIMPLB urged this course since its inception, but emphasized it starting in 1993. Besides, some conservative Muslim elites demanded that the state give sharia courts (that is, *darul qazas* and perhaps Muslim neighborhood councils) exclusive jurisdiction over Muslim family law cases. Legislators show no inclination to give Muslim institutions greater autonomy, and are unlikely to remove Muslim law cases from the jurisdiction of state courts. In recognition of this, many conservative Muslims accept the dual authority of state courts and community courts, but demand that state courts recognize all community court verdicts and direct the police to aid in their implementation. However, the state courts are likely to continue considering appeals of community court verdicts, especially as certain recent verdicts (for example, of caste *panchayats* against intercaste marriages) were clearly contrary to state policy. While resisting demands to give Muslim religious courts added powers, the executive opposed the plea in *Vishwa Lochan Madan v. Union of India* (2005) to disband these courts.[101] Although the formal powers of Muslim community courts are unlikely to change, the efforts of conservatives to urge more Muslims toward these courts may succeed, because they are more embedded among less-privileged groups, and the cost and duration of cases are lower in them.

V. CHANGES IN CHRISTIAN LAW

The important changes in Christian law since the 1990s have drawn far less public and scholarly attention than those in Muslim law. Alice Jacob, Flavia

Agnes, and Rita Monteiro outlined some of these changes, but did not address the legislation and case law of the last decade or explain the content, timing, and process of the reforms.[102]

The formation of a consensus about personal-law reform among the major Christian mobilizers by the 1990s contrasted with the resistance of conservative Muslim leaders to the majority of the reform proposals on offer. This reinforced the perception among policy elites that Christians were more inclined toward reform, and made them more willing to consider legislative changes in Christian law than in Muslim law. As a result, the Law Ministry drafted proposals that would increase individual autonomy and women's rights in Christian law in the 1960s, and then again in the 1990s and 2000s, but did not do so regarding Muslim law. But policy makers continued to resist Christian-law reforms that they feared would erode Hindu predominance in public life.

Various judges highlighted the need to change Christian divorce law from the late 1960s. As policy elites periodically considered legislative changes in Christian divorce law and adoption law, judges advocated legislation but did not change Christian law themselves until the 1990s. Judges began to change Muslim law earlier because they saw no signs of legislative initiative in this regard, and litigants demanded that they address the uncertain implications for Muslims of the changes in commonly applicable alimony laws.

Although policy elites considered Christian law reform at different points, their preferences differed from those of the Christian mobilizers about the precise nature of the reforms, and this delayed legislation until 2001. The majority of Christian mobilizers had agreed by the mid-1990s that they wanted to increase divorce rights, equalize the divorce rights of men and women, gain adoption rights, and give the ministers of all churches the right to solemnize marriages. Crucial political and bureaucratic elites were willing to accept the changes in divorce law alone, but wanted to give Christians the right to adopt only children with Christian biological parents, and wished to restrict Christian marriage law to couples in which both partners were Christians, because they were wary of enabling growth in the Christian population. The Christian mobilizers were unwilling to accept such restrictions on adoption rights and in the ICMA's application, and this suggested that there could be a prolonged delay in legislation. The failure of the executive to accommodate many reform demands even when the major Christian organizations had reached a consensus over them led certain judges to change divorce and adoption law in some states, especially as they believed these reforms were long overdue. The judicial reform of divorce law prompted legislation, which changed divorce law further and applied this reform throughout India. But the opposition of political elites and bureaucrats prevented legislation to apply the judicial changes in adoption law to all Christians. Legislators did increase widows' inheritance rights and divorcées' alimony entitlements, and abandoned a punitive response to adultery even though only certain Christian mobilizers prioritized these changes. They did so because giving widows better access to their husbands' property than extended kin conformed to their inclination to give the nuclear family priority: and ending punishment for adultery and increasing economic support for divorcées was consistent with their valuation of conjugal autonomy.

A. Divorce Rights

We saw that the IDA of 1869 provided men and women divorce on different grounds, and made it difficult for Christians to get divorce decrees. After independence, various women litigants challenged the differentiated divorce rights of Christian men and women on grounds including the constitutional rights to equality and equal treatment and current provisions of British law. However, as they ceased to rely on the divorce provisions of British law, starting in the 1950s, the courts made the limits to Christian divorce rights more binding. Moreover, the Madras High Court reinforced the judiciary's commitment to the gendered grounds for divorce in the IDA in *Dwaraka Bai v. Professor Nainan Mathews* (1953). Justice Panchapakesa Ayyar ruled that these provisions did not discriminate based on sex, insofar as they were based on the different consequences of adultery—a woman's adultery could lead to the birth of a child whom her spouse would be obliged to support—and found this a sound reason to limit the availability of divorce based solely on adultery to men.[103] The courts followed this precedent until 1995, initially endorsing *Dwaraka Bai*'s logic.

From 1968 onward, certain courts found the gendered grounds for divorce, the limited room for divorce, and the need for high court ratification of Christian divorce decrees out of date, but deemed legislators responsible to change these provisions. The first such judgment, *Solomon Devasahayam Selvaraj v. Chandirah Mary* (1968), highlighted the lack of correspondence between Christians having the least divorce rights in India and the social orientations of the community—"no one will consider that the Christians are a backward community compared to the other communities in the country."[104] However, its call for legislative reform was an *obiter dictum* in a response to a petition to restore conjugal rights. Certain subsequent judgments also took the widely noticed progressive social inclinations of Christians to particularly warrant an increase in their divorce rights, but did not introduce judicial reform.[105] *Swapna Ghosh v. Sadananda Ghosh* (1989) considered the different divorce rights of Christian men and women and the more limited availability of divorce to Christians discriminatory, and refused to accept *Dwaraka Bai*'s justification of the former, because it took the different consequences of adultery to be merely a result of gender differences.[106] This too remained an *obiter dictum* because divorce could be decreed in this case based on the existing provisions themselves. Various courts also called for the elimination of the requirement that high courts ratify Christian divorce decrees.[107]

The executive proposed no reforms to address the judiciary's concerns about Christian divorce law from the 1960s until the 1990s, although Christian mobilization for personal law reform grew starting in the 1980s. The inaction of the executive and the growth of Christian reformist mobilization prompted certain benches of the Kerala, Bombay, and Andhra Pradesh High Courts to change Christian divorce law in their jurisdictions.[108] Certain organizations engaged with Christian law participated in the first of these cases, *Mary Sonia Zachariah. v. Union of India* (1995), much as organizations involved in Muslim law had in the major Muslim maintenance cases. However, the major religious institutions, community organizations, and rights organizations united in pressing for reform in *Mary Sonia Zachariah*, unlike in *Shah Bano* and *Danial Latifi*, which pitted reformist organizations and lawyers against the most influential religious and community institutions. This was because many of the churches favored reform by then, contrary to the attitude of the Muslim religious institutions toward alimony law.

Two of Kerala's important reformed Orthodox churches, certain Christian reform organizations, and rights organizations that did not focus on Christian concerns were involved in *Mary Sonia Zachariah*.[109] They brought the visions of religion and gender that were motivating mobilization for Christian law reform to bear on the case. These organizations requested the court to delete the words "incestuous" before "adultery" and "adultery coupled with" before "cruelty" and "desertion" so that spousal adultery, cruelty, and desertion could become grounds for divorce on their own for Christian women, rather than adultery having to be combined with another spousal fault. They felt this would resolve the conflicts that they found between the existing divorce grounds and various constitutional rights. A vicar of the Saint Thomas Evangelical Church also argued in court that although spousal adultery was initially a precondition for divorce based on the Bible, the Biblical view of love as the basis for marriage also provided a justification to dissolve marriages no longer bound by love, reflecting the companionate yet sacramental understanding of marriage shared by many of the women mobilized to change Christian law. The Christian Institute for the Study of Religion and Society said that accessible divorce was necessary as a course of last resort to end dysfunctional marriages for the same reasons that euthanasia was needed to end miserable lives; this reflected a discussion that had recently begun in various churches in Kerala on euthanasia, leading the majority of them to accept the practice. The Indian government resisted the petition initially, on the grounds that many Christians opposed this change, that the Constitution enabled the differential treatment of groups, and that the changes the petitioners requested would create a new inequality in the grounds for divorce, which would be available to women but not to men based on cruelty or desertion alone. The lay organizations and churches had reached a consensus on divorce rights by the time the case neared its end, weakening the government's claim about Christian opposition. The government therefore abandoned its opposition in principle to increasing Christian divorce rights, but requested the court not to amend the law so that the legislature could pass comprehensive legislation that would better address the community's demands.[110]

    The court issued an interim order in 1989 directing the Indian government to decide within six months whether and how it would act on the suggestions in the Law Commission's *Ninetieth Report* to amend the IDA. It hoped to hasten legislation thereby, and indicated that it was the government's inaction on this directive, as well as on the previous recommendations of various courts and the Law Commission, that triggered its resort to reform: "It is after taking note of . . . the totally intransigent attitude adopted by the Central Government . . . that we have decided to consider the matter on merits and to grant the reliefs prayed for, assuming the role of reformer to the extent legally permissible." Justice T. Ramakrishnan claimed inspiration in *Shah Bano*'s statement that "inevitably, the role of the reformer has to be assumed by the Courts because it is beyond the endurance of sensitive minds to allow injustice to be suffered when it is palpable," and Justice Krishna Iyer's warning that "the sex equality clauses of our Constitution will remain frozen and be a perpetuation of ancient legal injustice unless activist judges share the new concerns and values."[111]

Mary Sonia Zachariah found the availability of divorce to men but not women on the ground of adultery alone, the unavailability of divorce to women on the grounds of cruelty or desertion alone, and the easier availability of divorce to all groups except Christians incompatible with constitutional equality and nondiscrimination on the bases of religion and gender; further, it found the disentitlement of Christian women to divorce based on cruelty and desertion contrary to the constitutional rights to life, personal liberty, and dignity. The court claimed that it was not breaking with judicial precedents that resisted the assessment of personal law with reference to the Constitution as it was amending only a particular provision of the IDA, rather than the entire act. It felt confirmed in its course because it found adultery "well nigh impossible" to prove, and because the increase in the divorce rights of Hindus and Parsis had not impaired family life among these groups, but rather had prompted demands for the further liberalization of divorce.

The second judgment that changed Christian divorce law, *Pragati Varghese v. Cyril George Varghese* (1997), found justification for the change in Christian doctrine and mobilization, as well as in constitutional rights. It indicated that the Protestant and Orthodox churches permit divorce, and that even the Roman Catholic Church, which considers marriage indissoluble, had amended its canon to offer divorce grounds more liberal than the IDA's. Moreover, it found the gap between Protestant canon and the statute that much greater, which was intolerable because of the extensive mobilization of Christians, including Catholics, for divorce law reform. *Pragati Varghese* found the easier availability of divorce to Christian women than to Christian men after the amendment it introduced acceptable, drawing justification from a Supreme Court judgment that defended such asymmetry with reference to the "muscularly weaker physique of the woman, her general vulnerable physical and social condition and her defensive and non-aggressive nature and role particularly in this country."[112] *Mary Sonia Zachariah* more specifically considered it appropriate to enable Christian women alone to access divorce on the grounds of cruelty and desertion, as it believed that women alone suffered the consequences of these spousal faults in India at that point. Both judgments left it to the legislature to equalize the divorce rights of Christian men and women, and to streamline Christian divorce procedures.

Much as with Muslim divorce and alimony law, judges changed Christian divorce law only to the extent that they considered this necessary to offer women redress, rather than with a view to equalizing matrimonial rights. The legislative amendment of the IDA in 2001 was prompted by judicial reform, but was more comprehensive, and equalized the divorce rights of Christian men and women. It (a) made divorce available to both Christian men and women based on a single spousal fault or mutual consent; (b) removed the requirement of high court confirmation of lower court divorce decrees; (c) increased alimony entitlements by eliminating the earlier ceiling of a fifth of the husband's earnings; and (d) abandoned a punitive approach to adultery by deleting the provision to transfer the property of adulterous women to their husbands and children on divorce and eliminating the need for adulterers to be corespondents and to pay damages. This rendered the divorce rights of Christians similar to those of Hindus, but not to those of Muslims, among whom alone unilateral male repudiation is possible.[113]

The courts considered group norms, practices, and initiatives relevant guidelines to change Christian divorce law, much as they did regarding Muslim law. So did the Law Commission, especially in its *Ninetieth Report*, presented when mobilization for Christian personal-law reform had begun, and its *164th Report*, presented when such mobilization had peaked. The Indian Divorce (Amendment) Act that was passed in 2001 also referred to the increased acceptance of divorce in the canons and by the leaders of various churches, the problems associated with the growth of dysfunctional marriages that could not be dissolved among Christians, and the initiatives of various Christian organizations for personal-law reform.[114]

B. Other Aspects of Christian Law

Legislation also changed other features of Christian law. It amended the ISA in 2002, based on demands of the more ambitious Christian mobilizers represented in the Ecumenical Committee for Changes in Christian Personal Laws. The amendments increased widows' rights in their husbands' property, specifically giving them priority over lineal descendants other than the couple's children; invalidated prenuptial contracts that might have deprived them of such property; and ensured that they would receive a third of their husbands' property irrespective of wills to the contrary.

Policy makers did not grant some of the demands of the Christian mobilizers, even though they were based on group preferences and interpretations of religious tradition, because these demands did not coincide with their normative vision. This was specifically the case regarding adoption rights, which they did not extend to Christians because of the concern of various political elites and bureaucrats that unlimited adoption rights could lead to a rapid rise in the Christian population. These actors were only willing to give Christian couples the right to adopt children of known Christian parentage; the Law Ministry drafted a bill to this effect in 2000, but it was not presented to parliament because the Christian organizations found such limits unacceptable while the adoption rights of Hindus, Sikhs, Buddhists, and Jains were not similarly restricted. When concerns to limit the religious minority populations had been weaker in the 1970s and early 1980s, the government had proposed to extend unlimited adoption rights to all Indians in 1972; in 1980, when faced with Muslim opposition to this proposal, it suggested granting this right solely to non-Muslims even though Christian mobilization for adoption-law reform was much lower then. Hindu nationalism had gained greater influence and the population shares of Christians and Muslims had risen since then, increasing Hindu anxieties about the further growth of the religious minority populations. This led enough legislators to resist unlimited adoption rights for Christians that even the Union Law Ministers of the past two decades who were open to this change (Arun Jaitley, Veerappa Moily, Salmad Khurshid, Ashwani Kumar, and Kapil Sibal) did not propose such legislation. Moreover, the disagreements of two other Union Law Ministers (Bharadwaj and Jethmalani) with the Christian organizations about the scope of the ICMA (the ministers wished to restrict it to couples in which both parties were Christians) blocked the other changes these organizations demanded in it, including the extension of the right to solemnize marriages to the ministers of all churches. Besides, Christian proposals to eliminate the right to demand the conjugal company of one's spouse and to grant spouses equal shares in matrimonial property, which the women's organizations primarily voiced, were based on valuing conjugal autonomy and women's property rights more than many policy makers did. Therefore, legislators did not introduce these changes in Christian law.

Certain judges did not share the opposition of crucial legislators and bureaucrats to Christian adoption rights, and a few high court benches granted couples these rights once the path to such legislation seemed blocked.[115] Other courts were reluctant to recognize such rights in the absence of legislation to this effect. The courts that granted adoption rights based their rulings on the canon of particular churches, and in some cases deduced these rights from the constitutional right to life. In the first such case, *Philips Alfred Malvin v. Y.J. Gonsalvis* (1999), a single judge of the Kerala High Court indicated that the canon of the Roman Catholic Church, to which the petitioner's parents belonged, accepted adoption if it was recognized in the civil law of the area. The court pointed out that Christian statutory law did not prohibit adoption although it did not recognize it either, Hindu law accepted it, and Muslim law could be taken to do so because certain statutes (the Oudh Estates Act, 1869 and the Sri Pratap Jammu and Kashmir Laws Consolidation Act, 1977) had accepted the adoption customs of particular Muslim groups. Justice Sreedevi treated these as signs that the civil law of India accepts adoption, and deduced that the Catholic canon would accept it as well. She reinforced this consideration with the construction that the constitutional right to life includes a right to what makes life meaningful, and surmised that the plaintiff's parents might have felt that the adoption of a son would make their lives more meaningful. Her justification of adoption with reference to canon or caste custom could only be extended to the members of churches and castes that accepted this practice, but the deduction of the right to adopt a child from the right to life could be extended to all citizens, including Muslims among whom resistance to adoption rights was strong.

Some courts drew from *Philips Alfred Malvin* the conclusion that all Christians have adoption rights; others used it to rely on church doctrine to assess whether particular Christian groups have adoption rights. The Karnataka High Court declared that all Christian couples have adoption rights, and the Rajasthan High Court inferred that the courts should recognize the adoption customs prevalent among particular Christian groups.[116] Another panel of the Kerala High Court declared that Christian law could be taken to recognize adoption, but its argument depended on church doctrine, specifically that of the Syrian Catholic Church that couples without biological children alone should enjoy this right.[117] Yet another Kerala High Court panel questioned the appropriateness of courts developing adoption rights for Christians in the absence of legislation, and a panel of the Allahabad High Court was divided in its reaction to *Malvin*.[118] The limited case law that has followed *Malvin* so far shows no definite trend, but suggests that more courts might recognize the adoption rights of Christian couples whose church canons accept adoption or whose castes or families have adoption customs. The courts that accepted Christian adoption did not identify legislative inaction as a reason why they did so, unlike those that amended the IDA. But the delivery of the adoption decrees after the blockage of Christian adoption legislation suggests that legislative inaction in the face of community initiative might have prompted these judicial reforms too.

Policy makers gave group traditions and practices priority over group statutes only when the former corresponded more with their normative vision. Thus, legislators wished to give state law priority over the rules of religious institutions, and leave state courts free to accept or reject the methods and results of community adjudication; for those reasons, they did not adopt the proposals of churches to invalidate marriages contrary to the rules of the church of either party, accept all marriage annulments by churches, or agree to base divorce proceedings in state courts on the records of earlier such proceedings in churches. Similarly, courts did not recognize certain church divorces and marriage annulments, starting with *Kurien v. Alphonsa* (1986) when canons considered marriages void under circumstances in which the IDA considered marriages neither void nor open to dissolution (such as the marriage of a Christian to a non-Christian and the marriage of individuals who took vows of chastity).[119] Such judgments led many priests to urge couples whose marriages they ended in church to seek civil divorces as well, to ensure that the church divorces would have their intended legal consequences; they took this position even while refusing to perform the later marriages of some individuals who had obtained civil divorces but not divorces or annulments in church.

The failure to effect legislation in favor of adoption rights did not deter Christian mobilizers. The organizations that had mobilized for Christian law reform through the 1980s and 1990s, as well as the rapidly growing churches that are part of the EFI and were not part of the earlier initiatives, continued to press for adoption rights over the last decade, and drafted a Christian Adoption and Maintenance Bill (2003) providing unlimited adoption rights. These efforts seem unlikely to succeed in the near future. However, the prospects recently became brighter for the accommodation of a demand that lay Christian reformers made until the 1990s but shelved to effect a compromise with certain churches—the grant of shares in matrimonial property to the spouses on divorce. Policy makers recently became willing to introduce this change among those governed by the HMA and the SMA, and parliament is currently considering a bill that would do so, as we saw in Chapter 4. If this change is introduced, the demand for a similar change in Christian law is likely to be revived, and policy makers seem likely to accommodate it.[120]

VI. PATTERNS OF MINORITY RECOGNITION

The experiences of Muslim law and Christian law reflect important aspects of the formation of the Indian nation and its religious minorities. Minority accommodation in the regulation of family life and the concern of political elites to build broad social coalitions would have been compatible with changing the laws of the Muslims and Christians soon after independence because initiatives for such reforms based on group traditions and group concerns were strong among Muslims and had emerged among Christians at the time. Moreover, support for personal-law reform was no weaker among Muslims than among Hindus. However, Hindu law was changed extensively as a means to make the postcolonial family, and the minority laws were not. Policy makers pursued this strategy because the majority of political elites took Hindu cultures to be dynamic and to offer the main bases on which to construct a culturally indigenous and modern Indian nation; they considered Muslims to be embedded in introverted cultures incompatible with modernity and postcolonial development. Such discourses about the nation and its religious groups made many of them less sensitive to minority reform initiatives and disinclined to change minority laws. Although prevalent stereotypes of Christians as having special affinities with modern values could have encouraged changes in Christian law, this did not happen in the first postcolonial generation because policy elites based their approaches to the other minority laws on those they adopted to Muslim law.

The growth of reform initiatives among the religious minorities, their greater attention to personal law, and the strengthening of networks between minority mobilizers, other civil society activists, and policy makers contributed to changes in policy elites' values and their perceptions of minority norms. These developments led certain policy makers to see minority cultures as more dynamic and varied, and to change minority laws based on these new understandings. However, the social vision of policy elites continued to restrict minority-law reform. The growth of Hindu nationalism since the 1980s led more political elites to see the religious minorities as culturally alien, and increased their inclination to limit the numerical strength and influence of these groups. This prevented the accommodation of certain demands for minority law reform—particularly to give Christians adoption rights. Even many policy makers with pluralistic orientations continued to see Muslim cultures as less compatible with the forms of modern family life they valued. As a result, even reformist judges did not feel that Indian Muslim culture provided grounds for them to stop recognizing unilateral male repudiation or polygamy, although reformists justified their demands to do so with reference to Islamic norms and Islamic state laws in other countries. The limited accommodation of such culturally grounded demands for legal change shows that there remains considerable room for reform while attending to cultural accommodation. Our analysis of the reasons for such policies indicates that policy elites would need to understand minority cultures better and weave more minority cultural threads into their tapestries of the nation for this potential to be realized.

The limits within which their demands were met did not restrain Muslim and Christian reformers. Drawing confidence from their successes in overcoming conservative resistance, winning the support of some religious elites and influencing policy, they pressed for further changes that would empower women or increase conjugal autonomy. For instance, Muslim reformers demanded that all women be given rights to inherit agricultural land and to access their dower on marriage, and that unilateral male repudiation not be recognized or require judicial approval. Meanwhile, Christian reformers demanded that unlimited adoption rights and shares in matrimonial property be recognized. The imaginative ways in which intellectuals and activists have interpreted and transformed the cultural traditions of India's Muslims and Christians suggest ways in which forms of multicultural accommodation might be changed.

Muslims and Christians were accommodated in different ways in personal law in some respects. Since independence, many policy makers saw Christians as more oriented than Muslims to social reform and to the state's initiatives to form the postcolonial citizen. This view was out of tune with mobilization being greater among Muslims than among Christians for personal-law reform in the last colonial decades. However, as Muslim mobilizers based their personal-law initiatives on religious discourses with which the political and bureaucratic elite were largely unfamiliar, these elites neither understood nor accommodated their reform aspirations.

Mobilization for personal-law reform increased much more among Christians than among Muslims from the 1980s, and gained the support of the majority of religious elites only within the former group. Levels of support in the two groups for changes in personal law thus coincided with policy makers' stereotypes from the 1980s, and reinforced those perceptions. This made policy elites promote changes more cautiously in Muslim law than in Christian law. Judges did not overrule any aspects of statutory Muslim law or rule that Islamic legal traditions were irrelevant, changing precedent only by drawing on interpretations of these statutes and traditions, sometimes in light of constitutional principles. The support of community mobilizers and major religious leaders made some judges willing, by way of contrast, to change Christian law, basing their rulings more crucially on constitutional principles. They overruled some features of Christian divorce statutes and constructed adoption provisions in certain states based on these principles, as well as on emergent community norms and initiatives. Moreover, the legislature reformed Christian law, but not Muslim law, to promote gender equality and individual liberty. Policy makers also saw more similarities in the practices emerging among Hindus and Christians and found it more feasible to promote similar practices among these groups, while continuing to regard Muslim practices as distinctive and rooted in irreducibly different traditions. As a result, they brought about partial convergence in Hindu law and Christian law, especially in their rules of marriage and divorce but also to some extent in their inheritance rules, while leaving Muslim law more distinctive, particularly with regard to its inheritance and divorce provisions. Thus, recognition involved more marginalization for Muslims than for Christians.

CHAPTER 6

NATIONALISM, MULTICULTURALISM, AND PERSONAL LAW

I. STATE, NATION, TRADITION, AND FAMILY: PATTERNS OF FORMATION

States formed family law in different ways in postcolonial societies and other developing societies over the course of the twentieth and early twenty-first centuries. We have seen that certain features of state-society relations and the discourses of nation and community salient among ruling elites took shape through mutual interaction, and their interactions influenced the approaches that states took to family law.

A variety of social institutions, such as local, lineage-based, ethnic, sectarian, and religious institutions, regulated aspects of family life and property control in these societies in the early twentieth century. The majority of colonial states, as well as certain indigenous monarchies, recognized the authority wielded by these institutions at the time. They did so either by delegating aspects of the formation and adjudication of personal law and customary law to these institutions or by having state courts apply laws that gave these institutions some influence over family life—for example, by recognizing marriages they solemnized or applying inheritance rules based on lineal descent. The new regimes that were established in these societies through the twentieth century could consolidate their authority by containing the power of these intermediate social institutions over family life and other aspects of social life, or by acknowledging their authority and building alliances with them. Trying to assume control over family life by curtailing the power of these social institutions could generate considerable conflict and impair the regime's popularity, authority, and stability. These were the consequences when leaders of the Turkish republic disbanded certain religious institutions, established state control over others, and transferred authority over matrimonial disputes to state courts. The delegation of authority to intermediate social institutions also had potential costs for state elites: it could weaken state authority and the autonomy of state institutions, blur the boundaries between state and society in various ways, constrain the ability of state elites to promote social change, and limit the stake of citizens in state policy and their incentive to respect state law. These were some of the effects of sectarian institutions being granted much authority over political, social, and family life in Lebanon, and they contributed to the onset of a prolonged civil war.

The Enlightenment encouraged various social actors to frame their projects as promoting universalistic values such as equality and liberty, although these projects were shaped in important ways by the specific contexts in which they emerged. The authors of modernist projects typically present them as promoting universalistic values as well as contextually specific goals. The promotion of such values often comes into conflict with pressures to accommodate culturally specific normative traditions, which are strong in various societies. Modernists sought to promote gender equality and individual autonomy in certain respects in family life, or at least framed their proposals as doing so. Such efforts had to contend with the value that many attached to cultural traditions and personal laws that gave men and kin groups authority over aspects of family life, intimacy, and property control, and the interest that many powerful actors had in such a distribution of authority. Policy makers could prioritize the promotion of universalistic values or the recognition of difference, or could seek to reconcile these aims by reconstructing cultural traditions to support goals conceptualized partly through universalistic modes of reasoning. A minority of states prioritized the promotion of universalistic values in developing societies (for example, in Turkey and Albania), but the majority either emphasized the accommodation of dominant cultural practices (as in Lebanon and Syria) or sought to reconstruct cultural traditions to promote social change (such as in Tunisia, Indonesia, and India).

States that emphasized the promotion of universalistic values drew most extensively from experience in more industrialized societies, while those that grounded their projects significantly in culturally specific traditions tended to retain or modify institutions with deeper indigenous roots. In the sphere of family law, a few of the former regimes replaced distinct personal laws with homogeneous laws largely drawn from Western precedents (for example, Turkey and Albania) and some of the latter regimes retained most of the personal laws they inherited (for example, Lebanon and Syria). The majority of states in developing countries changed personal laws based on reconstructing indigenous norms, partly in view of Western experiences (for example, Tunisia and Indonesia), and perhaps supplemented them with civil and criminal laws modeled on Western precedents (as did India and Israel).

Another related choice pertaining to family law was that between national consolidation and the accommodation of difference. The tensions between these goals were strong in the majority of developing societies, in which loyalties to the nations that states aimed to represent were weak or uncertain. Some states prioritized the recognition of diversity and others the formation of national cultures mainly from the ways of the dominant group. Yet other states sought to reconcile national consolidation and the recognition of difference by building national cultures drawn from the traditions of various ethnic and religious groups, especially the traditions that these groups shared; official discourses emphasized and promoted these shared traditions. The states that prioritized nation formation either homogenized the diverse personal laws they inherited or applied some of the politically dominant group's personal laws to other groups. While the former approach was taken in Turkey, the latter was considered in Egypt in the 1950s when policy makers proposed the application of family laws drawn largely from Islamic jurisprudence to Christians, and partly implemented there later when they gave *sharia* constitutional status and made it applicable in contexts for which statutes did not provide. The application of antipolygamy laws, based on particular versions of Christian tradition, to Mormons in the United States and to Muslims in several European countries also bore affinities with the latter approach. More states continued to recognize the personal laws of the minority and subordinate groups, but paid far greater attention to the content of the laws governing the majority/dominant group. This was the pattern in Morocco, Israel, Pakistan, and Bangladesh, where the minority laws were barely changed. Some states that promoted syncretic national cultures introduced reforms in the personal laws of the majority as well as those of various minorities. Indonesia especially experienced such wide-ranging reforms, and India also did so to some extent from the 1970s onward.

The efforts of secularist state elites to limit or change the public roles of religion often came into conflict with the power of religious institutions and influence of religious traditions, and sometimes with the proclaimed goals of these elites to respect religious freedom and to treat various religious groups similarly. Furthermore, the preponderant influence of some religious groups and sects frequently limited certain freedoms of other groups and hindered the state's ability to treat various religious groups similarly. Certain states, particularly various communist regimes, seriously limited the power of religious institutions and the public roles of religious norms and religious symbols, at a cost to religious freedom, and ended the recognition of religious laws. The French state also followed this path to a significant extent. More of the states that proclaimed commitments to secularism responded to the significant presence of religion in public life by continuing to recognize some religious norms and to engage in some ways with religious institutions. Some of them continued to apply personal laws based significantly on religious norms and traditions of religious jurisprudence, and attempted to reconcile this with other goals by limiting the sphere of application of religious law, supplementing religious laws with matrimonial laws not based on religious norms that were applied to all citizens, or changing religious laws by drawing from other aspects of the concerned groups' diverse and dynamic cultural repertoires. These were the approaches adopted in most postcolonial societies, especially in the Middle East, South Asia, and Southeast Asia. States that continued to apply religious laws varied in the roles they gave religious elites.

They gave religious courts much of the authority to adjudicate matrimonial disputes in Israel, shared such authority between state courts run by secular judges and religious courts in Indonesia and India, and took the preferences of religious elites into account at times in personal-law legislation and in how state courts adjudicated personal law in Egypt, India, and Indonesia. In societies in which religious elites gained considerable influence over the state, such as Iran and Afghanistan, official commitments to secularism (which were not strong at any point) were abandoned, personal laws were changed in light of the preferences of these elites, and the sphere of application of religious law was expanded.

In sum, policy makers varied considerably in the ways in which they responded to prior forms of patriarchal authority, other preexisting intermediate institutions, and strongly felt religious and other normative traditions in their approaches to build the state, consolidate the nation, accommodate cultural difference, and make family law in postcolonial and other developing societies over the past century. The Turkish state seriously limited the power of prior patriarchal, religious, and ethnic authority structures, promoted understandings of modernity derived largely from prior Western experiences and ideas, seriously limited certain public expressions of religion while establishing considerable control over others, and introduced uniform and secular family laws based on Western precedents. In the process, ruling elites gained only limited support, provoked considerable conflict, and did not effectively consolidate their control over society. The Lebanese state continued to delegate considerable authority to sectarian institutions at the cost of weakening the state and its transformative capacity, left personal law under the jurisdiction of the sectarian courts, and barely changed the country's various personal laws. Such extensive accommodation of sectarian elites did not, however, render the state stable.

In Malaysia, the ethnic and religious minorities were marginal to official nationalist discourse. Nevertheless, the multiethnic alliances that ruled the country managed to build a strong centralized state, maintain a stable regime for much of the postcolonial period, and introduce social- and family-law reforms that were moderate in scope and applied to both the ethnoreligious majority and the minorities in much of the country (except the eastern peninsula). Indonesian and Indian rulers built centralized states by engaging with authoritative social institutions, while erecting certain boundaries between state and society. They drew support from various ethnic and religious groups, promoted composite visions of national culture that engaged the imaginations and loyalties of many of their citizens, recognized cultural diversity in different ways, built secular states while accommodating public religion extensively, and gradually promoted social equality in various arenas including family life. This enabled them to build and maintain broad social coalitions even while experiencing considerable social conflict and occasional regime change. These regimes contained conflict over personal law by mobilizing credible and attractive cultural grounds for reform and forging compromises over the precise directions of legal change at different points. The postrevolutionary Iranian regime was run by unelected religious elites as well as by popularly elected republican institutions, both of which changed forms of social regulation and religious law significantly in light of their conservative visions. However, they also accommodated contrary preferences at times, and this enabled them to maintain somewhat broad support, but not to contain dissent.

II. INFLUENCES OVER APPROACHES TO MAKING STATE, NATION, TRADITION, AND FAMILY

A variety of factors set the background to the approaches states took to the formation of family law and the associated construction of nations and group traditions, but did not determine all features of their strategies. The drive to consolidate state authority urged new regimes to revise their relations with various social institutions, including those whose authority was recognized by the personal laws they inherited. However, this consideration did not determine the ability and inclination of these elites to centralize power. The new regimes that assumed power in the twentieth century inherited different levels of state autonomy, varied forms of state engagement with social institutions, and different resource endowments for further state building. Those that had more resources and were more autonomous of social institutions at the outset, such as the regimes of postcolonial Tunisia and republican Turkey, were in a better position to consolidate their power by containing the power of social institutions than those that inherited greater delegation of authority to social institutions, such as the postcolonial regimes of Lebanon and Egypt. This limited the options available to regimes, but did not determine the precise choices made. For instance, prior state autonomy enabled the new regimes of both Turkey and Tunisia to overcome the power of religious and ethnic institutions. But the Turkish rulers did so through the secularization of family law and the adoption of various other Western precedents, while the Tunisian state elites preferred to reform Islamic law as part of promoting revitalized religious traditions and a culturally indigenous nation. Although both the Ottoman and the colonial Indonesian states had delegated family-law adjudication to religious courts, the successor regime took over such authority more completely and transformed the basis of family law more in Turkey.

The experience of Western colonization was an important reason why rulers followed different strategies in Tunisia and Indonesia, from what they did in Turkey. Colonial rulers had devalued local traditions even while according them recognition in various forms in the former countries, much as in other colonies. In response, anticolonial nationalists felt pressed to uphold indigenous cultural traditions, rather than import many Western precedents in the cultural sphere as the Turkish republican leaders did. While postcolonial theorists highlighted such cultural challenges posed by colonial rule with much eloquence, they did not capture the rather diverse ways in which anticolonial nationalists and postcolonial states responded to these concerns. These actors sometimes asserted cultural traditions in the very forms in which colonial states had recognized them; but in other contexts, they rejected colonial understandings of local cultures and advocated other interpretations, incorporated certain colonial ideas into alternative visions, or championed cultural forms marginalized by colonial modernity. Moreover, some of them found the reform rather than the maintenance of indigenous traditions a more effective response to the colonial denigration of colonized societies as backward and static. Such alternative anticolonial cultural strategies informed the particular forms of multiculturalism and nationalism that postcolonial states adopted. They specifically shaped the retention of much of colonial-era personal law in Lebanon, Syria, and Algeria, in contrast with the adoption of moderate culturally grounded reform in Libya, Egypt, Jordan, India, Malaysia, and Indonesia and more extensive reform in Tunisia. Furthermore, they led some postcolonial states to continue to delegate family law to religious courts (as in Lebanon and Syria), others to give state courts sole authority over religious law (Tunisia), and yet others to grant state courts and religious courts joint adjudicative authority (for example, Indonesia and India).

Postcolonial states responded differently to other colonial cultural legacies too, retaining some, while modifying or abandoning others. For instance, the Indian state retained the colonial recognition of religion as a basis of personal law, but not for political representation, while the Lebanese state continued to accommodate religion in both spheres; the Indonesian state used the colonial emphasis on *adat* not to limit religious identification as colonial administrators tried to do, but to shape religious law based on various changing indigenous practices. More generally, the ways in which the predecessor regime (whether colonial or otherwise) engaged with authoritative social institutions and cultural traditions did not determine all aspects of the strategies of the new regimes. For instance, the Turkish republic's determination to distinguish itself from its predecessor led it to abandon certain aspects of the latter's engagement with religion (its close association with Islam, its delegation of family law to religious courts, and its recognition of various religious institutions) but not others (specifically, its control over Sunni religious institutions exerted by employing their elites and closely supervising their communication).

In sum, the following factors set the background to family-law policy, but did not determine all of its features: the drive to consolidate state authority, the inherited forms of state engagement with and autonomy from the social institutions that the prior family law systems authorized, the ways in which the predecessor regimes viewed and accommodated various cultural traditions pertaining to family life, and the orientations of state elites toward the predecessor regimes' cultural and institutional legacies. Two factors exercised reciprocal influence on each other and shaped approaches to family law—first, the ways in which regimes or segments of regimes aimed to change state-society relations, specifically the alliances they had and aimed to build; and second, the discourses about the nation, its cultural groups, and its traditions that framed the social visions of ruling elites.

The kind of social coalitions that regimes wished to build exercised some influence over their approaches to constructing nations, accommodating cultures, and making families. For instance, the Turkish and Tunisian rulers introduced more extensive reforms in family law than their Indian and Indonesian counterparts did. This was the case although the four regimes inherited states with comparable levels of autonomy from social institutions, the predecessor colonial states had engaged to a similar extent with religious institutions and lineages in Tunisia, India, and Indonesia, and the Ottoman regime had been more closely associated with religious institutions. The crucial difference was that the ruling elites valued the consolidation of broad social coalitions far more in India and Indonesia than in Tunisia and Turkey. The Indian and Indonesian regimes had support that cut across region, religion, ethnicity, and class, and wished to retain it. The Tunisian regime had broad support at the time of decolonization, but its dominant faction was inclined to abandon much of its support among rural lineages and religious elites, emphasize its association with urban groups, and promote the forms of modernity and reformed religious practice that its leaders valued. The early Turkish republic enjoyed less support at the outset, but its leaders were even more vanguardist than their Tunisian counterparts, and were willing to promote Westernizing social reforms although this further limited their support. As the Turkish regime's support became restricted to urban reformers who attached limited value to the public recognition of religion and indigenist constructions of the nation, it relied heavily on the military to repress the significant resistance it faced from certain religious institutions, rural groups, and ethnic minorities.

Thus, regimes engaged with society in significantly different ways although the prior histories of state-society relations were similar in various respects in the countries they governed. Nevertheless, the extent of state autonomy at the point of regime change from the social institutions authorized by the inherited personal-law systems mediated the influence of the coalition-building ambitions of governing elites over the approaches taken to reforming society and personal law. Thus, regimes that wished to maintain broad support varied in their strategies, with the rulers of Libya, Egypt, Jordan, India, Malaysia, and Indonesia changing personal law much more than those of Algeria, Lebanon, Syria, and until recently Morocco. The crucial reason for these different strategies was that the first set of regimes inherited states that were more autonomous of the social institutions that colonial personal laws had authorized, and were eager to consolidate such autonomy while they continued to engage with these institutions. These circumstances made them willing and able to gradually promote the culturally grounded forms of modernity they valued, although they encountered some resistance from conservatives. However, their preference to maintain broad coalitions led them to forge compromises to contain such resistance and prevent much erosion of their support. The second set of regimes relied too much on the social institutions invested in the personal law systems they inherited to be able to pursue even moderate reforms.

If regimes engaged with society in significantly different ways although state-society relations were similar under their predecessor regimes, this was principally due to the discourses about the nation, its cultural groups, and their traditions that oriented regime actors. Aside from influencing the kinds of social coalitions these actors wished to assemble, such discourses exercised independent influence over the approaches the regimes took to make the nation, recognize its traditions, and shape family law.

The effect of discourses of community on regime strategies to build social coalitions and regulate society is highlighted by a consideration of the alternative forms these strategies might have taken if governing elites had operated with different understandings of the nation and its traditions. Turkey's early republican regime included individuals who conceived the nation, its traditions, and its destiny differently—some wished to rebuild the nation based on reformed religious norms, others aimed to revive aspects of pre-Islamic Turkish social life as they imagined it, and yet others wanted to adopt Western institutions and drastically reduce the public roles of religion. If the religious reformists or indigenist secularists had retained significant space in the regime, they would most probably have restricted the extent to which Western civil codes and elements of French secularism were adopted. They might have reformed religious laws to a significant degree as happened in Tunisia, or on a less extensive scale as in Egypt and Jordan. Or they might have incorporated existing or imagined indigenous customs, whose relation to religious traditions was unclear, into religious law, along the lines of the Indonesian experience. Under any of these scenarios, the state would have engaged more closely and tolerantly with religious norms and religious institutions than it did under the hegemony of the Westernizing secularists, and

Turkey might have adopted a form of secularism akin to the Indian and Indonesian variants. The religious reformers and indigenist nationalists also valued broad support more than the Kemalists did, the reforms they favored would likely have been more popular, and their influence would have made the regime more stable in a society in which many citizens valued various religious norms and ethnic customs. As the Kemalists consolidated their control, they promoted their vision of a substantially secularized nation, represented by a highly centralized state. But they could not ensure that state institutions enjoyed popular legitimacy or regulated social life as closely as they wished, because many citizens continued to take their disputes to community institutions. Neither could they prevent the emergence of movements that sought to restore some of religion's public roles.

Alternative constructions of the nation and its traditions would also have led other regimes to engage differently with their societies and adopt different forms of multiculturalism and family law. In Tunisia, if the modernists had envisioned the nation less exclusively in terms of the cultures of the middle- and working classes of the coastal towns, they might have tried to retain the support of conservative rural groups, infringed less on the autonomy of lineages and religious elites, centralized the state less, and changed family law less extensively. If the Free Officers regime and its successors had emphasized the secularist and egalitarian features of their Arab nationalism more in Egypt, they might have paid less attention to allying themselves with major *ulama* and Coptic religious elites and introduced more extensive personal-law reforms. If proponents of an Islamic state such as the Sarekat Islam and the Masjumi had acquired greater influence over the early postcolonial Indonesian regime, they might have ensured the state's symbolic or substantive association with Islam, rather than with a nondenominational monotheism. While this would not have precluded the recognition of minority cultures, including in personal law, it would have made the regime less popular among religious minorities and less stable in the regions where they were concentrated. It might also have made the government less receptive to the imagination of national culture and religious traditions in light of a variety of indigenous customs. The bilateral and matrilineal customs of certain ethnic groups were important sources from which religious scholars and policy makers developed ideas of a national *adat* and framed changes in personal law, and an Islamic understanding of the nation was likely to have limited such changes. The more restricted space for the religious minorities in the ruling elite and the less extensive recognition of *adat* are likely to have particularly limited reforms in the personal laws of non-Muslims and given Indonesian secularism the kind of majoritarian bent seen in India.

If the cultural pluralists who led India's postcolonial regime had engaged more with religious minorities and woven more minority cultural threads into their national tapestries, they probably would have recognized these groups and framed social reform differently. Policy makers would most likely have recognized minority cultures in light of a wider variety of social currents among these groups, including emergent cultural forms, and relied less exclusively on Hindu concerns and initiatives to understand and reduce deep social inequalities. This would have enabled earlier and more extensive changes in the minority personal laws, along lines that enjoyed greater support among the concerned groups. Moreover, under these circumstances the state was likely to have better understood and accommodated minority autonomist initiatives, its preferential policies and other redistributive measures might have reached more members of the religious minorities, and these groups might have extended the state more enthusiastic and enduring support. This would have brought the Indian state closer to realizing its promise to engage similarly with various religious groups and thus made the Indian and Indonesian versions of secularism more similar. Such approaches would have helped the cultural pluralists represented in the regime link initiatives among different religious groups better, and thus have enabled them to counter Hindu majoritarianism more effectively.

Thus, inherited levels of state autonomy and prior forms of state-society engagement did not determine how far and in what ways ruling elites consolidated state authority, and how they regulated social life and family life. Particular constructions of the nation, its cultural groups, and their traditions framed the visions of these elites, and influenced these outcomes. They specifically shaped the forms of state engagement with major social institutions, the social coalitions that these elites assembled, the norms they promoted among the majority of citizens, the groups they recognized, and the forms in which they recognized various groups.

III. FORMATION OF NATION AND FAMILY IN INDIA

The colonial state had devalued indigenous traditions, yet recognized a variety of them and engaged with the social institutions whose authority these traditions upheld in India, as in most colonies. It recognized the importance of religion in public life in different ways, and specifically in family life, to enable stable governance.

The responses of Indian nationalists to colonial institutions and colonial discourse influenced the forms that multiculturalism and family law took after independence. Like the majority of anticolonial nationalists elsewhere, Indian nationalists wished to build a nation that was identifiably based in indigenous cultures. However, those who led the early postcolonial regime retained more colonial legacies and built more institutions modeled after Western precedents than many other opponents of colonial rule did, even while they altered some of these legacies to suit indigenous circumstances and their postcolonial aspirations. They specifically retained certain forms of colonial multiculturalism, including the recognition of particular public roles for religion. But they abandoned certain colonial forms of recognition, such as separate religious electorates, because they considered them incompatible with secularism and national cohesion, and the majority of them sought to modify certain cultural norms to promote social equality and individual liberties much more than colonial officials had—for instance, by outlawing untouchability and fostering lower-caste uplift. Moreover, they wished to deepen the representative character of colonial self-government institutions, and prioritized the consolidation of democracy more than most anticolonial nationalists did. The majority of Indian nationalists conceived of a culturally indigenous nation primarily in terms of Hindu cultures for two reasons: they accepted the frequent equation in colonial discourse of the Hindu and the culturally indigenous and the association of Muslims with transnational cultures; and they engaged primarily with initiatives among Hindus, especially those who belonged to the social elite. This meant that they conceived the modern Indian family primarily in terms of certain Hindu visions and practices, both enduring and emergent, and did not consider the formation of the religious minorities crucial to making the postcolonial nation.

Such visions of the Indian nation, its religious groups, and their future led postcolonial state elites to retain distinct personal-law systems and focus their reform initiatives solely on Hindu law until the 1970s. They changed only Hindu law soon after independence, although initiatives for culturally grounded personal-law reform were comparably strong among Muslims and Hindus. As they prioritized the consolidation of democracy and the maintenance of broad coalitions, the modernists and the conservatives forged compromises over moderate reforms. These reforms increased conjugal autonomy and women's rights in certain respects, for instance by giving individuals greater room to choose who to marry and whether to continue their matrimonial relationships, and by granting women rights to shares equal to those of their brothers in their parents' separate intestate property. But they maintained the authority of lineages and men in other respects, especially over the inheritance and control of jointly owned family property. Moreover, they signaled the family practices the state valued, for instance by enabling intercaste marriages and equalizing children's rights in intestate separate property, rather than enforcing their rapid adoption, such as by restricting testation. The moderate and culturally grounded nature of personal-law reform followed the predominant pattern in postcolonial societies, in contrast with the experience in former colonies that either retained much of colonial personal law (such as Lebanon), changed personal law more extensively (for example, Tunisia), abandoned distinct personal laws (as in Vietnam), or increased the scope of religious law and the authority of religious elites, men, and lineages (as Sudan did). The pattern of reform in India also differed from that in countries like Indonesia where the laws governing minorities were changed more extensively, in societies such as Pakistan and Bangladesh where they were not changed, and in societies like China and Turkey where distinct personal laws ceased to govern these groups.

Certain changes in patterns of mobilization, salient discourses of community, and values regarding the family enabled modifications in personal-law policy since the 1970s. Women's organizations and other civil-society organizations grew, promoted support for women's rights, and mobilized understandings of group tradition that provided grounds for extensive reforms. Moreover, ongoing socioeconomic changes made agrarian groups more open to the division of lineage property into individual shares. Hindu nationalists grew in strength, and highlighted demands for the speedy introduction of a UCC, but did not specify the content of such a code or initiate such a change. In response to the growth of Hindu nationalism and intolerance toward religious minorities, certain rights organizations, social movements, and political parties increased their engagement with minority initiatives and traditions, and proposed culturally grounded changes in the minority laws. As a result of these changes, support increased among the political elite for the autonomy of individuals and women in certain aspects of family life, and more of them found the pursuit of these goals compatible with broad social coalitions. Moreover, some policy elites became willing to base Hindu law on a wider cultural repertoire, including emergent practices and novel interpretations of Hindu traditions, and others grew more aware of minority norms and initiatives that supported greater rights for women and individuals.

These developments enabled further changes in personal law that increased women's rights and the autonomy of individuals and nuclear families, and departed from the primarily patrilineal constructions of kinship and inheritance that had shaped Hindu law. Besides, the later reforms extended to the minority laws. The main changes since the 1970s increased the divorce rights of Hindus, Christians, and Parsis; provided all women greater protection from domestic violence and gave them rights in the matrimonial home if they faced such abuse; gave Hindu daughters rights equal to those of their brothers in family joint property and in the ancestral home; made the inheritance rights of Hindu widows in their deceased husbands' property independent of their current civil status; equalized the divorce rights of Christian men and women; gave Muslim divorcees greater claims on their ex-husbands' income and property; and restricted unilateral male repudiation among Muslims.

However, policy makers remained more inclined to signal the practices they underwrote than to promote considerable social change. As a result, they indicated that they wanted women to own more property by making Hindu daughters coparceners in family joint property, but limited women's empowerment in the process by retaining testamentary freedom in Hindu law, which enabled parents to deprive their daughters of their entitlements through wills. They did so although civil society mobilizers emphasized that a failure to restrict testation would seriously limit women's gains, that limits on testation could be drawn from various Western and Islamic legal systems, and that Hindu law did not provide testamentary rights in joint property until the 1950s.

Moreover, the majority of political elites remained more connected to Hindu initiatives and traditions, which continued to be the main sources for their visions of the Indian nation, and more concerned to change Hindu practices. Therefore, their understandings of the modern Indian family continued to focus on Hindu law, which they changed far more than the minority laws. Understanding of minority traditions and opinion remained limited among policy elites, some of whom became more inclined to ensure Hindu hegemony. These circumstances continued to restrict the accommodation of culturally grounded demands for minority personal law reform. They specifically prevented the extension of adoption rights to all Christians and inheritance rights in agricultural land to all Muslim women, even though organizations of the relevant communities and rights organizations with support among different religious groups pressed these demands.

IV. THE AGENDA FOR FURTHER PERSONAL LAW REFORM IN INDIA

In the course of mobilizing in favor of the changes introduced in India's personal laws over the past two decades, civil-society organizations also offered other proposals to advance women's rights or individual autonomy in family life. Legislators are currently considering some of these proposals, have debated others since the 1990s but failed to adopt them, and have not so far examined yet others. Our analysis of the determinants of personal-law policy indicates that some of these proposals may be adopted in the near future, but that other demands will be accommodated only if certain features of policy makers' orientations to making nation, community, and family change.

Parliament is currently considering a bill to grant divorce rights under conditions of irretrievable marital breakdown even in the absence of spousal fault and mutual consent. The bill gives women the right to resist such divorce petitions if divorce would cause them grave financial hardship, and entitles them to a share in their matrimonial property (to be determined by the court) when they get divorced. When they made Hindu daughters coparceners in family joint property in 2004–5, legislators also debated the following proposals: the extension of coparcener status to Hindu widows, the decomposition of joint property into equal separate shares for each nuclear family member, and the limitation of testamentary rights to ensure that Hindu daughters receive a substantial proportion of the property to which they are entitled intestate. They did not make widows coparceners, mainly because many of them did not realize that the shares of widows would otherwise decline due to the rise in the shares of daughters. Parliament did not dissolve joint property, because certain proponents of increased inheritance rights for women shared the preference of conservatives to maintain the joint family's control over some property. It maintained testamentary freedom in joint property because many conservative legislators accepted making daughters coparceners only based on the silent assurance that people could still will most of their shares in such property to their sons.

Various legislators and bureaucrats resisted the demands of Christian organizations for unlimited adoption rights, because they believed this would enable an increase in the Christian share of the population. Muslim reformist organizations demanded that Muslim women's rights to access their dower be strengthened, and that men be deprived of the right to unilaterally repudiate their spouses or women be given that right as well. Moreover, certain conservative Muslim organizations joined reformers in demanding that Muslim women be given the right to inherit a Qur'anic share (half the share to which similarly positioned male kin are entitled) in family agricultural land in the regions where this right is not recognized (other than in Bengal, the northeastern states, Maharashtra, Gujarat, Andhra Pradesh, Tamil Nadu, Kerala, and parts of Karnataka). Policy elites were reluctant to accommodate these demands because they were uncertain about support for them among Indian Muslims and in Islamic tradition. Besides, the Hindu nationalists underlined demands to introduce a UCC since the 1980s, but did not explore such legislation either when they led the national government or when they governed particular states.

Of these proposals, legislators denied coparcener status to Hindu widows in joint property only because they did not adequately consider the implications of doing so. Even conservative representatives might accept this proposal soon. They should be more amenable to it than to making married daughters coparceners, which many of them agreed to do in 2005, as *Mitakshara* law and other patrilineal traditions consider widows members of the joint family but take married daughters to leave their natal lineages for those of their husbands.

The widespread concern among the political and judicial elite to provide an exit for couples in dysfunctional marriages should enable the acceptance of irretrievable marital breakdown as a ground for divorce, and the Rajya Sabha accepted this proposal in August 2013. Many civil society activists and some legislators are concerned about the potential deleterious economic consequences for divorcées and their children, but the room that the bill under consideration provides for women to oppose their spouses' divorce petitions on the ground of likely financial hardship and the share that it offers them in matrimonial property address this concern to some extent. These actors demanded that the bill specify divorcées' share in matrimonial property, in view of the inconsistent judicial record of ensuring support for divorcées and their children. However, many proponents of the proposed legislation are more inclined to demonstrate their belief that couples should share the property accumulated in the course of their marriages (as they contributed jointly to its acquisition) than to ensure that divorcées receive a substantial share. They left the divorcée's share to the court's discretion partly to accommodate conservative legislators who believe that matrimonial property should belong largely to the partner who earns more. The even greater reluctance of these legislators to accept the entitlement of divorcées to a share of their husband's residential property if it was not acquired with the couple's income during their marriage resulted in the deletion of this provision in the bill that the Rajya Sabha passed. The Lok Sabha is likely to pass this bill only if it retains its current form, not specifying the share of matrimonial property to accrue to the divorcée and not giving her a share in residential property that the husband inherited or acquired with his income prior to the couple's marriage. Such legislation will no doubt lead some courts to provide divorcées with limited support. Divorcées' entitlements are likely to be reinforced further only when more political elites believe that Hindu spouses should share matrimonial property equally.

The limitation of testamentary rights and the dissolution of joint property in Hindu law could empower women far more than the grant of coparcener status to daughters did, especially if people are allowed to will no more than a third of their property (as is the case in Islamic law and as certain policy planners have suggested be made the rule in Hindu law since the CSWI Report of 1974). These proposals will continue to face considerable resistance for precisely that reason. The argument of reformist mobilizers that restricting testamentary rights to a third of one's property would not take Indian law in entirely new directions because of the precedents in Islamic law will prove persuasive only when more political elites accept that one may borrow rules applied to Hindus from Islamic traditions. More of the political elite and mobilized citizens must embrace the equalization of gender roles and the democratization of families if testamentary rights are to be limited and joint property dissolved. Moreover, the dissolution of joint property is possible only if many Hindus cease to attach importance to the joint family as a unit that controls property, a change that would be compatible with the continued relevance of the joint family as a residential unit and a reference point in identity formation.

If the changes proposed in the minority laws are to be adopted, their proponents would need to overcome the resistance of those who find them contrary to their visions of desirable family organization, group tradition, or intergroup relations. Demands to reinforce Muslim women's access to their dower and to make unilateral repudiation equally available to Muslim men and women (or unavailable to both) were not seriously considered because there was limited mobilization in their favor, some conservative organizations opposed them, many policy elites did not understand how religious scholars justified such provisions in India and elsewhere, and the few that understood the relevant Islamic legal arguments were not convinced that they enjoyed support among many Indian Muslims. Even the support of the main conservative Muslim organizations for giving Muslim women Qur'anic shares in agricultural land throughout India did not bring about this change, because policy makers did not engage closely with this initiative and understand how it was based in widely accepted constructions of Islamic law; many of them did not grasp that the national government has the power to introduce this change; and conservative Muslim organizations did not mobilize strongly behind this demand because it remained unpopular among landed groups.

Islamic norms that distribute gendered authority more equally in families need to be mobilized much further, and gain the understanding and support of more policy elites, if the proposed changes in Muslim law are to be adopted. Moreover, for inheritance law to be changed, reformers would need to effectively press conservative Muslim organizations to give this demand much more attention, and policy elites would have to understand that conservatives cannot resist this change because it is indisputably grounded in the Qur'an, and that Indian federalism permits national legislation on this question.

Christian mobilization regarding personal law has emphasized adoption rights for over a decade. However, many Hindu policy makers remain unwilling to give Christians the right to adopt foundlings of unknown ancestry because of dystopian fears of a rapid growth in the population and social influence of the religious minorities. To circumvent this problem, religious pluralists would need to grow much stronger and effectively counter the demographic anxieties cultivated by the Hindu nationalists. If they do so, more policy elites will accept gradual increases in the non-Hindu share of the population or at least realize that unlimited adoption rights are unlikely to change population ratios much.

Although a UCC has been a motif of Hindu nationalist discourse since the 1980s, the BJP did not propose such legislation when it led the national government from 1998 to 2004 because most of its coalition partners opposed this move. Moreover, it neither took steps in this direction in the states that it ruled on its own nor initiated a debate about the content of a UCC, because its discourse about family law served mainly to portray the religious minorities as averse to national integration and modern values. The shift of most civil-society organizations that address family law from the aim of a UCC to that of culturally grounded personal-law reform has narrowed support for a UCC, and most political parties do not favor this goal as a result. These changes in civil-society mobilization and the minority law reforms they enabled since the 1970s have rendered less credible the claim that minority resistance to reform obliges modernists to introduce a UCC to promote the family practices they value. If the Hindu nationalists attempt to introduce a UCC in the future, they would face strong resistance from most political parties, which rely significantly on minority support.

V. LESSONS DRAWN FROM A COMPARATIVE PERSPECTIVE ON INDIAN EXPERIENCES

The book's exploration of the experience of Indian personal law in a comparative perspective indicates certain paths that multiculturalism, secularism, and family law may follow in India, as well as in other developing societies in which many citizens attach considerable value to various group traditions and to particular public roles for religion, and states recognize certain culturally specific norms in family life. In such societies, changes in family law are most likely to gain significant public support if they are based in the cultural traditions and practices of the concerned groups. The experiences of India and of other societies that saw comparable or higher levels of culturally grounded changes in personal law indicate that the traditions of many groups provide grounds for extensive reforms that enhance women's rights and individual liberties. Moreover, the demands of reformist mobilizers in various countries suggest ways in which cultural dynamism may be promoted to build social bases for further legal changes that advance these goals. The limited extent to which various states that employ multicultural policies have used the support that group norms and popular mobilization provide for culturally based reforms makes it more crucial to explore this avenue further.

We saw that states professing commitments to secularism accommodated many public roles for religion in countries such as India and Indonesia. Such extensive public recognition of religion met the expectations of many groups in these societies, and provided public institutions greater legitimacy. The pattern of secularism adopted in these societies and its consequences make for a sharp contrast with the experience in Turkey. The serious limits placed on the public roles of religious norms and religious symbols in Turkey enjoyed support only among a minority of citizens, and evoked considerable resistance. The country's rulers could sustain this form of secularism only by resorting to extensive repression or military rule at various points. Besides, the imposition of state tutelage over the most influential religious institutions was at odds with the rulers' claims to have erected a wall of separation between state and religion. Moreover, the limited public support for the secularization of family law during the early years of the Turkish republic meant that the state courts did not monopolize the adjudication of matrimonial disputes for at least a generation after they were granted exclusive jurisdiction over them. The acceptance of the simultaneous consideration of matrimonial and property cases by community courts in India and Indonesia was more pragmatic, since various groups felt a greater affinity with these courts or found them more accessible. The type of secularism seen in India and Indonesia offers a promising model for changing the public roles of religion in ways that are somewhat accountable and tolerant and that promote equality and liberty in some respects, while securing regimes a significant measure of legitimacy. It is worthy of emulation in the majority of societies, in which religious norms frame the expectations of many citizens in public life, if it is appropriately modified to suit the context. The early Turkish republican experience is less relevant for such societies. The widespread discontent with various features of Turkish policy enabled the growth of Islamic forces such as the Justice and Development Party, which have begun to accommodate public religion more, though not without provoking new conflicts.

A comparison of the forms of nationalism and secularism that the state adopted in India and Indonesia and the patterns of personal-law reform in these two countries highlights certain ways in which Indian policy makers could learn from Indonesian experiences. The personal laws of the religious minorities were changed earlier and more extensively in Indonesia. Certain features of the Indonesian experience enabled this outcome. Many religious scholars and policy elites incorporated in their constructions of indigenous Islam certain customs that were shared by the members of different religious groups and bore an uncertain relationship with classical Islamic traditions. Moreover, official constructions of the nation referred to elements of the different world religions present in the country, as well as various indigenous folk religious beliefs and practices. The prevalence of such nationalist and religious discourses led policy makers to draw from bilateral customs that gave women greater rights and nuclear families greater autonomy to reform the personal laws of both the Muslim majority and the religious minorities.

By way of contrast, nationalist discourses referred largely to Hindu cultures in India, and highlighted the transnational affinities of India's Muslims and Christians. Moreover, Islamic scholars were reluctant to incorporate customs shared by India's Muslims and non-Muslims into their constructions of religious tradition. These features of nationalist and religious discourse restricted connections between the reformist initiatives that emerged among different religious groups even though these mobilizers sometimes promoted similar social practices, and specifically contributed to the limited engagement of most policy makers with minority initiatives and traditions. These conditions led policy makers to focus on changing Hindu law soon after independence although culturally grounded initiatives for personal law reform were not weaker among Muslims than among Hindus. The strength of support for changes in personal law among the minorities at the point of decolonization shows that political elites missed an opportunity to change minority laws then. However, the comparison with Indonesia indicates that such a course was likely to have been followed only if influential nationalist discourses had included the religious minorities and their cultures more in India. It also shows that if more extensive changes are to be made in the minority personal laws and in other aspects of minority accommodation in India in the future, pluralistic constructions of the nation must be mobilized more and reformist initiatives should connect the members of different religious groups and their normative traditions more closely. This is particularly necessary insofar as Hindu majoritarian visions are popular and well organized. Such changes would enable reformers to draw more fully from the aspects of the country's diverse and dynamic cultural repertoires that hold promise for the democratic reconstruction of families, religious groups, and the nation, and thereby counter conservative efforts to resist such changes as contrary to indigenous cultures.

NOTES

CHAPTER ONE
1. *Mohammad Ahmed Khan v. Shah Bano Begum*, AIR 1985 SC 945.
2. For different understandings of the relative importance of these goals to democracy and how they might be reconciled, see Lijphart 1977; Horowitz 1985; Kymlicka 1995; Okin et al. 1999; Parekh 2006; Lipset 1981; Moore 1966; Rueschemeyer, Huber, and Stephens 1992.
3. Kandiyoti 1991a; Glendon 1989; Hooker 1975.
4. See: Hooker 1975; Mamdani 1996; Benton 2001; Asad 2003; Jacobsohn 2003; Taylor 2007; Bowen 2009; Beaman 2012.
5. For details of developments in Morocco, Tunisia and Algeria, see Charrad 2001; Charrad and Goeken 2006; Buskens 2010; in Senegal, D. Robinson 1992; Creevey 1996; in Libya, Mayer 1977; Layish 1991; in Egypt, Tucker 2008; Lombardi 2006; in Syria, Berger 1997; Hinnebusch 1993; in Lebanon, Bilani and el-Gemayel 1985; Joseph 1994; in Jordan, Sonbol 2002; Welchman 1988; in Nigeria, Harnischfeger 2008; Peters 2001; in Sudan, Massoud 2013; Fluehr-Lobban 1987; in Iraq, Joseph 1991; Stilt 2004; in Iran, Osanloo 2009; Mir-Hosseini 2000; in Afghanistan, Ghasemi 1998; in Pakistan, Nelson 2011; Yilmaz 2005; Mehdi 1994; in India, Menski 2001, 2003; Solanki 2011; Agnes 1999; Subramanian 2008, 2010; Vatuk 2005; Williams 2006; in Sri Lanka, Goonesekere 1980, 1990; in Bangladesh, Bhuiyan 2010; Hoque and Khan 2007; in Malaysia, Mohamad 2010; Peletz 2002; Horowitz 1994; in Indonesia, Bowen 2003; Feener 2007; Cammack and Feener 2007; Salim 2008; in the Philippines, Feliciano 1994.
6. Moore 1966; Huntington 1968, 1998; Rustow 1970; Rueschemeyer, Huber and Stephens 1992.

7. Gerschenkron 1962; Johnson 1982; Evans 1995; Amsden 2007.

8. Asad 1993; Asad 2003; Casanova 1994, 2006; Taylor 2007; Brown 2008; Eisenstadt 1987, 2003.

9. Anderson 1983; Smith 1986; Horowitz 1985; Marx 1998, 2003.

10. Hobsbawm and Ranger 1983; Anderson 1983; Cohn 1996; Viswanathan 1989; P. Chatterjee 1993.

11. India, Office of the Registrar General and Census Commissioner 2003; India, Census Commissioner 1943; Davis 1949; The population shares of religious groups changed significantly when predominantly Muslim Pakistan was partitioned from India at the point of independence. The population share of Christians changed considerably because of conversion, and there are very different estimates of the current Christian population. As the Indian censuses have estimated it, it rose from 0.7 percent in 1881 to 2.0 percent in 1941 (the last colonial census) and 2.3 percent in 2001. The censuses underestimate the changes since independence. Many recent lower-caste converts to Christianity from Hinduism do not officially claim a Christian identity even while practicing Christianity, because census officials usually provide those who declare themselves to be of the lower castes only three choices regarding religious identity—Hindu, Sikh or Buddhist. Many lower-caste Christians also do not declare themselves Christian to state officials because they would thereby lose preferences in education and government employment and special civil rights protections. The World Christian Database estimated the Christian share of the population to be as high as 6.7 percent in 2005 and to have increased sharply since 1995, when it was only 2.7 percent. Its estimates correct for the misreporting of religious identity to census officials by some practicing Christians. The Atlas of Global Christianity and Operation World, which rely on the figures provided by Christian churches rather than census officials, estimated Indian Christians to be 4.8 percent and 5.8 percent respectively of the Indian population in 2010. I rely hereafter on the figures of the World Christian Database which seem most reliable. See: Frykenberg 2008, vii; Lausanne Global Analysis 2011.

12. Viswanathan 1989; Dirks 2001; Kaviraj 1992.

13. *Qazi, a* word of Persian origin, is used most often in much of India, while the Arabic word *qadi* is used in much of the Muslim world.

14. For further details, see: Ewing 1988; Gilmartin 1988; Zaman 2002; Metcalf 1982, 2009a; Kugle 2001; Robinson 2008; Moosa 2009; Nelson 2011; De 2009.

15. See Halhed 2001; Strange 2007; Mulla 1975.

16. Lingat 1998, 176–206; Davis 2010, 144–65.

17. On the relationship of the *shastras* to colonial Hindu law, see: Rocher 1972; Cohn 1996, 57–75.

18. Jones 1989; Derrett 1976; Menski 2003; Newbigin 2011; India. RHLC 1941, 1947.

19. Derrett 1968, 1978; Menski 2003; Heimsath 1964.

20. Nehru 1959, 1990, 1996.

21. P. Chatterjee 1993; Tejani 2008; Jaffrelot 1996.

22. M. Gandhi 2008; Parekh 1989; Sinha 2006.

CHAPTER TWO

1. Pufendorf 1991; Bodin 1955; Filmer 1949.

2. Weber 1968, 1006–69.

3. Adams 2005 argued that early modern European states had pronounced patrimonial features; Adams and Charrad 2011 provided a comparative survey of modern patrimonialism; Eisenstadt 1973 offered the classic understanding of contemporary neopatrimonialism.

4. Cott 2000.

5. Cretney 2005; Glendon 1989; Colley 2009; Thompson 1966; Bell 2003; Hill 2008 on Britain and France. See Yilmaz 2005; Kuru 2009, 161–246; Charrad 2001 on Turkey and Tunisia.

6. Glendon 1989; Friedman 1994, 2004.

7. Foucault 1978, 1980, 2007; Ong and Peletz 1995; Mitchell 1991a; Rabinow 1995; Asad 2003; Peletz 2009.

8. Charrad 2001.

9. While Cott focused on visions of sovereignty, Charrad seemed to consider visions of nation and modernity concomitants of institutionalized state-society relations.

10. P. Chatterjee 1993.

11. "The modern state, embedded as it is within the universal narrative of capital, cannot recognize within its jurisdiction any form of community except the single, determinate, demographically enumerable form of the nation. It must therefore subjugate, if necessary by the use of state violence, all . . . aspirations of community identity." P. Chatterjee 1993, 238.

12. P. Chatterjee 1993; Mamdani 1996.

13. P. Chatterjee 1993, 1994.

14. Benton 2001; Merry 1991, 1999; Chanock 1991.

15. Everett 1979; Basu and Ray 1990; Nair 1996. Sinha 1999 and Nair 1996 equate the approaches of the major male leaders with those of Indian nationalists *tout court,* although understandings of Indian nationalism influenced the strategies of the AIWC and the WIA.

16. For an overarching view of multiple modernities, see Eisenstadt 1987, 2003. See also Chapter 1, notes 5–9.

17. Gerschenkron 1962; Johnson 1982; Evans 1995; Amsden 2001; Hill 2008.

18. Easton 1953; Almond and Coleman 1960.

19. Especially Nordlinger 1981; Krasner 1978.

20. Skocpol 1985, 1995; Bates 1981; Evans 1995.

21. Mitchell 1991b and Migdal 2001 highlight these problems.

22. Tilly 1975; Goldstone 1991; Marx 1998.

23. Friedman 1994, 2004.

24. Migdal 2001 is a particularly nuanced expression of this approach. Collier and Collier 1991; Migdal, Kohli, and Shue 1993; Jackman 1993; and Kohli 2004 are other important instances.

25. Various other theories also advance the first three claims. It is the combination of these and the fourth claim that is distinctive of the state-in-society school.

26. Khoury and Kostiner 1990; Charrad 2001; Adams and Charrad 2011.

27. Jackman 1993; Breuilly 1994; Marx 1998, 2003.

28. Microlevel discipline was the focus of his earlier work (Foucault 1973, 1977, 1978). His later lectures (Foucault 2007) emphasized macrolevel regulation.

29. Mitchell 1991a; Rabinow 1995; Peletz 2002, 2009; Asad 2003.

30. Scott 1998.

31. Said 1978; some of the essays in Hobsbawm and Ranger 1983; Cohn 1996; and Stoler 2009 explore colonial knowledge. Poststructuralist theory especially shaped Stoler's analysis, and bore affinities with the work of Said, Cohn, and Ranger. Cohn 1996; Appadurai 1996; Mamdani 1996; Nobles 2000; and Dirks 2001 discussed forms of colonial and postcolonial social classification. Dirks 2001; P. Chatterjee 1993; Mitchell 1991a; and Stoler 1985 highlighted ways in which social groups appropriated features of colonial discourse for counterhegemonic purposes.

32. Benton 2001; Merry 1999; and Chanock 1985 detail such trends in various societies.

33. Friedman 1994, 2004; Glendon 1987, 1989 and Goode 1993 agree with many of Friedman's claims, but offer more nuanced accounts.

34. Schwartz and Skolnick 1970; Stein 1980; Elliott 1985; Lowe and Douglas 2009.

35. Parashar 1992 also mistook the greater role of statute after decolonization to mean that the state modified religious rules and limited religious authority to a greater degree. Even colonial personal law was formed through considerable changes in prior norms and religious elites had limited roles in the state's legal system from the late nineteenth century, but various religious leaders continued to run community courts.

36. Women in matrilineal groups lost certain rights through the application of official Islamic law, but they were a small minority of Indian Muslims, mostly in Kerala and Lakshadweep. See Arunima 2003; Miller 1976.

37. Sunder Rajan 2003, 148–49 and Okin 2001 claimed that Muslim women had lost alimony rights over a decade after courts had increased these rights.

38. Bowen 2003; Cammack and Feener 2007.

39. But policy makers seriously considered the equalization of these shares in Indonesia.

40. Peletz 2002, 2009; Bowen 2003; Brewer 1999; Feliciano 1994.

41. Charrad 2001.

42. John Bowen especially helped me understand this.

43. Coulson 1971; Tucker 2008; Zaman 2002.

44. Sreenivas 2008.

45. For instance, she did not distinguish the greater orientation to reform among the less conservative traditionalists (e.g., C. Rajagopalachari, the first Indian Governor General (1948–50), who supported a minimum marriage age, inheritance rights for Hindu women in property earned by their parents, and the right of Hindus to a divorce after a period of judicial separation, while opposing giving daughters access to jointly owned ancestral property) than the more conservative ones (e.g., Rajendra Prasad, India's first President (1950–62), who opposed all of these proposals); nor did she distinguish variations among modernists, of whom the majority supported the right of males alone to partition jointly owned family property but a minority, including B.R. Ambedkar, the first postcolonial Law Minister, wished to extend this right to females as well.

46. Birla 2009.

47. Bourdieu 1977.

48. Bowen 2003; Peletz 1996; Feener 2007; Feener and Cammack 2007; Peletz 2002.

49. Powers 1986; Coulson 1971; Spooner 1966.

50. Rocher 1972; Cohn 1996, 57–75.

51. Agarwal 1995, 2008.

52. They offer an alternative to understandings that the French or the American version of secularism is the exemplar. For this older view, see: Berger 1967; and, with reference to India, D. Smith 1963.

53. Monsma and Soper 2009; Jacobsohn 1996; Asad 2003; Bhargava 1999, 2010; Casanova 1994, 2006; Taylor 2007.

54. Madan 2003; Nandy 1988. Madan and Nandy inappropriately focused their criticisms on Indian institutions.

55. Jacobsohn 1996, 2003.

56. Peled 2001, 70–71; Woods 2008. While the rabbinical courts do not usually register polygamous unions, "courts" composed of a hundred rabbis permit certain Jews to contract polygynous marriages. Edelman 1994, 143.

57. Jacobsohn 2003; Bhargava 2010; Brass 1991, 75–108; Chiriyankandath 2000; Mitra and Fischer 2002.

58. Gilmartin 1988; Nelson 2011.

59. The Muslim political elites who put forward the Shariat Act had said that they could not apply this central legislation to the inheritance of agricultural land, which was under provincial jurisdiction. But the Government of India Act of 1935 had placed the administration of agricultural land under provincial jurisdiction precisely due to the influence of one of the Shariat Act's architects, Mian Fazl-i-Husain (Nelson 2011, 100–102). The Indian Constitution made succession to all forms of property part of the "concurrent list," enabling either the national or the state governments to change laws regarding the inheritance of agricultural land. Bina Agarwal drew my attention to the implications of this change for amending the Shariat Act. Agarwal 2008, 337–38.

60. This change was introduced in the largest West Pakistani provinces of West Punjab and Sind in 1948 and 1950 respectively, and in the rest of West Pakistan in 1963. Islamic law was applied to agricultural land inheritance even before the passage of the Shariat Act in East Bengal. Nelson 2011, 161–69. Nelson showed that landed groups bypassed this legislation and maintained patrilineal inheritance, but did not discuss the motivations behind this reform. In India, the Shariat Act was similarly amended in two states in which bilateral and matrilineal kin practices were widespread—in Madras Presidency in 1949 and in Kerala in 1963. Islamic law had already been applied to the inheritance of agricultural land under colonial rule in West Bengal, Assam, Bombay Presidency, and Hyderabad state.

61. Asaf Ali Fyzee and Sharifa Hamid Ali were the chief proponents.

62. This is discussed in Chapters 3 and 5.

63. Pandey 1990, 2005; P. Chatterjee 1992; Mufti 2007.

64. The significant gap between the estimates of the Christian share of the population offered by the Indian census and the World Christian Database (2.3 percent and 6.7 percent respectively) suggests that many from the lower castes nevertheless converted to Christianity, but avoided reporting this to officials to retain their eligibility for preferences and special civil rights protections, and perhaps to reduce the prospect of Hindu nationalist attacks, which targeted Christian conversion activity over the past two decades. Minority religious identity does not, however, make individuals ineligible for the scheduled tribe and "other backward classes" (i.e., lower-middle and middle caste) preferences.

65. Most Nagas practice Christianity and folk religions, and the majority of Kashmiris are Muslim. See Galanter 1984 regarding preferential policies; Subramanian 1999

about the Dravidian movement; Baruah 1999 and 2005 concerning the Assamese and Naga movements; Brass 1991 and Singh 2000 regarding the Sikh movement; and Ganguly 1999 about Kashmiri nationalism.

66. For instance, Galanter 1984 and Mendelsohn and Vicziany 1998 noted the unavailability of preferences for Muslim and Christian lower castes, but did not explore the reasons. Brass 1991, Ganguly 1999, and Baruah 2005 did not address these aspects of state responses to the Sikh, Kashmiri, and Naga and Assamese movements respectively. Bhattacharyya 2003; Roy 2007; Ruparelia 2008; and Stepan, Linz, and Yadav 2011 did not examine these features of Indian multiculturalism.

67. See: Ahmed 1992; Ziadeh 1968; Kerr 1966; Tucker 2008, 65–77; Abu-Odeh 2004.

68. Ziadeh 1968, 117, 138; Abu-Odeh 2004, 1095–1101, 1126–46; Singerman 2005; Badran 2009, 1–54; Wickham 2002.

69. Regarding Malaysia, see Peletz 2002, Mohamad 2010, Sobotkova 2012, Horowitz 1994, and Hooker 1984, 48–60, 123–43, 148–50 on family law; Horowitz 1985, 398–440 and Camroux 1996 on ethnic politics and Islamism. Regarding Sri Lanka, see Goonesekere 1980; Goonesekere 1990 on family law; DeVotta 2004 on ethnic and religious politics; Bond 1988 on contemporary public Buddhism. Two of Sri Lanka's three personal law systems (Kandyan and Thesavalamai law) initially governed the inhabitants of particular regions, but the courts came to apply them, in combination with principles of Roman-Dutch and English law, largely to the Sinhalese and (non-Muslim) Tamil ethnic groups respectively.

70. Welchman 1988; Wiktorowicz 2001; Abu-Odeh 2000.

71. Regarding Indonesian nationalism and *Pancasila*, see Darmaputera 1988; Anderson 1998, 77–173; 1999; and Bertrand 2004, 28–34. Bowen 1988, 1998, 2003; Cammack, Young, and Heaton 1996; Feener and Cammack 2007; Salim 2008; Cammack 2002; and Cammack 2008 discuss personal law. Bowen 2003, 53–55; Cammack and Feener 2007; and Cammack 2002 explore the judicial deployment of notions of a national *adat*.

72. Of these countries, Malaysia comes closest to the Indonesian pattern. Both countries have Muslim majorities and significant religious minorities, widespread bilateral and matrilineal practices that colonial and postcolonial law recognized in some ways, the majority of Muslims adhere to the Shafiʿi *madhhab*, Islamic courts govern Muslims and civil courts govern the other religious groups, and policy makers gave Islamic law greatest attention, but also changed the minority laws.

73. This proposal is discussed in Feener 2007, 141–46, and Cammack 2002. Some Muslim women get no shares or negligible shares of certain properties, the inheritance of which is governed by ethnic custom rather than Islamic law. This is the case regarding agricultural land in much of India, and for most forms of property among the Berbers of Morocco and Algeria.

74. See Kuru 2009, 202–23, Kuru and Stepan 2012, and Berkes 1964 on Turkish secularism; Kandiyoti 1991b and Arat 1994 on its implications for women; and Yilmaz 2005, Yildirim 2005, Starr 1978 and 1989 on family law. The monarchy introduced very similar family law reforms just three years later in Albania, based on the French, Swiss, and Italian Civil Codes. Communist and postcommunist legislation increased women's rights further. Zace 1995.

75. Moroccan policy went further than the Tunisian precedents in giving spouses equal shares of matrimonial property on divorce, and making them jointly responsible for managing the nuclear family. Mir-Hosseini 2007; Wuerth 2005; Buskens 2010.

76. See Charrad 2001, 201–32; 2007; Charrad and Goeken 2006 on Tunisian Islamic law; Anderson 1986 on Tunisian nationalism and the Neo-Destour Party.

77. Arjomand 1989, 1988.

78. Osanloo 2009, Mir-Hosseini 2000, and Halper 2005 discuss changes in Islamic law. Osanloo 2009, Mir-Hosseini 1999, and Paidar 1995 place them in the context of women's changing experiences and debates on religion and gender.

79. Weiss 1986 and Mehdi 1994 explore the changes in Islamic law. Shaikh 2009, 107–15, 150–79 and Esposito 1990, 170–87 relate them to the politics of the dictatorship. Regarding conservative changes in Islamic law in Sudan, see Massoud 2013; Fluehr-Lobban 1987; in Nigeria, Harnischfeger 2008; Peters 2001; in Afghanistan, Ghasemi 1998; Middleton 2000.

80. Breuilly 1994, 390 elaborates on this connection.

81. Kuru 2009.

82. Yilmaz 2005.

83. Edelman 1994; Peled 2001.

84. The Pakistani state allowed Muslims to move from India to Pakistan and non-Muslims to leave for India soon after it was formed. The Israeli state encouraged the continued immigration of Jews, but denied Palestinians expelled when it was formed and their descendants a similar "right of return."

85. Important changes were made in 1938 in Orthodox Coptic Christian law, particularly in divorce rights. But further changes were not made in these laws, to accommodate the Orthodox Coptic Church. Shaham 2010; Rowberry and Khalil 2010; Hassan 2003.

86. See Bhuiyan 2007, 2010, and Hoque and Khan 2007 about the personal laws. See Baxter 1984 about nationalism in Bangladesh.

87. Siraj 1994. The changes in Islamic law varied across states, reflecting differences in party strength (modernist in the western peninsula where the National Front was strong, and conservative in the eastern peninsula where the Islamists were strong) and prevalent customs (with the courts incorporating certain matrilineal and bilateral customs in Sabah and Sarawak). Peletz 2002; Horowitz 1994.

88. State courts consider appeals of community court verdicts in many countries. This affects adjudication to the extent that appeals courts change community court verdicts.

89. These contrasting images of Hindus and Muslims drew significantly from colonial understandings, discussed in Cohn 1996; Parry 1972; Pandey 1990, 1–65.

90. Some of these groups were treated as minorities although they were numerically preponderant, such as the indigenous groups of settler colonies in parts of Africa and Latin America.

91. Mufti 2007.

92. For a discussion of varied group myths, see: Horowitz 1985, 141–84.

93. These states engaged religious norms and prior social organization more successfully than they promoted equality.

94. Their efforts to strengthen local government institutions were least successful.

95. This was true of even political forces that focused on Arab rather than Muslim identity, and reached out at some points to Christian minorities, such as Egypt's Free Officers Regime and Syria's Ba'ath Party. Concerns to accommodate Christians did not prevent policy makers from incorporating *shari'a* into constitutional law and considering the application of uniform laws drawn partly from Islamic tradition in Egypt. This contrasts with the refusal of Indonesian rulers to make a constitutional commitment to govern Muslim family life according to Islamic law.

96. Atatürk turned decisively against various Ottoman legacies, including the close association of the state with Islamic institutions, because of his confrontation with the Sultanate and the Allied Powers at the end of the First World War. See Barkey 2008 on the relationship of the Ottoman dynasts and the religious elite; Hanioglu 2011; Kuru 2009; Kandiyoti 1991b on early republican leaders' approach to public religion; Kuru 2009; Kerslake, Oktem, and Robins 2010; Berkes 1964 on secularism and nationalism; and Yilmaz 2005 on family law in Turkey.

97. See Hazard 1965 and Creevey 1996 on Senegal; Layish 1991, Mayer 1977, and Anderson 1986 on Libya; note 69 above on Malaysia and Sri Lanka; Sonbol 2002, Welchman 1988, and Abu-Odeh 2000 on Jordan; Joseph 1991 and Stilt 2004 on Iraq.

98. The Istiqlal Party was ambivalent about the monarchy, but the restriction of its support to urban areas limited its influence over Moroccan nationalism.

99. On Lebanon see Sulh 2004 and Joffe 1985; on Morocco and Algeria, Stora 2003, Maddy-Weitzman 2005, and Catalano 2010; on Syria, Devlin 1991 and Hinnebusch 1993; on Iraq, Joseph 1991 and Stilt 2004.

100. Even when the Hindu nationalists, who had little support among Muslims and Christians, led the Indian government from 1998 to 2004, they had coalition partners that enjoyed significant support among these groups.

101. Feener 2007; Hooker 2008; Cammack and Feener 2007.

102. Cohn 1996; van der Veer 1994.

103. Bowen 2003; Feener 2007; Cammack 2008.

104. Jaffrelot 1996 discusses Hindu nationalist claims to a monopoly over indigenous Indian culture.

105. Pandey 1990 highlights the forces that pulled Indian nationalists away from cosmopolitan modernism to Hindu majoritarianism.

106. Zaman 2002; Metcalf 1982.

107. This was the case although some civil society mobilizers demanded the incorporation of certain Islamic norms (e.g., regarding restrictions on testamentary rights) into Hindu law.

108. This was also because more extensive changes had been made in Muslim law through the last colonial decades.

CHAPTER THREE

1. Heimsath 1964; Jones 1989.
2. Forbes 1981; Minault 1998.
3. Sreenivas 2008; Newbigin 2009, 2010 2011; I. Chatterjee 2004 offers a more complex analysis.
4. Some of the relevant pieces of legislation were the Hindu Widows Remarriage Act, 1856; the Indian Divorce Act of 1869; the Indian Christian Marriage Act of 1872; the Age of Consent Act of 1891; the Criminal Procedure Code of 1898, Section 488; the Waqf

Validating Act of 1913; the Child Marriage Restraint Act of 1929; the Hindu Gains of Learning Act of 1930; the Hindu Women's Right to Property Act of 1937; the Dissolution of Muslim Marriages Act of 1939; and the Hindu Married Women's Right to Separate Residence and Maintenance Act of 1946.

5. Brass 1991, 75–108; Parashar 1992, 144–45, 158–60, 196–200; Jacobsohn 2003; Ruparelia 2008; Bhattaracharyya 2003; Mitra and Fischer 2002; Bhargava 2010; Chiriyankandath 2000.

6. Devji 1994; Minault 1998; Zaman 2002; Jalal 2001; Metcalf 2009b.

7. India, Constituent Assembly of India Debates (CAID) 1999.7, 541–43, 546.

8. Jacob 1999; India, Parliamentary Debates (PD) 1954, 2511–12; Interviews, Jyotsna Chatterji, founding President, Joint Women's Program; and John Dayal, President, All India Catholic Union; Chapter 5 elaborates on the early postcolonial debates about minority law.

9. This interpretation was offered in *Govind v. State of M.P.* (1975). Article 21 was taken to include the right to privacy in a minority opinion in *Kharak Singh v. State of U.P.* (1963). The view advanced in *Govind* that "any right to privacy must encompass and protect the personal intimacies of the home, the family, marriage, motherhood, procreation and child rearing" was of much potential significance for personal law.

10. Parashar 1992, 194–6, 201–29.

11. The right to a restitution of conjugal rights was incorporated in Sections 32 and 33 of the Indian Divorce Act, passed in 1869 and applied to Christians, and in Section 9 of the HMA in 1955.

12. *Narasu Appa Mali v. State of Bombay* (1952); Mansfield 1993; Bhattacharjee 1985.

13. PD 1951, 2466–67; India, Lok Sabha Debates (LSD) 1955, 7374–76.

14. PD 1951, 2754–55, 2772, 2933, cited in Parashar 1992, 86; LSD 1955, 7428.

15. Jacobsohn 2003, 95–119, 171–72.

16. Menski 2003.

17. Sarkar 1990; Parashar 1992; Som 1994; Agnes 1999; Newbigin 2009; Majumdar 2009.

18. However, certain presidencies (Bombay), princely states (Mysore, Baroda), and the Portuguese colony of Goa had given Hindu women limited inheritance rights in the 1930s and 1940s.

19. Parashar 1992; Agnes 2007.

20. Newbigin 2009, 2010.

21. Sreenivas 2008.

22. Majumdar 2009; Kishwar 1994.

23. Sreenivas 2008; Newbigin 2009, 2011; Agarwal 1994; 2008, 329.

24. Agarwal 1994, 2008.

25. PD 1951, 2754–55, 2772, 2933.

26. PD 1948, 3633–34; PD 1951, 2948; PD 1955, 7437–78.

27. PD 1951, 2465–57; LSD 1955, 7437–78, 8003.

28. Mantena 2010, 89–118 offers a nuanced discussion of the codification debates of the late nineteenth and early twentieth centuries, especially as they pertained to India.

29. This reversed the earlier claim of Macaulay, the first Law Member in the colonial government, that only an authoritarian regime could effectively codify the law.

30. Everett 1979; Forbes 1998; Mazumdar 1999.

31. PD 1951, 2948.

32. India. Constituent Assembly of India (Legislative) Debates Official Report (CAILD) 1948, 3647; PD 1951, 2470–22, 2945–56, 2948, 2951–52, 2992–94, 2999, 3004, 3029–30, 3077–78, 3185–86. The formation of Ambedkar's jurisprudence has to be understood based on limited materials. The arguments offered in favor of codification in British colonies and in India in particular must have contributed to his thinking, and that of various other Indian jurists. Ambedkar is also likely to have been exposed to similar discussions that preceded codification in some American states while he was at Columbia University in the 1910s and 1920s.

33. PD 1951, 2992–94, 2999, 3004, 3027–30, 3077–78, 3185–86.

34. Nehru 1996, 17, 189–190; PD 1955, 7438, 7487–88, 7488–89.

35. PD 1951, 2419, 2692, 2965, 3110–13, 3183–84; Gazette of India Extraordinary (GIE) 1954, 6890, 7474.

36. LSD 1955, 7674.

37. LSD 1955, 6473–75, 7673–74.

38. PD 1951, 2470–72; Rattigan and Aggarawala 1953; Gilmartin 1988; Oldenburg 2002.

39. G. V. Deshmukh claimed this precedent in Yajnavalkya's practice when he introduced a bill in the Central Legislative Assembly to make all female descendants and widows intestate heirs in 1937. Only widows gained inheritance rights from this initiative and only as limited estate. Pataskar cited Deshmukh in support of giving daughters joint property shares. LSD 1956, 6961–62.

40. India. Report of the Hindu Law Committee (RHLC) 1947, 15–36; CAILD 1948, 3629–33.

41. PD 1951, 2512, 2712–13, 2880–87, 2913, 2905–7; LSD 1955, 6843–50, 6856, 7693, 7705.

42. PD 1951: 2716, 2723, 2749, 2818, 2823; LSD 1955: 6504–6, 6514–15, 6835–42, 7796; On the presence of divorce customs among various groups, including a few higher castes, and their recognition in colonial courts, see: Sen 2000; Agnes 1999, 20–22; Pujari and Kaushik 1994, III: 310–12; Sharma 1989, 88–89; Virdi 1972, 33–36.

43. PD 1951, 2716; PD 1951, 2178, 2710–13, 2715–20, 2722–23.

44. PD 1951, 2374–45, 2392–2405, 2682–86, 2702, 2706–8, 2723, 2880–88, 2905–7, 3001–2, 3176–78; GIE 1954, 710–14; LSD 1955, 7452–55, 7479–81, 7490, 7497–98, 7697, 7760, 7925–29, 7933, 7978–79.

45. CAILD 1948, 3642–43; PD 1951, 2726–28; LSD 1955, 6477–78, 6487–89, 6498–99, 6845, 7432–35, 7707–8, 7957–58, 7962–63; Nehru 1996.10, 447–450; Nehru 1996.16, 76.

46. CAILD 1948, 3640–41; PD 1951, 2708–9, 2474–77, 2491–94, 2506–9, 2514, 2548–49, 2702, 2723, 2818, 2823, 2889–90, 2906; LSD 1955, 6533–36, 6891, 7374–76; Nehru 1996.17, 37, 59, 192–94, 434, 457. This is contrary to Menski's claim that there was "no official admission that low-caste Hindu rules were here being smuggled into the modern Hindu law in the garb of modernist Western-style reforms." Menski 2003, 446.

47. The illuminating discussion of the relationship between classical Hindu law and *achara* in Davis 2010, 144–165 and Lingat 1998, 176–206 suggests that this reformist understanding was in keeping with *shastric* tradition.

48. RHLC 1947, 23–24; LSD 1955, 6487–89, 6845, 7426, 7432–35, 7757–57; Nehru 1996.1, 443.

49. Menski 2003, 427.

50. CAILD 1949, 835–41; PD 1954, 2718–32; India. Report of the Joint Committee of the Houses of Parliament to Amend and Codify the Law Related to Intestate Succession Among the Hindus (Intestate Succession Report) 1955, 367–70; LSD 1956, 6970–72.

51. CAILD 1948, 3642–43, 3651; Intestate Succession Report 1955, 385–87; LSD 1956, 6884–85, 6965–71, 7164, 7190–91.

52. Intestate Succession Report 1955, 371–78, 381–83, 385–87; LSD 1956, 6865–68, 6884–88, 6899–6902, 7123–24, 7131, 7140–77, 7162–64, 7180–82.

53. CAILD 1948, 3637; CAILD 1949, 864; PD 1951, 2434–36, 2442, 2445, 2459–60, 2688, 2835–70, 2991, 3024–28, 3031, 3051–52, 3075–82, 3130–44, 3145–50; LSD 1955, 7783–84; LSD 1956, 6713–25, 6807–12, 6872–74, 6908–12.

54. CAILD 1948, 3640–42, 3648; CAILD 1949, 2533; PD 1951, 2753; PD 1955, 6895–96.

55. CAILD 1949, 840–41.

56. PD 1956, 6898–99.

57. PD 1956, 7163–64.

58. PD 1955, 7791.

59. PD 1951, 2713, 2716; LSD 1955, 6487–89, 6843–50, 6856, 7727–29, 7562, 7693, 7756, 7760.

60. Mahmood 1995, 145–56; Kusum 1975, 611; Menski 2003, 438–42; CAILD 1949, 832–33.

61. PD 1951, 2721–22; LSD 1955, 6888–89, 7555–56, 7579, 7727–29.

62. Divorce rights comparable to those introduced in 1955 for India's Hindus came into continued existence in France in 1884, in Sweden in 1915, in Britain in 1923, and in Germany in 1938, but only in the 1970s in Italy, Spain, and Portugal. Glendon 1989, 3, 17, 149–50, 160, 175–77, 182–85, 191.

63. CAILD 1948, 3631–32; GIE 1952, 675–714; LSD 1955, 6471–75.

64. CAILD 1948, 3629–31; Intestate Succession Report 1955, 369–70.

65. Agarwal 1995; Majumdar 2009.

66. LSD 1955, 7227.

67. CAILD 1948, 3651.

68. Some legislators suggested that married daughters be denied shares of parental property altogether or at least not be placed in the first tier of heirs.

69. GIE 1954; PD 1954, 2718.

70. The formula included shares in the property that a son might have partitioned notionally in the coparcenary prior to the intestate's death, and gave the daughter a share in this property equal to that of other Class I heirs. This meant that already partitioned sons got the highest share, and daughters and unpartitioned sons obtained lower shares.

71. Intestate Succession Report 1955, 371–78, 381–83, 385–87; LSD 1956, 6965–72.

72. Dumont 1983, 104–44; Arunima 2003, 157–90; and Jeffrey 1992 discuss changes in attitudes toward matriliny among historically matrilineal groups in Kerala through the nineteenth and early twentieth centuries.

73. Majumdar 2009, 227–237.

74. Frankel 2006; Mellor 1976; Subramaniam 1979.

75. Rajeshvar Prasad Narain Sinha, R. Seshagiri Rao, S. V. L. Narasimham, Renu Chakravartty, Parvathi Krishnan, S. S. More and R. P. Sinha attached such notes to the Committee's report. Intestate Succession Report 1955, 371–78, 381–83, 385–87.

76. LSD 1956, 6867–68, 6884–87, 6900–6902, 7236–37, 7261–66, 7275–77, 7609–46.

77. Mody 2008 and Majumdar 2009, 167–205 discuss the context in which the initial SMA was passed.

78. PD 1953, 2512; Various other parliamentarians made similar statements. LSD 1954, 794–95, 812, 818–19, 833, 892–93, 937.

79. PD 1953, 2507, 2523.

80. PD 1953, 2556.

81. PD 1953, 2507; LSD 1954, 897–98.

82. PD 1954, 2511–12.

83. PD 1953, 2547–51.

84. PD 1953, 2510–11, 2523, 2546, 2559–60; LSD 1954, 750–52; LSD 1955, 7935–36, 7997–98. An amendment of 1976 made the HSA rather than the ISA govern Hindu, Sikh, Buddhist, and Jain couples opting for the SMA, but did not offset the other factors discouraging a choice of the SMA.

85. The notes of dissent of eleven of the forty-five members of the Joint Committee that considered the SMA (B. K. Mukerjee, Tek Chand, Savitri Nigam, Sushama Sen, Violet Alva, K. A. Damodara Menon, Sucheta Kripalani, Renu Chakravartty, Rajendra Pratap Sinha, Venkat Krishna Dhage, and K. Rama Rao) opposed the severance of SMA couples from joint property. GIE, 1954: 148–52, 155–58, 173; Similar arguments were offered in parliament. PD 1953, 2508–9, 2523, 2527–28, 2545–46, 2549–56.

86. Mody 2008.

87. PD 1953, 2561–72; GIE 1954, 164–66; Parashar 1992, 161–62. Some AIMPLB leaders said they accepted the SMA because they felt that those of Muslim ancestry who choose the SMA place themselves beyond the Muslim fold. However, SMA couples have not been required to renounce their religious identities since 1923. Interviews, Mohammad Abdul Rahim Quraishi, Secretary, and Zafaryab Jilani, Member, Legal Committee, AIMPLB.

88. Many Christians and Muslims did not enjoy these rights, however, as they were governed by customary laws specific to region or sect.

89. Agnes 1999; Som 1994.

90. S. Basu 1999 is the most detailed account of patterns of property transmission. Patel 2007, Agarwal 1995, and U. Sharma 1983 support its findings.

91. S. Basu 1999.

92. Some practices of matrilineal groups were different from their colonial and postcolonial customary laws, and matriliny is in decline among some groups. Matriliny in erosion sometimes places various responsibilities on women without giving them access to the resources with which their ancestors fulfilled these responsibilities. For instance, this is the case with female ultimogeniture among the Khasis, Garos and, Jaintias of Meghalaya (which gives the youngest daughter control over the ancestral home and other family property, while making her responsible to maintain various kin). Changing practices led to disagreement over the laws to apply to these groups, with some younger men favoring assimilation in Hindu law, and women's organizations and older men preferring to retain matrilineal customary law. Agarwal 1995, 100–168 and Narwani 2004 provide overviews of India's tribal customary laws. Karve 1990; Dube 1997; Nakane 1967; Nongbri 2010; Trautmann 1982; Arunima 2003; Saradamoni 1999; Vijaya Kumar 2006 discuss changing practices among various matrilineal groups in India.

CHAPTER FOUR
1. India. Office of the Registrar General and Census Commissioner 1983.
2. India. Committee on the Status of Women in India 1975.
3. These parties initially opposed the Women's Reservation Bill because they believed that the quota it gave women in representation in parliament and the state assemblies would dilute the effects of the quotas for the lower castes and tribal groups unless the latter groups were assured a share of the women's quota as well. However, this consideration did not deter parties based among similarly ranked castes in other regions with more equitable gender relations (e.g., the DMK, the AIADMK, the PMK) from supporting this bill. When the Rajya Sabha passed this bill in 2010, the SP, the RJD and the BSP abstained from voting, and the majority of the Janata Dal (United)'s legislators voted in favor of the bill.
4. Sakshi and Global Fund for Women 1996.
5. State legislatures made a few changes in Hindu marriage law, such as the recognition in Tamil Nadu of "self-respect marriages," weddings conducted by some supporters of the Dravidian movement that dispensed with religious ceremonies involving Brahman priests. These changes did not influence matrimonial relations as much as those in divorce and inheritance law did.
6. Parashar 1992, 134.
7. India. Lok Sabha Debates (LSD) 1964, 3477–94, 4990–91.
8. This amendment did not change cruelty as a ground for divorce in the IDA and the DMMA, applied to Christians and Muslims respectively. Divorce was less accessible through the IDA than the HMA and the SMA, and the DMMA entitled a Muslim woman to a divorce based on spousal cruelty only if her husband

> habitually assaults her or makes her life miserable by cruelty of conduct even if such conduct does not amount to physical ill-treatment, or associates with women of evil repute or leads an infamous life, or attempts to force her to lead an immoral life, or disposes of her property or prevents her exercising her legal rights over it, or obstructs her in the observance of her religious profession or practice, or if he has more wives than one, does not treat her equitably in accordance with the injunctions of the Quran.

9. Menski 2001, 47–57, 63–138; Menski 2003, 427–83.
10. Menski 2003, 443.
11. Menski 2001, 86, 115–33; 2003, 429–30, 463–64.
12. India. Ministry of Law. Law Commission of India 1974, 2–9, 11–12, 25–26, 67, 71–72. Gajendragadkar produced a critical edition of the *Dattaka Mimamsa* (a classical treatise on the Hindu law of adoption) and was the general editor of a series on the *Upanishads*.
13. LSD 1975, 305–39; PD 1976, 112–52. The legislature rejected only one of the Law Commission's recommendations—to enable the consideration of divorce during the first year of a marriage—to give spousal reconciliation a better chance.
14. Committee on the Status of Women in India. 1975.
15. The Delhi High Court initially suggested that it would be appropriate to grant couples divorces when "the rift between them is complete," in *Ram Kali v. Gopal Das* (1971) and *Mrs. Swaraj Garg v. K.M. Garg* (1978). Justice H. R. Khanna, who authored *Ram Kali*, also chaired the Law Commission that recommended such legislation. Sivaramayya 1993;

India. Ministry of Law. Law Commission of India 1978; Marriage Laws (Amendment) Bill 1981. Saheli 1981 outlines women's organizations' objections to this bill.

16. This understanding (Menski 2003, 464–65) was also incompatible with Menski's recognition elsewhere that the resistance of women's organizations was the crucial reason why this proposal was shelved. Compare Menski 2003, 466–67 with Menski 2001, 72.

17. Mazumdar 1999.

18. *Chanderkala Trivedi v. S.P. Trivedi* (1993); *V. Bhagat v. Mrs. D. Bhagat* (1994); *Romesh Chander v. Savitri* (1995); *Smt. Kanchan Devi v. Promod Kumar Mittal* (1996); *Krishna v. Som Nath* (1996); *Ashok v. Rupa* (1996); *Ashok Hurra v. Rupa Bipin Zaveri* (1997); *Sabitanjali Pattanaik v. Priyabrata Pattanaik* (2001); *Sanghamitra Singh v. Kailash Singh* (2001); *Sudheer Singhal v. Ms. Neetha Singhal* (2001); *Shankar v. Puspita* (2005); *Naveen Kohli v. Neelu Kohli* (2006); *Rita Das Biswas v. Trilokesh Das Biswas* (2007); *Samar Ghosh v. Jaya Ghosh* (2007); and *Sanghamitra Ghosh v. Kajal Kumar Ghosh* (2007). Courts drew support from the Law Commission's *Seventy-First Report* in *Ashok Hurra, Samar Ghosh,* and *Sanghamitra Ghosh,* although legislators had not accepted this report's recommendations. The court misunderstood the marriage law reform of 1976 to have made irretrievable breakdown a divorce ground in *Keshaorao Krishnaji Londhe v. Nisha Londhe* (1984).

19. *Jorden Diengdeh v. S. S. Chopra* (1985); *Vinita Saxena v. Pankaj Pandit* (2006). Irretrievable marital breakdown was considered relevant to assess claims of cruelty in *V. Bhagat v. Mrs. D. Bhagat* (1994) and of desertion in *Neelam v. Vinod Kumar* (1986). Interview, Justice B. P. Jeevan Reddy (author of *Bhagat*).

20. *Lt. Col. Mohinder Pal Singh v. Kulwant Kaur* (1975); *Chinmoy Chakraborty v. Bharati Chakraborty* (1990); *Ashok Kumar Bhatnagar v. Shabnam Bhatnagar* (1989); *Smt. Smita Dilip Rane v. Dilip Dattaram Rane* (1990); *Nitu v. Krishan Lal* (1990); *B. v. A.* (1992); *A. v. H.* (1992); *Tapan Kumar Chakraborty v. Jyotsna Chakraborty* (1997); *Swapan Kumar Ganguly v. Smt. Smiritikana Ganguly* (2002); *Savitri Pandey v. Prem Chandra Pandey* (2002); *Geeta Mullick v. Brojo Gopal Mullick* (2003); *Rajendra Kumar Jajodia v. Puja Jajodia* (2009); *Brajesh Kumar v. Anjali* (2009); *Vishnu Dutt Sharma v. Manju Sharma* (2009).

21. *Jorden Diengdeh v. S. S. Chopra* (1985); *Naveen Kohli v. Neelu Kohli* (2006). The Delhi High Court had recommended such legislation much earlier, in *Ram Kali v. Gopal Das* (1971) and *Mrs. Swaraj Garg v. K. M. Garg* (1978).

22. India. Ministry of Law. Law Commission of India 2009. The chair of this Law Commission, Justice A. S. Lakshmanan, had authored a Supreme Court judgment that granted divorce based on irretrievable marital breakdown—*Vinita Saxena v. Pankaj Pandit* (2006).

23. Marriage Laws (Amendment) Bill 2010.

24. India. Parliament of India. Rajya Sabha. Department Related Parliamentary Standing Committee on Personnel, Public Grievances, Law and Justice 2011; Lawyers Collective Women's Rights Initiative 2010a. The following organizations deposed before the committee: the NCW, the Ministry of Women and Child Development, Majlis, Center for Women's Rights Discourse and Legal Initiative, Gender and Human Rights Society, Lawyers' Collective—Women's Rights Initiative, Mothers and Sisters Initiatives, the All India Democratic Women's Association (affiliated with the Communist Party of India-Marxist), Save Family Foundation, and Children's Rights Initiative for Shared

Parenting. The Married Women (Protection of Rights) Bill 1994 also proposed giving women shares in matrimonial property, but it was a private member's initiative.

25. Dhawan 2011.

26. India. Press Information Bureau 2010; Sobhana 2012; TNN 2012; Press Trust of India (PTI) 2012a; Special Correspondent 2012; Dhawan 2013.

27. PTI 2013, 2012b; Indo-Asian News Service 2013.

28. Agarwal 2013.

29. Agnes 2011b, 35.

30. Agnes 2011b, 34–41; Kusum 2000, 237–39; Menski 2001, 74–106.

31. *Sm. Pancho v. Ram Prasad* (1956) at 41.

32. *Shri Gurcharan Singh v. Shrimati Waryam Kaur* (1960) at 133.

33. *Putul Devi v. Gopi Mandal* (1963); This court held, at 97, that "having regard to the conditions obtaining in India and the importance attached to the purity of matrimonial relations, I cannot conceive of a case of greater mental distress and real apprehension of harm and injury for a wife than her husband's suspicion of faithlessness [sic] and unchastity on her part." It did not, however, find that the brothers involved in the case had been cruel to the sisters they had married by falsely accusing their father of having turned them into prostitutes.

34. *Kusum Lata v. Kamta Prasad* (1965) at 285–86. He declared that the man's unfounded allegations of adultery, his insistence on sexual intercourse when his wife was in delicate health, and his failure to arrange medical treatment when she was seriously ill amounted to cruelty and warranted judicial separation.

35. *Kuppuswami v. Alagammal* (1961); *Iqbal Kaur v. Pritam Singh S. Nanak Singh* (1963); *Smt. Umri Bai v. Chittar* (1966) (based on persistent false charges of adultery); *Rup Lal v. Kartaro Devi* (1970); *Dr. Narayan Ganesh Dastane v. Mrs. Sucheta Narayan Dastane* (1975) (discussed in the next paragraph); *Lalita Devi v. Radha Mohan* (1976) (based on the man's adultery and promise to marry his lover).

36. *Dastane* drew this standard from *Wright v. Wright* (1948) at 210 and *Blyth v. Blyth* (1966) at 536. The Madhya Pradesh High Court had applied the same standard, using the same precedents, in a Christian divorce case based on alleged adultery two years earlier, *Prem Masih v. Mst. Kumudani Bai* (1974), but *Dastane* and later cases did not rely on this precedent. The Supreme Court had earlier applied standards of proof beyond reasonable doubt to matrimonial cases too—*Bipin Chander Jaisinghbhai Shah v. Prabhavati* (1956); *John White v. Mrs. Kathleen Olive White* (1958); *Lachman Utamchand Kiriplani v. Meena Alias Mota* (1964); *Smt. Chandra Mohini Srivastava v. Shri Avinash Prasad Srivasatava* (1967); *Rohini Kumari v. Narendra Singh* (1972). Some courts continued to apply this standard after *Dastane*, in *Dr. Samir Kr. Das v. Aparna Das alias Tripti Das* (2000); *Ms. Santosh Kumari v. Shri Shiv Prakash Sharma* (2001); *Adhyatma Bhattar Alwar v. Adhyatma Bhattar Sri Devi* (2002); and *Dr.Vimla Balani v. Jai Krishan Balani* (2008).

37. In two brief telephone conversations in July 2007, Justice Chandrachud said that he considered *Dastane,* not *Shah Bano,* his most enduring contribution to personal law.

38. *Raj Kumar Manocha v. Smt. Anskuka Manocha* (1983); *Kamlesh v. Paras Ram* (1985).

39. Agnes 2011b, 35 inaccurately attributed this understanding to the Marriage Laws (Amendment) Act 1976. This act did not characterize cruelty; rather, it eliminated the earlier statutory characterization. This understanding was a construction of the courts,

beginning with *Ashwini Kumar Sehgal v. Smt. Swatantar Sehgal* (1979), well before *Meera v. Vijay Shankar Talchidia* (1994), which Agnes deemed crucial in this regard.

40. *Londhe*'s approach was followed in *Smt. Kamini Gupta v. Mukesh Kumar Gupta* (1985); *Ishwarlal Sarabhai Parikh v. Prabhawati Ishwarlal Parikh* (1988); *Gangadharan v. T.K. Thankam* (1988); *Dr. S.P. Trivedi v. Smt. Chandrakala Trivedi* (1990); *Smt. Nirmala Manohar Jagesha v. Manohar Shivram Jagesha* (1991); *Shri B. v. Smt. A* (1992); *Meera* (1994); *Shri Siba Prosad Basu v. Sm. Gouri Basu* (1994); *Vishnu B. Mayekar v. Smt. Laxmi V. Mayekar* (2000); and *Mrs. Manisha Sandeep Gade v. Sandeep Vinayak Gade* (2005). An earlier judgment that argued that cruelty should be assessed with regard to the parties' circumstances is *Bijoli v. Sukomal* (1979).

41. Also see *A. Viswanathan v. G. Lakshmi alias Seetha* (2006); *D. Nagappan v. T. Virgin Rani* (2009); *Amrithaa v. V. Krishna Kumar* (2010).

42. The appropriateness of such a construction of cruelty is argued in *Romesh Chander v. Savitri* (1995); *Rajan Vasant Revankar v. Mrs. Shobha Rajan Revankar* (1995); *Rupa Ashok Hurra v. Ashok G. Hurra* (1996); *Tapan Kumar Chakraborty v. Jyotsna Chakraborty* (1997); *Praveen Kumari Jaitly v. Surinder Kumar Jaitly* (2001); *Gananath Pattanaik v. State of Orissa* (2002); *Naveen Kohli v. Neelu Kohli* (2006); *Samar Ghosh v. Jaya Ghosh* (2007); *Rita Das Biswas v. Trilokesh Das Biswas* (2007); *Bharat Bhushan Sharma v. Pratibha* (2007); *Ramesh Kumar Sharma v. Smt. Akash Sharma* (2008); *Varalaxmi Charka @ Renuka v. Satyanarayana Charka* (2008); *Undavalli Narayana Rao v. State of Andhra Pradesh* (2010); *Hitesh Bhatnagar v. Deepa Bhatnagar* (2011). A minority of courts continued to use more stringent definitions—*Gurbachan Kaur v. Karnail Singh Resham Singh* (1999); *Naval Kishore Somani v. Poonam Somani* (1998).

43. *Rajani v. Subramoniam* (1990); *Tulasamma v. N. Seenan* (2002); *Smt. Anubha v. Vikas Aggarwal* (2002); *Smt. Sushma Kohli @ Satya Devi v. Shri Shyam Sunder Kohli* (2003); *Man Mohan Vaid v. Meena Kumari* (2003).

44. *Sukumar Mukherjee v. Tripti Mukherjee* (1992); *Dr. Samir Kr. Das v. Aparna Das @ Tripti Das* (2000); *Smt. Kusum v. Shri R.K. Saxena* (2004); *Seema v. Nilesh Chouhan* (2006); *Mrs.P.Manimekalai v. R.Kothandaraman* (2010).

45. *Smt. Kalpana Srivasta v. Surendra Nath Srivastava* (1985); *A.P. Ranga Rao v. Vijayalakshmi* (1990); *Smt. Surbhi Agrawal v. Sanjay Agrawal* (2000); *Smt. Bhagwanti v. Laxmandas Panjwani* (2000); *Mandeep Kaur v. Sukh Dev Singh* (2006); *P. Mohan Rao v. P. Vijayalakshmi* (2007); *Usha Rani v. Sham Lal* (2008).

46. Examples of the later trend include *Rakesh Goyal v. Deepika Goyal* (2007); *Ratna Banerjee v. Chandra Madhab Banerjee* (2007); *Arun Chettri v. Madhu Chettri* (2007), cited in Agnes 2011b, 37–38. The old approach persisted in *Ramesh Jangid v. Sunita* (2007).

47. Courts followed the interpretation in *Patala Atchamma v. Patala Mahalakshmi* (1907), which was laid out more fully in *Mahalingam Pillai v. Amsavalli* (1956).

48. Agnes 2011b, 124–28.

49. *Parami Ramayya v. Mahadevi Shankarappa* (1909) at 279.

50. Agnes 2011b, 127 maintained that courts made this distinction only from the 1990s.

51. *Kista Pillai v. Amirthammal* (1938); *Ma Mya Khin v. N. N. Godenho* (1936); *Dr. Hormusji M. Kalapesi v. Dinbai H. Kalapesi* (1955); *M. P. Subramaniyam v. T. T. Ponnakshiammal* (1958); *Audumbar Gangaram Gavandi v. Sonubai Audumbar Gavandi* (1960); *Amar Kanta Sen v. Sovana Sen* (1960); *Kasturi v. Ramasamy* (1979); *Gulab Jag-

dusa Kakwane v. Smt. Kamal Gulab Kakwane (1984) at 662; *Udaivir Singh v. Smt. Vinod Kumari* (1985); *Shravan Nathu Kannor v. Anjanabai Shravan Kannor* (1985); *Rachita Rout v. Basanta Kumar Rout* (1986); *Chhagan Lal Devman v. State of Maharashtra and Ors.* (1990); *Ravindra Singh v. Kapsi Bai* (1991); *Baishnab Charan Jena v. Ritarani Jena* (1993); *Chandrakant Gangaram Gawade v. Sulochana Chandakant Gawade* (1996); *Narnath Thazhakuniyil Sandha v. Kottayat Thazhakuniyil Narayanan* (1999); *Chanda Preetam Wadate v. Preetam Ganpatrao Wadate* (2002).

In one of the two cases that Agnes cited to indicate that Indian courts did not grant maintenance to adulterous women until the 1980s, *Sachindra Nath Biswas v. Sm. Benamala Biswas* (1960), the woman was found to be living in adultery. The court did deny a woman maintenance based on a finding of adultery *simpliciter* in the other case, *Sardari Lal v. Mst. Vishano* (1970), but the majority of courts did not rule thus even in the 1960s and some that did so were overruled by higher courts or larger benches of the same court (for example, *Raja Gopalan v. Rajamma* (1967), which was overruled by a larger panel of the Kerala High Court in *Kaithakulangara Kunhikannan v. Nellatham Veettil Malu* (1973)).

52. The *Yagnavalkya Smrti* was cited in: *Musunuru Nagendramma v. Musunuru Ramakotayya* (1953). This court also cited Apararka to the effect that "the Adhivinna, superseded wife, has the right to be maintained by the husband irrespective of whether she lives with her husband in his house or in the house of her parents," and Vijnaneswara to have said that "the husband who abandons an obedient and competent, son-bearing and pleasant speaking wife, should be made to give one-third of his property to the superseded wife. If he has no property he must maintain her."

53. For instance, women who committed adultery with men of a lower caste, leading to their expulsion from their caste, were ruled ineligible for spousal maintenance in *Ponnayee v. Periya Mooppan* (1908); *Ram-Autar v. Mt. Raghurai* (1926); and *Yesu Bai v. Parasram* (1933). But a man living in adultery was not required to provide his wife a separate home and maintenance because he was taken to be treating her in ways compatible with her status as his wife in *Gantapalli Appalamma v. Gantapalli Yellayya* (1897).

54. *Devyani Kantilal Shroff v. Kantilal Gamanlal Shroff* (1963) at 99; *Bhagwan Singh Sher Singh Arora v. Amar Kaur* (1962) at 145.

55. This approach was elaborated in *Mahalingam Pillai v. Amsavalli* (1956), based on precedents such as *Simon Lakra v. Bakla* (1932) and *Phillips v. Emperor* (1935).

56. *Mahalingam Pillai v. Amsavalli* (1956) at 298.

57. *Sanjukta Padhan v. Laxminarayan Padhan* (1991) at 42.

58. *Mahendra Manilal Nanavati v. Sushila Mahendra Nanavati* (1964); *Raji Pachori v. Kamlesh Pachori* (1993); *Smt. Leela Pande v. Shri Sachendra Kumar Pande* (1994).

59. As early as 1967, a court declined to find a married woman getting an "improper" letter from someone other than her husband a sign of adultery, in *Smt. Chandra Mohini Srivastava v. Shri Avinash Prasad Srivasatava* (1967).

60. *Smt. Swayamprabha v. A. S. Chandrasekhar* (1982); *Binod Anand Lakra v. Smt. Belulah Lakra* (1982).

61. *M. P. Subramaniyam v. T. T. Ponnakshiammal* (1958); *Bhagwan Singh Sher Singh Arora v. Amar Kaur* (1962); *Avinash Prasad Srivastava v. Smt. Chandra Mohini* (1964); *Smt. Chandra Mohini Srivastava v. Shri Avinash Prasad Srivasatava* (1967).

62. The lovers were estranged from their respective spouses in *Devyani Kantilal Shroff*, and the woman had left her matrimonial home of her own accord and refused her

father-in-law's invitation to leave her lover and live with her husband in *Sanjukta Padhan*.

63. There was strong evidence of the lovers living together in *Ammasi v. Smt. Amaravathi* (1997); *Chander Kumar Sharma v. Samriti Sharma* (1998); *Angoori v. Phool Kumar* (2003); and *Subal Chandra Saha v. Pritikana Saha* (2003).

64. Interview, Justice Aziz M. Ahmadi (author of *Vanamala*).

65. Maintenance was granted to women involved in other relationships in *Gopi v. Smt. Krishna* (2001); *Valsaraian v. Saraswathy* (2003); *Dalip Singh v. Rajbala* (2007); and *Sadanandan, K. v. Mepparamban Sreeja* (2009). Maintenance was granted to women who were found to have deserted their husbands in *Khandu Madhu Kadbhane v. Sitabai* (2001); *Ramavtar Sharma v. Smt. Santosh* (2002); *Subhadra v. Rajendra Prasad* (2003); *Smt. Kesari Devi v. Jagdev Singh* (2005); *Sajeev Kumar v. P.Dhanya* (2008); *R.Sunitha v. Gopalakrishnan alias Unni* (2008); and *Pareshkumar Chaturdas Patel v. State of Gujarat* (2010). It was awarded to a woman divorced on the ground of her cruelty toward her husband in *Nanisseri Mukundan v. M. Usha* (2007).

66. *Pola Venkateshwarlu v. Pola Lakshmi Devi and Ors.* (2005).

67. Menski 2001, 115–19.

68. Moreover, many cases of the colonial era concerned British couples—e.g., *Wood v. Wood* (1877); *Fowle v. Fowle* (1878); *Glancy v. Glancy* (1916); only a few related to Indian couples—e.g., *Appibai v. Khimji* (1936); *Stree v. Stree* (1935).

69. Agnes 2011b, 41–46.

70. Agnes 2011b, 42.

71. The Bombay Hindu Divorce Act, 1947, applicable to the couple when the case was considered, allowed divorce based on desertion for at least four years, until it was superseded by the HMA, which allowed only judicial separation for this reason until 1976.

72. This justification to recognize certain divorce customs was offered initially in *Kudomeo Dossee v. Joteeram Kolita* (1880) and *Lachu v. Dal Singh* (1896).

73. Derrett 1963; Holden 2008.

74. *Mt. Subhani v. Nawab* (1941). These standards for the recognition of custom were established in *Collector of Madura v. Moottoo Ramalinga Sethupathi* (1868). *Bai Jivatbai Jethmal v. Milkiram Deepchand* (1961) indicated that practices that have existed only for twenty years were not customary.

75. *Mst. Bhan Kaur v. Ishar Singh* (1958); *Smt. Premanbai v. Channoolal* (1963); *Edamma v. Hussainappa* (1965); *Velayudhan Kochappi v. Sirkar* (1915); *Sankaralingam Chetti v. Subban Chetti* (1894); *Nallathangal v. Nainan Ambalam* (1959); *Keshav Hargovan v. Bai Gandhi* (1915); *Are Lachia v. Are Raja Mallu* (1964); *Gurdit Singh v. Mst. Angrez Kaur Alias Gej Kaur Alias Malan* (1967); *Tara Singh v. Shakuntala* (1974); *Asha Rani v. Gulshan Kumar* (1995); *Bhaga Bai v. Mangali Bai* (1999); *Subramani v. M. Chandralekha* (2004); *Kunwar Singh Marko v. Shiv Dayal Sarote* (1999); *Virendra Kumar v. Preeta* (2009).

76. Holden 2008, 280 said that a woman-initiated divorce was also recognized among the Chetti potters of Tamil Nadu in *Sankaralingam Chetti v. Subban Chetti* (1894), but that judgment did not mention that the woman initiated the divorce, and *(Gedalu) Narayana v. Emperor* (1932) clarified that *Sankaralingam Chetti* dealt with a custom of mutual-consent divorce. *Velayudhan Kochappi* indicated: "the Ezhava wife is entitled to divorce her husband and take another . . . and the fact of the woman taking another husband is tantamount to her divorcing the first husband."

77. *Govindaraju v. Munisami Gounder* (1997) at 11; Menski 2001, 39.

78. In *Subramani*, the court held that divorce customs existing among Nattu Gounder does not show the existence of these customs among Kongu Vellala Gounder, a closely related subcaste. However, such customs were found to exist among the latter caste in *G. P. Rajendran v. M. Valarmathi* (2008). The Supreme Court sought similar caste-specific proof in *Vidyadhari v. Sukhrana Bai* (2008) and *Mahendra Nath Yadav v. Sheela Devi* (2010). Various high courts did so, for instance, in *Edla Neelaya v. Edla Ramada alias Ramadas* (1995); *Rita Rani v. Ramesh Kumar* (1996); *Jairam Somaji More v. Sindhubai* (1999); *Sulabha v. Suseela* (2007); *Latha Kunjamma v. Anil Kumar* (2008); *Virendra Kumar v. Preeta* (2009); *Kewal Kumar v. Pawna Devi* (2010); and *Satya Devi v. State of Himachal Pradesh* (2011).

79. *Sukri v. Khluji* (1981); *Radhakishan v. Shankarlal* (1982); *Ramkali v. Nathoosingh* (1983); *Bhaga Bai v. Mangali Bai* (1999); *Sushi Kumari v. Khairatilal* (1986); *Kunwar Singh Marko v. Shiv Dayal Sarote* (1999); *Harinarayan v. State of M.P.* (2005), discussed in Holden 2008, 164–66, 168–69.

80. As seen in *Sushi Kumari v. Khairatilal* (1986); *Vidyadhar v. Kamlabai* (1986); *Rameshchandra Daga v. Rameshwari Daga* (2005); *Savitaben Somabhai Bhatiya v. State of Gujarat* (2005). Holden 2008, 165–68, 170. The courts granted the women maintenance in the first three cases based on recognizing the customary divorces that had ended their earlier marriages, making their current marriages valid. The woman was denied maintenance in *Savitaben* insofar as she was the man's second concurrent wife, but the man paid 200,000 rupees to cover their child's maintenance, which would have benefited the woman too since she had custody of the child.

81. *Thangammal v. Gengayammal* (1945); *Nallathangal v. Nainan Ambalam* (1959); *Smt. Premanbai v. Channoolal* (1963); *Are Lachia v. Are Raja Mallu* (1964); and *K .P. Bhargavi Amma v. C .R. Kuttikrishnan* (1965). The invalidation of customary divorce claims accompanied maintenance decrees in *Edamma v. Hussainappa* (1965); and *Tara Singh v. Shakuntala* (1974).

82. *Rajeshbai*'s view that mistresses have the same maintenance rights as wives followed that in *Banwari Lal v. Emperor* (1914).

83. *Kaushalyabai Dinkar Mule v. Dinkar Mahadeorao Mule* (2001); *Thiyyakandi Ramachandran v. Sheena* (2009).

84. Chandra 1998 provided an engaging account of the varied responses to this case.

85. *Dadaji Bhikaji v. Rukhmabai* (1885); *Dadaji Bhikaji v. Rukhmabai* (1886).

86. This rule was the result of the opinions in *Moonshee Buzloor Ruheem v. Shumsoon-nissa Begum* (1848) and *Abdul Kadir v. Salima* (1886).

87. PD 1955, 7247, 7258–89, 7279–80, 7515–16, 7603–4, 7626, 7635–36, 7646; Renu Chakravartty suggested the adoption of a reconciliation clause instead.

88. *Shri Gurcharan Singh v. Shrimati Waryam Kaur* (1960); *Smt. Tirath Kaur v. Kirpal Singh* (1964); *Solomon Devasahayam Selvaraj v. Chandirah Mary* (1968); *Ratnaprabhabai Sheshrao Bhore v. Sheshrao Shankarrao Bhore* (1972); *Mrs. Swaraj Garg v. K.M.Garg* (1978); *Tarsem Lal v. Smt. Santosh* (1980).

89. *Bai Jiva v. Narsingh Lalbhai* (1927) at 268 declared that Hindu law "even while it lays down the duty of the wife of implicit obedience and return to her husband, has laid down no such sanction or procedure as compulsion by the courts to force her to return against her will."

90. *T. Sareetha v. T. Venkata Subbiah* (1983) at 367–70, 374; Interview, Justice P.A. Choudary.

91. Nussbaum 1999, 4, 91–93; Menski 2003, 558.

92. Menski 2003, 558 also inaccurately claimed that Sareetha "wanted to get rid of her rustic husband once she became famous." Agnes 2008, 244–47 understood the case better.

93. Agnes 2011a, 25–26.

94. *Mohan Lal v. Kalp Shikha* (1985); *Madhusudan v. Bhanumati* (1985).

95. *Smt. Harvinder Kaur v. Harmander Singh Choudhry* (1984) at 69–70, 75, 78–81; *Smt. Saroj Rani v. Sudarshan Kumar Chadha* (1984) at 1567–69. Section 22 of the SMA, Section 36 of the Parsi Marriage and Divorce Act, and Sections 32 and 33 of the Indian Divorce Act deal with restitution of conjugal rights.

96. In *Tarsem Lal v. Smt. Santosh* (1980) and *Dalbir Singh v. Simar Kaur Alias Simro* (2002), the court found the man's violence (and in the first case his adultery as well) a good reason for his wife not to live with him; in *Nirmala Devi v. Pritam Singh* (1998), the man and his parents had beaten the woman, evicted her, and resisted reconciliation efforts.

97. *Smt. Tirath Kaur v. Kirpal Singh* (1964); *Gaya Prasad v. Bhagwati* (1966); *Surinder Kaur v. Gurdeep Singh* (1973).

98. *A. Annamalai Mudaliar v. Perumayee Ammal* (1965) at 142.

99. The court found that the man had been cruel to his wife in *Baburao*, but felt that the relationship had deteriorated so far that it could not order the woman back to her husband even if cruelty had not been established.

100. Agnes 2011a, 24–25; Agnes 2008, 251–55.

101. Menski 2003, 484–542 provided an authoritative account of various precolonial traditions regarding the maintenance of married, widowed, separated, and divorced women, and indicated how colonial and postcolonial law built on these traditions. The scope of *stridhanam* was defined differently in various texts, epochs, and regions. See Agnes 1999, 14–18; S. Basu 2001, 75.

102. This requirement was in Section 536 of the Code of 1872, in Section 488 of its successor Code of 1898, and in a changed form in Section 125-8 of the Code of 1973.

103. These customs varied in the voice they gave women in the divorce process, and the compensation they provided them on divorce.

104. Agnes 1999, 46–52 discusses some of the relevant case law.

105. The Law Minister and parliamentarians emphasized the implications of this change for the maintenance provisions applicable to Muslims. Parashar 1992, 164–68. But Menski 2003, 486–87 indicated that it also addressed the limitations of Hindu maintenance law.

106. Glendon 1987 noted this trend in the West.

107. Agnes 2011b.

108. Litigants also disputed the maintenance entitlements of men and individuals with matrimonial faults, as well as the extent of maintenance payments, the status of extrajudicial deeds in which individuals relinquish maintenance claims on their spouses, and the constitutional status of various statutory maintenance provisions. For a discussion of the varied case law on these issues, see Agnes 2011b, 117–42, 164–207; Menski 2001, 261–75; 2003, 508–22, 535–42.

109. *Sree Raja Row Boochee Tummiah v. Sree Raja Row Venkata Neeladry Rao* (1805–47); *Viraswami Chetty v. Appaswami Chetty* (1864); *Pullamma v. Thatalingam* (1945).

110. *Sobhanadramma v. Varaha Lakshmi Narasimhaswami* (1934); *Vellayammal v. Ramaswami Naicken* (1934); *Rukmani Ammal v. T. R. S. Chari* (1935); *Mt. Lajwanti v. Bakshi Ram* (1935); *Seethayamma v. Venkataramana* (1940).

111. *Musunuru Nagendramma v. Musunuru Ramakotayya* (1953) applied this feature of the HMWRSRMA retrospectively, and interpreted certain Hindu legal classics to uphold the man's obligation to support his wife while she lived apart from him if he superseded her due to no matrimonial fault of hers, to marry another woman. (So did *Lakshmi Ammal v. Narayanaswami Naicker* (1950), without claiming support in classical Hindu law). But in *Kasubai v. Bhagwan Bhagaji Wanjari* (1955), the court argued against such a view of classical Hindu law and held the HMWRSRMA to enable separate maintenance only if the later marriage happened after the act's passage, and other courts came to the same conclusion without engaging Hindu classics in *Mt. Sukhribai v. Pohkalsingh* (1950) and *Ram Parkash v. Shrimati Savitri Devi* (1957) at 519.

112. *Viramallu Swarajya Lakshmi Mancharamma v. Viramallu Satyanarayana* (1950).

113. *Savithramma v. Ramanarasimhaiah* (1962); *A. P. K. Narayanaswami Reddiar v. Padmanabhan* (1966); *Banshidhar Jha v. Chhabi Chatterjee* (1967); *Pothula Manika Reddy v. Government of A. P.* (1978); *Yamunabai Anantrao Adhav v. Anantrao Shivram Adhav* (1988); and *Yamunabai Anantrao Adhav v. Anantrao Shivram Adhav* (1982) at 298. The last two were the rulings of the Supreme Court and the Bombay High Court respectively on the same dispute.

114. Menski 2003, 511–12.

115. *Bajirao Raghoba Tambre v. Tolanbai* (1980).

116. Menski 2001, 146, 224, 262; 2003, 395, 511; Agnes 2011b, 142

117. *Rajeshbai v. Shantabai* (1981); *Shantaram Patil v. Dagubai Patil* (1987); *Rudramma v. H. R. Pattaveerabhadrappa* (1987); *Vaijayantabai Gangarde v. Keru Anant Gangarde* (1991); *Sarabjit Singh v. Charanjit Kaur* (1997); *Krishnakant Mulashankar Vyas v. Reena Krishna Vyas* (1999); *Smt. Reeta Bharat Arora v. Bharat Yasodanandan Arora @ Dhingra* (2002); *Rameshchandra Daga* (2005).

118. Such assumptions were made about Muslim marriages in *Khajah Hidayut Oollah v. Rai Jan Khanum* (1844) and *Mohabbat Ali Khan v. Mahomed Ibrahim Khan* (1929). Similar claims were made about Hindu marriages in *Andrahennedige Dinohamy v. Wijetunge Liyanapatabendige Balahamy* (1927); *Nandamani Ananga Bhima Deo v. Suseela Mala Patta Mahadevi* (1932); *Shivalingiah* (1956); *Badri Prasad v. Dy Director of Consolidation* (1978); *Ramesh Chander Kaushal v. Veena Kaushal & Ors.* (1978); and *Boli Narajan Pawye v. Shiddeswari Morang* (1981).

119. Many of the cases Agnes cited to illustrate this trend (e.g., *Yamunabai Anantrao Adhav v. Anantrao Shivram Adhav* (1988) and *Savitaben Somabhai Bhatiya v. State of Gujarat* (2005)) continued the long-standing practice of denying such women maintenance under criminal law, rather than ruling with reference to Hindu law.

120. In *D. Velusamy v. D. Patchaiammal* (2010), the Supreme Court ruled that the PWDVA applies only to marital or quasi-marital relationships, rather than to the relationship of a man with a "'keep' whom he maintains financially and uses mainly for sexual purpose (sic) and/or as a servant."

121. Agarwal 1995, 1998, 2008; Sivaramayya 1997, 1999.

122. Rocher 1972 and Cohn 1996, 57–75 showed that the application of particular schools of Hindu law and subschools of Mitakshara law, based on specific commentaries on the *Yajnavalkya Smriti,* to certain regions and groups was a product of the colonial

encounter. The school relevant to an individual depended more on the region where his ancestors originated than on the region of his residence.

123. The executive and legislature did not highlight this aspect of Section 15 when they framed the HSA in the 1950s, but judges did in *Ayi Ammal v. Subramania Asari* (1966).

124. Agarwal 1995, 222.

125. For further details, see: Agarwal 2008, 312–17; Sivaramayya 1997.

126. *Narasimhamurthy v. Sushilabai* (1996).

127. *Shiramabai v. Kalgonda Bhimgonda* (1964); *P. Govinda Reddy v. Golla Obulamma* (1971); *Yethirejulu Neelaya v. Mudummuru Ramaswami* (1973).

128. This interpretation was adopted thereafter in *Ananda Naik v. Haribandhu Naik* (1967); *Vidyaben v. Jagdishchandra Nandshankar Bhatt* (1972); and *Sushilabai Ramchandra Kulkarni v. Narayanrao Gopalrao Deshpande* (1975).

129. Parashar 1992, 110–11, 125–29; Newbigin 2009, 2010, 2011.

130. This change was mainly meant to encourage more Hindu couples to opt for the SMA by applying Hindu law to the inheritance of their property.

131. Committee on the Status of Women in India 1975; India. National Commission for Women 1995; Agarwal, Sivaramayya, and Sarkar 1998.

132. Sections 3 to 6 of the Kerala Act were similar to Sections 86 to 89 of this version of the HCB. Section 4(1) said that "all members of an undivided Hindu family governed by the Mitakshara law holding any coparcenary property on the day this Act comes into force shall with effect from that day, be deemed to hold it as tenants-in-common" and Section 4(2) that "all members of a joint Hindu family, other than an undivided Hindu family referred to in sub-section (1), holding any joint family property on the day this Act comes into force, shall, with effect from that day be deemed to hold it as tenants-in-common, as if a partition of such property per capita had taken place."

The Madras Marumakkathayam Act, the Madras Aliyasanthana Act, the Travancore Nayar Act, the Travancore Ezhava Act, the Nanjinad Vellala Act, the Travancore Kshatriya Act, the Travancore Krishnavaka Marumakkathayee Act, the Cochin Thiyya Act, the Cochin Nayar Act, the Cochin Marumakkathayam Act, and the Kerala Nambudiri Act recognized Kerala's matrilineal systems, in somewhat changed forms. Agarwal 1995, 168–80, Fuller 1976, and Arunima 2003 discuss matrilineal practices and their relationship to legislation in Kerala since the early colonial period.

133. Sivaramayya 1997; Agarwal 2008; Parameswaran Moothath 1973.

134. Many *shastras* recommended that the inheritance rights of unmarried daughters be greater than those of married daughters. Among the major commentaries that influenced colonial law, Jimutavahana's *Dayabhaga* recommended that unmarried daughters receive only shares that would cover their wedding expenses, but Vijnaneswara's *Mitakshara* suggested that they get more.

135. *Pulla Reddy v. I. Seshi Reddy* (1987); *S. Sai Reddy v. S. Narayana Reddy* (1991); *G. Valli alias Rayaprolu v. State of Andhra Pradesh* (2003); *Merla Narayudu v. M. Bramaramba* (2006); *Sugalabai v. Gundappa Adiveppa Maradi* (2007); *Prema v. Nanje Gowda* (2011); Lawyers Collective—Women's Rights Initiative 2010a.

136. *Sundarambal v. Deivanaayagam* (1991); *Sheela Devi v. Lal Chand* (2007); *Valliammal v. Muniyappan* (2008); and *S. Seshachalam v. S. Deenadayalan* (2009); Lawyers Collective, Women's Rights Initiative 2010a.

137. *Smt. Nanjamma and Another v. State of Karnataka* (1999); *R. Mahalakshmi v. A. V. Anantharaman* (2009). However, a daughter married before the passage of the Karnakata amendment was deemed a coparcener because the case was pending when national legislation that made married daughters coparceners as well was passed, and the latter legislation took precedence over the former, in *Sugalabai v. Gundappa Adiveppa Maradi* (2007).

138. Sivaramayya 1988.

139. Agarwal 2008.

140. Matriliny is also widely prevalent in some of the smaller states of northeast India, but Hindu law is less relevant there because tribal customary laws govern much of the region's population, particularly in Meghalaya, Mizoram, Manipur, Nagaland, and Arunachal Pradesh.

141. For a discussion of Kerala politics, see Nossiter 1982. For the Telugu Desam, see Reddy 1989. For the DMK and the AIADMK, see Subramanian 1999. Interviews, D. Purandeswari (daughter of Telugu Desam's founding leader, N. T. Rama Rao, currently a Congress Party MP); Justice M. Jagannadha Rao (Justice of Andhra Pradesh High Court, 1982–91, and Chair of Law Commission, 2002–2006); Justice P. A. Choudary (Justice of Andhra Pradesh High Court, 1980–95); Pappa Umanath (of the CPI-M, who welcomed the amendment in the Tamil Nadu legislative assembly); P. H. Pandian (AIADMK); Durai Murugan (DMK; Law Minister of Tamil Nadu, 2006–11).

142. Tamil Nadu. Legislative Assembly 1989 (6 May), 418–67.

143. Uttar Pradesh Land Laws (Amendment) Act, 1982; Agarwal 2008, 339.

144. India. National Commission for Women 1997; India. Ministry of Law. Law Commission of India 2000; *The Observer* 2000; *The Hindu* 2000; *The Tribune* 2000.

145. The responses were not entirely consistent. While a definite majority recommended the dissolution of coparcenaries, a plurality favored the adoption of the Andhra Pradesh precedent rather than the Kerala model although coparcenaries were dissolved only in Kerala. Moreover, only a slight majority favored enabling married daughters to reside in the ancestral home. However, most who wished to retain joint property wanted to make daughters and mothers coparceners, and to protect widows' rights to reside in the ancestral home.

146. The Chair of the Commission that presented the Report, Justice B. P. Jeevan Reddy, adopted a more cautious approach than some other members, notably Justice Leila Seth. Interviews, Justices B. P. Jeevan Reddy; Leila Seth.

147. India. Ministry of Law. Law Commission of India 2000.

148. The Hindu Succession (Amendment) Bill, 2004.

149. She carefully documented various steps in this process in Agarwal 2007, and generously shared with me these documents and her insights on the process. I am also grateful to E. M. Sudarsana Natchiappan, Chair of the Department Related Parliamentary Standing Committee on Personnel, Public Grievances, Law and Justice, for giving me access to the committee's proceedings, and informing me of other discussions of this initiative.

150. Agarwal 2007, 30–45; Although only the AIWC enjoyed significant support across India, many other organizations involved in the process had carved niches for themselves in the fields of women's rights, child rights, agrarian development, housing and land rights, lower caste rights, legal reform, workers and peasants' rights, and civil liberties.

151. Agarwal 2005a; 2005b; 2007, 1; Saheli 2005; Interviews, Sudha Sundararaman, General Secretary, AIDWA; Subhashini Ali, President, AIDWA; Kirti Singh, Legal Convenor, AIDWA; Pramila Loomba, Vice-President, NFIW; Colin Gonsalves, Founder, Human Rights Law Network.

152. Agarwal 2008.

153. T. K. Viswanathan, Secretary, Ministry of Law and Justice, also said to the committee: "The Law Commission noted that women who are already married would have taken their share by way of dowry, jewellery and other things." Department Related Parliamentary Standing Committee on Personnel, Public Grievances, Law and Justice 2005.

154. Agarwal 2005a; 2005b; 2008, 346; Department Related Parliamentary Standing Committee on Personnel, Public Grievances, Law and Justice 2005; Interviews, Bina Agarwal; Kirti Singh; Pramila Loomba; E. M. Sudarsana Natchiappan.

155. Panda and Agarwal 2005; Deininger, Nagarajan and Goyal 2010.

156. Department Related Parliamentary Standing Committee on Personnel, Public Grievances, Law and Justice 2005; LSD 2005; Report of the Standing Committee of Parliament on Law and Justice: Hindu Succession Amendment Bill 2005.

157. Bal Apte, the vice-president of the party and member of the committee, evidently expressed his misgivings privately; in parliament, P. S. Gadhavi opposed enabling married daughters to partition the ancestral home. Interview, E. M. Sudarsana Natchiappan; LSD 2005.

158. The Committee takes note of the fact that the joint family system is a unique feature of the Indian society. Though not impervious to various inadequacies and anomalies, the joint family system has been in existence since time immemorial and is continuing with many a change in its structure and ideology to keep pace with the changing needs of time. While noting the concern regarding discrimination of women in the patrilineal, patriarchal joint family set up, the Committee also comprehends the fact that strong public sentiment is attached regarding the sanctity of the joint family system. Moreover, it is beyond the scope of the present Bill to consider any such step regarding abolition of the joint family system in the Hindu household.

Report of the Standing Committee of Parliament on Law and Justice: Hindu Succession Amendment Bill 2005; Interview, E. M. Sudarsana Natchiappan.

159. While the Chair of the Law Commission, Justice M. Jagannadha Rao, wanted married daughters not to be made coparceners (as D. Purandeswari (Congress Party) indicated in parliament), state agrarian legislation to retain priority over the HSA's rules, and testamentary freedom to be retained, another member, Justice S. Muralidhar, urged the Law Ministry to follow the opposite course in all these respects. A Law Commission member said that an intermediate version of the bill ended testamentary rights over half of one's property, but that an important minister got the cabinet to remove this provision. The last claim could not be verified. Muralidhar 2004; LSD 2005; Interviews, Justices M. Jagannadha Rao; S. Muralidhar

160. LSD 2005; the Law Minister promised to explore with state governments the changes these legislators suggested in agrarian legislation, but no such effort was made.

161. This was the case with R. S. Gadhavi (BJP), Raja Ram Pal (Congress Party), Shailendra Kumar, and Tufani Saroj (SP). LSD 2005.

162. *Assistant Commissioner of Gift Tax v. C. Krishnan and Ors.* (2002); and *Sugalabai v. Gundappa Adiveppa Maradi* (2007).

163. Courts rejected pleas to give widows their pre-amendment shares in cases such as *Anar Devi v. Parmeshwari Devi* (2006), *Pravat Chandra Pattnaik v. Sarat Chandra Pattnaik* (2008), *Smt. Bhagirathi v. S. Manivanan* (2008), and *M. Yogendra v. Leelamma N.* (2010).

CHAPTER FIVE

1. See: Cohn 1996; Pandey 1990; Dalmia and Von Stietencron 1995; Jaffrelot 1996; Mufti 2007.

2. Douglas 1988; Hasan 1992; Madani 2005; Mufti 2007, 129–76; F. Robinson 2007; Metcalf 2009b.

3. Brass 1991, 75–108.

4. Metcalf 1982; Minault 1982; Baljon 1986; Zaman 2002; Sanyal 2005.

5. ibn Abidin's major work, *Radd al-mukhtar 'ala al-Durr al-mukhtar*, remained a part of the curricula of major Hanafi religious institutions. Interviews, Maulana Jaseemuddin, Chief Qazi, Imarat-e-Shariah; Maulana Mohammad Burhanuddin Sambhali, Chief Qazi, Darul Uloom Nadwatul Ulama and President, Fiqh Committee, AIMPLB; Mufti Mukarram Ahmed, Shahi Imam of Fatehpuri Masjid; Maulana Yasin Akhtar Misbahi, Founder & President, Darul Qalam.

6. Ewing 1988; Masud 1996; Zaman 2002, 2008; Metcalf 2009b; Kugle 2001; F. Robinson 2008; De 2009; Moosa 2009; Sanyal 2005. However, the DUMI promotes certain religious practices shared by many Hindus and Sikhs, notably the reverence of saints and their gravesites.

7. Ansari 2009; M. Ali 2010. Interviews: Ali Anwar, President, All India Pasmanda Muslim Mahaz; Dr. Ejaz Ali, President, All India United Muslim Morcha.

8. Gilmartin 1981, 1988; Nelson 2011. As we saw in Chapter 2, the Government of India Act of 1935 placed the administration of agricultural land under the exclusive jurisdiction of the provincial governments, crucially due to the influence of one of the Shariat Act's architects, Mian Fazl-i-Husain (Nelson 2011, 100–102), and succession to other forms of property under the concurrent control of the national and the provincial governments.

9. The DMMA enabled Muslim women to gain divorces if their husbands had not been heard from for four years, did not provide them maintenance for two years, were sentenced to prison for seven years, did not perform their marital obligations for three years, were impotent since the couple's marriage, had been insane for two years, had leprosy or a virulent venereal disease, or had been cruel toward them (by habitually assaulting them, frequenting prostitutes, forcing them into prostitution, obstructing their religious practice, or not treating them on a par with their other wives), or if the women were married before they turned fifteen and repudiated their marriages before they turned eighteen.

10. Minault 1998; Devji 1994; Gilmartin 1981; Fyzee 1999, 474; Jalal 2001.

11. Joshi, Srinivas and Bajaj 2003, 179; Oddie 1991, Appendices A and B.

12. Frykenberg 2008; Forrester 1980.

13. Harper 1988; Webster 1992.

14. Oddie 1998, 2001; Frykenberg 2008; Boyd 1969; Thomas 1979.

15. *Sarabai v. Rabiabai* (1905) at 537.

16. Repudiation was recognized although it was declared in the woman's absence in such cases as *Sarabai* (1905), *Ful Chand v. Nazab Ali Chowdhry* (1908), *Asha Bibi v. Kadir*

Ibrahim Rowther (1909), *Ma Mi v. Kallander Ammal* (1927), *Saiyid Rashid Ahmad v. Mt. Anisa Khatun* (1932), and *Ahmad Kasim Molla v. Khatun Bibi* (1933); only on the date of the man's written divorce statement, which was later than when repudiation was verbally pronounced, in *Asmata Ullah v. Khatun-unnisa* (1939); and only when the woman learned of the divorce in *Kathiyamma v. Urathel Marakkar* (1931) and *Abdul Khader v. Aziza Bee* (1944).

17. *Sarabai* (1905) at 538; *Asha Bibi* (1909) at 33.
18. *Muhammad Muin-ud-din v. Jamal Fatima* (1921).
19. This was because these laws were initially said to apply to the residents of the territory of British India, rather than a group, that is, to residents not covered by group-specific personal laws (Hindu, Muslim, Parsi, and Jewish law).
20. N. Chatterjee 2010.
21. Divorce grounds were similarly asymmetric and based on English matrimonial law for Parsis, but this was changed in 1936. They remain asymmetric for Muslims.
22. *Miss. Shireen Mall v. Mr. John James Taylor* (1952) set the precedent in this regard. *George Swamidoss Joseph v. Harriett Sundari Edward* (1955) deemed current British legislation relevant three years later, but other courts did not follow this precedent.
23. Women could also get divorces if their husbands either engaged in rape, sodomy, or bestiality, or converted to another religion and married another woman.
24. CAID 1999.7, 540–41, 544–46.
25. CAID 1999.7, 541–43, 546.
26. PD 1951, 2550–52.
27. Jacob 1999; PD 1954, 2511–12.
28. Gandhi and Shah 1992; Epp 1998; Agarwal 2008; Mazumdar 1999.
29. Ram Jethmalani and Arun Jaitley, who were the Law Ministers when the BJP led a national government, admitted they had no concrete plans about the content of a UCC. Interviews, Ram Jethmalani; Arun Jaitley (Union Law Minister, 2000–2004).
30. Mazumdar 1999; Agnes 1999; AIDWA 1999, 2010; Interviews, Jyotsna Chatterji; Subhashini Ali; Maimoona Mollah, Convenor, Muslim Women Sub-Committee, AIDWA; Mary Khemchand, former President, YWCA.
31. Vatuk 2008.
32. The Shia Women's Personal Law Board is inactive. Hasan 2005; Awasthi 2006; Chauhan 2007; Schwartz 2012; Interviews, Maulana Mirza Mohammad Athar, President, and Shikoh Azad, Joint Secretary, All India Shia Personal Law Board; Maulana Mohammad Burhanuddin Sambhali; Maulana Khalid Rashid, Naib Imam, Firangi Mahal; Shaista Amber, President, All India Muslim Women's Personal Law Board; Mohammad Abdul Rahmin Quraishi; Syeda Saiyidain Hameed, former President, and Dr. Sughra Mehdi, current President, Muslim Women's Forum; D.Sharifa, President, STEPS.
33. Islamic Fiqh Academy 2004; Zaman 2008; Sikand 2003, 2008; Interviews, Maulana Khalid Saifullah Rehmani, President and Maulana Amin Osmani, Vice President, Islamic Fiqh Academy; Dr. Tahir Mahmood.
34. Hameed 2000; TNN 2004; AIDWA 2005; Engineer 2005; All India Muslim Personal Law Board 2002; Interviews, Syeda Saiyidain Hameed, former President, Muslim Women's Forum; Maulana Ateeq Ahmed Bastvi, Convenor, Darul Qaza Committee, AIMPLB.

35. This was because some members resisted further dialogue with women who did not wear the *hijab*.

36. Indeed, Maulana Jasemuddin, the Chief Qazi of the Imarat-e-Shariah, admitted that the central *dar'ul qaza* of the Imarat-e-Shariah did not have a copy of this model marital contract. Interviews, Maulana Jaseemuddin; Maulana Khalid Saifullah Rehmani, Convenor, Nikahnama Committee, AIMPLB; Begum Naseem Iktidhar Ali, only woman member, AIMPLB Executive Committee.

37. Shahabuddin 1992, 1999; Sikand 2005, 2010; Ahmad 2008; Express News Service 2006; PTI 2006; Women Living Under Muslim Laws 2006; Jamaat Ahl-i-Hadith 1994; Interviews, Maulana Mirza Athar, President, and Shikoh Azad, Joint Secretary, All India Shia Personal Law Board; Maulana Abdul Wahab Khilji, former General Secretary, Jamaat Ahl-i-Hadith, and President, All India Milli Council; Syed Shahabuddin, President, Muslim Majlis-e-Mushawarat.

38. Interviews, Syed Mohammad Rabey Hasni Nadwi, President, AIMPLB; Dr. Qasim Rasool Ilyas, Secretary and Convenor, Babri Masjid Committee, AIMPLB; Maulana Jalaluddin Umri, President, Jamaat-i-Islami Hind; Maulana Mehmood Madani, President, Jamiyat Ulama-i-Hind; Maulana Abdul Wahab Khilji.

39. Jacob 1999; Agnes 1999, 141–63; Monteiro 1992; N. Chatterjee 2004 ; and N. Chatterjee 2010 discuss aspects of Christian mobilization regarding personal law.

40. Parashar 1992, 189–92; Monteiro 1992; Jacob 1999; India. Ministry of Law. Law Commission of India 1960, 1961; The Christian Marriage and Matrimonial Causes Bill, 1962.

41. Chatterji 1979, 1982, 1983, 1984, 1986, 1989; AIDWA 2002, 35–36; The personal law files in the offices of the YWCA and the CNI indicate the various ways in which many individuals involved in these discussions based the policies they sought in their religious visions. Young Women's Christian Association n.d.; Church of North India n.d.

42. India. Ministry of Law. Law Commission of India 1983; The appendices include many of the letters and articles of the proponents of Christian law reform.

43. Christian Marriage and Matrimonial Causes Act, 1990; Christian Adoption and Maintenance Bill, 1993; Christian Marriage Bill 1994, 1997; Indian Succession (Amendment) Bill 1994; Indian Divorce Bill 1997 (Draft Bill of CBCI, NCCI and JWP).

44. However, some courts recognized a right to a share of the matrimonial home on separation or divorce, the PWDVA did so too in 2005 if there had been spousal violence, and giving Hindu divorcées a share in matrimonial property is under consideration, as we saw in Chapter 4.

45. Chatterji 1984; Interviews, Jyotsna Chatterji; Dr. John Dayal; Jos Chiramel, former National Secretary for Legal Affairs, AICU, and Legal Counsel, CBCI; Dr. Julian Francis, Legal Counsel, NCCI; Mary Khemchand, former President, YWCA; Rev. Richard Howell, General Secretary, EFI; Justice Vikramjit Sen, Delhi High Court; Cardinal Oswald Gracias, Archbishop of Bombay, Roman Catholic Church and President, CBCI; Bishop Santhram, former General Secretary, CNI; Fr. Savio Coutinho, former Secretary, CBCI; Dr. Kande Prasada Rao, General Secretary, Christian Law Review Committee.

46. Watson 1983, 2001; Horowitz 1994; Habermas 1991; Rueschemeyer and Skocpol 1996.

47. The relevant judgments of Baharul Islam were *Jiauddin Ahmed v. Anwar Begum* (1978) and *Rukia Khatun v. Abdul Khalique Laskar* (1981). Those of Krishna Iyer were *A. Yousuf Rawther v. Sowramma* (1971), *Bai Tahira v. Ali Hussain Fisalli Chothia* (1979), and

Fuzlunbi v. Khader Vali (1980). Krishna Iyer called for personal-law reform in Krishna Iyer 1984a, 1984b.

48. Bhattacharjee 1985, 1994.

49. The Christian law cases in which women's divorce rights were increased were *Mary Sonia Zachariah v. Union of India* (1995) (also called *Ammini E. J. v. Union of India*), *Pragati Varghese v. Cyril George Varghese* (1997), and *N. Sarada Mani v. G. Alexander* (1997); those in which adoption rights were recognized were *Philips Alfred Malvin v. Gonsalvis* (1999), *Maxin George & Mary George v. Indian Oil Corporation Ltd.* (2005), *Vasanti v. Pharez John Abraham* (2007), and *Mrs. T. Crauford v. Ms. Maary Disilva* (2008). Interviews, Justices S. Rajendra Babu, former Chief Justice of India; V. R. Krishna Iyer, retired judge, Supreme Court.

50. The more recent treatises include Verma 2002, Kader 1998, and Mahmood 1997; for examples of the older texts frequently used in courts, see Ameer Ali 1929, Mulla 1968, and Fyzee 1999.

51. Interviews, Justice S. A. Kader, retired judge, Madras High Court; Dr. Tahir Mahmood.

52. Cossman and Kapur 2002.

53. Interview, Dr. Rajeev Dhavan (Khatoon Nisa's lawyer).

54. Interviews, Sona Khan; Indira Jaising (lawyers in *Danial Latifi*).

55. Frykenberg 2008, vii; Pew Research Center 2011, 78.

56. Iyer 2000; Christian Marriage Bill 2000; AICU 2000; CBCI 2000a, 2000b; Centre for Policy Research and Communication 2000; Interviews, Arun Jaitley; Jyotsna Chatterji; Dr. John Dayal; Dr. Julian Francis; Jos Chiramel; Rev. Richard Howell.

57. Parashar 1992; Kapur and Cossman 1996; Sunder Rajan 2003.

58. Narain 2008.

59. Vatuk 2005; Basu 2003, 2008; Agnes 2005; Solanki 2011; Subramanian 2008.

60. Parashar 1992, 164–68; Menski 2003, 515–22.

61. These legislators disregarded the distinction that Islamic legal traditions make between the husband's obligation to pay dower and his maintenance obligations after divorce. Judges distinguished the two obligations in many cases, such as *Hamira Bibi v. Zubaide Bibi* (1916), *Syed Sabir Husain v. Farzand Hasan* (1938), *Shah Bano* (1985), and *Abdul Khader v. Smt. Razia Begum* (1990).

62. Some of the high court cases following this pattern were: *Khurshid Khan Amin Khan v. Husnabanu* (1976) and *Mehbubabi Nasir Shaikh v. Nasir Farid Shaikh* (1976). The relevant Supreme Court judgments were *Bai Tahira (1979)*, *Fuzlunbi (1980)*, and *Shah Bano* (1985). Courts required maintenance for just three months in other cases, such as *Rukhsana Parvin v. Sheikh Mohammad Hussain* (1977) and *Aluri Sambaiah v. Shaikh Zahirabi* (1977).

63. The relevant verses say: "For divorced women, let there be a fair provision. This is an obligation on those who are mindful of god"; and "Let the divorced women dwell where ye dwell, according to your means, and do not harm them, to reduce them to straits." Latif 1969. The courts have so far not followed the suggestion that the latter verse gives divorced women rights in the matrimonial home.

64. The following prominent Indian Hanafis nevertheless accepted that *mata* should be mandatory: Maulana Mujahidul Islam Qasmi, who founded the Islamic Fiqh Academy and was the AIMPLB's President; Maulana Khalid Saifullah Rehmani, current President, Islamic Fiqh Academy; Mufti Mukarram Ahmed, Shahi Imam of Fatehpuri

Masjid; and Athar Hussain, whose book on Muslim personal law the AIMPLB published. They and certain prominent Ithna Asharis, such as Maulana Kalbe Sadiq, the Vice-President of the AIMPLB, and Ayatollah Syed Aqeel-ul Gharavi, the Vice-President of the Muslim Majlis-e-Mushawarat, believed *mata* was meant to be a lump-sum amount. Interviews, Maulana Kalbe Sadiq; Maulana Khalid Saifullah Rehmani; Mufti Mukarram Ahmed; Ayatollah Syed Aqeel-ul Gharavi.

65. Syed Ameenul Hasan Rizvi, a legal advisor to the Hanafi Islamist organization, the Jamaat-i-Islami Hind, offered this suggestion in 1980 and reported that certain important Hanafi *ulama* supported this proposal. Latifi and Rizvi 1998, 66–67. Interview, Maulana Jalaluddin Umri (whom Rizvi had consulted).

66. Latifi 1988; Latifi and Rizvi 1998.

67. Sethi, Nauriya, and Thapar 2000.

68. Latifi and Rizvi 1998, 27–29.

69. Latifi 1988. Section 125(3) enabled a woman to live apart from her husband and claim maintenance from him if he had another conjugal relationship. Justice Chandrachud considered this contrary to the permission Muslim law gave men to have up to four wives, and so found in this section a basis to override Muslim law. However, twenty-five years earlier in *Itwari v. Smt. Asghari Begum and Others* (1960), a high court had allowed a Muslim woman to gain judicial separation and maintenance from a bigamous husband based on the construction that in current social conditions, bigamy amounted to cruelty to one's spouse and cruelty was a ground on which Muslim law allowed separation. Later, the Supreme Court enabled a Muslim woman to divorce her bigamous husband for the same reason, in *Begum Subanu alias Saira Banu and another v. A. M. Abdul Gafoor* (1987).

70. He quoted Tahir Mahmood as saying: "instead of wasting their energies in exerting theological and political pressure in order to secure an 'immunity' for their traditional personal law from the State's legislative jurisdiction, the Muslims will do well to begin exploring and demonstrating how the true Islamic laws, purged of their time-worn and anachronistic interpretations, can enrich the common civil code of India." *Shah Bano* (1985) at 955.

71. Carroll 1998, 144; Interview, Dr. Tahir Mahmood.

72. Williams 2006, 144–45.

73. LSD 1986, 309–18.

74. The AIDWA gathered the signatures of a million women, including 252,000 Muslim women, in the largest signature campaign against the MWPRDA. Writ Petition No. 1001 of 1986, 5.

75. For instance, H. A. Dora of the Telugu Desam party, who wished to require alimony among Muslims, voiced such concerns. LSD 1986, 335–37. The Prime Minister's office is said to have pressed the AIMPLB officials to accept the act as initially drafted or take the risk that no legislation might result. Interviews, Yusuf Hatim Muchchala, Convenor, AIMPLB Legal Committee; Dr. Qasim Rasool Ilyas; Maulana Syed Jalaluddin Umri.

76. *Ramzan v. Smt. Salma* (1987); *Abid Ali v. Mst. Rasia Begum* (1988); *Mehboobkhan v. Parvinbanoo* (1988); *Rupsan Begum v. Md. Abdus Sattar* (1990); *Abdul Rashid v. Sultana Begum* (1992); *Mohamed Ibrahim v. Ramzan Begum* (1993); *Begum Bibi v. Abdul Rajak Khan* (1994); *Mrs. Nazimunnissa Begum v. Abdul Majeeth* (1994); *Shahadabi M. Isak v. Abdul Ajij Abdul Latif* (1996); *Shahida Begum v. Abdul Majid* (1996); *Noor Jehan. v. State*

of Maharashtra (1996); *Abdul Haq v. Yasmin Talat* (1998); and *Aziza Khan v. Dr. Amir Hussain* (1999).

77. *Usman Khan Bahamani v. Fathimunnisa Begum* (1990) (also called *All India Muslim Advocates Forum v. Osman Khan Bahmani*).

78. *G. M. Jeelani v. Shanswar Kulsum* (1992).

79. *M. H. Hameed v. Arif Jan, alias Shahida Begum* (1990); *Abdul Khader v. Smt. Razia Begum* (1990).

80. *Syed Fazal Pookaya Thangal v. Union of India* (1993); *Sadique Ali v. Apar Sessions Naiyai Dheesh, Basti & Ors.* (1995).

81. The major high court judgments along these lines were *Arab Ahmedhia Abdullah v. Arab Bail Mohmuna Saiyadbhai* (1988) (the first such decree); *Ali v. Sufaira* (1988); *Aliyar v. Pathu* (1988); *Mohd. Tajuddin v. Quomarunnisa Begum* (1989); *Ahmed v. Aysha* (1990); *Abdul Khader v. Smt. Razia Begum* (1990); *M. Subhan v. Smt. Mazbul Be* (1991); *Jaitunbi Mubarak Shaikh v. Mubarak Fakruddin Shaikh* (1993); *Smt. Hamidan v. Mohd. Rafiq* (1994); *Banu v. Kutubuddin Selumanji Vimanwala* (1995); *Kunhammed Haji v. K. Amina* (1995); *K. Zunaideen v. Ameena Begum* (1998); *Kaka v. Hassan Bano* (1998); *Mumtazben Jusabbhai Sipahi v. Mahebubkhan Usmankhan Pathan* (1998); *Majitha Beevi v. Yakoob* (1999); *Shaikh Babbu v. Sayeda Masarat Begum* (1999); *Karim Abdul Rehman Shaikh v. Shehnaz Karim Shaikh* (2000); *Abdul Latif Mondal v. Anuwara Khatun* (2001); *Shamshad Begum v. Md. Noor Ahemad Khan* (2001); *Hasenara Begum v. Fazar Ali* (2002); and *Naseemunisa Begum v. Shaikh Abdul Rehman* (2002).

82. *Arab Ahmedhia Abdullah v. Arab Bail Mohmuna Saiyadbhai* (1988).

83. *Ali v. Sufaira* (1988); *Aliyar v. Pathu* (1988).

84. *Abdullah Rauf Khan v. Halemon Bibi* (1989); *Noor Saba Khatoon v. Mohammad Quasim* (1997).

85. Writ Petitions No. 996, 1001, 1055, 1062 of 1986, 868 of 1996 in *Danial Latifi and Ms. Susheela Gopalan v. Union of India*.

86. This was in contrast with Justice Chandrachud, who was unwilling to speak about *Shah Bano* over two decades after his judgment. Interviews, Justices S. Rajendra Babu; Shivaraj C. Patil; G. B. Pattanaik; D .P. Mohapatra; Doraiswamy Raju (members of the bench); Yusuf Hatim Muchchala; Sona Khan; Kamini Jaiswal; Indira Jaising; Syed Saif Mahmood (lawyers in the case); Dr. Tahir Mahmood.

87. *Danial Latifi* (2001) at 742–43.

88. *Danial Latifi* (2001) at 746–47.

89. *Danial Latifi* (2001) at 742–43, 757–58.

90. *Danial Latifi* (2001) at 744, 762.

91. Sunder Rajan 2003, 148–49; Okin 2001.

92. *Shabana Bano v. Imran Khan* (2009).

93. *Iqbal Bano v. State of Uttar Pradesh* (2007).

94. See discussion on pp. 34, 51.

95. The verse quoted in the last judgment was: "If ye fear a breach between them twain, appoint two Arbiters, one from his family, and the other from hers. If they seek to set things aright, Allah will cause their reconciliation. For Allah hath full knowledge; and is acquainted with all things."

96. Jamaat Ahl-i-Hadith 1994; Shahabuddin 1992, 1999; All India Muslim Personal Law Board 2002. Interviews, Maulana Abdul Wahab Khilji; Syed Shahabuddin; Ayatollah Syed Aqeel ul-Gharavi; Habeebulla Basha (lawyer); Justices S. A. Kader; A. Abdul

Hadi, retired judge, Madras High Court; Badar Durrez Ahmed, judge, Delhi High Court.

97. For instance, the Islamic Shariat Board (based in Kerala) intervened in *Shamim Ara v. State of U.P.* (2002), and the Tamil Nadu Advocates Meelad Forum in *Parveen Akhtar v. Union of India* (2002). An AIMPLB lawyer, Zafaryab Jilani, intervened in *Rahmat Ullah*, but in his individual capacity. Interviews, Zafaryab Jilani, lawyer and Member, AIMPLB Legal Committee; Zaffarullah Khan; Habeebulla Basha; Bader Sayeed; P. V. S. Giridhar (lawyers in the relevant cases); K. A. Sukkur (litigant); Justice S. A. Kader; Dr. Tahir Mahmood.

98. The following judgments deemed the *talaq-ul ba'in* revocable in this period: *Rukia Khatun v. Abdul Khalique Laskar* (1981); *Zeenat Fatema Rashid v. Md. Iqbal Anwar* (1993); *Motiur Rahaman v. Sabina Khatun* (1994); *Rahmat Ullah v. State of U. P. and Khatoon Nisa v. State of U. P* (1994); *Shaikh Mobin v. State of Maharashtra* (1996); *Saleem Basha v. Mumtaz Begum* (1998); *Kadar Mian v. Jahera Khatun* (1998); *Saira Bano v. Mohd. Aslam Ghulam Mustafa Khan* (1999); *Zulekha Begum alias Rahmathunnisa Begum v. Abdul Raheem* (2000); *M.Shahul Hameed v. Salima* (2003); and *Shamim Ara v. State of U.P. (2002)*. The triple *talaq* was deemed irrevocable in the majority of these cases, including *Ramzan v. Smt. Salma* (1987); *Sheikh Mohiuddin v. Hasina Bibi* (1988); *Abid Ali* (1988); *Sayed Newaj Ali alias Neti v. Rasida Begum* (1991); *Mohammad Umar Khan v. Gulshan Begum* (1992); *Begum Bibi v. Abdul Rajak Khan* (1994); *Shahadabi M. Isak* (1996); *Sheikh Saber Ali v. Smt. Sahmim Banu* (1996); *Shahida Begum* (1996); *Alimuddin Khan v. Nasiran Bibi* (1998); *Jaitunbi Mubarak Shaikh* (1993); and *Aziza Khan* (1999). The lower courts seem to have accepted the triple talaq in a higher proportion of cases.

99. Interviews, Justices Ramesh Chandra Lahoti; P. Venkatarama Reddi (*Shamim Ara* judges); Aziz M. Ahmadi, former Chief Justice of India; Badar Durrez Ahmed (*Masroor Ahmed* judge).

100. Interview, Justice Aziz M. Ahmadi (author of *Ahmedabad Women's Action Group*).

101. Redding 2010.

102. Jacob 1999; Agnes 1999, 141–63; Monteiro 1992.

103. *Dwaraka Bai* (1953) at 799–800.

104. *Solomon Devasahayam Selvaraj* (1968) at 294.

105. *T. M. Bashiam v. M. Victor* (1970) at 14; *Abedabi d/o Doud Shaikh & Anr. v. Sikandar Akabar Mujawar & Anr.* (1980); *Reynold Rajamani v. Union of India* (1982); *Jorden Diengdeh v. S. S. Chopra* (1985); *Swapna Ghosh v. Sadananda Ghosh* (1989); *Ramish Francis Toppo v. Violet Francis Toppo* (1989); *Ahmedabad Women's Action Group (AWAG) and Others v. Union of India* (1997); *P. E. Mathew v. Union of India* (1999).

106. *Swapna Ghosh* (1989) at 2–4.

107. *Solomon Devasahayam Selvaraj* (1968) at 294; *Neena v. John Pormu* (1985) at 87; *Swapna Ghosh* (1989) at 3; *Ramish Francis Toppo* (1989) at 325; *Binoy Mathew v. Sabu Abraham* (1998).

108. The three judgments were *Mary Sonia Zachariah v. Union of India* (1995), *Pragati Varghese v. Cyril George Varghese* (1997), and *N. Sarada Mani v. G.Alexander* (1997). The third judgment did not refer to its two predecessors and attracted limited attention among lawyers.

109. The churches were the Saint Thomas Evangelical Church and the Assyrian Church of the East. The Christian reform organizations were the Christian Institute for the Study of Religion and Society (the JWP's parent organization), the World Student Christian Federation, and the Janakiya Vimochana Viswas Prasthanam, an organization for lower-caste liberation affiliated with the Church of South India. The Church of South India is the largest Indian Christian church other than the Roman Catholic Church, and was born of a union of the Anglican, Congregational, Presbyterian, and Reformed churches in south India. The other rights organizations were the Indian Federation of Women Lawyers and the People's Council for Social Justice.

110. Writ Petitions Nos. 8505 of 1988-N and 4319 of 1991-N; *Mary Sonia Zachariah* (1995) at 33–37.

111. *Mary Sonia Zachariah* (1995) at 57.

112. *Anil Kumar Mahsi v. Union of India* (1994).

113. There are still minor differences between the divorce rights of Christians and Hindus. For instance, the nonresumption of cohabitation after judicial separation is a ground for divorce among Hindus, but not among Christians. Indian Divorce (Amendment) Act, 2001; Joint Women's Programme 2000.

114. India. Ministry of Law. Law Commission of India 1983, 1998; Ministry of Law, Justice and Company Affairs 2001; India. Parliament Standing Committee on Home Affairs 2001, 5–7.

115. A high court (*Sohan Lal v. A. Z. Makuin* (1929)) recognized the adoption rights of certain Punjabi Christians in 1929, based on the argument that various agrarian castes in the region had retained, after their conversion to Christianity, their adoption customs, which were meant to provide them heirs if they did not have sons, rather than to serve a religious or ritual purpose. But other courts do not seem to have followed this precedent, and another bench of the late colonial period (*Ranbir Karam Singh v. Jogindra C. Bhattachargi* (1940) at 139) found insufficient evidence that adoption customs existed among Punjabi Christians.

116. *Vasanti v. Pharez John Abraham* (2007); *Mrs. T. Crauford v. Ms. Maary Disilva* (2008).

117. *Maxin George & Mary George v. Indian Oil Corporation Ltd.* (2005); Moreover, it made the recognition of adoption contingent on authorized individuals having given the child in adoption.

118. *Biju Ramesh v. J. P. Vijayakumar* (2005); *Ajit Dutt v. Mrs. Ethel Walters* (2000). The first bench did not however overrule *Malvin* because it was not satisfied that adoption had indeed taken place in the case it considered, and the second bench's divided opinion about *Malvin* did not prevent it from delivering a judgment, since it too did not find that adoption had been proven.

119. *Jose v. Alice* (1988); *George Sebastian @ Joy v. Molly Joseph @ Nish* (1995).

120. The Marriage Laws (Amendment) Bill, 2010 does not specify the spouses' shares, and the Christian women's organizations may not soon gain the equal shares they have sought.

REFERENCES

BOOKS, PERIODICALS, AND GOVERNMENT DOCUMENTS

Abu-Odeh, Adnan. 2000. "Jordanians, Palestinians and the Hashemite Kingdom in the Middle East Peace Process." *Peace Research Abstracts* no. 37 (1).

Abu-Odeh, Lama. 2004. "Modernizing Muslim Family Law: The Case of Egypt." *Vanderbilt Journal of Transnational Law* no. 37: 1043–146.

Adams, Julia. 2005. *The Familial State: Ruling Families and Merchant Capitalism in Early Modern Europe*. Ithaca, NY: Cornell University Press.

Adams, Julia, and Mounira M. Charrad, eds. 2011. *Patrimonial Power in the Modern World*. Thousand Oaks, CA: Sage Publications.

Agarwal, Bina. 1994. "Gender and Command Over Property: A Critical Gap in Economic Analysis and Policy in South Asia." *World Development* no. 22 (10): 1455–78.

———. 1995. *A Field of One's Own: Gender and Land Rights in South Asia*. Cambridge: Cambridge University Press.

———. 1998. "Widows Versus Daughters or Widows as Daughters? Property, Land, and Economic Security in Rural India." *Modern Asian Studies* no. 32 (1): 1–48.

———. 2005a. "A Landmark Step to Gender Equality." *The Hindu*. September 25. Accessed May 30, 2013. http://hindu.com/thehindu/mag/2005/09/25/stories/2005092500050100.htm.

———. 2005b. "Women's Inheritance: Next Steps." *The Indian Express*. October 17.

———. 2007. *Amending the Hindu Succession Act, 1956: Documenting the Process*. Manuscript.

———. 2008. "Bargaining, Gender Equality and Legal Change: The Case of India's Inheritance Laws." In *Redefining Family Law in India: Essays in Honour of B. Sivara-

mayya, edited by Archana Parashar and Amita Dhanda, 30–54. Delhi: Routledge India.

———. 2013. "A House Divided," *Indian Express*, Monday, September 02. http://m.indianexpress.com/news/a-house-divided/1163180/; consulted: October 2, 2013.

Agarwal, Bina, B. Sivaramayya, and Lotika Sarkar. 1998. Report of the Committee on Gender Equality in Land Devolution in Tenurial Laws. Report submitted to the Department of Rural Development, Government of India, February.

Agnes, Flavia. 1999. *Law and Gender Inequality: The Politics of Women's Rights in India*. New Delhi: Oxford University Press.

———. 2001. "Minority Identity and Gender Concerns." *Economic and Political Weekly* no. 36 (42): 3973–76.

———. 2005. "Islamic Jurisprudence and Rights of Muslim Women in India". *Yahoo Group: india-unity*. Accessed October 7, 2013. http://groups.yahoo.com/group/india-unity/message/3177.

———. 2007. "The Supreme Court, the Media, and the Uniform Civil Code Debate in India." In *The Crisis of Secularism in India*, edited by Anuradha Dingwaney Needham and Rajeswari Sunder Rajan, 294–315. Durham, NC: Duke University Press.

———. 2008. "Hindu Conjugality: Transition from Sacrament to Contractual Obligations." In *Redefining Family Law: Essays in Honour of B. Sivaramayya*, edited by Archana Parashar and Amita Dhanda, 236–57. Delhi: Routledge India.

———. 2011a. *Family Law, Vol. 1, Family Laws and Constitutional Claims*. New Delhi: Oxford University Press.

———. 2011b. *Family law. Volume II: Marriage, Divorce, and Matrimonial Litigation*. New Delhi: Oxford University Press.

Ahmad, Irfan. 2008. "Cracks in the 'Mightiest Fortress': Jamaat-e-Islami's Changing Discourse on Women." *Modern Asian Studies* no. 42 (2–3): 549–75.

Ahmed, Leila. 1992. *Women and Gender in Islam: Historical Roots of a Modern Debate*. New Haven, CT: Yale University Press.

AIDWA. 1999. *Not a Uniform Civil Code but Equal Rights, Equal Laws*. New Delhi: All India Democratic Women's Association.

———. 2002. *Perspectives, Interventions and Struggles, 1998–2001*. New Delhi: All India Democratic Women's Association.

———. 2005. "AIDWA Response to Muslim Personal Law Board Model Nikahnama." *All India Democratic Women's Association*. Accessed May 31, 2013. http://aidwaonline.org/issues_of_concern/aidwa-response-muslim-personal-law-board-model-nikahnama.

———. 2010. *Muslim Women: AIDWA's Interventions and Struggles*. New Delhi: All India Democratic Women's Association.

Ali, Manjur. 2010. "Politics of 'Pasmanda' Muslims: A Case Study of Bihar." *History and Sociology of South Asia* no. 4 (2): 129–44.

Ali, Syed Ameer. 1985. *Mahommedan Law: Compiled from Authorities in the Original Arabic*. New Delhi: Himalayan Books.

All India Catholic Union (AICU). 2000. Letter of Convenor for Christian Personal Laws, AICU, to Secretary, Ministry of Law. April 22.

All India Muslim Personal Law Board. 2002. *Compendium of Islamic laws: A Section-wise Compilation of the Rules of Shari'at Relating to Muslim Personal Law*. 2nd ed. Delhi: All India Muslim Personal Law Board.

Almond, Gabriel A., and James Smoot Coleman. 1960. *The Politics of the Developing Areas.* Princeton, NJ: Princeton University Press.
Ameer Ali, Syed. 1929. *Mahommedan Law: Tagore Law Lectures.* Calcutta, India: Kitab Bhavan.
Amsden, Alice H. 2001. *The Rise of "the Rest": Challenges to the West from Late-Industrializing Economies.* Oxford: Oxford University Press.
———. 2007. *Escape from Empire: The Developing World's Journey Through Heaven and Hell.* Cambridge, MA: MIT Press.
Anderson, Benedict R. O'G. 1983. *Imagined Communities: Reflections on the Origin and Spread of Nationalism.* New York: Verso.
———. 1998. *The Spectre of Comparisons: Nationalism, Southeast Asia, and the World.* New York: Verso.
———. 1999. "Indonesian Nationalism Today and in the Future." *Indonesia* no. 67 (April): 1–11.
Anderson, Lisa. 1986. *The State and Social Transformation in Tunisia and Libya, 1830–1980.* Princeton, NJ: Princeton University Press.
An-Na'im, Abdullahi Ahmed. 2008. *Islam and the Secular State: Negotiating the Future of Shari'a.* Cambridge, MA: Harvard University Press.
Ansari, Khalid Anis. 2009. "Rethinking the Pasmanda Movement." *Economic and Political Weekly* no. 44 (13): 8–10.
Appadurai, Arjun. 1996. *Modernity at Large: Cultural Dimensions of Globalization.* Minneapolis: University of Minnesota Press.
Arat, Zehra F. 1994. "Kemalism and Turkish Women." *Women and Politics* no. 14 (4): 57–80.
Arjomand, Said Amir. 1988. *The Turban for the Crown: The Islamic Revolution in Iran.* New York: Oxford University Press.
———. 1989. "Constitution-Making in Islamic Iran: The Impact of Theocracy on the Legal Order of a Nation-State." In *History and Power in the Study of Law: New Directions in Legal Anthropology,* edited by June Starr and Jane F. Collier, 113–30. Ithaca, NY: Cornell University Press.
Arunima, G. 2003. *There Comes Papa: Colonialism and the Transformation of Matriliny in Kerala, Malabar, c. 1850–1940.* New Delhi: Orient Longman.
Asad, Talal. 1993. *Genealogies of Religion: Discipline and Reasons of Power in Christianity and Islam.* Baltimore, MD: Johns Hopkins University Press.
———. 2003. *Formations of the Secular: Christianity, Islam, Modernity.* Stanford, CA: Stanford University Press.
Awasthi, Pooja. 2006. "Muslim Women: Our Own Personal Law Board." *India Together.* 21 September. Accessed May 30, 2013. http://www.indiatogether.org/2006/sep/wom-aimwplb.htm#continue.
Badran, Margot. 2009. *Feminism in Islam: Secular and Religious Convergences.* Oxford: Oneworld Publications.
Baljon, J. M. S. 1986. *Religion and Thought of Shah Wali Allah Dihlawi, 1703–1762.* Leiden: Brill.
Barkey, Karen. 2008. *Empire of Difference: The Ottomans in Comparative Perspective.* Cambridge: Cambridge University Press.
Baruah, Sanjib. 1999. *India Against Itself: Assam and the Politics of Nationality.* Philadelphia: University of Pennsylvania Press.

———. 2005. *Durable Disorder: Understanding the Politics of Northeast India.* New Delhi and New York: Oxford University Press.
Basu, Aparna, and Bharati Ray. 1990. *Women's Struggle: A History of the All India Women's Conference, 1927–1990.* New Delhi: Manohar.
Basu, Srimati. 1999. *She Comes to Take Her Rights: Indian Women, Property, and Propriety.* Albany: State University of New York Press.
———. 2001. "The Personal and the Political: Indian Women and Inheritance Law." In *Religion and Personal Law in Secular India: A Call to Judgment,* edited by Gerald J. Larson, 163–83. Bloomington: Indiana University Press.
———. 2003. "Shading the Secular: Law at Work in the Indian Higher Courts." *Cultural Dynamics* no. 15 (2): 131–52.
———. 2008. "Separate and Unequal: Muslim Women and Un-Uniform Law in India." *International Feminist Journal of Politics* no. 10 (4): 495–517.
Bates, Robert H. 1981. *Markets and States in Tropical Africa: The Political Basis of Agricultural Policies.* Berkeley: University of California Press.
Baxter, Craig. 1984. *Bangladesh: A New Nation in an Old Setting.* Boulder, CO: Westview Press.
Beaman, Lori G, ed. 2012. *Reasonable Accommodation: Managing Religious Diversity.* Vancouver, BC: UBC Press.
Bell, David Avrom. 2003. *The Cult of the Nation in France: Inventing Nationalism, 1680–1800.* Cambridge, MA: Harvard University Press.
Benton, Lauren A. 2001. *Law and Colonial Cultures: Legal Regimes in World History, 1400–1900.* Cambridge: Cambridge University Press.
Berger, Maurits S. 1997. "The Legal System of Family Law in Syria." *Bulletin d'études orientales*: T.49: 115–27.
Berger, Peter L. 1967. *The Sacred Canopy: Elements of a Sociological Theory of Religion.* Garden City: Doubleday.
Berkes, Niyazi. 1964. *The Development of Secularism in Turkey.* Montreal, QC: McGill University Press.
Bertrand, Jacques. 2004. *Nationalism and Ethnic Conflict in Indonesia.* Cambridge: Cambridge University Press.
Bhargava, Rajeev, ed. 1999. *Secularism and Its Critics.* New Delhi: Oxford University Press.
———. 2010. *The Promise of India's Secular Democracy.* New Delhi: Oxford University Press.
Bhattacharjee, A. M. 1985. *Muslim Law and the Constitution: Calcutta University Ibrahim Saliman Salahjee Lectures 1981.* Calcutta: Eastern Law House.
———. 1994. *Hindu Law and the Constitution.* Calcutta: Eastern Law House.
Bhattacharyya, Harihar. 2003. "Multiculturalism in Contemporary India." *International Journal on Multicultural Societies (UNESCO)* no. 5 (2): 148–61.
Bhuiyan, Rabia. 2007. "The Personal Laws of Muslim and Hindu Women in Marriage and Divorce in Bangladesh: Addressing the Critical Issues from a Feminist Perspective." PhD diss., Cornell University.
———. 2010. *Gender and Tradition in Marriage and Divorce: An Analysis of Personal Laws of Muslim and Hindu Women in Bangladesh.* Dhaka: United Nations Educational, Scientific, and Cultural Organization.

Bilani, Najjar, and Antoine Elias El-Gemayel. 1985. "Personal Status." In *The Lebanese Legal System*, edited by Antoine Elias El-Gemayel, 267–390. Washington, D.C.: University Press of America.

Birla, Ritu. 2009. *Stages of Capital: Law, Culture, and Market Governance in Late Colonial India*. Durham, NC: Duke University Press.

Bodin, Jean. 1955. *Six Books of the Commonwealth*. Oxford: Basil Blackwell.

Bond, George D. 1988. *The Buddhist Revival in Sri Lanka: Religious Tradition, Reinterpretation, and Response*. Columbia: University of South Carolina Press.

Bourdieu, Pierre. 1977. *Outline of a Theory of Practice*. Cambridge: Cambridge University Press.

Bowen, John R. 1988. "The Transformation of an Indonesian Property System: Adat, Islam, and Social Change in the Gayo Highlands." *American Ethnologist* no. 15 (2): 274–93.

———. 1998. "'You May Not Give It Away': How Social Norms Shape Islamic Law In Contemporary Indonesian Jurisprudence." *Islamic Law and Society* no. 5 (3): 382–408.

———. 2003. *Islam, Law, and Equality in Indonesia: An Anthropology of Public Reasoning*. Cambridge: Cambridge University Press.

———. 2009. *Can Islam be French? Pluralism and Pragmatism in a Secularist State*. Princeton, NJ: Princeton University Press.

Boyd, Robin H. S. 1969. *An Introduction to Indian Christian Theology*. Madras: Christian Literature Society.

Brass, Paul R. 1991. *Ethnicity and Nationalism: Theory and Comparison*. New Delhi: Sage Publications.

Breuilly, John. 1994. *Nationalism and the State*. Chicago: University of Chicago Press.

Brewer, Carolyn. 1999. "Baylan, Asog, Transvestism, and Sodomy: Gender, Sexuality, and the Sacred in Early Colonial Philippines." *Intersections: Gender, History and Culture in the Asian Context* no. 2: 1–5.

Brown, Wendy. 2008. *Regulating Aversion: Tolerance in the Age of Identity and Empire*. Princeton, NJ: Princeton University Press.

Buskens, Léon. 2010. "Sharia and National Law in Morocco." In *Sharia Incorporated: A Comparative Overview of the Legal Systems of Twelve Muslim Countries in Past and Present*, edited by Jan Michiel Otto, 89–135. Leiden: Leiden University Press.

Constituent Assembly of India. India. 1948. *Constituent Assembly of India (Legislative) Debates (CAILD), Official Report*. New Delhi: Lok Sabha Secretariat.

———. 1949. *Constituent Assembly of India (Legislative) Debates (CAID), Official Report*. New Delhi: Lok Sabha Secretariat.

———. 1999. *Constituent Assembly of India Debates (CAID)*. New Delhi: Lok Sabha Secretariat.

Cammack, Mark E. 2002. "Islamic Inheritance Law in Indonesia: The Influence of Hazairin's Theory of Bilateral Inheritance." *Australian Journal of Asian Law* no. 4 (3): 295.

———. 2008. "Marital Property in California and Indonesia: Community Property and Harta Bersama." *Washington and Lee Law Review* no. 64 (4): 1417.

Cammack, Mark E., and R. Michael Feener. 2007. "Joint Marital Property in Indonesian Customary, Islamic, and National Law." in *The Law Applied: Contextualizing the Islamic Shari'a*, edited by Mark E. Cammack, Michael Feener, and Ruud Peters, 104–27. London: I. B. Tauris.

Cammack, Mark E., L. A. Young, and T. Heaton. 1996. "Legislating Social Change in an Islamic Society—Indonesia's Marriage Law." *American Journal of Comparative Law* no. 44 (1): 45.

Camroux, David. 1996. "State Responses to Islamic Resurgence in Malaysia: Accommodation, Co-Option, and Confrontation." *Asian Survey* no. 36 (9): 852–68.

Carroll, Lucy. 1998. *Shah Bano and the Muslim Women Act a Decade On: The Right of the Divorced Muslim Woman to Mataa*. Grabels Cèdex, FR: Copubished by Women Living Under Muslim Laws, International Solidarity Network, and Women's Research Action Group.

Casanova, José. 1994. *Public Religions in the Modern World*. Chicago: University of Chicago Press.

———. 2006. "Rethinking Secularization: A Global Comparative Perspective." *Hedgehog Review* no. 8 (1/2): 7–22.

Catalano, S. L. 2010. "Shari'a Reforms and Power Maintenance: The Cases of Family Law Reforms in Morocco and Algeria." *Journal of North African Studies* no. 15 (4): 535–55.

Catholic Bishops Conference of India (CBCI). 2000a. Press Statement, New Delhi, April 28.

———. 2000b. Letter to Union Minister of Law, May 4.

Centre for Policy Research and Communication. 2000. Amendments Proposed by the Christian Community in the Government's Christian Marriages Bill, 2000. Delhi.

Chandra, Sudhir. 1998. *Enslaved Daughters: Colonialism, Law, and Women's Rights*. Delhi: Oxford University Press.

Chanock, Martin. 1985. *Law, Custom, and Social Order: The Colonial Experience in Zambia and Malawi*. Cambridge: Cambridge University Press.

———. 1991. "A Peculiar Sharpness: An Essay on Property in the History of Customary Law in Colonial Africa." *Journal of African history* no. 32 (1): 65–88.

Charrad, Mounira M. 2001. *States and Women's Rights: The Making of Postcolonial Tunisia, Algeria, and Morocco*. Berkeley, CA: University of California Press.

———. 2007. "Tunisia at the Forefront of the Arab World: Two Waves of Gender Legislation." *Washington and Lee Law Review* no. 64: 1513.

Charrad, Mounira M., and Allyson Goeken. 2006. "Continuity or Change: Family Law and Family Structure in Tunisia." In *African Families at the Turn of the Twenty-First Century*, edited by Yaw Oheneba-Sakyi and Baffour K. Takyi, 27–48. Westport, CT: Praeger.

Chatterjee, Indrani. 2004. *Unfamiliar Relations: Family and History in South Asia*. New Brunswick: Rutgers University Press.

Chatterjee, Nandini. 2004. *Christian Personal Law in India: The Modern Origins of Yet Another Tradition*. Cambridge: Centre of South Asian Studies, University of Cambridge.

———. 2010. "Religious Change, Social Conflict and Legal Competition: The Emergence of Christian Personal Law in Colonial India." *Modern Asian Studies* no. 44 (6): 1147–95.

Chatterjee, Partha. 1992. "History and the Nationalization of Hinduism." *Social Research* no. 59 (1): 111–49.

———. 1993. *The Nation and Its Fragments: Colonial and Postcolonial Histories*. Princeton, NJ: Princeton University Press.

———. 1994. "Secularism and Toleration." *Economic and Political Weekly* no. 29 (28): 1768–77.
Chatterji, Jyotsna. 1979. *Good News for Women*. New Delhi: Joint Women's Programme and William Carey Study and Research Centre.
———. 1982. *Women in Praise and Struggle*. Delhi: The India Society for Promoting Christian Knowledge.
———. 1983. *Wake Up and Live*. Delhi: The India Society for Promoting Christian Knowledge.
———. 1984. *Changes in Christian Personal Laws*. Delhi: The India Society for Promoting Christian Knowledge, for WCSRC-CISRS-JWP.
———. 1986. *Vision and Service*. Delhi: The India Society for Promoting Christian Knowledge.
———. 1989. *The Authority of the Religions and the Status of Women*. Delhi: WCSRC-CISRS Joint Women's Programme and the William Carey Study and Research Centre.
Chauhan, Chetan. 2007. "Muslim Women Challenge Shariat Laws." *Hindustan Times*. January 10. Accessed May 30, 2013; http://www.hindustantimes.com/News-Feed/NM21/Muslim-women-challenge-Shariat-laws/Article1-198940.aspx.
Chiriyankandath, James. 2000. "'Creating a Secular State in a Religious Country': The Debate in the Indian Constituent Assembly." *Journal of Commonwealth & Comparative Politics* no. 38 (2): 1–24.
Church of North India. n.d. Personal Law File, CNI Office, Delhi.
Cohn, Bernard S. 1996. *Colonialism and Its Forms of Knowledge: The British in India*. Princeton, NJ: Princeton University Press.
Colley, Linda. 2009. *Britons: Forging the Nation, 1707–1837*. New Haven, CT: Yale University Press.
Collier, Ruth Berins, and David Collier. 1991. *Shaping the Political Arena: Critical Junctures, the Labor Movement, and Regime Dynamics in Latin America*. Princeton, NJ: Princeton University Press.
Cossman, Brenda, and Ratna Kapur. 2002. *Secularism's Last Sigh? Hindutva and the (Mis) Rule of Law*. New Delhi: Oxford University Press.
Cott, Nancy F. 2000. *Public Vows: A History of Marriage and the Nation*. Cambridge, MA: Harvard University Press.
Coulson, Noel J. 1971. *Succession in the Muslim Family*. Cambridge: Cambridge University Press.
Creevey, Lucy. 1996. "Islam, Women and the Role of the State in Senegal." *Journal of Religion in Africa* no. 26 (3): 268–307.
Cretney, Stephen Michael. 2005. *Family Law in the Twentieth Century: A History*. Oxford University Press.
Dalmia, Vasudha, and Heinrich Von Stietencron, eds. 1995. *Representing Hinduism: The Construction of Religious Traditions and National identity*. Thousand Oaks, CA: Sage Publications.
Darmaputera, Eka. 1988. *Pancasila and the Search for Identity and Modernity in Indonesian Society: A Cultural and Ethical Analysis*. Leiden: Brill.
Davis, Donald R. 2010. *The Spirit of Hindu Law*. Cambridge: Cambridge University Press.
Davis, Kingsley. 1949. "India and Pakistan: The Demography of Partition." *Pacific Affairs* no. 22 (3): 254–64.

De, Rohit. 2009. "Mumtaz Bibi's Broken Heart: The Many Lives of the Dissolution of Muslim Marriages Act." *Indian Economic & Social History Review* no. 46 (1): 105–30.
Deininger, Klaus, Hari Nagarajan, and Aparajita Goyal. 2010. *Inheritance Law Reform and Women's Access to Capital: Evidence from India's Hindu Succession Act.* Washington, D.C.: World Bank.
Derrett, J. Duncan M. 1963. "Divorce by Caste Custom." *Bombay Law Reporter* no. 65: 161–69.
———. 1968. *Religion, Law, and the State in India.* New York: Free Press.
———. 1976. *Essays in Classical and Modern Hindu Law.* 4 vols. Leiden: Brill.
———. 1978. *The Death of a Marriage Law: Epitaph for the Rishis.* Durham, NC: Carolina Academic Press.
Devji, Faisal F. 1994. "Gender and the Politics of Space: the Movement for Women's Reform, 1857–1900." In *Forging Identities: Gender, Communities and the State*, edited by Zoya Hasan, 35–63. Delhi: Kali for Women.
Devlin, John F. 1991. "The Baath Party: Rise and Metamorphosis." *American Historical Review* no. 96 (5): 1396–407.
DeVotta, Neil. 2004. *Blowback: Linguistic Nationalism, Institutional Decay, and Ethnic Conflict in Sri Lanka.* Stanford, CA: Stanford University Press.
Dhawan, Himanshi. 2011. "BJP, Left Unite over Divorce Law." *The Times of India*, March 8. Accessed May 31, 2013. http://articles.timesofindia.indiatimes.com/2011-03-08/india/28667786_1_irretrievable-breakdown-marriage-laws-divorce-by-mutual-consent.
———. 2013. "Union Cabinet Refers Marriage Laws to GoM". *The Times of India*, May 1. Accessed May 31, 2013. http://articles.timesofindia.indiatimes.com/2013-05-01/india/38956341_1_union-cabinet-law-ministry-child-development.
Dirks, Nicholas B. 2001. *Castes of Mind: Colonialism and the Making of Modern India.* Princeton, NJ: Princeton University Press.
Douglas, Ian H. 1988. *Abul Kalam Azad: An Intellectual and Religious Biography.* Delhi: Oxford University Press.
Dube, Leela. 1997. *Women and Kinship: Comparative Perspectives on Gender in South and South-East Asia.* Tokyo: United Nations University Press.
Dumont, Louis. 1983. *Affinity as a Value: Marriage Alliance in South India, with Comparative Essays on Australia.* Chicago: University of Chicago Press.
Easton, David. 1953. *The Political System: An Inquiry into the State of Political Science.* New York: Knopf.
Edelman, Martin. 1994. *Courts, Politics, and Culture in Israel.* Charlottesville: University Press of Virginia.
Eisenstadt, Shmuel N. 1973. *Traditional Patrimonialism and Modern Neopatrimonialism.* Beverly Hills, CA: Sage Publications.
———, ed. 1987. *Patterns of Modernity.* 2 vols. New York: New York University Press.
———. 2003. *Comparative Civilizations and Multiple Modernities.* 2 vols. Boston: Brill.
Elliott, E. Donald. 1985. "The Evolutionary Tradition in Jurisprudence." *Columbia Law Review* no. 85 (1): 38–94.
Engineer, Asghar Ali. 2005. "Model Nikahnama—A Hope or Disappointment?" *Center for the Study of Society and Secularism.* Accessed May 31, 2013. http://www.csss-isla.com/arch%2014.htm.
Epp, Charles R. 1998. *The Rights Revolution: Lawyers, Activists, and Supreme Courts in Comparative Perspective.* Chicago: University of Chicago Press.

Esposito, John L. 1990. *Islam and Politics*. 2nd ed. Syracuse: Syracuse University Press.
Evans, Peter B. 1995. *Embedded Autonomy: States and Industrial Transformation*. Princeton, NJ: Princeton University Press.
Everett, Jana Matson. 1979. *Women and Social Change in India*. New York: St. Martin's Press.
Ewing, Katherine Pratt, ed. 1988. *Shari'at and Ambiguity in South Asian Islam*. Berkeley, CA: University of California Press.
Express News Service. 2006. "Shia Board Proposes New Nikahnama." *The Indian Express Online*, May 31. Accessed May 31, 2013. http://www.indianexpress.com/news/shia-board-proposes-new-nikahnama/5491/.
Feener, R. Michael. 2007. *Muslim Legal Thought in Modern Indonesia*. Cambridge: Cambridge University Press.
Feener, R. Michael, and Mark E. Cammack. 2007. *Islamic Law in Contemporary Indonesia: Ideas and Institutions*. Cambridge, MA: Harvard University Press.
Feliciano, Myrna S. 1994. "Law, Gender, and the Family in the Philippines." *Law & Society Review* no. 28 (3): 547–60.
Filmer, Robert. 1949. *Patriarcha and Other Political Works*. Oxford: B. Blackwell.
Fluehr-Lobban, Carolyn. 1987. *Islamic Law and Society in the Sudan*. London: Frank Cass.
Forbes, Geraldine. 1981. "The Indian Women's Movement: A Struggle for Women's Rights or National Liberation?" In *The Extended Family: Women and Political Participation in India and Pakistan*, edited by Gail Minault, 49–82. Delhi: Chanakya Publications.
———. 1998. "Women in Independent India." In *Women in Modern India*, 223–54. Cambridge: Cambridge University Press.
Forrester, Duncan B. 1980. *Caste and Christianity: Attitudes and Policies on Caste of Anglo-Saxon Protestant Missions in India*. London: Curzon Press.
Foucault, Michel. 1973. *The Birth of the Clinic: An Archaeology of Medical Perception*. New York: Pantheon Books.
———. 1977. *Discipline and Punish: The Birth of the Prison*. New York: Pantheon Books.
———. 1978. *The History of Sexuality*. Vol. 1. New York: Pantheon Books.
———. 1980. *Power/Knowledge: Selected Interviews and Other Writings, 1972–1977*. New York: Pantheon Books.
———. 2007. *Security, Territory, Population: Lectures at the Collège de France, 1977–78*. New York: Palgrave Macmillan.
Frankel, Francine R. 2006. *India's Political Economy, 1947–2004: The Gradual Revolution*. New Delhi: Oxford University Press.
Friedman, Lawrence M. 1994. "Is There a Modern Legal Culture?" *Ratio Juris* no. 7 (2): 117–31.
———. 2004. *Private Lives: Families, Individuals, and the Law*. Cambridge, MA: Harvard University Press.
Frykenberg, Robert Eric. 2008. *Christianity in India from Beginnings to the Present*. Oxford: Oxford University Press.
Fuller, Christopher J. 1976. *The Nayars Today*. Cambridge: Cambridge University Press.
Fyzee, Asaf Ali Asghar. 1999. *Outlines of Muhammadan Law*. Delhi: Oxford University Press.

Galanter, Marc. 1984. *Competing Equalities: Law and the Backward Classes in India*. Berkeley: University of California Press.
Gandhi, Mohandas Karamchand. 2008. *Hind Swaraj or Indian Home Rule*. Ahmedabad: Navajivan Publishing House.
Gandhi, Nandita, and Nandita Shah. 1992. *The Issues at Stake: Theory and Practice in the Contemporary Women's Movement in India*. New Delhi: Kali for Women.
Ganguly, Sumit. 1999. *The Crisis in Kashmir: Portents of War, Hopes of Peace*. Cambridge: Cambridge University Press.
Gerschenkron, Alexander. 1962. *Economic Backwardness in Historical Perspective: A Book of Essays*. Cambridge, MA: Belknap Press of Harvard University Press.
Ghasemi, Marjon E. 1998. "Islam, International Human Rights and Women's Equality: Afghan Women under Taliban Rule." *Southern California Review of Law and Women's Studies* no. 8: 445.
Gazette of India Extraordinary (GIE). 1952. Gazette of India Extraordinary. New Delhi: Government of India Press.
———. 1954. Gazette of India Extraordinary. New Delhi: Government of India Press.
Gilmartin, David. 1981. "Kinship, Women, and Politics in Twentieth-Century Punjab." In *The Extended Family: Women and Political Participation in India and Pakistan*, edited by Gail Minault, 151–70. Delhi: Chanakya Publications.
———. 1988. *Empire and Islam: Punjab and the Making of Pakistan*. Berkeley, CA: University of California Press.
Glendon, Mary Ann. 1987. *Abortion and Divorce in Western Law*. Cambridge, MA: Harvard University Press.
———. 1989. *The Transformation of Family Law: State, Law, and Family in the United States and Western Europe*. Chicago: University of Chicago Press.
Goldstone, Jack A. 1991. *Revolution and Rebellion in the Early Modern World*. Berkeley: University of California Press.
Goode, William Josiah. 1993. *World Changes in Divorce Patterns*. New Haven, CT: Yale University Press.
Goonesekere, Savitri. 1980. *The Legal Status of the Female in the Sri Lanka Law on Family Relations*. Colombo: Gunasena.
———. 1990. "Status of Women in the Family Law of Sri Lanka." In *Women at the Crossroads: A Sri Lankan Perspective*, edited by Sirima Kiribamune and Vidyamali Samarasinghe, 152–81. Delhi: Vikas Publishers, with International Centre for Ethnic Studies.
Habermas, Jurgen. 1991. *The Structural Transformation of the Public Sphere: An Inquiry Into a Category of Bourgeois Society*. Cambridge, MA: MIT Press.
Halhed, Nathaniel Brassey. 2001. *A Code of Gentoo Laws, or, Ordinations of the Pundits: From a Persian Translation, Made from The Original, Written in the Shanscrit Language*. Holmes Beach, FL: Gaunt.
Halper, Louise. 2005. "Law and Women's Agency in Post-Revolutionary Iran." *Harvard Journal of Law & Gender* no. 28 (1): 85–142.
Hameed, Syeda Saiyidain. 2000. *Voice of the Voiceless: Status of Muslim Women in India*. Delhi: National Commission for Women.
Hanioglu, M. Sükrü. 2011. *Atatürk: An Intellectual Biography*. Princeton, NJ: Princeton University Press.
Harnischfeger, Johannes. 2008. *Democratization and Islamic Law: The Sharia Conflict in Nigeria*. Frankfurt: Campus Verlag.

Harper, Susan B. 1988. "The Politics of Conversion: The Azariah-Gandhi Controversy over Christian Mission to the Depressed Classes in the 1930s." *Indo-British Review* no. 15 (1): 147–75.
Hasan, Masood. 2005. "Women's personal law board." The Milli Gazette Online. 16–28 February. Accessed May 30, 2013. http://www.milligazette.com/Archives/2005/16-28feb05-Print-Edition/162802200512.htm.
Hasan, Mushirul. 1992. *Islam and Indian Nationalism: Reflections on Abul Kalam Azad*. New Delhi: Manohar Publications.
Hassan, Sana. 2003. *Christians Versus Muslims in Modern Egypt: The Century-Long Struggle for Coptic Equality*. Oxford: Oxford University Press.
Hazard, John N. 1965. "Negritude, Socialism and the Law." *Columbia Law Review* no. 65 (5): 778–809.
Heimsath, Charles H. 1964. *Indian Nationalism and Hindu Social Reform*. Princeton, NJ: Princeton University Press.
Hill, Christopher L. 2008. *National History and the World of Nations: Capital, State, and the Rhetoric of History in Japan, France, and the United States*. Durham, NC: Duke University Press.
The Hindu. 2000. "States Told to Amend Hindu Succession Act." 7 February. Accessed May 30, 2013. http://www.hindu.com/thehindu/2000/02/07/stories/0207000h.htm.
Hinnebusch, Raymond A. 1993. "State and Civil Society in Syria." *Middle East Journal* no. 47 (2): 243–57.
Hobsbawm, Eric, and Terence Ranger, eds. 1983. *The Invention of Tradition*. Cambridge: Cambridge University Press.
Holden, Livia. 2008. *Hindu Divorce: A Legal Anthropology*. Aldershot, UK: Ashgate.
Hooker, M. B. 1975. *Legal Pluralism: An Introduction to Colonial and Neo-Colonial Laws*. Oxford: Clarendon Press.
———. 1984. *Islamic Law in South-East Asia*. Singapore: Oxford University Press.
———. 2008. *Indonesian Syariah: Defining a National School of Islamic Law*. Singapore: Institute of Southeast Asian Studies.
Hoque, Ridwanul, and Md. Morshed Mahmud Khan. 2007. "Judicial Activism and Islamic Family Law: A Socio-Legal Evaluation of Recent Trends in Bangladesh." *Islamic Law and Society* no. 14 (2): 204–39.
Horowitz, Donald L. 1985. *Ethnic Groups in Conflict*. Berkeley, CA: University of California Press.
———. 1994. "The Qur'an and the Common Law: Islamic Law Reform and the Theory of Legal Change." *American Journal of Comparative Law* no. 42 (2–3): 233–93, 543–80.
Huntington, Samuel P. 1968. *Political Order in Changing Societies*. New Haven, CT: Yale University Press.
———. 1998. *The Clash of Civilizations and the Remaking of World Order*. New York: Simon and Schuster.
India. Census Commissioner. 1943. *India (Census 1941): Abstract of Tables Giving the Main Statistics of the Census of the Indian Empire of 1941, with a Brief Introductory Note*. H.M. Stationery Off.
India. Committee on the Status of Women in India. 1975. *Towards Equality: Report of the Committee on the Status of Women in India*. New Delhi: Government of India, Ministry of Education & Social Welfare, Dept. of Social Welfare.

India. Department Related Parliamentary Standing Committee on Personnel, Public Grievances, Law and Justice. 2005. *Proceedings of the Parliamentary Standing Committee on Personnel, Public Grievances, Law and Justice: Hindu Succession (Amendment) Bill, 2004.* 3 & 16 February, 19 & 27 April. (electronic copy, provided courtesy Mr. E.M. Sudarsana Natchiappan, Committee Chair).

India. Ministry of Law. Law Commission of India. 1960. Fifteenth Report: Law Relating to Marriage and Divorce Among Christians in India. Delhi: Government of India Press.

———. 1961. Twenty-Second Report: Christian Marriage and Matrimonial Causes Bill, 1961. Delhi: Government of India Press.

———. 1974. Fifty-Ninth Report on Hindu Marriage Act, 1955 and Special Marriage Act, 1954. Delhi: Government of India Press.

———. 1978. Seventy-First Report on the Hindu Marriage Act, 1955—Irretrievable Breakdown of Marriage as a Ground of Divorce. Delhi: Government of India Press.

———. 1983. Ninetieth Report on the Grounds of Divorce Amongst Christians in India: Section 10 of the Indian Divorce Act, 1869. Delhi: Government of India Press.

———. 1998. One Hundred Sixty-Fourth Report on the Indian Divorce Act (IV of 1869). Delhi: Government of India Press.

———. 2000. Property Rights of Women: Proposed Reforms under the Hindu Law. Delhi: Government of India Press.

———. 2009. Irretrievable Breakdown of Marriage—Another Ground for Divorce. Delhi: Government of India Press.

India. National Commission for Women. 1995. Review of Laws and Legislative Measures Affecting Women. No. 19. The Hindu Succession Act, 1956 (30 of 1956). Accessed May 29, 2013. http://ncw.nic.in/frmReportLaws19.aspx.

———. 1997. Review of Laws Relating to Women. New Delhi: National Commission for Women.

India. Office of the Registrar General and Census Commissioner. 1983. *Census of India, 1981. Series 1, India.* Delhi: Controller of Publications.

———. 2003. *Census of India, 2001. Series 1, India.* Delhi: Controller of Publications.

India. Parliament of India. Rajya Sabha. Department Related Parliamentary Standing Committee on Personnel, Public Grievances, Law and Justice. 2011. *Forty Fifth Report on the Marriage Laws (Amendment) Bill, 2010.* New Delhi: Rajya Sabha Secretariat.

India. Parliament Standing Committee on Home Affairs. 2001. *Proceedings of the Department Related Parliamentary Standing Committee on Home Affairs Which Met at 11:00 a.m. on Friday, the 9th February, 2001, in Main Committee Room, Parliament House Annexe, New Delhi.* New Delhi: Rajya Sabha Secretariat.

India. Press Information Bureau. Government of India. 2010. Cabinet Approves the Marriage Laws (Amendment) Bill, 2010 to amend the Hindu Marriage Act. Accessed May 31, 2013. http://pib.nic.in/newsite/erelease.aspx?relid=62464.

India. Report of the Hindu Law Committee (RHLC). 1941. Simla: Government of India Press.

———. 1947. New Delhi: Government of India Press.

India. Report of the Joint Committee of the Houses of Parliament to Amend and Codify the Law Related to Intestate Succession Among the Hindus. 1955. Delhi: Government of India Press.

India. Report of the Standing Committee of Parliament on Law and Justice. 2005. *Hindu Succession Amendment Bill*. Delhi: Government of India Press.
Indo-Asian News Service. 2013. "Marriage Laws Bill on Hold over Women's Property Share." *NDTV.com*, May 1. Accessed May 31, 2013. http://www.ndtv.com/article/india/marriage-laws-bill-on-hold-over-women-s-property-share-361473.
Islamic Fiqh Academy. 2004. *Important Fiqh Decisions: Juristic Decisions on Contemporary Issues*. New Delhi: IFA Publications.
Iyer, Lakshmi. 2000. "Christian Marriage Bill: On the Rocks." *India Today*, May 22. Accessed May 31, 2013. http://www.india-today.com/itoday/20000522/nation.html.
Jackman, Robert W. 1993. *Power without Force: The Political Capacity of Nation-States*. Ann Arbor: University of Michigan Press.
Jacob, Alice. 1999. "Uniform Civil Code: Reforms in Christian Family Law." In *Engendering Law*, edited by Amita Dhanda and Archana Parashar, 375–86. Lucknow: Eastern Book Co.
Jacobsohn, Gary J. 1996. "Three Models of Secular Constitutional Development: India, Israel, and the United States." *Studies in American Political Development* no. 10 (1): 1–68.
———. 2003. *The Wheel of Law: India's Secularism in Comparative Constitutional Context*. Princeton, NJ: Princeton University Press.
Jaffrelot, Christophe. 1996. *The Hindu Nationalist Movement in India*. New York: Columbia University Press.
Jalal, Ayesha. 2001. *Self and Sovereignty: Individual and Community in South Asian Islam Since 1850*. London: Routledge.
Jamaat Ahl-i-Hadith. 1994. "Fatwa of Ahl-i-Hadith: Talaq, Talaq, Talaq Is Not Final Talaq." in *Triple Talaq: An Analytical Study with Emphasis on Socio-Legal Aspects*, edited by Furqan Ahmad, 140–41. New Delhi: Regency Publications.
Jeffrey, Robin. 1992. *Politics, Women, and Well-Being: How Kerala Became "A Model."* London: Macmillan Press.
Joffe, E. G. H. 1985. "The Moroccan Nationalist Movement: Istiqlal, the Sultan, and the Country." *Journal of African History* no. 26 (4): 289–307.
Johnson, Chalmers. 1982. *MITI and the Japanese Miracle: The Growth of Industrial Policy, 1925–1975*. Stanford, CA: Stanford University Press.
Joint Women's Programme (JWP). 2000. *Changes in Indian Divorce Act, 1869*, December 5 (mimeo).
Jones, Kenneth W. 1989. *Socio-Religious Reform Movements in British India*. Cambridge: Cambridge University Press.
Joseph, Suad. 1991. "Elite Strategies for State-Building: Women, Family, Religion, and the State in Iraq and Lebanon." In *Women, Islam, and the State*, edited by Deniz Kandiyoti, 176–200. Philadelphia: Temple University Press.
———. 1994. "Problematizing Gender and Relational Rights: Experiences from Lebanon." *Social Politics* no. 1 (3): 271–85.
Joshi, A. P., M. D. Srinivas, and J. K. Bajaj. 2003. *Religious Demography of India*. Chennai: Centre for Policy Studies.
Kapur, Ratna and Brenda Cossman. 1996. *Subversive Sites: Feminist Engagements with Law in India*. New Delhi; Thousand Oaks, CA: Sage Publications.
Kader, S. A. 1998. *Muslim Law of Marriage and Succession in India: A Critique with a Plea for Optional Civil Code*. Calcutta: Eastern Law House.

Kandiyoti, Deniz. 1991a. "Identity and its Discontents: Women and the Nation." *Millennium: Journal of International Studies* no. 20 (3): 429–43.

———. 1991b. "End of Empire: Islam, Nationalism and Women in Turkey." In *Women, Islam, and the State*, edited by Deniz Kandiyoti, 22–47. Philadelphia: Temple University Press.

Karve, Irawati Karmarkar. 1990. *Kinship Organization in India*. Bombay: Asia Publishing House.

Kaviraj, Sudipta. 1992. "The Imaginary Institution of India." In *Subaltern Studies VII: Writings on South Asian History and Society*, edited by Partha Chatterjee and Gyanendra Pandey, 1–39. Delhi: Oxford University Press.

Kerr, Malcolm H. 1966. *Islamic Reform: The Political and Legal Theories of Muhammad Abduh and Rashid Rida*. Berkeley, CA: University of California Press.

Kerslake, Celia, Kerem Oktem, and Philip Robins, eds. 2010. *Turkey's Engagement with Modernity: Conflict and Change in the Twentieth Century*. Basingstoke, UK: Palgrave MacMillan.

Khoury, Philip S., and Joseph Kostiner, eds. 1990. *Tribes and State Formation in the Middle East*. Berkeley, CA: University of California Press.

Kishwar, Madhu. 1994. "Codified Hindu Law: Myth and Reality." *Economic and Political Weekly* no. 29 (33): 2145–61.

Kohli, Atul. 2004. *State-Directed Development: Political Power and Industrialization in the Global Periphery*. Cambridge: Cambridge University Press.

Krasner, Stephen D. 1978. *Defending the National Interest: Raw Materials Investments and US Foreign Policy*. Princeton, NJ: Princeton University Press.

Krishna Iyer, V. R. 1984a. *Law and Religion*. New Delhi: Deep & Deep.

———. 1984b. *Woman Unbound: A Plea for Gender Justice*. Madurai: Society for Community Organisation Trust.

Kugle, Scott Alan. 2001. "Framed, Blamed and Renamed: The Recasting of Islamic Jurisprudence in Colonial South Asia." *Modern Asian Studies* no. 35 (2): 257–313.

Kuru, Ahmet T. 2009. *Secularism and State Policies Toward Religion: The United States, France, and Turkey*. New York: Cambridge University Press.

Kuru, Ahmet T., and Alfred C. Stepan. 2012. *Democracy, Islam, and Secularism in Turkey*. New York: Columbia University Press.

Kusum. 1975. "Marriage Laws (Amendment) Bill, 1974: A Critique." *Journal of the Indian Law Institute* no. 17 (4): 611–17.

———. 2000. "Matrimonial Adjudication under Hindu Law." In *Fifty Years of the Supreme Court of India: Its Grasp and Reach*, edited by S. K. Verma and Kusum, 231–68. Delhi: Oxford University Press.

Kymlicka, Will. 1995. *Multicultural Citizenship: A Liberal Theory of Minority Rights*. Oxford: Oxford University Press.

Latif, Syed Abdul. 1969. *al-Quran: Rendered into English*. Hyderabad: Academy of Islamic Studies.

Latifi, Danial. 1988. "The Muslim Women Bill." In *The Shah Bano Controversy*, edited by Asghar Ali Engineer, 102–7. Bombay: Orient Longman.

Latifi, Danial, and Syed Ameenul Hasan Rizvi. 1998. "Views on Maintenance for Divorced Women." In *Shah Bano and the Muslim Women Act, a Decade on: The Right of the Divorced Muslim Woman to Mataa*, edited by Lucy Carroll, 65–68. Grabels Cédex, FR: Copublished by Women Living Under Muslim Laws, International Solidarity Network, and Women's Research Action Group.

Lausanne Global Analysis. 2011. *Number of Christians in China and India*. Accessed October 6, 2013. http://conversation.lausanne.org/en/conversations/detail/11971#article_page_1.

Lawyers Collective—Women's Rights Initiative. 2010. *Mapping Women's Gains under the Hindu Succession Act, 1956*. Accessed May 31, 2013. http://www.lawyerscollective.org/files/LCWRI%20INHERITANCE%20REPORT.pdf.

Layish, Aharon. 1991. *Divorce in the Libyan Family: A Study Based on the Sijills of the Shari'a Courts of Ajdabiyya and Kufra*. New York: New York University Press.

Lijphart, Arend. 1977. *Democracy in Plural Societies: A Comparative Exploration*. New Haven, CT: Yale University Press.

Lingat, Robert. 1998. *The Classical Law of India*. Delhi: Oxford University Press.

Lipset, Seymour Martin. 1981. *Political Man: The Social Bases of Politics*. Baltimore, MD: Johns Hopkins University Press.

Lok Sabha Debates (LSD). India. 1954. New Delhi: Lok Sabha Secretariat.

———. 1955. New Delhi: Lok Sabha Secretariat.

———. 1956. New Delhi: Lok Sabha Secretariat.

———. 1964. New Delhi: Lok Sabha Secretariat.

———. 1975. New Delhi: Lok Sabha Secretariat.

———. 1986. New Delhi: Lok Sabha Secretariat.

———. 2005. Fourteenth Series. New Delhi: Lok Sabha Secretariat.

Lombardi, Clark B. 2006. *State Law as Islamic Law in Modern Egypt: The Incorporation of the Shari'a into Egyptian Constitutional Law*. Leiden: Brill.

Lowe, Nigel V., and Gillian Douglas. 2009. *The Continuing Evolution of Family Law*. Bristol, UK: Jordan Publishing.

Madan, Triloki Nath. 2003. *Modern Myths, Locked Minds: Secularism and Fundamentalism in India*. Oxford: Oxford University Press.

Madani, Sayyid Husain Ahmad. 2005. *Composite Nationalism and Islam*. New Delhi: Manohar Publishers.

Maddy-Weitzman, B. 2005. "Women, Islam, and the Moroccan State: The Struggle over the Personal Status Law." *Middle East Journal* no. 59 (3): 393–410.

Mahmood, Tahir. 1995. *Statute-Law Relating to Muslims in India: A Study in Constitutional and Islamic Perspectives*. New Delhi: Institute of Objective Studies.

———. 1997. *Islamic Law in Indian Courts Since Independence: Fifty Years of Judicial Interpretation*. New Delhi: Institute of Objective Studies.

Majumdar, Rochona. 2009. *Marriage and Modernity: Family Values in Colonial Bengal*. Durham, NC: Duke University Press.

Mamdani, Mahmood. 1996. *Citizen and Subject: Contemporary Africa and the Legacy of Late Colonialism*. Princeton, NJ: Princeton University Press.

Mansfield, John H. 1993. "The Personal Laws of a Uniform Civil Code?" In *Religion and Law in Independent India*, edited by Robert D. Baird, 139–77. New Delhi: Manohar Publishers.

Mantena, Karuna. 2010. *Alibis of Empire: Henry Maine and the Ends of Liberal Imperialism*. Princeton, NJ: Princeton University Press.

Marx, Anthony W. 1998. *Making Race and Nation: A Comparison of South Africa, the United States, and Brazil*. New York: Cambridge University Press.

———. 2003. *Faith in Nation: Exclusionary Origins of Nationalism*. New York: Oxford University Press.

Massoud, Mark F. 2013. *Law's Fragile State: Colonial, Authoritarian, and Humanitarian Legacies in Sudan*. New York: Cambridge University Press.

Masud. Muhammad Khalid. 1996. "Apostasy and Judicial Separation in British India." In *Islamic Legal Interpretation: Muftis and their Fatwas*, edited by Muhammad Khalid Masud, Brinkley Morris Messick, and David Stephan Powers, 193–203. Cambridge, MA: Harvard University Press.

Mayer, Ann Elizabeth. 1977. *Islamic Law in Libya: Analyses of Selected Laws Enacted Since the 1969 Revolution*. London: School of Oriental and African Studies, Department of Law.

Mazumdar, Vina. 1999. "Political Ideology of the Women's Movement's Engagement with Law." In *Engendering Law: Essays in Honour of Lotika Sarkar*, edited by Amita Dhanda and Archana Parashar, 339–74. Lucknow: Eastern Book Co.

Mehdi, Rubya. 1994. *The Islamization of the Law in Pakistan*. London: Curzon Press.

Mellor, John W. 1976. *The New Economics of Growth: A Strategy for India and the Developing World*. Ithaca, NY: Cornell University Press.

Mendelsohn, Oliver, and Marika Vicziany. 1998. *The Untouchables: Subordination, Poverty, and the State in Modern India*. Cambridge: Cambridge University Press.

Menski, Werner. 2001. *Modern Indian Family Law*. Richmond, UK: Curzon Press.

———. 2003. *Hindu Law: Beyond Tradition and Modernity*. New Delhi: Oxford University Press.

Merry, Sally Engle. 1991. "Law and Colonialism." *Law and Society Review* no. 25 (4): 889–922.

———. 1999. *Colonizing Hawai'i: The Cultural Power of Law*. Princeton, NJ: Princeton University Press.

Metcalf, Barbara Daly. 1982. *Islamic Revival in British India: Deoband, 1860–1900*. Princeton, NJ: Princeton University Press.

———, ed. 2009a. *Islam in South Asia in Practice*. Princeton, NJ: Princeton University Press.

———. 2009b. *Husain Ahmad Madani: The Jihad for Islam and India's Freedom*. Oxford: Oneworld.

Middleton, Shannon A. 2000. "Women's Rights Unveiled: Taliban's Treatment of Women in Afghanistan." *Indiana International & Comparative Law Review*. no. 11: 421.

Migdal, Joel S. 2001. *State in Society: Studying How States and Societies Transform and Constitute One Another*. New York: Cambridge University Press.

Migdal, Joel S., Atul Kohli, and Vivienne Shue, eds. 1993. *State Power and Social Forces: Domination and Transformation in the Third World*. New York: Cambridge University Press.

Miller, Roland E. 1976. *Mappila Muslims of Kerala: A Study in Islamic Trends*. Madras: Orient Longman.

Minault, Gail. 1982. *The Khilafat Movement: Religious Symbolism and Political Mobilization in India*. New York: Columbia University Press.

———. 1998. *Secluded Scholars: Women's Education and Muslim Social Reform in Colonial India*. New Delhi: Oxford University Press.

Ministry of Law, Justice, and Company Affairs. 2001. *Proposal Regarding the Christian Marriage Bill, 2000: Background Note*. New Delhi: Government of India, Ministry of Law, Justice and Company Affairs.

Mir-Hosseini, Ziba. 1999. *Islam and Gender: The Religious Debate in Contemporary Iran.* Princeton, NJ: Princeton University Press.
———. 2000. *Marriage on Trial: Islamic Family Law in Iran and Morocco.* London: I. B. Tauris.
———. 2007. "How the Door of Ijtihad Was Opened and Closed: A Comparative Analysis of Recent Family Law Reforms in Iran and Morocco." *Washington and Lee Law Review* no. 64 (4): 1499.
Mitchell, Timothy. 1991a. *Colonising Egypt.* Berkeley, CA: University of California Press.
———. 1991b. "The Limits of the State: Beyond Statist Approaches and Their Critics." *American Political Science Review* no. 85 (1): 77–96.
Mitra, Subrata K., and Alexander Fischer. 2002. "Sacred Laws and the Secular State: An Analytical Narrative of the Controversy over Personal Laws in India." *India Review* no. 1 (3): 99–130.
Mody, Perveez. 2008. *The Intimate State: Love-Marriage and the Law in Delhi.* New Delhi: Routledge.
Mohamad, Maznah. 2010. "Making Majority, Undoing Family: Law, Religion and the Islamization of the State in Malaysia." *Economy and Society* no. 39 (3): 360–84.
Monsma, Stephen V., and J. Christopher Soper. 2009. *The Challenge of Pluralism: Church and State in Five Democracies.* Lanham, MD: Rowman & Littlefield Publishers.
Monteiro, Rita. 1992. "Belief, Law and Justice for Women: Debate on Proposed Christian Marriage and Matrimonial Causes Bill, 1990." *Economic and Political Weekly* no. 27 (43/44):WS74-WS80.
Moore, Barrington. 1966. *Social Origins of Dictatorship and Democracy: Lord and Peasant in the Making of the Modern World.* Boston: Beacon Press.
Moosa, Ebrahim. 2009. "Colonialism and Islamic Law." In *Islam and Modernity: Key Issues and Debates*, edited by Muhammad Khalid Masud, Armando Salvatore, and Martin van Bruinessen, 158–81. Edinburgh: Edinburgh University Press.
Mufti, Aamir. 2007. *Enlightenment in the Colony: The Jewish Question and the Crisis of Postcolonial Culture.* Princeton, NJ: Princeton University Press.
Mulla, Dinshah Fardunji. 1968. *Principles of Mahomedan Law.* Calcutta: Eastern Law House.
———. 1975. *Principles of Hindu law.* Bombay: N. M. Tripathi Private.
Muralidhar, S. 2004. *Hindu Succession (Amendment) Bill, 2004: Note to Law Ministry* (received courtesy of the author).
Nair, Janaki. 1996. *Women and Law in Colonial India: A Social History.* New Delhi: Kali for Women in collaboration with the National Law School of India University.
Nakane, Chie. 1967. *Garo and Khasi: A Comparative Study in Matrilineal Systems.* Paris: Mouton.
Nandy, Ashis. 1988. "The Politics of Secularism and the Recovery of Religious Tolerance." *Alternatives: Global, Local, Political* no. 13 (2): 177–94.
Narain, Vrinda. 2008. *Reclaiming the Nation: Muslim Women and the Law in India.* Toronto: University of Toronto Press.
Narwani, G. S. 2004. *Tribal Law in India.* Jaipur: Rawat Publications.
Nehru, Jawaharlal. 1959. *The Discovery of India.* Garden City, NY: Anchor Books.
———. 1990. *Glimpses of World History: Being Further Letters to His Daughter, Written in Prison, and Containing a Rambling Account of History for Young People.* Oxford: Oxford University Press.
———. 1996. *Jawaharlal Nehru Speeches.* Delhi: Ministry of Information and Broadcasting.

Nelson, Matthew J. 2011. *In the Shadow of Shari'ah: Islam, Islamic Law, and Democracy in Pakistan*. New York: Columbia University Press.

Newbigin, Eleanor. 2009. "The Codification of Personal Law and Secular Citizenship." *Indian Economic & Social History Review* no. 46 (1): 83–104.

———. 2010. "A Post-Colonial Patriarchy? Representing Family in the Indian Nation-State." *Modern Asian Studies* no. 44 (1): 121–44.

———. 2011. "Personal Law and Citizenship in India's Transition to Independence." *Modern Asian Studies* no. 45 (1): 7–32.

Nobles, Melissa. 2000. *Shades of Citizenship: Race and the Census in Modern Politics*. Stanford, CA: Stanford University Press.

Nongbri, Tiplut. 2010. "Family, Gender and Identity: A Comparative Analysis of Trans-Himalayan Matrilineal Structures." *Contributions to Indian Sociology* no. 44 (1–2): 155–78.

Nordlinger, Eric A. 1981. *On the Autonomy of the Democratic State*. Cambridge, MA: Harvard University Press.

Nossiter, T. J. 1982. *Communism in Kerala: A Study in Political Adaptation*. Berkeley, CA: University of California Press for the Royal Institute of International Affairs, London.

Nussbaum, Martha C. 1999. *Sex and Social Justice*. New York: Oxford University Press.

The Observer. 2000. "Law Commission Considers Family Property for Women." 7 February.

Oddie, Geoffrey A. 1991. *Religion in South Asia: Religious Conversion and Revival Movements in South Asia in Medieval and Modern Times*. New Delhi: Manohar.

———, ed. 1998. *Religious Traditions in South Asia: Interaction and Change*. Richmond: Curzon Press.

———. 2001. "Indian Christians and National Identity, 1870–1947." *Journal of Religious History* no. 25 (3): 346–66.

Okin, Susan Moller. 2001. "When Cultural Values Clash with Universal Right: Is Multiculturalism Bad for Women?" *Markkula Center for Applied Ethics Lecture Series*. Accessed May 31, 2013. http://www.scu.edu/ethics/publications/submitted/okin/multicultural.html/.

Okin, Susan Moller, Joshua Cohen, Matthew Howard, and Martha Craven Nussbaum. 1999. *Is Multiculturalism Bad for Women?* Princeton, NJ: Princeton University Press.

Oldenburg, Veena Talwar. 2002. *Dowry Murder: The Imperial Origins of a Cultural Crime*. Oxford: Oxford University Press.

Ong, Aihwa, and Michael G. Peletz, eds. 1995. *Bewitching Women, Pious Men: Gender and Body Politics in Southeast Asia*. Berkeley, CA: University of California Press.

Osanloo, Arzoo. 2009. *The Politics of Women's Rights in Iran*. Princeton, NJ: Princeton University Press.

Paidar, Parvin. 1995. *Women and the Political Process in Twentieth-Century Iran*. Cambridge: Cambridge University Press.

Panda, P., and Bina Agarwal. 2005. "Marital Violence, Human Development and Women's Property Status in India." *World Development* no. 33 (5): 823–50.

Pandey, Gyanendra. 1990. *The Construction of Communalism in Colonial North India*. New Delhi: Oxford University Press.

———. 2005. *Routine Violence: Nations, Fragments, Histories*. Stanford, CA: Stanford University Press.

Parameswaran Moothath, P. 1973. "The Kerala Joint Family System (Abolition) Bill—A Study." *Kerala Law Times*: 91–95, 99–101.

Parashar, Archana. 1992. *Women and Family Law Reform in India: Uniform Civil Code and Gender Equality.* New Delhi: Sage Publications.

Parekh, Bhikhu C. 1989. *Colonialism, Tradition, and Reform: An Analysis of Gandhi's Political Discourse.* New Delhi: Sage Publications.

———. 2006. *Rethinking Multiculturalism: Cultural Diversity and Political Theory.* New York: Palgrave Macmillan.

Parry, Benita. 1972. *Delusions and Discoveries: Studies on India in the British Imagination, 1880–1930.* Berkeley, CA: University of California Press.

Patel, Reena. 2007. *Hindu Women's Property Rights in Rural India: Law, Labour and Culture in Action.* Farnham, UK: Ashgate.

Parliamentary Debates (PD). India. 1948. New Delhi: Lok Sabha Secretariat.

———. 1951. New Delhi: Lok Sabha Secretariat.

———. 1953. New Delhi: Lok Sabha Secretariat.

———. 1954. New Delhi: Lok Sabha Secretariat.

———. 1955. New Delhi: Lok Sabha Secretariat.

———. 1956. New Delhi: Lok Sabha Secretariat.

———. 1976. New Delhi: Lok Sabha Secretariat.

Peled, Alisa Rubin. 2001. *Debating Islam in the Jewish State: The Development of Policy Toward Islamic Institutions in Israel.* Albany: State University of New York Press.

Peletz, Michael G. 1996. *Reason and Passion: Representations of Gender in a Malay Society.* Berkeley, CA: University of California Press.

———. 2002. *Islamic Modern: Religious Courts and Cultural Politics in Malaysia.* Princeton, NJ: Princeton University Press.

———. 2009. *Gender Pluralism: Southeast Asia Since Early Modern Times.* New York: Routledge.

Peters, Ruud. 2001. *Islamic Criminal Law in Nigeria.* Ibadan: Spectrum Books.

Pew Research Center. 2011. *The Future of the Global Muslim Population: Projections for 2010–2030.* Washington, D.C.: Pew Research Center Forum on Religion & Public Life. Accessed May 31, 2013. http://www.pewforum.org/uploadedFiles/Topics/Religious_Affiliation/Muslim/FutureGlobalMuslimPopulation-WebPDF-Feb10.pdf.

Powers, David Stephan. 1986. *Studies in Qur'an and Hadith: The Formation of the Islamic Law of Inheritance.* Berkeley, CA: University of California Press.

Press Trust of India (PTI). 2006. "Model Nikahnama: Shia Women Gain Right to Divorce." *The Times of India Online*, November 26. Accessed May 31, 2013. http://articles.timesofindia.indiatimes.com/2006-11-26/india/27793729_1_divorce-maulana-mirza-mohammad-athar-groom.

———.2012a. "Redrafted Marriage Laws Bill Seeks to Make Divorce Process Easier." *India.com*, March 23. Accessed May 31, 2013. http://www.dnaindia.com/india/report_redrafted-marriage-laws-bill-seeks-to-make-divorce-process-easier_1666590.

———. 2012b. "Women to Get Share in Husband's Property in Case of Divorce." *NDTV.com*, May 17. Accessed May 231 2013. http://www.ndtv.com/article/india/women-to-get-share-in-husband-s-property-in-case-of-divorce-212354.

———. 2013. "Cabinet Fails to Clear Amendment to Marriage Laws (Amendment) Bill." *The Hindu*, May 1. Accessed May 31, 2013. http://www.thehindu.com/news/national/cabinet-fails-to-clear-amendment-to-marriage/article4673576.ece.

Pufendorf, Samuel 1991. *On the Duty of Man and Citizen According to Natural Law*, edited by James Tully, translated by Michael Silverthorne. Cambridge: Cambridge University Press.

Pujari, Premlata, and Vijay Kumari Kaushik. 1994. *Women Power in India*. Delhi: Kanishka Publishers.

Rabinow, Paul. 1995. *French Modern: Norms and Forms of the Social Environment*. Chicago: University of Chicago Press.

Rattigan, W. H., and Om Prakash Aggarawala. 1953. *A Digest of Civil Law for the Punjab, Chiefly Based on the Customary Law as at Present Ascertained*. 13th ed. Allahabad: University Book Agency.

Redding, Jeffrey A. 2010. "Institutional v. Liberal Contexts for Contemporary Non-State, Muslim Civil Dispute Resolution Systems." *J. Islamic St. Prac. Int'l L.* no. 6 (2): 1–25.

Reddy, G. Ram. 1989. "The Politics of Accommodation: Caste, Class and Dominance in Andhra Pradesh." In *Dominance and State Power in Modern India: Decline of a Social Order, Vol. 1*, edited by Francine R. Frankel and M. S. A. Rao, 265–321. New Delhi: Oxford University Press.

Robinson, David. 1992. "Ethnography and Customary Law in Senegal." *Cahiers d'études africaines* no. 32 (126): 221–37.

Robinson, Francis. 2007. *Separatism Among Indian Muslims: The Politics of the United Provinces' Muslims, 1860–1923*. 2nd ed. Cambridge: Cambridge University Press.

———. 2008. "Islamic Reform and Modernities in South Asia." *Modern Asian Studies* no. 42 (2–3): 259–81.

Rocher, Ludo. 1972. "Schools of Hindu Law." In *India Maior. Congratulatory Volume Presented to J. Gonda*, edited by J. Gonda, J. Ensink, and Peter Gaeffke, 167–76. Leiden: Brill.

Rowberry, Ryan M., and John Khalil. 2010. "A Brief History of Coptic Personal Status Law." *Berkeley Journal of Middle Eastern & Islamic Law* no. 3 (1): 81–139.

Roy, Srirupa. 2007. *Beyond Belief: India and the Politics of Postcolonial Nationalism*. Durham, NC: Duke University Press.

Rueschemeyer, Dietrich, Evelyne Huber, and John D. Stephens. 1992. *Capitalist Development and Democracy*. Chicago: University of Chicago Press.

Rueschemeyer, Dietrich, and Theda Skocpol, eds. 1996. *States, Social Knowledge, and the Origins of Modern Social Policies*. Princeton, NJ: Princeton University Press.

Ruparelia, Sanjay. 2008. "How the Politics of Recognition Enabled India's Democratic Exceptionalism." *International Journal of Politics, Culture and Society* no. 21 (1–4): 39–56.

Rustow, Dankwart A. 1970. "Transitions to Democracy: Toward a Dynamic Model." *Comparative Politics* no. 2 (3): 337–63.

Saheli. 1981. The Marriage Laws (Amendment) Bill, 1981. New Delhi. Manuscript.

———. 2005. "Hindu Succession Amendment Bill: Women's Groups Join to Plug Loopholes." *Newsletter* (Jan-Apr).

Said, Edward W. 1978. *Orientalism*. New York: Vintage Books.

Sakshi and Global Fund for Women. 1996. *Gender and Judges: A Judicial Point of View*. New Delhi: Sakshi.

Salim, Arskal. 2008. *Challenging the Secular State: The Islamization of Law in Modern Indonesia*. Honolulu: University of Hawaii Press.

Sanyal, Usha. 2005. *Ahmad Riza Khan Barelwi: In the Path of the Prophet*. Oxford: Oneworld.

Saradamoni, Kunjulekshmi. 1999. *Matriliny Transformed: Family, Law, and Ideology in Twentieth Century Travancore.* New Delhi: Sage Publishers.

Sarkar, Lotika. 1990. "Jawaharlal Nehru and the Hindu Code Bill." In *Indian Women, From Purdah to Modernity*, edited by B. R. Nanda, 87–98. New Delhi: Sangram.

Schwartz, Richard D., and Jerome H. Skolnick. 1970. *Society and the Legal Order: Cases and Materials in the Sociology of Law.* New York: Basic Books.

Schwartz, Stephen. 2012. "An Indian Revolution in Islamic Law." *Center for Islamic Pluralism.* February 12. Accessed May 30, 2013. http://www.islamicpluralism.org/1983/an-indian-revolution-in-islamic-law.

Scott, James C. 1998. *Seeing Like a State: How Certain Schemes to Improve the Human Condition Have Failed.* New Haven, CT: Yale University Press.

Sen, Samita. 2000. "Offences against Marriage: Negotiating Custom in Colonial Bengal." In *A Question of Silence? The Sexual Economies of Modern India*, edited by Janaki Nair and Mary E. John, 77–110. London: Zed Books.

Sethi, Sunil, Anil Nauriya, and Valmik Thapar. 2000. "In Memoriam of Krishna Riboud, Danial Latifi and S. P. Godrej." *India Seminar.* Accessed May 31, 2013. www.india-seminar.com/2000/492/492%20memoriam.htm.

Shahabuddin, Syed. 1992. "Should Muslims Follow the Qur'anic Modality for Divorce?" *Religion and Law Review* no. 1 (1): 27–35.

———. 1999. "No More Talaq Talaq Talaq." *Religion and Law Review*: 63–77.

Shaham, Ron. 2010. "Communal Identity, Political Islam and Family Law: Copts and the Debate over the Grounds for Dissolution of Marriage in Twentieth-Century Egypt." *Islam and Christian-Muslim Relations* no. 21 (4): 409–22.

Shaikh, Farzana. 2009. *Making Sense of Pakistan.* New York: Columbia University Press.

Sharma, B. K. 1989. *Divorce Law in India: Inter-Spousal Conflicts in Relation to Maintenance, Property, and Custody of Children.* New Delhi: Deep & Deep Publications.

Sharma, Ursula. 1983. *Women, Work, and Property in North-West India.* London: Tavistock.

Sikand, Yoginder. 2003. "Towards a Contextually Relevant Fiqh for India." *Sikh Spectrum* (November). Accessed May 31, 2013. http://sikhspectrum.com/2003/11/towards-a-contextually-relevant-fiqh-for-india/.

———. 2005. "Interrogating Triple Talaq: The Ahl-i Hadith Counter-Perspective." *Qalandar: Islam and the Interfaith Relations in South Asia* (July).

———. 2008. "Madrasa Reforms and Interfaith Dialogue: Interview with Maulana Khalid Saifullah Rehmani." Accessed May 13, 2013. http://mrzine.monthlyreview.org/2008/sikand171208p.html.

———. 2010. "New Shia Nikahnamah: Reform Muslim Law Through the Back Door." *TwoCircles.* Accessed May 30, 2013. http://twocircles.net/2010feb23/new_shia_nikahnamah_reforming_muslim_law_through_backdoor.html.

Singerman, Diane. 2005. "Rewriting Divorce in Egypt: Reclaiming Islam, Legal Activism, and Coalition Politics." In *Remaking Muslim Politics: Pluralism, Contestation, Democratization*, edited by Robert W. Hefner, 161–88. Princeton, NJ: Princeton University Press.

Singh, Gurharpal. 2000. *Ethnic Conflict in India: A Case-Study of Punjab.* Basingstoke, UK: Macmillan Press.

Sinha, Mrinalini. 1999. "The Lineage of the 'Indian' Modern: Rhetoric, Agency and the Sarda Act in Late Colonial India." In *Gender, Sexuality and Colonial Modernities*, edited by Antoinette M. Burton, 207–20. London: Routledge.

———. 2006. *Specters of Mother India: The Global Restructuring of an Empire*. Durham, NC: Duke University Press.

Siraj, Mehrun. 1994. "Women and the Law: Significant Developments in Malaysia." *Law and Society Review* no. 28 (3): 561–72.

Sivaramayya, B. 1988. "The Hindu Successsion (Amendment) Act, 1985: A Move in the Wrong Direction." *Journal of the Indian Law Institute* no. 30 (2): 166–73.

———. 1993. "Irretrievable Breakdown of Marriage as a Ground for Divorce." In *Women, March Towards Dignity: Social and Legal Perspectives*, edited by K. Kusum, 56–62. New Delhi: Regency Publications.

———. 1997. "Coparcenary Rights to Daughters: Constitutional and Interpretational Issues." *3 SCC (Jour)* no. 25.

———. 1999. *Matrimonial Property Law in India*. New Delhi: Oxford University Press.

Skocpol, Theda. 1985. "Bringing the State Back In: Strategies of Analysis in Current Research." In *Bringing the State Back In*, edited by Peter B. Evans, Dietrich Rueschemeyer, and Theda Skocpol, 3–43. Cambridge: Cambridge University Press.

———. 1995. *Protecting Soldiers and Mothers: The Political Origins of Social Policy in the United States*. Cambridge, MA: Belknap Press of Harvard University Press.

Smith, Anthony D. 1986. *The Ethnic Origins of Nations*. Oxford: Blackwell Publishers.

Smith, Donald Eugene. 1963. *India as a Secular State*. Princeton, NJ: Princeton University Press.

Sobhana, K. 2012. "Equality in Marriage Law—Cabinet Clears Proposals to Ease Divorce Deterrents." *The Telegraph*, March 24. Accessed May 31, 2013. http://telegraphindia.com/1120324/jsp/frontpage/story_15289659.jsp#.UajjnZVNCK8.

Sobotkova, V. 2012. "The Major Trends of Islam in Contemporary Malaysia and Their Influence on the Form of Islamic Family and Penal Law." *Archiv Orientalni* no. 80 (3): 389–416.

Solanki, Gopika. 2011. *Adjudication in Religious Family Laws: Cultural Accommodation, Legal Pluralism, and Gender Equality in India*. New York: Cambridge University Press.

Som, Reba. 1994. "Jawaharlal Nehru and the Hindu Code: A Victory of Symbol over Substance?" *Modern Asian Studies* no. 28 (1): 165–94.

Sonbol, Amira E.A. 2002. *Women of Jordan: Islam, Labor, and the Law*. Syracuse, NY: Syracuse University Press.

Special Correspondent. 2012. "Marriage Law Amendment Bill Discriminatory: AIDWA." *The Hindu*, May 1. Accessed May 31, 2013. http://www.thehindu.com/news/national/marriage-law-amendment-bill-discriminatory-aidwa/article3374531.ece.

Spooner, Brian. 1966. "Iranian Kinship and Marriage." *British Institute of Persian Studies* no. 4: 51–59.

Sreenivas, Mytheli. 2008. *Wives, Widows, and Concubines: The Conjugal Family Ideal in Colonial India*. Bloomington: Indiana University Press.

Starr, June. 1978. *Dispute and Settlement in Rural Turkey: An Ethnography of Law*. Leiden: Brill.

———. 1989. "The Role of Turkish Secular Law in Changing the Lives of Rural Muslim Women, 1950–1970." *Law & Society Review* no. 23 (3): 497–523.

Stein, Peter. 1980. *Legal Evolution: The Story of an Idea*. Cambridge: Cambridge University Press.
Stepan, Alfred C., Juan J. Linz, and Yogendra Yadav. 2011. *Crafting State-Nations: India and Other Multinational Democracies*. Baltimore, MD: Johns Hopkins University Press.
Stilt, Kristen. 2004. "Islamic Law and the Making and Remaking of the Iraqi Legal System." *George Washington International Law Review* no. 36: 695.
Stoler, Ann L. 1985. *Capitalism and Confrontation in Sumatra's Plantation Belt, 1870–1979*. New Haven, CT: Yale University Press.
———. 2009. *Along the Archival Grain: Epistemic Anxieties and Colonial Common Sense*. Princeton, NJ: Princeton University Press.
Stora, B. 2003. "Algeria/Morocco: The Passions of the Past: Representations of the Nation that Unite and Divide." *Journal of North African Studies* no. 8 (1): 14–34.
Strange, Thomas. 2007. *Hindu Law VI: Principally with Reference to Such Portions of It as Concern the Administration of Justice, in the King's Courts, in India*. Whitefish: Kessinger Publishing.
Subramaniam, Chidambaram. 1979. *The New Strategy in Indian Agriculture: The First Decade and After*. New Delhi: Vikas Publishing House.
Subramanian, Narendra. 1999. *Ethnicity and Populist Mobilization: Political Parties, Citizens, and Democracy in South India*. New York: Oxford University Press.
———. 2008. "Legal Change and Gender Inequality: Changes in Muslim Family Law in India." *Law and Social Inquiry* no. 33 (3): 631–72.
———. 2010. "Making Family and Nation: Hindu Marriage Law in Early Postcolonial India." *The Journal of Asian Studies* no. 69 (3): 771–98.
Sulh, Raghid. 2004. *Lebanon and Arabism: National Identity and State Formation*. London and New York: I. B. Tauris.
Sunder Rajan, Rajeswari. 2003. *The Scandal of the State: Women, Law, Citizenship in Postcolonial India*. Durham, NC: Duke University Press.
Tamil Nadu. Legislative Assembly. 1989. *Tamilnatu Cattap Peravai Natavatikkaikal*. (Tamil Nadu Legislative Assembly Debates). Madras: Secretariat.
Taylor, Charles. 2007. *A Secular Age*. Cambridge, MA: Belknap Press of Harvard University Press.
Tejani, Shabnum. 2008. *Indian Secularism: A Social and Intellectual History, 1890–1950*. Bloomington: Indiana University Press.
Thomas, George. 1979. *Christian Indians and Indian Nationalism, 1885–1950: An Interpretation in Historical and Theological Perspectives*. Frankfurt: Lang.
Thompson, E. P. 1966. *The Making of the English Working Class*. New York: Pantheon Books.
Tilly, Charles. 1975. *The Formation of National States in Western Europe*. Princeton, NJ: Princeton University Press.
TNN. 2004. "Triple Talaq to Go Out Softly." *The Times of India*. July 5. Accessed May 31, 2013. http://articles.timesofindia.indiatimes.com/2004-07-05/india/27146046_1_nikahnama-shariat-triple-talaq.
———. 2012. "Cabinet Gives Nod to Quick Divorces." *The Times of India*. March 24. Accessed May 31, 2013. http://articles.timesofindia.indiatimes.com/2012-03-24/india/31233652_1_irretrievable-breakdown-divorce-marriage-act.

Trautmann, Thomas R. 1982. *Dravidian Kinship*. Cambridge: Cambridge University Press.
The Tribune. 2000. "Law Commission Considers Hindu Inheritance Reform." 22 March.
Tucker, Judith E. 2008. *Women, Family, and Gender in Islamic Law*. Cambridge: Cambridge University Press.
Van der Veer, Peter. 1994. *Religious Nationalism: Hindus and Muslims in India*. Berkeley, CA: University of California Press.
Vatuk, Sylvia J. 2005. "Moving the Courts: Muslim Women and Personal Law." In *The Diversity of Muslim Women's Lives in India*, edited by Zoya Hasan and Ritu Menon, 18–58. New Brunswick, NJ: Rutgers University Press.
———. 2008. "Islamic Feminism in India: Indian Muslim Women Activists and the Reform of Muslim Personal Law." *Modern Asian Studies* no. 42 (2–3): 489–518.
Verma, B. R. 2002. *Commentaries on Mohammedan Law (in India, Pakistan and Bangladesh)*. 8th ed. Allahabad: Law Publishers.
Vijaya Kumar, V. 2006. *Traditional Futures: Law and Custom in India's Lakshadweep Islands*. New Delhi: Oxford University Press.
Virdi, P. K. 1972. *The Grounds for Divorce in Hindu and English Law: A Study in Comparative Law*. Delhi: Motilal Banarsidass.
Viswanathan, Gauri. 1989. *Masks of Conquest: Literary Study and British Rule in India*. New York: Columbia University Press.
Watson, Alan. 1983. "Legal Change: Sources of Law and Legal Culture." *University of Pennsylvania Law Review* no. 131 (5): 1121–57.
———. 2001. *Society and Legal Change*. 2nd ed. Philadelphia: Temple University Press.
Weber, Max. 1968. *Economy and Society: An Outline of Interpretive Sociology*, edited by Guenther Roth and Claus Wittich. New York: Bedminster Press.
Webster, John C. B. 1992. *The Dalit Christians: A History*. Delhi: Indian Society for Promoting Christian Knowledge.
Weiss, Anita M., ed. 1986. *Islamic Reassertion in Pakistan: The Application of Islamic Laws in a Modern State*. Syracuse, NY: Syracuse University Press.
Welchman, Lynn. 1988. "The Development of Islamic Family Law in the Legal System of Jordan." *International and Comparative Law Quarterly* no. 37 (4): 868–86.
Wickham, Carrie Rosefsky. 2002. *Mobilizing Islam: Religion, Activism, and Political Change in Egypt*. New York: Columbia University Press.
Wiktorowicz, Quintan. 2001. *The Management of Islamic Activism: Salafis, the Muslim Brotherhood, and State Power in Jordan*. Albany: State University of New York Press.
Williams, Rina Verma. 2006. *Postcolonial Politics and Personal Laws: Colonial Legal Legacies and the Indian State*. New Delhi: Oxford University Press.
Women Living Under Muslim Laws. 2006. "India: Shia Women Too Can Initiate Divorce." From *The Times of India Online*, November 6. Accessed May 31, 2013. http://www.wluml.org/node/3332.
Woods, Patricia J. 2008. *Judicial Power and National Politics: Courts and Gender in the Religious-Secular Conflict in Israel*. Albany: State University of New York Press.
Wuerth, Oriana. 2005. "The Reform of the Moudawana: The Role of Women's Civil Society Organizations in Changing the Personal Status Code in Morocco." *Hawwa* no. 3 (3): 309–33.

Yildirim, Seval. 2005. "Aftermath of a Revolution: A Case Study of Turkish Family Law." *Pace International Law Review* no. 17 (2): 347–71.
Yilmaz, Ihsan. 2005. *Muslim Laws, Politics, and Society in Modern Nation States: Dynamic Legal Pluralisms in England, Turkey, and Pakistan*. Farnham, UK: Ashgate.
Young Women's Christian Associaton. n.d.. Personal Law Files, consulted at YWCA offices in Delhi, Chennai, and Kochi.
Zace, Valentina. 1995. "Albania: Family Law Under the Dictatorship of the Proletariat." *Journal of Family Law* no. 33 (2): 259.
Zaman, Muhammad Qasim. 2002. *The Ulama in Contemporary Islam: Custodians of Change*. Princeton, NJ: Princeton University Press.
———. 2008. *Ashraf 'Ali Thanawi: Islam in Modern South Asia*. Oxford: Oneworld.
Ziadeh, Farhat Jacob. 1968. *Lawyers, the Rule of Law and Liberalism in Modern Egypt*. Stanford, CA: Hoover Institution on War, Revolution, and Peace, Stanford University.

CASES CITED

A. Annamalai Mudaliar v. Perumayee Ammal, AIR 1965 Madras 139
A. Bhagavathi Ammal v. Sethu, 1986 INDLAW MAD 181
A.E. Thirumal Naidu v. Rajammal, AIR 1968 Madras 201
A. P. K. Narayanaswami Reddiar v. Padmanabhan, AIR 1966 Mad 394
A. P. Ranga Rao v. Vijayalakshmi, I (1990) DMC 567
A. v. H. 1992 Mh. L. J. 790
A. Viswanathan v. G. Lakshmi alias Seetha (on 20 November 2006). Accessed May 28, 2013. (http://www.indiankanoon.org/doc/1341139/)
A.Yousuf Rawther v. Sowramma, AIR 1971 Kerala 261
Abbas Ali v. Mt. Rabia Bibi, 1951 All LJ 346
Abbayolla M. Subba Reddy v. Padmamma, 1998 (5) ALT 152
Abdul Haq v. Yasmin Talat, 1998 Cri LJ 3433
Abdul Kadir v. Salima, (1886) ILR 8 All 149
Abdul Khader v. Aziza Bee, AIR 1944 Madras 227
Abdul Khader v. Smt. Razia Begum, 1990 INDLAW KAR 35
Abdul Latif Mondal v. Anuwara Khatun, 2001 INDLAW CAL 310
Abdul Rashid v. Sultana Begum, 1992 Cri LJ 76
Abdullah Rauf Khan v. Halemon Bibi, 1989, 67 Cut LT 285
Abedabi d/o Doud Shaikh & anr. V. Sikandar Akabar Mujawar & Anr., 1980 Bom. CR 240
Abid Ali v. Mst. Rasia Begum, 1988 RCC 51
Adhyatma Bhattar Alwar v. Adhyatma Bhattar Sri Devi (2002) 1 SCC 308
Ahmad Kasim Molla v. Khatun Bibi, AIR 1933 Calcutta 27
Ahmed v. Aysha, II (1990) DMC 110 Kerala
Ahmedabad Women's Action Group (AWAG) and Others v. Union of India (1997) 3 SCC 573
Ajit Dutt v. Mrs. Ethel Walters, 2000(4) AWC 3270
Ali v. Sufaira, 1988 (3) Crimes 147 [Kerala]
Alimuddin Khan v. Nasiran Bibi, 1998 14 Orissa Cri R 224
Aliyar v. Pathu, 1988 (2) KLT 446
Aluri Sambaiah v. Shaikh Zahirabi, 1977 INDLAW AP 90

Amar Kanta Sen v. Sovana Sen, AIR 1960 Cal 438
Ammasi v. Smt. Amaravathi, 1997 (4) RCR (Criminal) 301 (Madras)
Amrithaa v. V. Krishna Kumar, 2010 INDLAW MAD 2407
Ananda Naik v. Haribandhu Naik, AIR 1967 Orissa 194
Anar Devi v. Parmeshwari Devi, AIR 2006 SC 3332
Andrahennedige Dinohamy v. Wijetunge Liyanapatabendige Balahamy, 1927 INDLAW PC 88
Angoori v. Phool Kumar, II (2003) DMC 688
Anil Kumar Mahsi v. Union of India, (1994) 5 SCC 704
Appibai v. Khimji, AIR 1936 Bom 138
Arab Ahmedhia Abdullah v. Arab Bail Mohmuna Saiyadbhai, AIR 1988 Guj 141
Are Lachia v. Are Raja Mallu, 1964(1) Cri LJ 237
Arun Chettri v. Madhu Chettri, AIR 2007 NOC 563 MP
Aruna Parmod Shah v. Union Of India (on 7 April, 2008). Accessed May 28, 2013. (http://indiankanoon.org/doc/511970/)
Arya Kumar Bal v. Smt. Ila Bal, AIR 1968 Cal 276
Asha Bibi v. Kadir Ibrahim Rowther, (1909) ILR 33 Madras 22
Asha Rani v. Gulshan Kumar, II (1995) DMC 198
Ashok Hurra v. Rupa Bipin Zaveri, AIR 1997 SC 1266
Ashok Kumar Bhatnagar v. Shabnam Bhatnagar, AIR 1989 Del 121
Ashok v. Rupa, 1996 (2) HLR 512 (Guj)
Ashwini Kumar Sehgal v. Smt. Swatantar Sehgal, 1979 Mat LR 26 (Punj & Har)
Asmata Ullah v. Khatun-unnisa, AIR 1939 Allahabad 592
Assistant Commissioner of Gift Tax v. C. Krishnan and Ors., (2002) 109 TTJ 516
Audumbar Gangaram Gavandi v. Sonubai Audumbar Gavandi (1960) 63 Bom LR 595
Avinash Prasad Srivastava v. Smt. Chandra Mohini, AIR 1964 All 486
Ayi Ammal v. Subramania Asari, AIR 1966 Madras 369
Aziza Khan v. Dr. Amir Hussain, 1999 INDLAW RAJ 158
B. v. A., 1992 Mh. L. J. 748
Baburao v. Mst. Sushila Bai, AIR 1964 MP 73
Badri Prasad v. Dy Director of Consolidation, AIR 1978 SC 1557
Bai Jiva v. Narsingh Lalbhai, (1927) ILR Bom 264
Bai Jivatbai Jethmal v. Milkiram Deepchand, 1961(2) Cri LJ 469
Bai Tahira v. Ali Hussain Fisalli Chothia, AIR 1979 SC 362
Baishnab Charan Jena v. Ritarani Jena, 1993 Cri LJ 238 (Ori)
Bajirao Raghoba Tambre v. Tolanbai, 1980 Cri LJ 473
Banshidhar Jha v. Chhabi Chatterjee, AIR 1967 Pat 277
Banu v. Kutubuddin Selumanji Vimanwala, II (1995) DMC 392
Banwari Lal v. Emperor, AIR 1914 Lah 455
Begum Bibi v. Abdul Rajak Khan, 1994 INDLAW ORI 125
Begum Subanu alias Saira Banu and another v. A. M. Abdul Gafoor, 1987 INDLAW SC 235
Bhaga Bai v. Mangali Bai, 1999 MPJR 74
Bhagwan Singh Sher Singh Arora v. Amar Kaur, AIR 1962 Punj 144
Bharat Bhushan Sharma v. Pratibha, I (2007) DMC 767
Bhausaheb alias Sandu Magar v. Leelabai, AIR 2004 Bom 283
Bijoli v. Sukomal, AIR 1979 Cal 87

Biju Ramesh v. J. P. Vijayakumar, AIR 2005 Ker 196
Binod Anand Lakra v. Smt. Belulah Lakra, AIR 1982 Patna 213
Binoy Mathew v. Sabu Abraham, 1998 (2) Ker LJ 688
Bipin Chander Jaisinghbhai Shah v. Prabhawati, 1956 INDLAW SC 34
Blyth v. Blyth, 1966, 1 AER 524
Boli Narajan Pawye v. Shiddeswari Morang, 1981 Cri LJ 674
Brajesh Kumar v. Anjali, I (2009) DMC 579 Allahabad
C. Obula Konda Reddy v. C. Pedda Venkata Lakshmamma, AIR 1976 AP 43
C. T. Radhakrishnan v. C. T. Viswanathan Nair, 2006 INDLAW SC 13
C. Vathsalan v. Kotta Madathil Narayanankutty, 2007 INDLAW KER 1432
Chanda Preetam Wadate v. Preetam Ganpatrao Wadate, 2002(2) Mh LJ 331
Chander Kumar Sharma v. Samriti Sharma, 1998 (3) RCR (Criminal) 135 (P & H)
Chanderkala Trivedi v. S. P. Trivedi, (1993) 4 SCC 232
Chandrakant Gangaram Gawade v. Sulochana Chandakant Gawade, 1996(2) Mh.L.J. 341
Chanmuniya v. Virendra Kumar Singh Kushwaha, 2010 INDLAW SC 845
Chhagan Lal Devman v. State of Maharashtra and ors., 1990 (1) DMC 533
Chinmoy Chakraborty v. Bharati Chakraborty, 1990(2) HLR 128
Collector of Madura v. Moottoo Ramalinga Sethupathi, (1868) 12 MIA 397
D. Nagappan v. T. Virgin Rani, 2009 INDLAW MAD 1125
D. Velusamy v. D. Patchaiammal, 2010 INDLAW SC 876
Dadaji Bhikaji v. Rukhmabai, (1885) ILR 9 Bom 529
Dadaji Bhikaji v. Rukhmabai, (1886) ILR 10 Bom 301
Dalbir Singh v. Simar Kaur Alias Simro, II (2002) DMC 371
Dalip Singh v. Rajbala, II (2007) DMC 273
Danial Latifi v. Union of India, 2001 (7) SCC 740
Dayal Singh v. Bhajan Kaur, AIR 1973 P & H 44
Devyani Kantilal Shroff v. Kantilal Gamanlal Shroff, AIR 1963 Bom 98
Dharmambal v. S. Lakshmi Ammal, 2002 INDLAW KER 285
Dr. Hormusji M. Kalapesi v. Dinbai H. Kalapesi, AIR 1955 Bom 413
Dr. Narayan Ganesh Dastane v. Mrs. Sucheta Narayan Dastane, AIR 1975 SC 1534
Dr. Samir Kr. Das v. Aparna Das alias Tripti Das. 9 August 2000. Accessed May 28, 2013. (http://www.indiankanoon.org/doc/681097/)
Dr. S. P. Trivedi v. Smt. Chandrakala Trivedi, 1990(2) HLR 67
Dr. Vimla Balani v. Jai Krishan Balani, 2008 INDLAW Del 1996
Dwaraka Bai v. Professor Nainan Mathews, AIR 1953 Madras 792
Edamma v. Hussainappa, AIR 1965 AP 45
Edla Neelaya v. Edla Ramada alias Ramadas, I (1995) DMC 19
Fowle v. Fowle (1878) ILR 4 Cal 260
Ful Chand v. Nazab Ali Chowdhry, (1908) ILR 36 Calcutta 184
Fulchand Maganlal v. Unknown, AIR 1928 Bom 59
Fuzlunbi v. Khader Vali, AIR 1980 SC 1730
G. M. Jeelani v. Shanswar Kulsum, 1992 INDLAW AP 11
G. P. Rajendran v. M. Valarmathi, 2008 INDLAW MAD 3460
G. V. N. Kameshwara Rao v. G. Jabille, I (2002) DMC 266 (SC)
G. Valli alias Rayaprolu v. State of Andhra Pradesh, 2003 INDLAW AP 329
Gananath Pattanaik v. State of Orissa, 2002 (2) SCC 619
Gangadharan v. T. K. Thankam, AIR 1988 Ker 244

Gantapalli Appalamma v. Gantapalli Yellayya (1897) ILR 20 Mad 470
Gaya Prasad v. Bhagwati, AIR 1966 MP 212
(Gedalu) Narayana v. Emperor, AIR 1932 Mad 561
Geeta Mullick v. Brojo Gopal Mullick, AIR 2003 Calcutta 321
George Sebastian @ Joy v. Molly Joseph @ Nish, II (1995) DMC 168 (FB)
George Swamidoss Joseph v. Harriett Sundari Edward, AIR 1955 Madras 341
Gita Masand v. Narain Dass, I (1985) DMC 349
Glancy v. Glancy (1916) 31 IC 264
Gopi v. Smt. Krishna, 2001 (4) RCR (Crl) 624 (P&H)
Gopi Krishna Kasaudhan v. Musammat Jaggo (1936) LR 63 IA 295
Govind v. State of M. P., AIR 1975 SC 1378
Govindaraju v. Munisami Gounder, AIR 1997 SC 10
Govindrao Ranoji Musale v. Sou. Anandibai, AIR 1976 Bom 433
Gulab Jagdusa Kakwane v. Smt. Kamal Gulab Kakwane, 86 Bom LR (1984): 662
Gurbachan Kaur v. Karnail Singh Resham Singh, II (1999) DMC 686
Gurdit Singh v. Mst. Angrez Kaur Alias Gej Kaur Alias Malan, 1967 INDLAW SC 501
Gurupad Khandappa Magdum v. Hirabai Khandappa Magdum, 1978 INDLAW SC 232
Hamira Bibi v. Zubaide Bibi, AIR 1916 PC 46
Harinarayan v. State of M. P., 2005(1) MPLJ 196
Hasenara Begum v. Fazar Ali, I (2002) DMC 385
Hitesh Bhatnagar v. Deepa Bhatnagar, (2011) 5 SCC 234
Honamma v. Timannabhat (1877) ILR 1 Bom 559
Iqbal Bano v. State of Uttar Pradesh, 2007 INDLAW SC 618
Iqbal Kaur v. Pritam Singh S. Nanak Singh, AIR 1963 Punj 242
Ishwarlal Sarabhai Parikh v. Prabhawati Ishwarlal Parikh, 1988 (1) Bom CR 464
Itwari v. Smt. Asghari Begum and others, AIR 1960 All 684
Jairam Somaji More v. Sindhubai, Mh LJ 1999(3) 872
Jaitunbi Mubarak Shaikh v. Mubarak Fakruddin Shaikh, 1993 (3) Mh LJ 694
Jal Kaur v. Pala Singh, AIR 1961 Punj 391
Jeebo Dhon Banyah v. Mt. Sundhoo (1872), 17 W. R. C. R. 522
Jiauddin Ahmed v. Anwar Begum, (1978) 1 GLR 375
Jina Magan Pakhali v. Bai Jethi (1941) 43 Bom LR 651
John White v. Mrs. Kathleen Olive White, AIR 1958 SC 441
Jorden Diengdeh v. S. S. Chopra, AIR 1985 SC 935
Jose v. Alice (1988) 2 Ker LT 890
Jyotish Chandra Guha v. Meera Guha, 1969 INDLAW CAL 162
K. P. Bhargavi Amma v. C. R. Kuttikrishnan, 1965 INDLAW KER 118
K. Zunaideen v. Ameena Begum, II (1998) DMC 468 (DB)
Kadar Mian v. Jahera Khatun, 1998 INDLAW ORI 12
Kadia Harilal Purshottam v. Kadia Lilavati Gokaldas, AIR 1961 Guj 202
Kailash Wati v. Ayodhia Parkash, 1977 Hindu LR 175
Kaithakulangara Kunhikannan v. Nellatham Veettil Malu, AIR 1973 Ker 273
Kaka v. Hassan Bano, II (1998) DMC 85 (FB*)*
Kamala Sharma v. Suresh Kumar Sharma, II (2001) DMC 680 Raj
Kamlesh v. Paras Ram, AIR 1985 P&H 19
Karim Abdul Rehman Shaikh v. Shehnaz Karim Shaikh, 2000 Cri LJ 3560
Karumpa Kochappi v. Sirkar, 1911 TLR (24) 157

Kasturi v. Ramasamy, 1979 Cri LJ 741
Kasubai v. Bhagwan Bhagaji Wanjari, AIR 1955 Nagpur 210
Kathiyamma v. Urathel Marakkar, AIR 1931 Madras 647
Kaushalyabai Dinkar Mule v. Dinkar Mahadeorao Mule, 2001 INDLAW MUM 443
Keshaorao Krishnaji Londhe v. Nisha Londhe, AIR 1984 Bom 413
Keshav Hargovan v. Bai Gandhi (1915) ILR 39 Bom 538
Kewal Kumar v. Pawna Devi, 2010 INDLAW HP 444
Khajah Hidayut Oollah v. Rai Jan Khanum, (1844) 3 Moo IA 295
Khandu Madhu Kadbhane v. Sitabai, 2001 Cri LJ 4339
Kharak Singh v. State of U. P., AIR 1963 SC 1295
Khemchand Om Prakash Sharma v. State of Gujarat, 2000 INDLAW SC 181
Khurshid Khan Amin Khan v. Husnabanu, 1976 Cri LJ 1584 (Bom)
Kishenlal v. Prabhu, AIR 1963 Raj 95
Kista Pillai v. Amirthammal, AIR 1938 Mad 833
Krishna v. Som Nath, (1996) DMC 667 (P & H)
Krishnakant Mulashankar Vyas v. Reena Krishna Vyas, AIR 1999 Bom 127
Kudomeo Dossee v. Joteeram Kolita, (1880) ILR 3 Cal 305
Kunhammed Haji v. K. Amina, II (1995) DMC 260 (DB)
Kunwar Singh Marko v. Shiv Dayal Sarote, 1999(1) MPJR 563
Kuppanna Goundan v. Palani Ammal, AIR 1955 Mad 471
Kuppuswami v. Alagammal, AIR 1961 Mad 391
Kurien v. Alphonsa, 1986 Ker LT 731
Kusum Lata v. Kamta Prasad, AIR 1965 Allahabad 280
L. Mallya Naika v. Somli Bai, (1978) ILR 28 Karn 1706
Lachman Utamchand Kiriplani v. Meena Alias Mota, 1964 SCR (4) 331
Lachu v. Dal Singh, 33 PR 1896
Lakshmi Ammal v. Narayanaswami Naicker, AIR 1950 Mad 321
Lalita Devi v. Radha Mohan, AIR 1976 Raj 1
Laserbai v. Jugribai, 1978 MPWN 336
Latha Kunjamma v. Anil Kumar, 2008 INDLAW Ker 74
Laxmansingh v. Kasharbai, 1965 MPLJ 702
Lt. Col. Mohinder Pal Singh v. Kulwant Kaur, 1975 INDLAW Del 77
M. H. Hameed v. Arif Jan, alias Shahida Begum, 1990 Cri LJ 96
M. Kanniappan v. Akilandammal, AIR 1954 Mad 427
M. P. Subramaniyam v. T. T. Ponnakshiammal, AIR 1958 Mys 41
M. Shahul Hameed v. Salima, 2003-1-LW 183
M. Subhan v. Smt. Mazbul Be, 1991 INDLAW AP 19
M. Yogendra v. Leelamma N., 2010(1) All LR (SC) 490
Ma Mi v. Kallander Ammal, AIR 1927 PC 15
Ma Mya Khin v. N.N. Godenho AIR 1936 Rang 446
Madanlal Sharma v. Smt. Santosh Sharma 1980 Mah LJ 391
Madhusudan v. Bhanumati, I (1985) DMC 413
Mahalingam Pillai v. Amsavalli (1956) 2 MLJ 289
Maharshi Avadhesh v. Union of India 1994 Supp (1) SCC 7313
Mahendra Manilal Nanavati v. Sushila Mahendra Nanavati, 1964 SCR (7) 267
Mahendra Nath Yadav v. Sheela Devi, 2010 INDLAW SC 667
Majitha Beevi v. Yakoob, 1999 (1) KLT 796

Malti v. State of U. P., I (2001) DMC 204 All
Man Mohan Vaid v. Meena Kumari, 107 (2003) DLT 195
Mandeep Kaur v. Sukh Dev Singh, AIR 2006 HP 97
Mary Roy v. State of Kerala, AIR 1986 SC 1011
Mary Sonia Zachariah v. Union of India (also called *Ammini E. J. v. Union of India*), II (1995) DMC (FB) 27
Masroor Ahmed v. State (NCT) of Delhi, Crl MC 10078/ in Bail Appln. 4746/2006
Maxin George & Mary George v. Indian Oil Corporation Ltd., 2005 INDLAW KER 23
Meera v. Vijay Shankar Talchidia, AIR 1994 Raj 33
Mehboobkhan v. Parvinbanoo, 1988 Mh LJ 781
Mehbubabi Nasir Shaikh v. Nasir Farid Shaikh, 1976 INDLAW MUM 98
Merla Narayudu v. M. Bramaramba, 2006(2) ALT 730
Miss. Shireen Mall v. Mr. John James Taylor, Punj LR 1952 (IV) 125
Mohabbat Ali Khan v. Mahomed Ibrahim Khan, 1929 INDLAW PC 3
Mohamed Ibrahim v. Ramzan Begum, I (1993) DMC 60
Mohammad Ahmed Khan v. Shah Bano Begum, AIR 1985 SC 945
Mohammad Umar Khan v. Gulshan Begum, 1992 Cri LJ 899
Mohammed Hanifa v. Pathummal Beevi, 1972 Ker LT 512
Mohan Lal v. Kalp Shikha, (1985) 77 PLR 44
Mohd. Tajuddin v. Quomarunnisa Begum, II (1989) DMC 204 AP
Moonshee Buzloor Ruheem v. Shums-oon-nissa Begum (1848) 11 Moo IA 551
Motiur Rahaman v. Sabina Khatun, 1994 (3) Crimes 236
Mrs. Manisha Sandeep Gade v. Sandeep Vinayak Gade, AIR 2005 Bom 180
Mrs. Nazimunnissa Begum v. Abdul Majeeth, 1994 INDLAW MAD 79
Mrs. P. Manimekalai v. R. Kothandaraman (August 4, 2010). Accessed May 28, 2013. (http://www.indiankanoon.org/doc/1733146/)
Mrs. Swaraj Garg v. K. M. Garg, AIR 1978 Delhi 296
Mrs. T. Crauford v. Ms. Maary Disilva, AIR 2008 Raj 189
Ms. Santosh Kumari v. Shri Shiv Prakash Sharma, AIR 2001 Delhi 376
Ms. Suresh Khullar v. Mr. Vijay Khullar, 2002 INDLAW DEL 503
Mst. Bhan Kaur v. Ishar Singh, 50 PLR (1958) 156
Mt. Kishan Devi v. Mangal Sen, AIR 1935 All 927
Mt. Lajwanti v. Bakshi Ram, AIR 1935 Lah 110
Mt. Subhani v. Nawab, AIR 1941 PC 21
Mt. Sukhribai v. Pohkalsingh, AIR 1950 Nag 33
Muhammad Muin-ud-din v. Jamal Fatima, AIR 1921 Allahabad 152
Mumtazben Jusabbhai Sipahi v. Mahebubkhan Usmankhan Pathan, 1998 INDLAW GUJ 67
Musunuru Nagendramma v. Musunuru Ramakotayya, 1953 INDLAW MAD 148
N. R. Radhakrishnan v. N. Dhanalakshmi, (1975) 1 MLJ 439
N. Sarada Mani v. G.Alexander, INDLAW 1997 AP 277
Nallathangal v. Nainan Ambalam, 1959 INDLAW MAD 254
Nandamani Ananga Bhima Deo v. Suseela Mala Patta Mahadevi, 1932 INDLAW PC 51
Nanisseri Mukundan v. M. Usha (2007). Accessed May 28, 2013. (http://www.indiankanoon.org/doc/471387/)
Narasimhamurthy v. Sushilabai, AIR 1996 SC 1826
Narasu Appa Mali v. State of Bombay, AIR 1952 Bom 84
Narayan Bharthi v. Laving Bharthi (1877) ILR 2 Bom 140

Narnath Thazhakuniyil Sandha v. Kottayat Thazhakuniyil Narayanan, 1999 Cri LJ 1663
Naseemunisa Begum v. Shaikh Abdul Rehman, 2002 (2) Mh LJ 115
Naval Kishore Somani v. Poonam Somani, 1998 (5) ALD 349
Naveen Kohli v. Neelu Kohli, AIR 2006 SC 1675
Neelam v. Vinod Kumar, AIR 1986 P&H 253
Neena v. John Pormu, AIR 1985 Madhya Pradesh 85
Nirmala Devi v. Pritam Singh, II (1998) DMC 376
Nitu v. Krishan Lal, AIR 1990 Del 1
Noor Jehan. v. State of Maharashtra, I (1996) DMC 120
Noor Saba Khatoon v. Mohammad Quasim, 1997 (7) JT SC 104
P. E. Mathew v. Union of India, 1999 INDLAW KER 367
P. Govinda Reddy v. Golla Obulamma, AIR 1971 AP 363
P. Mariammal v. Padmanabhan, AIR 2001 Madras 350
P. Mohan Rao v. P. Vijayalakshmi, 2007 (5) ALT 19
Parami Ramayya v. Mahadevi Shankarappa (1909) ILR 34 Bom 278
Pareshkumar Chaturdas Patel v. State of Gujarat (2010). Accessed May 28, 2013. (http://www.indiankanoon.org/doc/317432/)
Parveen Akhtar v. Union of India, Writ Petition No. 744 of 1992 (2002)
Patala Atchamma v. Patala Mahalakshmi, (1907) ILR 30 Mad 332
Perumal Naicker v. Sithalakshmi Ammal, 1955 INDLAW MAD 141
Philips Alfred Malvin v. Y. J. Gonsalvis, AIR 1999 Ker 187
Phillips v. Emperor, AIR 1935 Oudh 506
Pola Venkateshwarlu v. Pola Lakshmi Devi and Ors. 2005 (1) R.C.R. (Criminal) 1004 (AP)
Ponnayee v. Periya Mooppan (1908) 18 MLJ 150
Pothula Manika Reddy v. Government of A. P. 1978 (1) APLJ 360
Pragati Varghese v. Cyril George Varghese, AIR 1997 Bombay 349
Pravat Chandra Pattnaik v. Sarat Chandra Pattnaik, AIR 2008 Ori 133
Praveen Kumari Jaitly v. Surinder Kumar Jaitly, I (2001) DMC 308
Prem Masih v. Mst. Kumudani Bai, AIR 1974 MP 88
Prema v. Nanje Gowda, 2011 INDLAW SC 361
Pritam Kaur v. Surjit Singh, (1984) 86 PLR. 202 (F. B.)
Pritam Singh v. Nasib Kaur, 1956 PLR 424
Pulla Reddy v. I. Seshi Reddy, 1987(2) ALT 210
Pullamma v. Thatalingam, AIR 1945 Mad 4
Puthiyadath Jayamathy Avva and Others v. K. J. Naga Kumar, 2000 INDLAW KER 276
Putul Devi v. Gopi Mandal, AIR 1963 Patna 93
R. Mahalakshmi v. A. V. Anantharaman, (2009) 9 SCC 52
R. Sunitha v. Gopalakrishnan alias Unni (2008). Accessed May 29, 2013. (http://www.indiankanoon.org/doc/81471/)
Rachita Rout v. Basanta Kumar Rout, (1986) 2 DMC 448
Radhakishan v. Shankarlal, 1982 JLJ SN 77
Rahmat Ullah v. State of U. P. and Khatoon Nisa v. State of U. P., II (1994) DMC 64
Raj Kumar Manocha v. Smt. Anskuka Manocha, 1983 Cur LJ (Civ & Cri) 134
Raja Gopalan v. Rajamma, AIR 1967 Ker 181
Rajan Vasant Revankar v. Mrs. Shobha Rajan Revankar, AIR 1995 Bom 246
Rajani v. Subramoniam, AIR 1990 Ker 1
Rajani Prabhakar Lokur v. Prabhakar Raghavendra Lokur, AIR 1958 Bom 264

Rajendra Kumar Jajodia v. Puja Jajodia, I (2009) DMC 332 Calcutta
Rajesh Kumar Madaan v. Mrs. Mamta alias Veena, (2005) 140 PLR 196
Rajeshbai v. Shantabai, 1981 Mh LJ 820
Raji Pachori v. Kamlesh Pachori, 1993 JLJ 565
Rakesh Goyal v. Deepika Goyal, I (2007) DMC 457 P&H
Ram Kali v. Gopal Das, (1971) ILR 1 Delhi 10
Ram Parkash v. Shrimati Savitri Devi, 59 PLR (1957) 519
Ram Sarup Aggarwal v. Shrimati Dev Kumari, 52 PLR (1950) 297
Ram-Autar v. Mt. Raghurai, AIR 1926 Oudh 604
Ramavtar Sharma v. Smt. Santosh, I (2002) DMC 515
Ramesh Chander Kaushal v. Veena Kaushal & Ors., AIR 1978 SC 1807
Ramesh Jangid v. Sunita, AIR 2007 Raj 160
Ramesh Kumar Sharma v. Smt. Akash Sharma, AIR 2008 HP 78
Rameshchandra Daga v. Rameshwari Daga, I (2005) DMC 1
Ramish Francis Toppo v. Violet Francis Toppo, I (1989) DMC 322
Ramkali v. Nathoosingh, 1983 WN 396
Ramzan v. Smt. Salma, 1987 Cri LJ 324 (Raj)
Ranbir Karam Singh v. Jogindra C. Bhattachargi, AIR 1940 All 134
Rangubai v. Laxman Lalji Patil AIR 1966 Bom 169
Ratna Banerjee v. Chandra Madhab Banerjee, I (2007) DMC 566 Cal
Ratnaprabhabai Sheshrao Bhore v. Sheshrao Shankarrao Bhore, (1972) 74 Bom LR 434
Ravindra Singh v. Kapsi Bai, II (1991) DMC 422
Reg. v. Karsan Goja and Reg. v. Bai Rupa, (1864) 2 Bom HCR 117
Rekha v. B. Susheelendra, 2010 INDLAW AP 427
Renganayaki v. Arunagiri, AIR 1993 Mad 174
Rewaram Balwant Khati v. Ramratan Khati, AIR 1963 MP 160
Reynold Rajamani v. Union of India, AIR 1982 SC 1261
Rita Das Biswas v. Trilokesh Das Biswas, AIR 2007 Gau 122
Rita Rani v. Ramesh Kumar, I (1996) DMC 511
Rohini Kumari v. Narendra Singh, AIR 1972 SC 459
Rohtash Singh v. Smt. Ramendri & Ors., AIR 2000 SC 952
Romesh Chander v. Savitri, AIR 1995 SC 851
Rudramma v. H. R. Pattaveerabhadrappa, (1987) Cri LJ 677
Rukhsana Parvin v. Sheikh Mohammad Hussain, 1977 Cri LJ 1041
Rukia Khatun v. Abdul Khalique Laskar, (1981) 1 GLR 375
Rukmani Ammal v. T. R. S. Chari, AIR 1935 Mad 616
Rup Lal v. Kartaro Devi, AIR 1970 J&K 153
Rupa Ashok Hurra v. Ashok G. Hurra, (1996) 3 GLR 668
Rupsan Begum v. Md. Abdus Sattar, II (1990) DMC 253
S. S. Manickam v. Arputha Bhavani Rajam, 1980 Cri LJ 354
S. Sai Reddy v. S. Narayana Reddy, 1991 INDLAW SC 465
S. Seshachalam v. S. Deenadayalan, 2009 INDLAW MAD 2148
Sabitanjali Pattanaik v. Priyabrata Pattanaik, AIR 2001 Orissa 84
Sachindra Nath Biswas v. Sm. Benamala Biswas, AIR 1960 Cal 575.
Sadanandan, K. v. Mepparamban Sreeja (2009). Accessed May 29, 2013. (http://www.indiankanoon.org/doc/406164/)
Sadasivan Pillai v. Vijayalakshmi, 1986 INDLAW KER 140

Sadhu Singh v. Jagdish Kaur, AIR 1969 P&H 139
Sadique Ali v. Apar Sessions Naiyai Dheesh, Basti & Ors., II (1995) DMC 222
Saira Bano v. Mohd. Aslam Ghulam Mustafa Khan, 1999 (3) Mh LJ 716
Saiyid Rashid Ahmad v. Mt. Anisa Khatun, AIR 1932 PC 25
Sajeev Kumar v. P. Dhanya (2008). Accessed May 29, 2013. (http://www.indiankanoon.org/doc/1665058/)
Saleem Basha v. Mumtaz Begum, 1998 Cri LJ 4782
Samar Ghosh v. Jaya Ghosh (2007) 4 SCC 511
Sanghamitra Ghosh v. Kajal Kumar Ghosh, (2007) 2 SCC 220
Sanghamitra Singh v. Kailash Singh, AIR 2001 Orissa 151
Sanjukta Padhan v. Laxminarayan Padhan, AIR 1991 Orissa 39
Sankaralingam Chetti v. Subban Chetti (1894) ILR 17 Mad 479
Sarabai v. Rabiabai (1905) ILR 30 Bombay 537
Sarabjit Singh v. Charanjit Kaur, AIR 1997 P H 66
Sardari Lal v. Mst. Vishano, AIR 1970 J&K 150
Sarla Mudgal v. Union of India, AIR 1995 SC 1531
Satya Devi v. State of Himachal Pradesh, 2011 INDLAW HP 7
Savita Samvedi v. Union of India, AIR 1985 SC 716
Savitaben Somabhai Bhatiya v. State of Gujarat, AIR 2005 SC 1809
Savithramma v. Ramanarasimhaiah, 1963(1) Cri LJ 131
Savitri Pandey v. Prem Chandra Pandey, AIR 2002 SC 591
Sayed Newaj Ali alias Neti v. Rasida Begum, 1991 22 OJD 212 (Criminal)
Seema v. Nilesh Chouhan, AIR 2006 MP 46
Seethayamma v. Venkataramana, AIR 1940 Mad 906
Shabana Bano v. Imran Khan, 2009 INDLAW SC 1702
Shahadabi M. Isak v. Abdul Ajij Abdul Latif, 1996 INDLAW MUM 81
Shahida Begum v. Abdul Majid, 1996 INDLAW RAJ 17
Shaikh Babbu v. Sayeda Masarat Begum, 1999 Cri LJ 4822
Shaikh Mobin v. State of Maharashtra, 1996 (1) Mh LJ 810
Shamim Ara v. State of U. P., 2002 AIR SCW 4162
Shamlal v. Rajkumar, 1958 MPLJ 139
Shamshad Begum v. Md. Noor Ahemad Khan, 2001 INDLAW ORI 48
Shankar v. Puspita, AIR 2005 Jharkhand 92
Shanta v. Sahadevan, 2011 INDLAW KER 222
Shantaram Patil v. Dagubai Patil, AIR 1987 Bom 182
Sheela Devi v. Lal Chand, 2007(1) MLJ 797 (SC)
Sheikh Mohiuddin v. Hasina Bibi, 1988 2 Orissa LR 163
Sheikh Saber Ali v. Smt. Sahmim Banu, 1996 INDLAW CAL 54
Shiramabai v. Kalgonda Bhimgonda, AIR 1964 Bom 263
Shivalingiah v. Chowdamma, AIR 1956 Mysore 17
Shobha Rani v. Madhukar Reddi, AIR 1988 SC 121
Shravan v. Anjanabai, 1985 Cri LJ 1213 (Bom)
Shravan Nathu Kannor v. Anjanabai Shravan Kannor 1985 (2) Bom CR 495
Shri B. v. Smt. A, (1992) 94 Bom LR 160
Shri Gurcharan Singh v. Shrimati Waryam Kaur, LXIII-1960 PLR 127
Shri Kishan Chand v. Smt. Munni Devi, AIR 2003 Delhi 382
Shri Siba Prosad Basu v. Sm. Gouri Basu, 1994 (1) CHN 324

Shyam Chand v. Janki, 1966 INDLAW HP 12
Simon Lakra v. Bakla, (1932) ILR 11 Pat 627
Sirigiri Pullaiah v. Sirigiri Bushings Amma, 1962 INDLAW AP 142
Sitaram v. Demai, 1949 Cri LJ 29
Sm. Pancho v. Ram Prasad, AIR 1956 All 41
Smt. A. v. Sri B, 1990 Mh LJ 35
Smt. Alopbai v. Ramphal Kunjilal, AIR 1962 MP 211
Smt. Anubha v. Vikas Aggarwal, 2002 INDLAW DEL 973
Smt. Asha Handa v. Baldev Raj Handa, 1984 INDLAW DEL 227
Smt. Bhagirathi v. S. Manivanan, AIR 2008 Mad 250
Smt. Bhagwanti v. Laxmandas Panjwani, AIR 2000 MP 190
Smt. Chandra Mohini Srivastava v. Shri Avinash Prasad Srivasatava, AIR 1967 SC 581
Smt. Hamidan v. Mohd. Rafiq, 1994 Cri LJ 348
Smt. Harvinder Kaur v. Harmander Singh Choudhry, AIR 1984 Delhi 66
Smt. Kalpana Srivasta v. Surendra Nath Srivastava, AIR 1985 All 253
Smt. Kamini Gupta v. Mukesh Kumar Gupta, AIR 1985 Delhi 221
Smt. Kanchan Devi v. Promod Kumar Mittal, AIR 1996 SC 3192
Smt. Kesari Devi v. Jagdev Singh, 2005 Cri LJ 1091
Smt. Kusum v. Shri R. K. Saxena, I (2004) DMC 654
Smt. Leela Pande v. Shri Sachendra Kumar Pande, AIR 1994 MP 205
Smt. Nanjamma and Another v. State of Karnataka, 1999 (2) Kar LJ 109
Smt. Nirmala Manohar Jagesha v. Manohar Shivram Jagesha, AIR 1991 Bom 259
Smt. Premanbai v. Channoolal, AIR 1963 MP 57
Smt. Reeta Bharat Arora v. Bharat Yasodanandan Arora @ Dhingra, I (2002) DMC 136
Smt. Saroj Rani v. Sudarshan Kumar Chadha, AIR 1984 SC 1562
Smt. Smita Dilip Rane v. Dilip Dattaram Rane, AIR 1990 Bombay 84
Smt. Sumitra Devi v. Narender Singh, (1993) 103 PLR 422
Smt. Surbhi Agrawal v. Sanjay Agrawal, AIR 2000 MP 139
Smt. Surrinder Kaur v. Mohinder Singh, PLR 55 (1967) 774
Smt. Sushma Kohli @ Satya Devi v. Shri Shyam Sunder Kohli, I (2003) DMC 52
Smt. Swayamprabha v. A. S. Chandrasekhar, AIR 1982 Kar 295
Smt. Tirath Kaur v. Kirpal Singh, AIR 1964 Punjab 28
Smt. Umri Bai v. Chittar, AIR 1966 MP 205
Smt. Vanamala v. Shri H. M. Ranganatha Bhatta, 1995 SCC (5) 299
Snehlata Seth v. Kewal Krishan Seth, AIR 1986 Delhi 162
Sobhanadramma v. Varaha Lakshmi Narasimhaswami, AIR 1934 Mad 401
Sohan Lal v. A. Z. Makuin, AIR 1929 Lahore 230
Solomon Devasahayam Selvaraj v. Chandirah Mary, 1968(1) Madras LJ 289
Sonubai Yeshwant Jadhav v. Bala Govind Yadav, AIR 1983 Bom 156
Sree Raja Row Boochee Tummiah v. Sree Raja Row Venkata Neeladry Rao, (1805–47) 1 Mad DSDSA 366 (B)
Stree v. Stree, (1935) 68 MLJ 606
Subal Chandra Saha v. Pritikana Saha, 2003 Cri LJ 2200
Subhadra v. Rajendra Prasad, 2003 (3) MPHT 452
Subramani v. M. Chandralekha, 2004 INDLAW SC 1011
Sudheer Singhal v. Ms. Neetha Singhal, AIR 2001 Del 116
Sugalabai v. Gundappa Adiveppa Maradi, 2007 INDLAW KAR 422

Sukri v. Khluji, 1981(2) WN 82
Sukumar Dhibar v. Smt. Anjali Dasi, 1983 Cri LJ 36
Sukumar Mukherjee v. Tripti Mukherjee, AIR 1992 Pat 32
Sulabha v. Suseela, 2007 INDLAW KER 2045
Sulochana v. Selva Madhavan, 1974 TNLJ 351
Sundarambal v. Deivanaayagam, 1991(2) MLJ 199
Sundari Devi v. Ram Lal, I (1995) DMC 252
Surinder Kaur v. Gurdeep Singh, AIR 1973 P&H 134
Sushi Kumari v. Khairatilal, 1986 MPWN 134
Sushilabai Ramchandra Kulkarni v. Narayanrao Gopalrao Deshpande, AIR 1975 Bom 257
Swapan Kumar Ganguly v. Smt. Smiritikana Ganguly, I (2002) DMC 433 (DB)
Swapna Ghosh v. Sadananda Ghosh, AIR 1989 Calcutta 1
Syed Fazal Pookaya Thangal v. Union of India, AIR 1993 Kerala 308
Syed Sabir Husain v. Farzand Hasan, AIR 1938 PC 80
T. M. Bashiam v. M. Victor, AIR 1970 Madras 12
T. Sareetha v. T. Venkata Subbiah, AIR 1983 AP 356
Tai v. Harishchandra, II (1984) DMC 91
Tapan Kumar Chakraborty v. Jyotsna Chakraborty, AIR 1997 Calcutta 134
Tara Singh v. Shakuntala, AIR 1974 Raj 21
Tarsem Lal v. Smt. Santosh, 1980 HLR 344
Teerth Ram v. Parvati Devi, AIR 1995 Raj 86
Thangammal v. Gengayammal (1945) 1 MLJ 299
Thiyyakandi Ramachandran v. Sheena (2009). Accessed May 29, 2013. (http://www.indiankanoon.org/doc/63982/)
Tulasamma v. N. Seenan, ILR 2002 Kar 4941
Udaivir Singh v. Smt Vinod Kumari, (1985) Cri LJ 1923
Uji v. Hathi Lalu (1870) 7 BHCR 133
Undavalli Narayana Rao v. State of Andhra Pradesh, AIR 2010 SC 3708
Usha Rani v. Sham Lal, (2008) 149 PLR 454
Usman Khan Bahamani v. Fathimunnisa Begum (also called: *All India Muslim Advocates Forum v. Osman Khan Bahmani*), AIR 1990 AP 225
V. Bhagat v. Mrs. D. Bhagat, AIR 1994 SC 710
Vaijayantabai Gangarde v. Keru Anant Gangarde, 1991 (2) Bom CR 336
Valliammal v. Muniyappan, 2008(4) CTC 773
Valsaraian v. Saraswathy, II (2003) DMC 344
Varalaxmi Charka @ Renuka v. Satyanarayana Charka, AIR 2008 AP 134
Vasanti v. Pharez John Abraham, AIR 2007 Kant 121
Velayudhan Kochappi v. Sirkar, 1915 TLJ (5) 398
Vellayammal v. Ramaswami Naicken, 1934 Mad W N 825
Vidyaben v. Jagdishchandra Nandshankar Bhatt, 1972 INDLAW GUJ 45
Vidyadhar v. Kamlabai, 1986 (II) MPWN 259
Vidyadhari v. Sukhrana Bai, 2008 INDLAW SC 79
Vineeta Devi v. Bablu Thakur & State of Jharkhand, 2011 INDLAW JHKD 239
Vinita Saxena v. Pankaj Pandit, JT 2006 (3) SC 587
Viramallu Swarajya Lakshmi Mancharamma v. Viramallu Satyanarayana, AIR 1950 Mad 356
Virasangappa v. Rudrappa, (1885) ILR 8 Mad 444

Viraswami Chetty v. Appaswami Chetty, (1864) 1 Mad HCR 375
Virendra Kumar v. Preeta, 2009 INDLAW MUM 212
Vishnu B. Mayekar v. Smt. Laxmi V. Mayekar, II (2000) DMC 727
Vishnu Dutt Sharma v. Manju Sharma, I (2009) DMC 515 SC
Vishwa Lochan Madan v. Union of India Writ Petition (Civil) No. 386/2005
Vuyyuri Potharaju v. Vuyyuri Radha, AIR 1965 AP 407
Wood v. Wood, (1877) ILR 3 Cal 485
Wright v. Wright (1948) 77 CLR 191
Writ Petition No. 1001 of 1986
Writ Petition No. 8505 of 1988-N
Writ Petition No. 4319 of 1991-N
Writ Petitions No. 996, 1001, 1055, 1062 of 1986, 868 of 1996 in *Danial Latifi v. Union of India and Ms. Susheela Gopalan v. Union of India*
Yamanji H. Jadhav v. Nirmala, 2002 INDLAW SC 81
Yamunabai Anantrao Adhav v. Anantrao Shivram Adhav, 84 Bom LR (1982), 298
Yamunabai Anantrao Adhav v. Anantrao Shivram Adhav, AIR 1988 SC 644
Yesu Bai v. Parasram, AIR 1933 Bom 21
Yethirejulu Neelaya v. Mudummuru Ramaswami, AIR 1973 AP 58
Zeenat Fatema Rashid v. Md. Iqbal Anwar, I (1993) DMC 49
Zulekha Begum alias Rahmathunnisa Begum v. Abdul Raheem, 2000(2) Kar LJ 70

STATUTES, AMENDMENTS, AND BILLS CITED

Age of Consent Act, 1891
Bombay Hindu Divorce Act, 1947
Child Marriage Restraint Act, 1929
Christian Adoption and Maintenance Bill (1982, 1993, 2003)
Christian Marriage and Matrimonial Causes Act, 1990
Christian Marriage and Matrimonial Causes Bill, 1962
Christian Marriage and Matrimonial Causes Bill, 1990
Christian Marriage Bill (1994, 1997, 2000)
Cochin Marumakkathayam Act (XXXIII of 1113)
Cochin Nayar Act, 1920
Cochin Thiyya Act (VII of 1107)
Cohin Makkathayam Thiyya Act (XVII of 1115)
Criminal Procedure Code, 1898
Criminal Procedure Code, 1973
Dissolution of Muslim Marriages Act, 1939
English Matrimonial Causes Act, 1857
Hindu Code Bill (HCB), 1948
Hindu Gains of Learning Act, 1930
Hindu Marriage Act (HMA), 1955
Hindu Marriage and Divorce Bill, 1952
Hindu Married Women's Right to Separate Residence and Maintenance Act (HMWRSRMA), 1946
Hindu Succession (Amendment) Act, 2005
Hindu Succession (Amendment) Bill, 2004
Hindu Succession (Andhra Pradesh Amendment) Act, 1986

Hindu Succession (Karnataka Amendment) Act, 1994
Hindu Succession (Maharashtra Amendment) Act, 1994
Hindu Succession (Tamil Nadu Amendment) Act, 1989
Hindu Succession Act, 1956
Hindu Widows Remarriage Act, 1856
Hindu Women's Right to Property Act, 1937
Indian Christian Marriage Act (ICMA), 1872
Indian Divorce (Amendment) Act, 2001
Indian Divorce Act (IDA), 1869
Indian Divorce Bill, 1997 (Draft Bill of CBCI, NCCI and JWP)
Indian Succession (Amendment) Bill, 1994
Kerala Joint Hindu Family System (Abolition) Act, 1975
Kerala Nambudiri Act, 1958
Madras Aliyasanthana Act, 1949
Madras Marumakkathayam Act, 1932
Madras Nambudiri Act, 1932
Marriage Laws (Amendment) Act, 1976
Marriage Laws (Amendment) Bill, 1981
Marriage Laws (Amendment) Bill, 2010
Married Women (Protection of Rights) Bill, 1994
Muslim Women (Protection of Rights On Divorce) Act (MWPRDA)), 1986
Mussulman Wakf Validating Act (MWVA), 1913
Travancore Ezhava Act (III of 1100K)
Travancore Krishnavaka Marumakkathayee Act (VII of 1115K)
Travancore Kshatriya Act (VII of 1108K)
Travancore Nanjinad Vellala Act (IV of 1101K)
Travancore Nayar Act, 1912 and 1925
Uttar Pradesh Land Laws (Amendment) Act, 1982

INTERVIEWS
Ali Anwar, President, Pasmanda Muslim Mahaz. (Delhi), July 20, 2007
Arun Jaitley, Union Law Minister, 2000–2004 (Delhi), June 30, 2007
Ayatollah Syed Aqeel-ul Gharavi, Vice-President, Muslim Majlis-e-Mushawarat (Delhi), July 30, August 4, 2007
Bader Sayeed, lawyer (Chennai), January 15 and February 12, 2003
Begum Naseem Iktidhar Ali, only woman member, AIMPLB Executive Committee (Lucknow), August 11, 2006
Bina Agarwal, scholar of property and inheritance law and mobilizer to amend HSA and Shariat Act (Delhi), June 9, 28, July 13, 17, 19, 31, 2007
Bishop Santhram, former General Secretary, Church of North India (Agra), July 14, 2007
Cardinal Oswald Gracias, Archbishop of Bombay, Roman Catholic Church, and President, Catholic Bishops' Conference of India (Mumbai), August 3, 2007
Colin Gonsalves, Founder, Human Rights Law Network (Delhi), June 12, 2007
D. Purandeswari, Congress Party parliamentarian and daughter of N.T. Rama Rao, who piloted Hindu Succession (Andhra Pradesh Amendment) Act, July 29, 2007
D. Sharifa, President, STEPS (Chennai), February 22, 2003

Dr. Ejaz Ali, President, All India United Muslim Morcha (Delhi), August 5, 2007
Dr. John Dayal, President, All India Catholic Union (Delhi), July 26 and 29, 2006
Dr. Julian Francis, Legal Counsel, National Council of Churches of India (Delhi), July 24, 2006
Dr. Kande Prasada Rao, General Secretary, Christian Law Review Committee, July 1 & 5, 2007
Dr. Qasim Rasool Ilyas, Secretary and Convenor of Babri Masjid Committee, AIMPLB (Delhi), April 10, 2003; July 20, 2007
Dr. Rajeev Dhavan, lawyer and legal scholar (Delhi), April 15, 2001; April 18, 2003; June 15, 20, 2006
Dr. Sughra Mehdi, President, Muslim Women's Forum (Delhi), July 18, 2006
Dr. Tahir Mahmood, legal scholar; former member, Minorities Commission; member, Law Commission of India (Delhi), April 5, 2003, July 21, 2006
Dr. Veena Mazumdar, former member, Committee on the Status of Women in India (Delhi), April 10, 12, 2001, May 3, 2003
Durai Murugan, DMK; Law Minister of Tamil Nadu, 2006–2011 (Chennai), August 15, 2007
E. M. Sudarsana Natchiappan, Congress Party parliamentarian and Chair of the Department Related Parliamentary Standing Committee on Personnel, Public Grievances, Law and Justice that reframed Hindu Succession (Amendment) Act, 2005 (Delhi), June 14, 18, 25, 2007
Fr. Savio Coutinho, former Secretary, Catholic Bishops Conference of India (Delhi), June 28, 2006
Gargi Chakravartty, Working President, NFIW (Delhi), July 19, 2007
Geeta Ramaseshan, lawyer (Chennai), January 13, 15, 20, February 1, 3, 7, 2003
Habeebulla Basha, lawyer (Chennai), February 28, 2003
Indira Jaising, lawyer (Delhi), July 3, 2006
Jos Chiramel, former National Secretary for Legal Affairs, AICU, and Legal Counsel, CBCI (Delhi), August 3, 2006
Justice A. Abdul Hadi, retired judge, Madras High Court (Chennai), February 24, 2003
Justice Aziz M. Ahmadi, Former Chief Justice of India (Delhi), July 9, 2007
Justice B. P. Jeevan Reddy, retired Supreme Court justice and Chair of Law Commission, 1997–2001 (Chennai), August 13, 2007
Justice Badar Durrez Ahmed, judge, Delhi High Court (Delhi), August 1, 2007
Justice D. P. Mohapatra, retired judge, Supreme Court of India (Delhi), August 2, 2007
Justice Doraiswamy Raju, retired judge, Supreme Court of India (Chennai), August 7, 2007
Justice G. B. Pattanaik, retired judge, Supreme Court of India (Delhi), June 30, 2007
Justice K. Chandru, lawyer and former judge, Madras High Court, February 3, 2003
Justice Leila Seth, retired judge, Supreme Court of India, member of Law Commission, 1997–2000 (Delhi), June 5, 2007
Justice M.B. Shah, former judge, Gujarat High Court & Supreme Court, July 5, 2007
Justice M. Jagannadha Rao, retired judge, Supreme Court of India, Chair of Law Commission, 2002–6 (Delhi), June 28, 2007
Justice P. A. Choudary, judge of Andhra Pradesh High Court, 1980–95 (Hyderabad, over phone), February 23, 2003
Justice P. Venkatarama Reddi, retired judge, Supreme Court of India (Delhi), July 2, 2007

Justice S. Rajendra Babu, former Chief Justice of India (Delhi), July 2 and 3, 2007
Justice Ramesh Chandra Lahoti, former Chief Justice of India (Delhi), June 26, 2007
Justice S. A. Kader, retired judge, Madras High Court (Chennai), February 2, 2003
Justice S. Muralidhar, judge, Delhi High Court, and member, Law Commission, 2003–2006 (Delhi), July 29, August 1, 3, 5, 2007
Justice Shivaraj C. Patil, retired judge, Supreme Court of India (Delhi), June 21, 2007
Justice V. R. Krishna Iyer, retired judge, Supreme Court of India (Kochi), August 1, 2006
Justice Vikramjit Sen, judge, Delhi High Court (Delhi), July 24, 2007
Justice Y. V. Chandrachud, former Chief Justice of India (Mumbai, over phone), July 15, 30, 2007
Jyotsna Chatterji, founding President, Joint Women's Programme (Delhi), May 3, 2003, June 19 and 24, 2006
K. A. Sukkur, litigant in *Parveen Akhtar* case (Chennai), March 20, 2003
Kamini Jaiswal, lawyer (Delhi), April 15, 2003
Kirti Singh, Legal Convenor, AIDWA (Delhi), April 30, 2003, June 10, 2006
Maimoona Mollah, Convenor, Muslim Women Sub-Committee, AIDWA (Delhi), April 15, 2003
Mary Khemchand, former President, YWCA (Delhi), July 5, 2006
Maulana Abdul Wahab Khilji, former General Secretary, Jamaat Ahl-i-Hadith, and President, All India Milli Council (Delhi), July 2, 2006
Maulana Amin Osmani, Vice-President, Islamic Fiqh Academy (Delhi), July 18 and 29, 2006
Maulana Ateeq Ahmed Bastvi, Convenor, Darul Qaza Committee, AIMPLB (Lucknow), August 10, 2006
Maulana Jaseemuddin, Chief Qazi, Imarat-e-Shariah (Phulwari Sharif, Bihar), August 1 and 2, 2006
Maulana Kalbe Sadiq, Vice-President, AIMPLB (Lucknow), August 11, 2006
Maulana Khalid Rashid, Naib Imam, Firangi Mahal (Lucknow), August 10, 2006
Maulana Khalid Saifullah Rehmani, President, Islamic Fiqh Academy, and Convenor, Nikahnama Committee, AIMPLB (Delhi), July 16, 2007
Maulana Mehmood Madani, President, Jamiat Ulama-i-Hind (Delhi), July 7, 2007
Maulana Mirza Mohammad Athar, President, All India Shia Personal Law Board (Lucknow), August 10, 2006
Maulana Mohammad Burhanuddin Sambhali, Chief Qazi, Darul Uloom Nadwatul Ulama, and President, Fiqh Committee, AIMPLB (Lucknow), August 10, 2006
Maulana Syed Jalaluddin Umri, President, Jamaat-i-Islami Hind (Delhi), April 10, 2003
Maulana Yasin Akhtar Misbahi, Founder & President, Darul Qalam (Delhi), June 15, 2007
Mohammad Abdul Rahim Quraishi, Secretary, AIMPLB (Delhi), July 22, 2006, July 15, 2007
Mufti Mukarram Ahmed, Shahi Imam of Fatehpuri Masjid (Delhi), July 3, 2007
M. Nizamuddin, General Secretary, AIMPLB and President, Imarat-e-Shariah (Delhi), July 15, 2007
Obaidullah Khan Azmi, Member of Parliament, Congress Party and later Samajwadi Party, (Delhi), June 17, 2007
Pappa Umanath, CPI-M (Chennai), February 15, 2003

P. H. Pandian, AIADMK (Chennai), August 10, 2007
Pramila Loomba, Vice-President, National Federation of Indian Women, June 16, 2007
P. V. S. Giridhar, lawyer (Chennai), February 28, March 3, 2003
Ram Jethmalani, Union Law Minister, 1998–2000 (Delhi), July 5, 2007
Rev. Richard Howell, General Secretary, Evangelical Fellowship of India (Delhi), August 19, 2006
Shaista Amber, President, All India Muslim Women's Personal Law Board (Lucknow), August 11, 2006
Sheila Jayaprakash, lawyer (Chennai), January 4, 2003
Shikoh Azad, Joint Secretary, All India Shia Personal Law Board (Lucknow), August 10, 2006
Soli Sorabjee, former Attorney General and former Solicitor General of India, July 14, 2007
Sona Khan, lawyer in *Danial Latifi* (Delhi), May 5, 2003, July 5, 2006
Subhashini Ali, President, AIDWA (Delhi), June 25, 2006
Sudha Ramalingam, lawyer (Chennai), January 18, 23, 27, 2003
Sudha Sundararaman, General Secretary, AIDWA (Delhi), June 20, 22, 2006
Syed Mohammad Rabey Hasni Nadwi, President, AIMPLB (Lucknow), August 10, 2006
Syed Saif Mahmood, lawyer (Delhi), July 21, 2006
Syed Shahabuddin, President, Muslim Majlis-e-Mushawarat (Delhi), April 25, 2003
Syeda Saiyidain Hameed, former President, Muslim Women's Forum (Delhi), July 16, 2006
Yusuf Hatim Muchchala, Convenor, AIMPLB Legal Committee (Delhi), July 1, 14 and 31, 2007
Zafaryab Jilani, lawyer and Member, AIMPLB Legal Committee (Delhi), July 12, 2006
Zaffarullah Khan, lawyer (Chennai), February 6, 2003

INDEX

Page numbers in italic indicate tables.

A. Annamalai Mudaliar v. Perumayee Ammal (1965), 170, 171
Abbayolla M. Subba Reddy v. Padmamma (1998), 179
Abduh, Muhammad, 48
A. Bhagavathi Ammal v. Sethu (1986), 160
adat: defined, 37; Dutch attitudes toward, 78–79; family disputes regulated according to, 37, 51, 273; Indonesian judges and, 51, 273, 277–278, 294n71; and Indonesian minority law reform, 80–81, 276–277; orientations of Indonesian nationalists toward, 50, 79–81; religious judges' orientation toward, 37, 277–278
adoption, *illatom*, 173
adoption rights: and agenda for further personal-law reform in India, 282; bill to provide, for all Indians, 86, 221, 235, 259; Christian law reform and, 218, 226–227, 253–254, 259–262, 265, 320nn115–118; Christian mobilization for, 65, 87, 226–228, 234, 253, 262, 264, 285; for Christians, 65, 87, 90, 205, 215, 218, 235–236, 263, 281–282, 285, 320n115; of Hindus, 107, 111, 301n12; and Muslims, 221–222, 235, 252; and recognition of custom, 111, 218, 233, 260–261, 320n115; Special Marriage Act and, 111, 128, 129; in Turkey and Tunisia, 54
adultery: false charges of, and divorce, 149–150, 160, 171–172, 303nn34–35; as grounds for divorce, 12, 110–111, 119–120, 128, 143–145, 153–158, 197, 254–258, 303n36, 305n39; Indian Divorce Act and, 128, 218–219, 254–258; maintenance rights and, 157–158, 305n51, 305n53
Afghanistan, 6, 71–72
Agarwal, Bina: on conjugality, 106; on determinants of legal change, 105–106; on federalism and Shariat Act amendment, 293n59; on Hindu inheritance law reforms, 104–105; on Kerala Joint Hindu Family System (Abolition) Act, 186; on kinship practices, 39–40, 121;

Agarwal, Bina (*continued*)
    on kinship practices and inheritance, 39–40, 104–105, 187; on land rights, 39–40, 104–105, 125, 180; on national inheritance law reform, 191–192; on regional customs and orientations to family law, 39–40; role in national inheritance reform, 191, 193; on succession law, 180
Agnes, Flavia: on adultery as grounds for divorce, 154; on changes in Hindu law, 101–102; on cruelty as grounds for divorce, 148–149; on desertion as grounds for divorce, 159; on judicial view of choice of residential location, 172; on polygamy and maintenance rights, 177; on women's rights, 132–133
Ahmad, Naziruddin, 97, 220
Ahmedabad Women's Action Group (AWAG) v. Union of India (1997), 251
Algeria, regime, coalitions and limited reform in, 47–48, 57, 71, 77
Ali, Begum Sharifa Hamid, 212, 223, 240, 293n61
Ali, Subhashini, 193
alimony. *See* maintenance rights
All India Anna Dravida Munnetra Kazhagam (AIADMK), 188, 301n3
All India Catholic Union (AICU), 226, 228, 229, 231
All India Muslim (Jadeed) Personal Law Board, 223
All India Muslim Personal Law Board (AIMPLB), 86–87, 211, 221–226, 244
All India Shia Personal Law Board, 223
All India Women's Conference (AIWC), 25, 94, 97, 191, 212, 291n15, 311n150
Ambedkar, B. R.: on application of Hindu law to Sikhs, Jains, and Buddhists, 111; on divorce rights, 85, 113–114, 119; formation of jurisprudence of, 109–110, 298n32; on Hindu inheritance law reforms, 85, 88, 103, 114–116, 122; on judicial interpretation, 109–110, 134; personal-law reform under, 83; as proponent of legal consolidation, 109–110; on recognition of customs, 85, 110, 113–114, 134; reliance on *shastras*, 85,

113–114; on Special Marriage Act, 128; on Uniform Civil Code, 108
Anjuman-Khavatin-i-Islam, 97, 212
anticolonial nationalists: and colonial discourse, institutions, and policies, 23–28; in India, 24–25, 28, 69, 83–87; indigenous cultural traditions and, 67, 272, 278; modernity and authenticity and, 23, 68–69; support of, for social reform efforts, 24–25
Article 13 of Constitution, 98, 99
Article 25 of Constitution, 98, 102
Aruna Parmod Shah v. Union of India (2008), 179
Arya Kumar Bal v. Smt. Ila Bal (1968), 178
Asha Rani v. Gulshan Kumar (1995), 164
Ashwini Kumar Sehgal v. Smt. Swatantra Sehgal (1979), 151–152
Ataturk, Mustafa Kemal Pasa, 72–75, 276, 296n96
authenticity: and modernity in national narratives, 66–70; visions of, in India, 83–87
autonomist movements, responses to, 44–45
A. Yousuf Rawther v. Sowramma (1971), 248
Ayyar, Panchapakesa, 254

Babu, S. Rajendra, 233, 244–245
Baburao v. Mst. Sushila Bai (1964), 170
Baig, Mahboob Ali, 219–220
Bai Jiva v. Narsingh Lalbhai (1927), 307n89
Bai Tahira v. Ali Hussain Fisalli Chothia (1979), 238–239
Bangladesh, 6, 39, 56, 60, 200–201
Basu, Srimati, 133, 237
Beg, Mirza Hameedullah, 150
Belgium, 64
Bhagat (1994), 152–153
Bhargava, Rajeev, 42, 44–45
Bhargava, Thakur Das, 115, 116
Bhattacharjee, A. M., 232–233
Bhausaheb alias Sandu Magar v. Leelabai (2004), 179
bigamy: and assessment of desertion claims, 159; Christian law reform and, 236; as grounds for divorce, 120, 159, 205, 218, 237, 317n69; and Hindu marriage law

reform, 116, 118, 119, 133; and Hindu norms, 118–119; laws against, 118–119; maintenance rights and, 133, 162, 170, 171, 178–179; prevalence of practice, 42, 118; restitution of conjugality and, 170, 171; women's rights and laws against, 118, 132–133. *See also* polygyny

Bipin Chander Jaisinghbhai Shah v. Prabhawati (1956), 159

Birla, Ritu, 36

Biswas, Charu Chandra, 108, 115, 127, 128

Bombay Hindu Divorce Act (1947), 306n71

Bourguiba, Habib, 53, 72–73

Bowen, John, 37

Brass, Paul, 42–43, 207

Britain, 19, 39, 64, 69, 109

Buddhists, application of Hindu law to, 111

Cammack, Mark, 37

Canada, 5, 39, 64

caste: adultery and spousal maintenance and, 305n53; and Christian adoption, 260–261, 320n115; Christian conversion and, 204, 213, 214, 290n11, 293n64; and Christian religious practice and Christian mobilization, 213–214, 229; customary divorces and, 86, 161–164, 307n78; customs, Hindu cultural mobilization, and Hindu law, 12–15, 38, 40, 86, 95, 113–114, 298n46; customs and their judicial recognition, 9, 79, 85, 110, 161–164, 173, 260–261; and divorce, 85, 86, 101, 113–114, 119, 229, 298n42; Muslim law reforms and, 43, 95, 209–210; and Muslim reform initiatives, 82, 209, 224; and patriliny, patrilocality, and matrimonial relations, 170, 174, 187; and preferential policies, 7, 44, 83, 87, 294n66, 301n3; and social relations, 10, 14–15, 67, 83. *See also* intercaste marriage, recognition of

catchall regimes, 47, 48–49, 52, 57

Catholic Church: adoption and, 260, 261; Christian mobilization and, 213; divorce law reform and, 226, 229, 257; and marriage solemnization, 218, 226; and mobilization regarding Christian law, 226, 229–230

Chakravartty, Renu, 115, 117, 122, 125, 299n75, 300n85, 307n87

Chandrachud, Y. V., 150, 240–241, 303n37, 317n69, 318n86

Chanmuniya v. Virendra Kumar Singh Kushwaha (2010), 179–180

Charrad, Mounira: on Islamic law, 21–22, 35–37; on nationalism, 22, 291n9; on state, lineage, and family law, 21–22, 31, 35

Chatterjee, Partha, 23–24, 25, 26, 44, 291n11, 292n31

Chatterji, Jyotsna, 227

China, 63, 199–200

Chiriyankandath, James, 42–43

Choudary, P. A., 167–168

Christian Institute for the Study of Religion and Society, 227, 256, 320n109

Christian law: and adoption, 90, 111, 205, 228, 235–236, 259–261, 264, 282, 285, 320n115; basis of, 8, 96; and conjugal rights, 99; courts and contentious questions in, 217–219; divorce rights and reform to, 87, 89, 128, 153, 168, 205, 218–219, 227, 228, 229–230, 234–235, 254–259, 320n113; in Egypt, 60, 65, 295n85; as influence on Hindu law, 116; judges reforming, 233; legal reform and, 44; mobilization regarding, 87, 213–214, 226–231, 264–265, 315n42; Muslim law reform and, 263, 268–269; postcolonial policy formation and, 96; reforms in, 87, 233–234, 252–262; understandings of religious tradition's influence on, 87, 234–235; women's rights under, 116, 131–132. *See also* minority law

Christians: accommodation for, 65, 264, 296n95; perceptions of postcolonial roles of, 202, 203–204; population share of, 230, 290n11, 293n64. *See also* Christian law

Church of North India, 227, 228, 231, 315n41

Church of South India, 320n109

coalitions: and accommodation of minorities, 65, 200–201; influence of, 273–274; opposing *Shah Bano*, 239; regimes and, 47–57; and regimes in nation and family formation, 274–275; state-society relations and personal-law reform and, 71–72

C. Obula Konda Reddy v. C. Pedda Venkata Lakshmamma (1976), 177, 178, 179
Code of Criminal Procedure, 153–154, 174–175, 176, 237, 238, 239–240, 241–242, 243, 244–245, 246, 247, 249
colonial personal law: changes to, after independence, 4–6, 33–34, 292n35; colonial knowledge and classification schemes' influence on, 32; in India, 8–16; postcolonial policy formation and, 94, 111–114; property control under, 37; regional customs incorporated in, 38–39; religious norms in, 33; and rights and strategies of colonized groups, 24
colonial state(s): consolidation of state authority in, 272–273; and formation of nation and family in India, 278; interference of, in religious practice, 95–96; support for reform efforts of, 24–25
Committee on the Status of Women in India (CSWI), 140, 144, 146, 147, 185, 284
Congress Party: anticolonial mobilization by, 25; and Christian law, 236–237; decline of, 138; and early postcolonial personal law reform, 16, 74, 76, 103, 115, 117; Hindu Code Bill and, 117; inheritance law reform and, 187, 188, 191, 192; and Muslim law, 42, 212–213, 220, 242; national inheritance reform and, 192; social outlooks in, 16, 28, 81, 83–85; and women's organizations, 94
conjugal rights: Christian law reform and, 260; enforcement of, 165–166; Hindu law reform and, 99, 106–107; maintenance rights and, 176–177; restitution and contestation of, 166–173, 196–197
Constituent Assembly, 84, 97–99, 219–220, 242
Constitution of India, 43, 45, 84, 87, 92, 98–100, 101, 102, 105, 108, 145, 183, 185, 193, 219–220, 293n59; and case law, 99, 147, 167–169, 171, 172–173, 197, 206, 221, 233, 236, 237, 238–239, 243–245, 249–251, 256–257, 260, 264–265, 308n108
constitutional law, comparative, 1, 2, 33, 42, 45, 50–51, 52, 60, 67, 80, 145, 296n95
constructive desertion, 159, 160

Cott, Nancy, 19
Criminal Procedure Code Sections 125 and 127(3)(b), 237, 238, 239–240, 241–242, 243, 244–245, 246, 247, 249
cruelty, as grounds for divorce, 110–111, 143–145, 148–153, 156, 173, 196, 218, 256, 257, 258, 301n8, 302n19, 303nn33–34, 303–304n39, 304n40, 304n42, 317n69
cruelty *simpliciter*, 149
cultural accommodation: forms of, 40–41, 60–61, 64, 73, 78–81, 89–90, 198–201; national consolidation and, 267–269
cultural accommodation in India: and alimony rights of Muslim women, 247; forms of, 7; minority-law reform and, 42–43, 97–98, 201–206, 262–264
cultural change, 65–66
cultural diversity, 59–62, 199–201, 268–269
cultural stability, 65–66
cultures, indigenous. *See* indigenous cultures
customary divorces, 161–165, 307n78, 307n80
custom(s): adjudication and, 78–79; debates over inheritance law and recognition of, 114–116; and determination of extent of *mata*, 247; divorce and recognition of, 161–165; Hindu consolidation and recognition of, 111; of *illatom* adoption, 173; Muslim law reforms and, 82, 209–210; policy makers' views on recognition of, 110, 113–114; religious norms and social structure and, 33–40; responses of Islamic scholars to, 37, 79–83
Czechoslovakia, 64

Dadaji Bhikaji v Rukhmabai (1885–6), 166–167
Danial Latifi v. Union of India (2001), 233, 234, 244, 245–247, 255, 317n69
Darul Uloom Deoband, 10, 97, 208, 209, 223, 224
Darul Uloom Manzar-e-Islam, 208, 209, 223, 224
Dastane (1975), 150–151, 303nn36–37
Dayabhaga law, 79, 104; influence of, on postcolonial policy formation, 85, 111–112, 120–121; inheritance under, 112, 114, 121, 310n134; joint property under, 104, 135
Dayal Singh v. Bhajan Kaur (1973), 178

INDEX

Dehlavi, Shah Waliullah, 207
Deo, R. N. Singh, 117
Department of Women and Child Development, 140–141, 188
desertion, as grounds for divorce, 158–160, 173, 218, 256, 257, 258, 302n19, 306n71
Deshmukh, G. V., 298n39
Deshpande, V. G., 113
Deshpande, V. S., 172
Dhanalakshmi (1975), 172–173
discourses of community: development of, 58–59; features of state-society relations and, 47; modernity and authenticity in, 66; nation-community and modernity-authenticity in, 45–46; purposes of, 57–58; state-society relations and, 28–32
Dissolution of Muslim Marriages Act (DMMA), 11, 12, 211, 301n8, 313n9
diversity, cultural, 59–62
divorce: adultery as grounds for, 12, 110–111, 119–120, 128, 143–145, 153–158, 197, 254–258, 303n36, 305n39; bigamy as grounds for, 120, 159, 205, 218, 237, 317n69; under Christian law, 87, 89, 128, 153, 168, 205–206, 217–219, 227, 228, 229–230, 234–235, 254–259, 261–262, 320n113; conditions of, 196–197; cruelty as grounds for, 110–111, 143–145, 148–153, 156, 173, 196, 218, 256, 257, 258, 301n8, 302n19, 303nn33–34, 303–304n39, 304n40, 304n42, 317n69; customary, 161–165, 307n78, 307n80; desertion as grounds for, 158–160, 173, 218, 256, 257, 258, 302n19, 306n71; under Dissolution of Muslim Marriages Act, 313n9; Hindu law reform and, 142–160; irretrievable marital breakdown as grounds for, 147–148; and mobilization regarding Christian law, 87, 226–230; and mobilization regarding Muslim law, 222–223, 224–225; Muslim initiatives regarding, 211–212; under Muslim law, 205–206, 215–217; unilateral male repudiation and, 43, 55, 89, 160, 163–164, 205, 212, 215–216, 224–225, 232, 234, 247–251, 263–264, 282, 284; women-initiated, 118–119, 163–164, 251, 306n76. *See also* divorce rights

divorce rights: and agenda for further personal-law reform in India, 281, 283; Christian law reform and, 87, 89, 128, 153, 168, 205–206, 217–219, 227, 228, 229–230, 234–235, 254–259, 261–262, 320n113; of Christians and Hindus, 320n113; Hindu law reform and, 88, 89, 106–107, 118–120, 142–160; under Hindu Marriage Act, 175; modernist reforms and, 34; in postcolonial policy formation, 113–114; Special Marriage Act and, 128, 130; women's rights and, 135, 316n63. *See also* maintenance rights
Dravida Munnetra Kazhagam (DMK), 188, 301n3
Dravida subschool of *Mitakshara* law, 181, 186
Dr. Narayan Ganesh Dastane v. Mrs. Sucheta Naryan Dastane (1975), 150–151, 303n36
Dwaraka Bai v. Professor Nainan Mathews (1953), 254–255

economy: and postcolonial social reforms, 26–28; women's inheritance rights and, 124–125
Ecumenical Committee for Changes in Christian Personal Laws, 228–229, 259
Edla Neelaya v. Edla Ramada alias Ramadas (1995), 165
Egypt: constitutional role of *sharia* in, 60, 268–269; Coptic Christian law in, 60, 65, 200–201; cultural diversity in, 60; as example of catchall regime, 48–49, 57; as example of moderate reform, 5–6, 6, 7, 19, 57, 76–77; marginalization of Christian minority in, 65; state courts in family law in, 61
employment, restitution of conjugality and, 172–173
European states, and regulation of family, 19

family: discourses of nation and community and regulation of, 59–62; formation of, 35–37, 266–271; formation of, in India, 278–281; influences over approaches to formation of, 45–47, 271–277; inheritance and patrilineal visions of, 121–126; modernist views on, 137–138; modernity

family (continued)
    and authenticity and regulation of, 66–70; shift from lineage to nuclear, 5, 21–22, 70, 88, 96, 139; visions of, in India, 83–87. See also inheritance; joint family system
family law. See personal law
Feener, Michael, 37
female ultimogeniture, 300n92
fiqh, 11, 94
Fischer, Alexander, 42–43
Foucault, Michel, 20, 31–32
France, recognition of religion in, 40–41, 59, 68
Free Officers regime, 48–49, 276
Friedman, Lawrence, on changes in Western family law, 20, 30, 33
Front de Libération Nationale (FLN), 48, 77
Fulchand Maganlal v. Unknown (1928), 154
Fuzlunbi v. Khader Vali (1980), 238–239
Fyzee, Asaf Ali, 97, 203, 208, 240, 293n61

Gajendragadkar, P. B., 145–146, 301n12
Gandhi, Mohandas ("Mahatma"), 15–16, 24, 28, 81, 204, 214
Gandhi, Rajiv, 242
Gandhi, Sonia, 191, 194
Gandhians, 83–84
gender equality: in Christian divorce rights, 254–258; Christian law reform and, 265
gender inequalities: in inheritance law, 181–184; in personal law, 4
Gerschenkron, Alexander, 27
Gita Masand v. Narain Dass (1985), 156–157
Gokalp, Ziya, 73
Government of India Act (1935), 293n59, 313n8
Govindaraju v. Munisami Gounder (1997), 163–164
Govindrao Ranoji Musale v. Sou. Anandibai (1976), 177, 178, 179
Govind v. State of M.P. (1975), 297n9
G.V.N. Kameshwara Rao v. G. Jabilli (2002), 152–153

Hafeezuddin, Begum, 212
Hanafi law, 11–12, 56, 209, 211, 212, 215, 216, 217, 239–240, 251

Hanumanthappa, N. Y., 192
Harvinder Kaur (1984), 168–169
Hill, Christopher, 27
Hindu Adoptions and Maintenance Act (HAMA), 107, 175–176, 177, 178
Hindu Code Bill (HCB), 107, 116, 117, 120–121, 122, 124, 128, 185, 310n132
Hindu Gains of Learning Act, 36
Hindu law: application of, to non-Hindus, 79, 111, 220; basis of, 8, 12, 94–95; changes proposed in, soon after independence, 111–112; conjugal rights under, 99, 143–144, 166–173; consolidation of, 107, 108, 110–111, 116; focus on, reform in postcolonial policy formation, 97–100; Indian postcolonial reforms in, 87–89, 137–138, 279; influence of other personal-law systems on, 116–117; legal reform and, 16, 42; lineage authority under, 93–94, 102–103, 104–105, 115–116, 123, 138, 139, 180–181, 182–183, 186–188, 279; nature of changes in, in postcolonial policy formation, 100–107; proposals to codify, 109–110; regional customs and, 38–39; relationship of reform proposals in, to classical and colonial Hindu law, 111–115; religious mobilization and, 12–13; traditional elites' views on, 84–85; women's rights under, 131–133. See also postcolonial policy formation
Hindu Law (Mulla), 170
Hindu Law Committees, 107, 111–112, 113, 114, 120, 166
Hindu Marriage Act (HMA): adultery as grounds for divorce under, 144; adultery as grounds for separation under, 110–111, 119–120, 143, 153; antibigamy clause of, 118, 133; bigamy as grounds for divorce under, 120; conjugal rights under, 167, 173; custom defined under, 162; desertion as grounds for divorce under, 158–159; Hindu consolidation and, 110–111; maintenance and divorce rights under, 175; polygamy and maintenance rights under, 177; solemnization and dissolution of marriage under, 161; Special Marriage Act versus, 127

INDEX 367

Hindu Married Women's Right to Separate Residence and Maintenance Act (HMWRSRMA), 175, 177, 309n111
Hindu nationalism: and claim to advocate secular and gender-equal laws, 135–136,; and demand to adopt a UCC, 15, 113, 115–116, 139, 222, 241, 279–280, 282, 285; growth of, 205, 225–226, 279–280; Indian nationalists and, 15; influence of, 223, 225, 233–234, 259, 263; minority law and, 222, 233–234, 259, 263; and Muslim resistance to personal-law reform, 247; and opposition to early postcolonial Hindu law reform, 113; Pataskar and, 108, 110, 111; *Shah Bano* and, 1–2, 222; women's rights and, 141
Hindu Succession (Amendment) Act, 190–195, 312n159
Hindu Succession Act (HSA), 101, 107, 122–124, 125, 175, 181–184, 300n84, 310n123
Holden, Livia, 161, 162, 163, 164, 306n76
home, matrimonial: location of, 170–171, 172–173, 196–197; rights to share of, 104, 134, 142–143, 158, 197, 280, 315n44, 316n63
homogeneity, cultural, 59–62
Honamma v. Timannabhat (1877), 154
Hussain, Kazi Ahmad, 130

ibn Abidin, Muhammad Amin, 209, 313n5
iddat, 117; maintenance during and perhaps after, 237–238, 239, 242, 243, 245, 246, 248, 249, 251; and validity of unilateral repudiation, 216–217
ijtihad, 11, 94, 207–208, 211, 215
illatom adoption, 173
Imam, Hussain, 97, 220
Indian Christian Marriage Act (ICMA), 218, 236, 253, 260
Indian Divorce (Amendment) Act, 258–259
Indian Divorce Act (IDA): adjudication with reference to, 235, 254–259; amendment of, 256–257; and cruelty as grounds for divorce, 301n8; gendered grounds for divorce in, 128, 254; limitations of, 128; stipulations of, 218–219
Indian nationalism: and colonial institutions, 69, 278–279; and formation of nation and family in India, 278; and Hindu majoritarianism, 44, 61–62, 92–93, 201–202, 203; legal reform and, 14–16; modernity and authenticity and, 69; Muslim approaches to, 203, 209; and perception of Christians, 203–204, 214; and perception of Muslims, 92, 203; and pluralism, 67, 81, 201–202; support of, for social reform efforts, 24–25, 103
Indian Succession Act (ISA), 129, 130, 184, 217, 227, 229, 259
indigenous cultures: changing, 66; and Indian minority law reform, 81; Indian Muslim law and, 82; Indonesian Islamic law and, 83; recognition of, 278
Indonesia: coalitions and family-law reforms in, 274; consolidation of state authority in, 272; cultural diversity in, 22, 61, 62; as example of moderate reform, 19, 50–52, 76–77; formation of, 270–271; kin relations in, 37; matrimonial property, 34, 247; minority law reform in, 61–62, 78–83, 269; minority laws in Malaysia and, 294n72; modernity and authenticity in, 67; multiculturalism and family law in, 268, 276–277; nationalism and secularism adopted in, 27, 276–277, 287–288; perception of minorities, 65; regimes and personal-law reform in, 50–52, 76–77; religious law and ethnic custom in, 38, 39, 61, 62, 201, 273
inheritance: and agenda for further personal-law reform in India, 281–285; of agricultural land among Muslims, 11, 43, 210–211, 293nn59–60; changes in provisions in particular states concerning, after passage of Hindu Succession Act, 184–188; and changes to Hindu Code Bill, 117; Christian law and, 217, 218, 227, 229, 259; colonial marriage law and, 126; consequences of Hindu Succession Act, 181–184; under *Dayabhaga* and *Mitakshara* schools, 96, 112, 114, 310n134; and formation of Hindu Succession Act, 120–126; Hindu law reform and, 88–89, 101–102, 104–105, 279; and Indonesian minority law reform, 80–81; Indonesian

inheritance (*continued*)
    personal-law reform and, 51, 52; and
    mobilization regarding Christian law, 228;
    and mobilization regarding Muslim law,
    222–223; under Muslim law, 104, 210–211,
    215; in postcolonial policy formation,
    114–116, 120–126; process of national
    reform of laws concerning, 188–195; reform
    to, 142–143, 180, 197–198; regional customs
    and, 38; Shariat Act and, 43, 210–211,
    293nn59–60; under Shia law, 37; Special
    Marriage Act and, 130; testamentary rights
    and, 54, 115, 117, 122, 123, 125–126, 132, 133,
    135, 182, 187, 189, 190, 191, 193–195, 198,
    280–281, 282, 283–284, 312n159; Turkish
    and Tunisian personal-law reforms and,
    54; views on Indian laws regarding, 85–86;
    women's rights and, 39–40, 132, 133,
    280–281, 298n39
intercaste marriage, recognition of, 88, 107,
    112, 117–118, 126, 127, 129, 252, 279
intrakin marriage, 117–118, 130, 187
Iqbal, Mohammad, 208
Iran, kinship in, and Ithna Ashari law, 37;
    conservative Islamization in, 54–56;
    modernity and authenticity in, 66–67,
    69–70
Iraq, 77
irretrievable marital breakdown, 138, 144, 146,
    147–148, 281, 283, 302n19, 302n22
Islam, Baharul, 232, 233, 248
Islamic *Fiqh* Academy, 223–224, 316n64
Islamic law. *See* Muslim law
Ismail, Mohammad, 219–220
Israel: immigration and, 295n84; majoritarian
    nationalism in, 59–60; minority laws in,
    60, 201; polygyny in, 42; religious courts
    in, 270
Itwari v. Smt. Asghari Begum and Others
    (1960), 317n69
Iyer, V. R. Krishna, 232, 233, 248, 257

Jacobsohn, Gary, 41–43, 45, 100
Jairam Somaji More v. Sindhubai (1999), 165
Jaitley, Arun, 233–234, 259, 314n29
Jal Kaur v. Pala Singh (1961), 178
Jethmalani, Ram, 194, 235, 260, 314n29

Jiauddin Ahmed v. Anwar Begum (1978), 248, 250
Jina Magan Pakhali v. Bai Jethi, 162
Jinnah, Mohammad Ali, 24, 210
Joint Committees of the Central Legislative
    Assembly, 111–112, 114, 122
joint family system: abolition of, 187; decline of,
    135; and efforts to dissolve joint property,
    114, 120–121, 122, 193–194, 197, 282,
    283–284; and joint property, 96, 102–105,
    112, 122, 193–194; landholding groups and,
    36, 104–105; Majumdar on, 102–103; and
    Mitakshara law, 112; Natchiappan on,
    192; in organization of colonial Indian
    mercantile activity, 36; recognition of, 192,
    194; strong sentiment attached to, 114–115,
    117, 121, 312n158; support for, 104–105, 121,
    142; women's rights and, 184. *See also*
    inheritance; land ownership
Joint Women's Program (JWP), 226, 227–228,
    231
Jordan, 50
judicial separation, 119–120, 143, 150

Kaarvendhan, S. K., 192
*Kadia Harilal Purshottam v. Kadia Lilavati
    Gokaldas* (1961), 178
Kailash Wati v. Ayodhia Parkash (1977), 171
Karumpa Kocahppi v. Sirkar (1911), 162
Kasubai v. Bhagwan Bhagaji Wanjari (1955),
    309n111
Kerala, 105, 124, 134, 162, 165, 181, 183, 185,
    187–188, 211, 229, 230, 232, 234, 255, 256,
    260, 261, 292n36, 293n60
Kerala Joint Hindu Family System (Abolition)
    Act, 185–186, 189, 192, 193, 310n132
Keshaorao Krishnaji Londhe v. Nisha Londhe
    (1984), 152
Keshav Hargovan v. Bai Gandhi (1915), 162
Khan, Sayyid Ahmed, 208
Khomeini, Ayatollah, 54–55, 69–70
Kuppanna Goundan v. Palani Ammal (1955), 159
Kurien v. Alphonsa (1986), 261–262
Kusum Lata v. Kamta Prasad (1965), 303n33

Lahoti, Ramesh Chandra, 250–251
land ownership: Hindu law reform and, 103;
    Muslim women's rights and, 234, 281–283;

and postcolonial social reforms, 27;
Shariat Act and, 43, 210–211, 293nn59–60;
urbanization and industrialization's effect
on, 139; women's rights and, 39–40.
See also inheritance; property
Latif, Baji Rashida, 212
Latifi, Danial, 2, 239, 240, 241, 244
Law Commission: Christian law reform and,
168, 226, 228, 234–235, 256–257, 258; and
codification of Indian legal system, 109;
divorce law reform and, 144–146, 147,
152; *Fifty-Ninth Report*, 145, 152; national
Hindu inheritance law reform and,
188–190; *Ninetieth Report*, 256, 258
Law Ministry: Christian law reform and,
234–235, 253, 259; divorce law reform and,
119, 146, 148; inheritance law and, 122;
national inheritance reform and, 190, 191,
192, 194; women's rights and, 146
Lebanon, 19, 48, 64, 77, 200, 267
Lee Kuan Yew, 27
lineage authority: decline of, 180; over family
regulation, 21–22; Hindu law reform
and, 279; inheritance and, 182–183;
postcolonial policy formation and, 93–94;
urban groups and, 35
L. Mallya Naika v. Somli Bai (1978), 173

Madan Lal Sharma v. Smt. Santosh Sharma
(1980), 151, 152
Mahalingam Pillai v. Amsavalli (1956), 155
Maharshi Avadhesh v. Union of India (1994), 251
Mahmood, Tahir, 241
maintenance rights, 174–180; adultery and,
153–155, 157–158, 305n51, 305n53; customary
divorces and, 164–165, 307n80; and
mobilization regarding Muslim law, 225;
under Muslim and Christian law, 205–206;
under Muslim law, 217; Muslim law reforms
and, 237–247; MWPRDA and, 237;
precolonial traditions regarding, 308n101;
restitution of conjugality and, 170, 197;
unilateral male repudiation and, 247–250
Majumdar, Rochona, 102–103, 121, 124–125
Malankara Orthodox Syrian Church, 230
Malaysia, 5, 6, 49–50, 60, 65, 76, 200–201,
270, 294n72

Malviya, Madan Mohan, 15
Mamdani, Mahmood, 23–24
marriage: under Christian law, 217–218;
Christian law reform and, 236, 253; gender
equality in inheritance and, 186, 189;
Hindu law reform and, 279; initiatives
regarding, 211–212; intercaste, 107,
117–118, 127, 129; irretrievable marital
breakdown, 146, 147–148; maintenance
rights and obligations in, 174–180; and
mobilization regarding Christian law,
226–230; and mobilization regarding
Muslim law, 222–225; under Muslim law,
215; national inheritance reform and, 194;
and regulation of family, 19, 20. See also
bigamy; divorce, divorce rights; polygyny
Marriage Laws (Amendment) Act (1976), 144,
151–152, 184
Marriage Laws (Amendment) Bill (2010),
147–148, 281, 283
Mary Sonia Zachariah v. Union of India (1995),
255–256, 257–258
Masroor Ahmed v. State of Delhi (2007), 251
mata, 89, 217, 238–240, 241, 243, 244–245, 246,
247, 249, 316–317n64
matriliny, 21, 35, 37, 39, 45, 51, 62, 82, 88–89, 105,
124, 132, 134, 142, 185–186, 187, 247, 277,
292n36, 293n60, 294n72, 295n87, 299n72,
300n92, 310n132, 311n140; and customary
law, 124, 131, 134
matrimonial home: location of, 170–173,
196–197; rights to share of, 315n44
matrimonial property: bill to grant shares in,
in India, 138, 148, 198, 281, 283, 315n44;
discussion of and mobilization about, in
India, 138, 144, 146, 148, 228, 230, 247,
252, 260, 262, 264, 281, 283, 303n24,
315n44; in Indonesia, 34, 61, 247; in Iran,
56; Moroccan law, 34, 295n75
Menski, Werner: on approaches to divorce
law reform, 144–145, 146; on changes in
Hindu law, 100–101, 114; on "constructive
desertion", 158; on cruelty as grounds for
divorce, 149, 151; on polygamy and
maintenance rights, 177, 180; on roles of
women's organizations, 144, 146–147; on
T. Sareetha v. T. Venkata Subbiah, 167

mental cruelty, 149, 150, 151, 152
Migdal, Joel, 291n21, 291n24
Ministry of Women and Child Development, 148
minorities: cultural diversity and, 59–62, 199–200; in nationalist narratives, 62–65; policy regarding, in personal law, *66*; postcolonial policy formation and, 92–93; traditions of, 232–233. *See also* minority law
minority law: and agenda for further personal-law reform in India, 284; changes in policy makers' outlook on, 231–236; courts and contentious questions in, 214–219; cultural and legal mobilization regarding, 221–222; and focus on Hindu law in postcolonial policy formation, 97–99; formation of early postcolonial, 219–221; limited changes to, 134; and multiculturalism in state formation, 277; overview of, 262–265; overview of approaches to, 199–206; postcolonial policy formation and, 92; reform in India, 89–90; reform in India and Indonesia, 78–83; restrictions in reforms of, 281; significant changes in, 131. *See also* Christian law; Muslim law
Mitakshara law: application of, 309–310n122; dissolution of coparcenaries under, 189; gender equality in inheritance and, 185–186; influence of, on postcolonial policy formation, 111–112; inheritance under, 86, 115–116, 122–123, 181; joint property under, 135; lineage authority under, 93–94; property under, 96; women's inheritance rights under, 193
Mitra, Subrata, 42–43
modernity: and authenticity in national narratives, 66–70; formation of legal culture of, 33; minorities and, 65; and postcolonial social reforms, 23–28; Special Marriage Act and, 126, 127; visions of, in India, 83–87
modes of imagination of nations: cultural change and stability in, 65–66; discourses of community and, 57–59; homogeneity and diversity in, 59–62; modernity and authenticity in, 66–70; nations and minorities in, 62–65
Mohammed Ahmad Khan v. Shah Bano Begum (1985), 1–2, 3, 222, 238–242, 244, 245, 246, 257, 303n37, 317n70, 318n86
Mohammed Hanifa v. Pathummal Beevi (1972), 248
Mookerjee, Shyama Prasad, 113
Mrs. Swaraj Garg v. K.M. Garg (1978), 172–173
Mt. Subhani v. Nawab (1941), 162
Mufti, Aamir, 44, 63
multiculturalism: and alternative constructions of nation, 275–277; consequences of, 3–4; and formation of nation and family in India, 278–281; influences on, *47*; major features of Indian, 7; secularism and recognition of religion and, 40–45, 286–287
Muslim law: and agenda for further personal-law reform in India, 282, 284–285; alimony and reforms in, 237–247; authority of patrilineage under, 35; basis of, 8, 10–11; Christian law reform and, 253, 263, 268–269; conjugal rights under, 165–166; courts and contentious questions in, 215–217; in Egyptian, 48–49, 60, 268–269; and family regulation in Tunisia, 21–22, 53–54, 74–76; Hindu nationalists call to abandon, 222; Indian diversity and, 62; and Indian minority law reform, 81–83; Indian nationalists' views on, 203; Indonesian diversity and, 61–62; and Indonesian minority law reform, 78–80; Indonesian personal-law reform and, 50–52; as influence on Hindu law, 116–117; inheritance and property under, 37; interpretations of, reforms, 236–237; legal reform and, 16; limits in reform to, 34–35, 234; mobilization regarding, 206–213, 222–226, 264; modernity and authenticity and, 68–69; nation formation and, 75; opposition to reform of, 221–222; in Pakistani, 43, 56; patterns of change in, 251–252; postcolonial policy formation and, 92, 96; reforms in Indian, 86–87; regional customs and, 38–39; religious mobilization and, 10–12; secularism and

multiculturalism and, 42–44; Turkish personal-law reform and, 73–74; and unilateral male repudiation, 247–251; variations in, in Malaysia, 295n87; women's rights under, 33, 88, 131–132. *See also* minority law

Muslim Personal Law (Shariat) Application Act (1937). *See* Shariat Act (1937)

Muslims: accommodation of, 16, 44–45, 264; application of Hindu law to, 136, 220; divorce rights for, 11, 118–119, 211; perceptions of postcolonial roles of, 202–203; population share of, 8. *See also* Muslim law

Muslim Women (Protection of Rights on Divorce) Act (MWPRDA): effects on Muslim alimony rights, 241–245, 246, 247; interpretation of, 237, 242–246; passing of, 1–2, 241–242

Muslim Women's Personal Law Board, 223

Mussulman Wakf Validating Act (MWVA), 11, 211

Musunuru Nagendramma v. Musunuru Ramakotayya (1953), 305n52, 309n111

nafaqa, 217, 245

Natchiappan, E. M. Sudarsana, 192–193

National Commission for Women (NCW), 140–141, 185, 186, 188, 244, 302n24

National Council of Women in India (NCWI), 25, 94

nationalist narratives: cultural change and stability in, 65–66; family law and, 22–23, 59, *71*; formation of, 268–269; homogeneity and diversity in, 59–62, 63; in India and Indonesia, 287–288; influence of Orientalist representations of, *adat* on Indonesian, 80; minority accommodation and, 199–202; modernity and authenticity in, 66–70; nations and minorities in, 62–65; of pluralist nationalists, 64, 76, 139; variations in, 58–59. *See also* anticolonial nationalists; Hindu nationalism; Indian nationalism

nation(s): formation of, 266–271; formation of, and family in India, 278–281; influences over formation of, 271–277; modernities

and, 23–28; modes of imagination of, 57–78; and regulation of family, 22–23

Nehru, Jawaharlal: and Ambedkar, 83, 85, 110, 111, 113–114; and cosmopolitan nationalism, 81; on divorce rights, 113; and Gandhi, 16, 24, 28; jurisprudential vision of, 85, 110; and Kemal Atatürk, 73; legal reform and, 14, 24, 76, 83; political experiences of, 74; political vision of, 14, 28, 74; support of, for social reform efforts, 24

Nehru, Shivrajwati, 116

Neo-Destour Party, 53, 72–73, 74, 75

Newbigin, Eleanor, 101, 102, 103–104, 106, 120, 184

New Order regime, 51

Nigeria, 69, 71–72

N. R. Radhakrishnan v. N. Dhanalakshmi (1975), 172–173

Nussbaum, Martha, 167

Orthodox Coptic Christian law, 60, 65, *66*, 201, 295n85

Pakistan: cultural diversity in, 59–60; effect of, movement on cultural policy in India, 44, 81; effect of, movement on personal law in India, 16, 43, 95, 220; immigration and, 60, 295n84; Indian *ulama* and, movement, 209; kinship and land rights in, 39; nationalism, multiculturalism, and personal law in, 59–60, 64–65, 66, *66*, *71*, 200; official nationalism and Muslim law in, 56; regimes and personal-law in, *6*, *7*, 21, 56, *57*; Shariat Act in, 43

Pancasila, 50, 80–81

Pandey, Gyanendra, 44

Parami Ramayya v. Mahadevi Shankarappa (1909), 154

Parashar, Archana, 33, 98, 101, 106, 111, 120, 134, 143, 184, 236, 239, 292n35

Pataskar, Hari Vinayak: on application of Hindu law, 108, 111; on Hindu inheritance law reforms, 114–115, 121, 122, 123, 298n39; and Hindu nationalism, 110; jurisprudential vision of, 110–111; on recognition of custom, 110

Patil, Shivaraj, 244–245
patrilineage: authority of, 21–22, 35–36, 47, 138; and construction of family identity, 132; Hindu inheritance law and, 38, 45, 86, 88–89, 102–105, 115–116, 121–126, 138, 139; Muslim inheritance law and, 11, 37, 43; opposition to proposals threatening, 117; and personal law, 5–6, 21–22, 35, 47, 48, 53, 71, 72–73, 77, 93–94; women's rights and, 43, 116, 117, 183–184, 186–187
Pattanaik, G. B., 245
Peletz, Michael, 37
personal law: agenda for further, reform in India, 281–285; background and approaches to, 273; in colonial India, 8–16; comparative perspective on formation of, 3–8, 18–23; context of formation of, 3–8; culturally grounded changes in, 72–77, 286–288; effects of changes in, on women's rights and individual autonomy, 7; modes of imagination of nation and approaches to, 57–78; nationalist narratives and, 71; nature of change in, after independence/regime change, 6; reforms to Indian, 87–90, 279–280; regimes and reforms to, 49–56, 57; religious norms, social structure, and regional customs and, 33–40; and secularism in India and Indonesia, 287–288; social coalitions' influence on, 47–57; state-society relations and, 28–32. *See also* colonial personal law
Perumal Naicker v. Sithalaksmi Ammal (1955), 160
Philippines, 6, 34–35, 63
Philips Alfred Malvin v. Y.J. Gonsalvis (1999), 260–261
pluralistic nationalism: marriage law reform and, 139; minorities in, 64
P. Mariammal v. Padmanabhan (2001), 164
polygyny: Hindu law reform and, 42, 101–102, 118, 119; in Israel, 42; in Judaism, 293n56; maintenance rights and, 176–180; multiculturalism and, 41, 42. *See also* bigamy
postcolonial policy formation: background to, 93–97; considerations influencing proposals for, 108–117; continuities between later reform and, 141–142; focus on Hindu law reform in, 97–100; Hindu inheritance law and, 120–126; Hindu marriage law and, 117–120, 137–138; legislation in, 117–130; nature of changes in Hindu law in, 100–107; options and choices in, 107–108; outcomes and consequences of, 131–136; overview of, 91–93; Special Marriage Act and, 126–130
postcolonial social reforms: anticolonial nationalists' support for, 24–25; in India, 87–90; introduction of, 25–28; religious norms and, 33
poststructuralists, 31–32, 292n31
Pragati Varghese v. Cyril George Varghese (1997), 257–258
Prasad, Rajendra, 84, 292n45
preferential policies: Indian multiculturalism and, 7, 44–45, 83; uniformity of, 87
property: under colonial personal law, 37; divorce and women's rights to matrimonial, 34, 56, 61, 138, 144, 146, 147–148, 198, 228, 230, 247, 252, 260, 262, 264, 281, 283, 295n75, 303n24, 315n44; Hindu law reform and, 101–106, 180–195; under *Mitakshara* school, 96; regulation of conjugality and, 106–107; Shariat Act and, 43; urbanization and industrialization's effect on landed, 139; women's rights and, 39–40, 135, 280–281. *See also* inheritance; land ownership
Protection of Women from Domestic Violence Act (PWDVA), 176, 177, 179–180, 309n120
Putul Devi v. Gopi Mandal (1963), 303n33

Qasmi, Maulana Mujahidul Islam, 224

Radhakrishnan, V., 193–194
Rahmat Ullah v. State of U.P. and Khatoon Nisa v. State of U.P. (1994), 234
Rajagopalachari, C., 292n45
Rajani Prabhakar Lokur v. Prabhakar Raghavendra Lokur (1958), 157
Rajeshbai v. Shantabai (1981), 165

Rajesh Kumar Madaan v. Mrs. Mamta alias Veena (2005), 165
Ramakrishnan, T., 257
Rasul, Begum Qudsia Aizaz, 116, 212
regimes: and change in personal law, 57; coalitions and, 47–57; conflict containment and, 270–271; and consolidation of state authority, 271–272; and minority accommodation, 199–201; modernity and authenticity and, 67–69; nation and family formation and, 273–277; nature of change in personal law following change in, 6; state-society relations and personal-law reform and, 71–72
religion: as basis of Indian personal law, 8–9; as basis of personal law and political representation, 273; colonial state's interference in, 95–96; cultural homogeneity and, 59; Egyptian diversity and, 60; freedom of, 44, 102; Free Officers regime and, 48–49; Hindu law reform and, 103–104; and Indonesian and Indian minority law reform, 78–83; Indonesian diversity and, 61; Indonesian personal-law reform and, 50–52; maintenance rights and, 175–176; in moderate reform cases, 76; Pakistani personal-law reform and, 56; in personal-law legislation, 269–270; and personal-law reform in Malaysia and Sri Lanka, 49–50; postcolonial policy formation and, 94–95; and postcolonial social reforms, 27–28; recognition of, 4–5, 40–45, 273, 286–287; Special Marriage Act and, 126–127, 129; Tunisian personal-law reform and, 53–54; Turkish and Tunisian personal-law reforms and, 74–76; Turkish personal-law reform and, 52; Turkish republican regime and, 275–276
religious groups, population shares of, 213, 235–236, 290n11, 293n64
religious mobilization, colonial personal law and, 9–14
religious norms: social structure and regional custom and, 33–40; visions of, in India, 84–87

Republican People's Party, 74–76
Rida, Rashid, 48
rights organizations: Christian law reform and, 226–229, 255–256; mobilization of, 221–223, 279–280; national inheritance reform and, 190–192; proliferation and growth of, 140–141. *See also* women's organizations
Rita Rani v. Ramesh Kumar (1996), 165
Rizvi, Syed Ameenul Hasan, 317n65
Rohatgi, Avadh Behari, 168–169

Sachindra Nath Biswas v. Sm. Benamala Biswas (1960), 305n51
Sadasivan Pillai v. Vijayalakshmi (1986), 165
Sadhu Singh v. Jagdish Kaur (1969), 171–172
Sahib, B. Pocker, 130, 219–220
Sarkar, Lotika, 101, 102
Sarla Mudgal v. Union of India (1995), 236
Scott, James, 37
secularism: approaches to family law shaped by, 131; in India, 42–43, 44–45, 76, 99–100; in India and Indonesia, 287–288; in Indonesia, 48, 50–51; multiculturalism and recognition of religion and, 40–45, 286–287; and state, nation, tradition, and family formation, 269–270; in Turkey, 74–76, 272, 275–276
Sen, Ashoke Kumar, 242
Senegal, 6, 7, 57, 71, 76
Senghor, Leopold, 76
separation, judicial, 17, 20, 87, 88, 89, 101, 106, 110–111, 119–120, 130, 135, 138, 143–144, 145, 148, 149, 150–153, 155, 157–160, 168–169, 174, 196, 197, 218, 227, 229, 233, 237, 303n34, 306n71, 315n44, 317n69, 320n113
Shafi'i law: divorce under, 216, 251; in Indonesia and Malaysia, 37, 51, 294n72; unilateral repudiation among adherents of, in India, 251; view of *mata* in, 239; women's rights and, 215, 216, 239
Shah Bano (1985), 1–2, 3, 222, 238–242, 244, 245, 246, 257, 303n37, 317n70, 318n86
Shamim Ara v. the State of U.P. (2002), 225, 249, 250–251, 309n97

Shariat Act (1937): agricultural inheritance and, 43, 210–211, 293nn59–60; consolidation of Muslim community through, 86, 95; in Pakistan, 43, 293n60; passage of, 11, 43, 86, 95, 210–211, 293nn59–60; postcolonial policy formation and, 95
Sharma, Nand Lal, 113
shastras: and adultery as grounds for divorce, 154–155; Hindu divorce law and, 113–114; Hindu personal law based on, 12, 85–86, 290n17; inheritance rights and, 186, 310n134; maintenance rights and obligations in, 174, 175
Shia Personal Law Board, 225
Shivalingiah v. Chowdamma (1956), 162
Shri Gurcharan Singh v. Shrimati Waryam Kaur (1960), 149–150
Shri Kishan Chand v. Smt. Munni Devi (2003), 160
Shyam Chand v. Janki (1966), 160
Singh, Kirti, 193
Sirigiri Pullaiah v. Sirigiri Bushings Amma (1962), 159
Sitaram v. Demai (1941), 162
Sivaramayya, B., 180, 186
Sm. Pancho v. Ram Prasad (1956), 149
Smt. Anubha v. Vikas Aggarwal (2002), 160
Smt. Asha Handa v. Baldev Raj Handa (1984), 160
Smt. A. v. Sri B. (1990), 173
Smt. Harvinder Kaur v. Harmander Singh Choudhry (1984), 168–169
Smt. Leela Pande v. Shri Sachendra Kumar Pande (1994), 156
Smt. Saroj Rani v. Sudarshan Kumar Chadha (1984), 168, 169–170
Smt. Sumitra Devi v. Narender Singh (1993), 173
Smt. Surrinder Kaur v. Mohinder Singh (1967), 171
Smt. Swayamprabha v. A.S. Chandrasekhar (1982), 156
Smt. Tirath Kaur v. Kirpal Singh (1964), 170–171
Smt. Vanamala v. Shri H.M. Ranganatha Bhatta (1995), 157–158
Snehlata Seth v. Kewal Krishan Seth (1986), 160
social institutions: Foucault's study of, 31–32; state authority and, 18–19, 20, 21, 266–267, 271–272, 273–275
social projects: discursive practices and, 31–32; influences on, 28–29; state-society relations and, 29–31
social solidarity, as consideration influencing policy proposals, 110–111, 113
social structure: personal-law reform and, 71–72; religious norms and regional custom and, 33–40
Solomon Devasahayam Selvaraj v. Chandirah Mary (1968), 170, 255
Som, Reba, 101, 106, 133
Sonubai Yeshwant Jadhav v. Bala Govind Yadav (1983), 182
Special Marriage Act (SMA): adultery as grounds for separation under, 153, 155; changes in, 92; compared to Hindu Marriage Act, 120, 130; constraints on choice to be governed by, 92, 126–127, 129, 300n87; polygamy and maintenance rights under, 177; in postcolonial policy formation, 126–130; as step to a Uniform Civil Code, 127
spousal reconciliation: and adultery as grounds for divorce, 156; encouragement for, 144–146, 156, 162–163, 165, 169, 196, 216, 225, 234, 248–249, 251; restitution of conjugality and, 165, 168–169
Sreenivas, Mytheli, 36, 102–104, 292n44
Sri Lanka, 39, 49–50, 76, 294n69
Sri Lanka Freedom Party, 49–50
state: formation of, 266–271; formation of, and lineage authority, 18–19, 21–22; influences over approaches to formation of, 271–277; minorities and formation of, 62–64; secular, and recognition of religion, 40–41, 269–270. *See also* state authority; colonial state(s); state-society relations
state authority: consolidation of, 271–273, 277; and regulation of family, 18–23, 100; state-society relations and, 29–30
state-society relations, 18–19, 28–32; and consolidation of state authority, 271–273, 277; discourses of community and, 45–46,

72, 266; personal-law reform and, 70–72; relevant features of, 45, 47; Turkish and Tunisian personal-law reforms and, 74–76
stridhanam, 114, 174, 308n101
Subramani v. Chandralekha (2004), 164
succession. *See* inheritance
Sudan, 69, 71–72, 279
Sukumar Dhibar v. Smt. Anjali Dasi (1983), 157
Sumitra Devi v. Narender Singh (1993), 173
Sunder Rajan, Rajeswari, 236, 239, 246, 292n37
Swapna Ghosh v. Sadananda Ghosh (1989), 255
Swaraj Garg v. K.M. Garg (1978), 172–173
Syria, 77, 296n95
Syro-Malabar Catholic Church, 230, 261

Tai v. Harishchandra (1984), 156
takhayyur, 94, 207, 240
talaq-ul ba'in, 215–216, 225, 247–251. *See also* unilateral male repudiation
Tara Singh v. Shakuntala (1974), 162–163
Taylor, Charles, 45
Telugu Desam, 188
testamentary rights, 54, 115, 117, 122, 123, 125–126, 132, 133, 135, 182, 187, 189, 190, 191, 193–195, 198, 280–281, 282, 283–284, 312n159
Thailand, 111
Tilak, Bal Gangadhar, 15
traditional elites: and minority laws, 64; regimes dominated by, 47–48, 57; regimes with links with, 5, 71
traditionalists, orientation of, towards family law, 15–16, 28, 53–54, 64, 83, 84–86, 88, 89, 103, 207, 292n45
tradition(s): Christian law and understanding of religious, 214, 234–235; dynamic, 5, 6–7, 8, 9–22, 30–31; dynamic, and family law, 54, 67, 94–95; formation of, 266–277; and Hindu law, 12–13, 45; Islamic, and Muslim law, 2–3, 8, 35–36, 206–209, 222–225; Islamic and other indigenous, 81–83; policy makers' understanding of minority, 232–233; recognition of indigenous, 14, 37, 81–83, 278
tribal groups: Christian mobilization and, 204, 213–214, 229; customary law and women's rights among, 131, 134, 300n92, 311n140; customs and law applied to, 9, 162; laws applied to, 8, 9, 110, 124; preferences in education, government employment, and political representation, and land rights of, 7, 44, 293n64, 301n3
T. Sareetha v. T. Venkata Subbiah (1983), 167–168, 169, 308n92
Tunisia: authority over family regulation in, 21–22, 34; coalitions and family-law reforms in, 274, 276; consolidation of state authority in, 271–272; as example of extensive early reform, 72–76; personal law in, 5, 71; regimes and personal-law reform in, 53–54
Turkey: coalitions and family-law reforms in, 52, 274; consolidation of state authority in, 271–272; early republican regime of, 275–276; as example of extensive early reform, 72–76; homogenist nationalist narratives and policy in, 59–60, 63, 275; modernity and authenticity in, 67, 68; personal law in, 5, 54, 71; power of social institutions limited in, 267, 270; regimes and personal-law reform in, 52–53, 54, 72–73; secularism in, 68, 273, 275–276, 286–287, 296n96
Tyabji, Badruddin, 208

UCC (Uniform Civil Code). *See* Uniform Civil Code (UCC)
ulama: and adjudication in Indonesia, 37, 51; alimony and, 238, 239–240, 241; and Dissolution of Muslim Marriages Act, 211; Free Officers regime and, 49; and Islamic law in Tunisian reforms, 75; and Muslim law reform, 10–11, 97, 203, 206–211, 223–224; oppose restriction of Islamic law, 10; and patrilineages, 35, 43; recognition of custom and, 43, 210; reform initiatives of, 231; Shariat Act and, 43, 203, 211
ultimogeniture, female, 300n92
Uniform Civil Code (UCC): and agenda for further personal-law reform in India, 285; Christians and, 87, 204, 227; consolidation and reform of Hindu law as

Uniform Civil Code (UCC) (*continued*)
step toward, 85, 108, 128, 131, 135, 139; constitutional status of, 84, 95, 100, 219–220; Hindu nationalists' support for, 15, 135–136, 203, 222, 279–280, 282, 285, 314n29; Indian nationalists' views on religious minorities and, 203; judiciary and, 86, 234, 241, 245, 250; and mobilization regarding Christian law, 227; Muslims and, 219–220, 221, 241; Muslim support for, 97, 219–220; postcolonial policy formation and, 95, 131; sources of, 92, 129, 203, 212, 227, 241, 279–280; Special Marriage Act as step toward, 92, 127; support for, 84, 139, 146, 203, 220, 241; time frame to introduce, 95, 117, 222, 242, 285; women's organizations and, 222, 227, 228

unilateral male repudiation: AIMPLB and, 224, 225, 249; Allahabad High Court's treatment of, 234; Bombay High Court on, 216; demands to limit recognition of, 146, 212, 222–223, 225; judicial limits on, 89, 160, 205, 232, 234, 247–251, 263; Justice Baharul Islam on, 248; among Muslims, 215–216; recognition of, 153, 163–164, 216, 313–314n16. *See also talaq-ul ba'in*

United Malay National Organization, 49–50

United National Party, 49–50

United Progressive Alliance (UPA), 190, 191, 198

United States: constitution in, 42; family law in, 19–20, 34, 39, 269; recognition of religion in, 40–41

urban groups: family formation and, 36–37; Moroccan monarchy's relationship with, 48; and lineage power, 35

vanguardist regimes, 47–48, 52–54, 57, 71, 274

V. Bhagat v. Mrs. D. Bhagat (1994), 152–153, 302n19

Venkataraman, R., 116–117

Vietnam, 279

violence: and cruelty as grounds for divorce, 148–150, 152; ethnic, 220, 225–226, 247; laws to support women and children facing domestic, 176, 179–180, 193; Muslim law reform and, 247

Viswanathan, T.K., 312n153

Western cultural practices and institutions: accommodation of, in India, 69; modernity and authenticity and, 68, 69–70; and nature of changes in Hindu law, 100, 101; recognition of religion and, 33, 42; and regulation of family, 20–21, 33; Turkish personal-law reform and, 52–53, 75; Turkish republican regime and, 68, 74–76, 275–276

Western education: influence over reform initiatives, 93; Muslim law mobilization and legislation and, 206–208

widows: and agenda for further personal-law reform in India, 282–283; Christian law reform and inheritance rights of, 228, 230, 254, 259; early inheritance reform initiatives and, 197; gender equality in inheritance and, 188; and Hindu Widows Right to Property Act, 13, 175, 298n39; inheritance rights in Indonesia, 80–81; inheritance rights of, under amended Indian Succession Act, 259; and inheritance under Hindu Succession Act, 88, 114, 121–122, 123–124, 132, 181–182, 183–184; and inheritance under *Mitakshara* law, 181–182, 298n39; and inheritance under proposal to modify *Dayabhaga* law, 112; maintenance rights and, 174, 175; national Hindu Succession Act reform and inheritance rights, 190, 193, 194, 195, 197, 282–283, 313n163; reforms in Hindu Succession Act in particular states and inheritance rights, 186–187, 188; remarriage, 14, 88, 96, 125, 132

William Carey Study and Research Center, 227

Women's Indian Association (WIA), 25, 94

women's organizations: cultural and legal mobilization and, 221–222; and demands for a Hindu Code, 109; and demands for Muslim law reform, 212, 222–223, 244; divorce law reform and, 146–147; and enhancement of women's rights, 105–106,

135, 212; gender equality in inheritance and, 185, 187–188; and gender-relevant policy bureaucracies, 140–141; mobilization of, 140–141, 222–223, 279–280; on a Uniform Civil Code or culturally grounded personal law reform, 139, 144, 222; women's inheritance rights and, 125, 190

Women's Research and Action Group, 223

Women's Reservation Bill, 301n3

women's rights: adultery and spousal maintenance and, 153–155, 157; Agarwal on, 39–40, 104–106; and agenda for further personal-law reform in India, 281–285; and changes to Hindu Code Bill, 117; under *Dayabhaga* and *Mitakshara* schools, 86, 96, 102, 104, 112; divorce and, 144–145, 147, 163, 254–258, 316n63; effects of personal-law changes since 1970s on, 7; expansion of, 106–107, 131–133, 138, 205; family nuclearization and, 35; under Free Officers regime, 49; under Hindu law, 88–89, 101–102, 104–107, 131–133, 142–143, 196–198, 279–281; Indonesian personal-law reform and, 51–52; Iranian personal-law reforms and, 55–56; Islamic *Fiqh* Academy's recommendations for, 224; maintenance rights and obligations and, 174–180; minority law reform and, 263–264; and mobilization regarding Muslim law, 222–225; modernist reforms of religious law and, 34; Muslim, 33, 205–206, 234, 282, 284–285; Mussulman Wakf Validating Act and Dissolution of Muslim Marriages Act and, 211; postcolonial policy formation and, 131–135; Shariat Act's impact on, 43; Turkish and Tunisian personal-law reforms and, 54; Turkish personal-law reform and, 52–53; women's organizations' mobilization for, 105–106, 135, 141, 212, 222–223. *See also* inheritance; women's organizations

Yugoslavia, 64

Zia-ul-Haq, Muhammad, 56